TROLLEYS OF PENNSYLVANIA

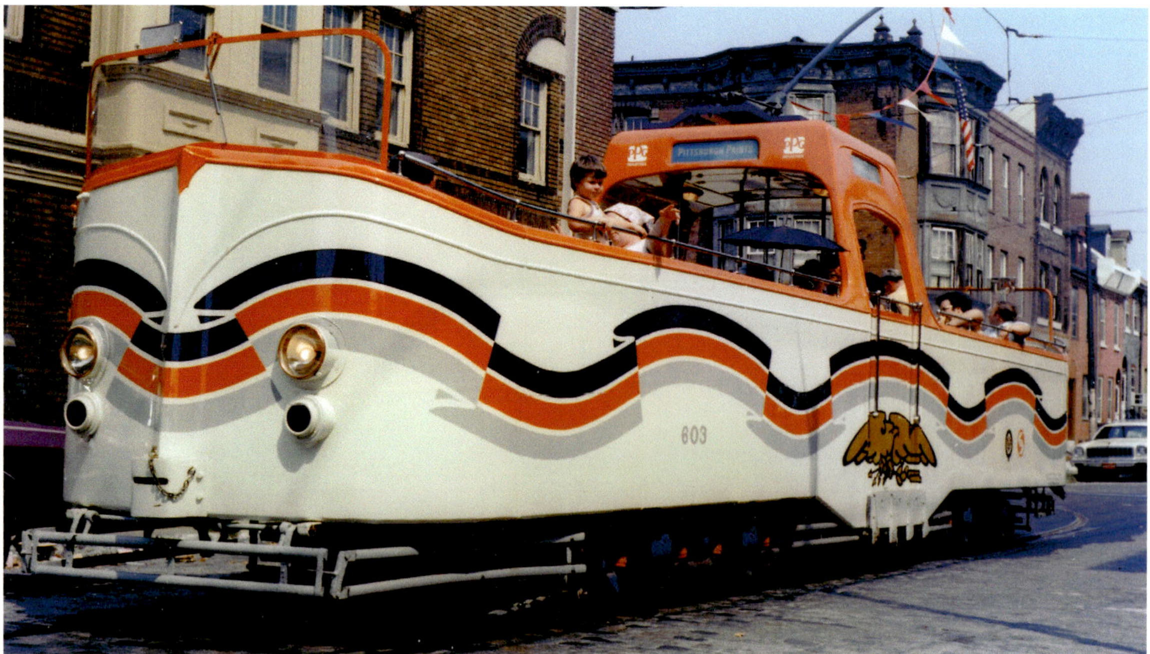

"Boat trolley" car No. 603 is on 4th at Catherine Street operating along a portion of Southeastern Pennsylvania Transportation Authority (SEPTA) Route 50 in Philadelphia on August 14, 1976. In 1977, the "boat trolley" was operated over a portion of Route 15. It was later returned to Blackpool and was acquired in 1984 by the Market Street Railway for the San Francisco Municipal Railway. This was originally car No. 228 from Blackpool, England where it was one of twelve "boat trams" that were built by English Electric in 1934 for the Blackpool Tramways. Weighing 20,000 pounds, the 42.25 foot long car seats forty-four and is powered by two English Electric type 305 motors. Founded in 1976, the Market Street Railway is a member supported non-profit organization that is not part of the San Francisco Municipal Railway but is a preservation partner. Its mission is to preserve historic transit in San Francisco by advocating for historic streetcar and cable car improvements and educating the public on the importance of public transit.

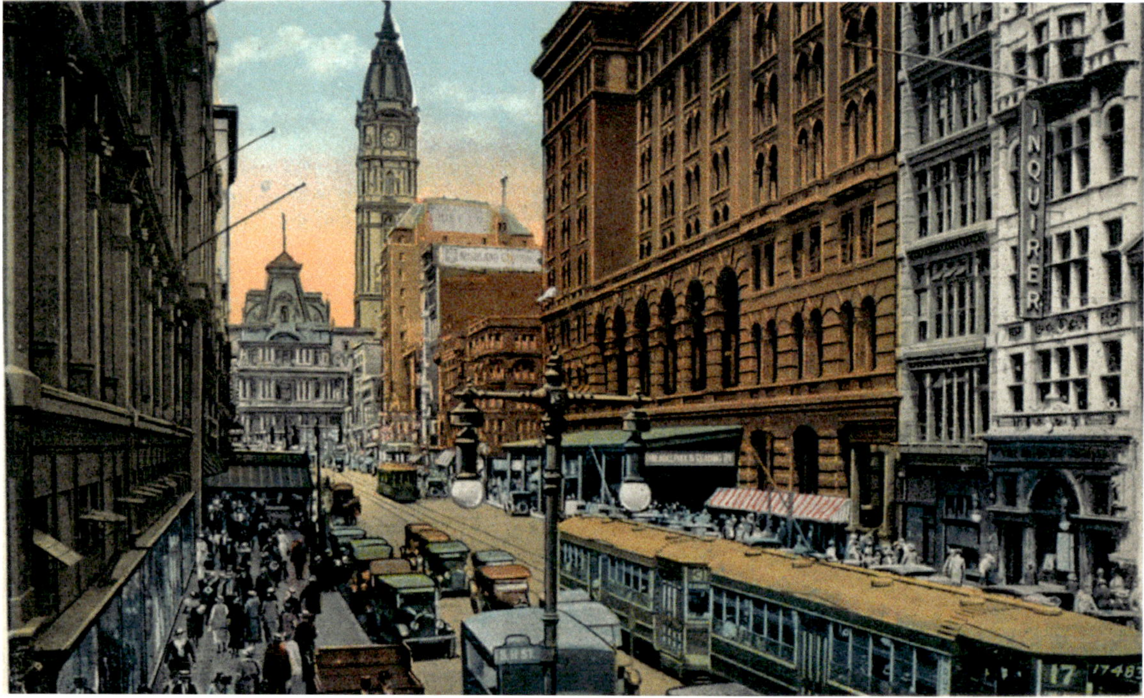

Downtown Philadelphia looking west from 11th Street was busy with trolley cars and numerous automobiles in this 1920s postcard scene. On December 29, 1957, the Philadelphia Transportation Company (PTC) converted Route 17 to bus operation, and combined Trolley Car Route 32 with Bus Routes 2 and 21 into one Bus Route 2 ending all surface trolley car service in downtown Market Street.

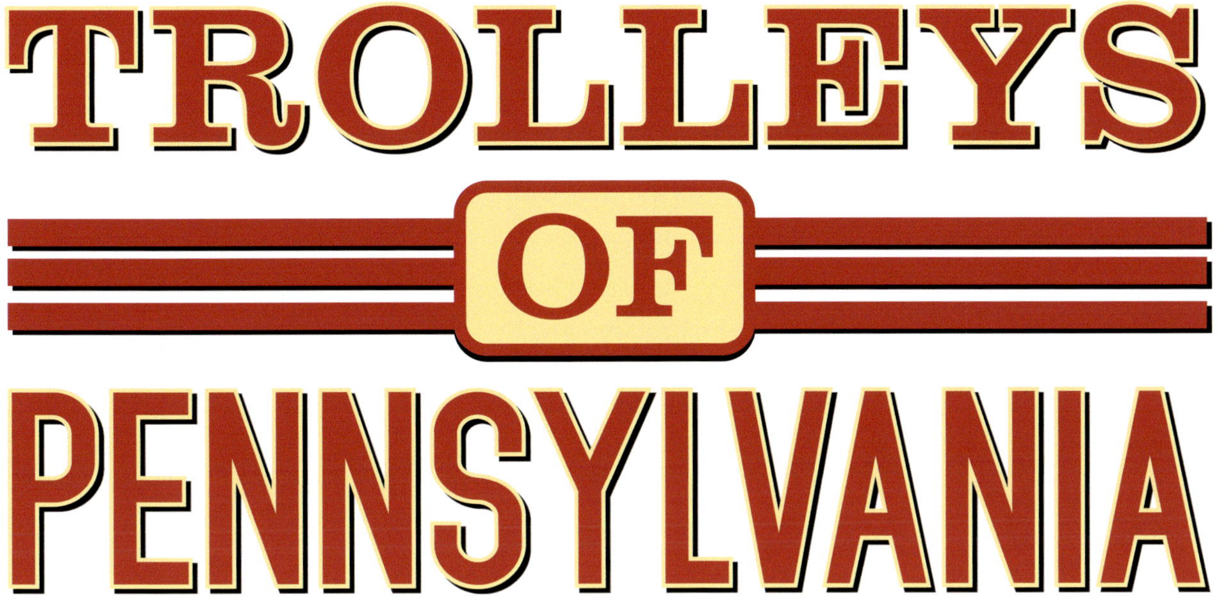

KENNETH C. SPRINGIRTH

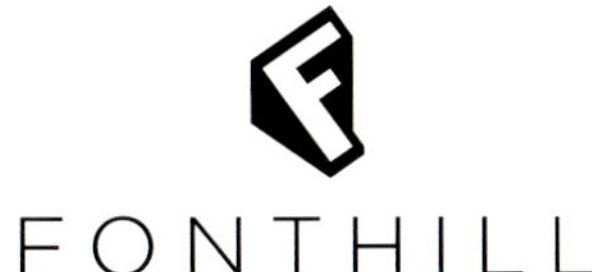

FONTHILL

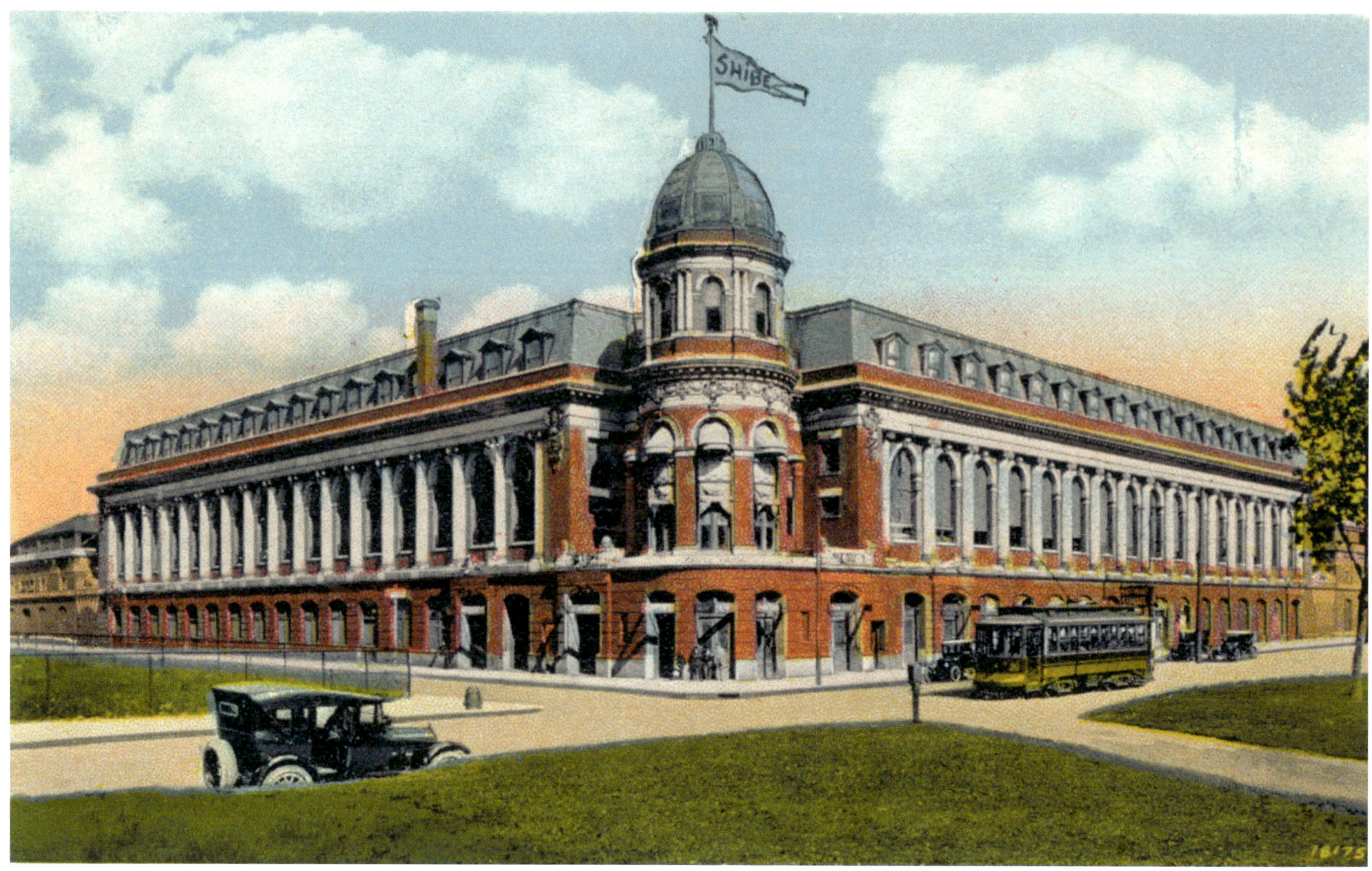

A Route 54 trolley car is westbound on Lehigh Avenue approaching 21st Street in North Philadelphia passing by the ornate French Renaissance style baseball stadium Shibe Park (later known as Connie Mack Stadium) in this postcard around 1910. Buses replaced Route 54 trolley cars on June 4, 1955.

On the cover: Pittsburgh Railways Company Route 22 Presidents' Conference Committee (PCC) car No. 1559 (built by St. Louis Car Company as part of sixty-five cars Nos. 1500-1564 that were received by 1945) is at North Avenue and Sandusky Street on the north side of Pittsburgh displaying a colorful advertisement for the Allegheny Fair in this August 3, 1963 view. Route 22, connecting the North Side of Pittsburgh (business district) with downtown Pittsburgh, opened in 1918. The Port Authority of Allegheny County known as Port Authority Transit (PAT), which took over Pittsburgh Railways and thirty independent bus companies on March 1, 1964, replaced Route 22 on July 5, 1964 by an extension of Bus Route 16D.

Back cover: On August 13, 1976, Southeastern Pennsylvania Transportation Authority Route 50 Presidents' Conference Car No. 2284 is northbound on 5th Street at Chestnut Street passing by the Federal style Old City Hall in the Independence National Historical Park in Center City Philadelphia. Car No. 2284 was originally car No. 766 built by the St. Louis Car Company in 1946 for Kansas City Public Service Company and acquired by the Philadelphia Transportation Company in 1955.

Fonthill Media Inc.
www.fonthillmedia.com
office@fonthillmedia.com

First published 2021

Copyright © Kenneth C. Springirth 2021

ISBN 978-1-62545-034-0

Typeset in Utopia Std
Printed and bound in England

Contents

Acknowledgments

Thanks to the Erie County Public Library system with its excellent staff and interlibrary loan system. Photographs on Altoona & Logan Valley, Reading Street Railway, and Lehigh Valley Transit trolleys were from the collection of Cliff Scholes. All of the vintage postcards were from the author's collection, and the remainder of the photographs was taken by the author.

Pennsylvania has a number of excellent rail museums. The Rockhill Trolley Museum, located in Rockhill Furnace, Huntingdon County, in south central Pennsylvania, is a wonderful place where you can learn about trolley cars, take a ride through the sylvan countryside, and see a fleet of cars that have been carefully restored by skilled volunteers. The museum address is Rockhill Trolley Museum, 430 Meadow Street, PO Box 203, Rockhill Furnace, PA 17249.

Rev. Edward J. Casey was the source of detailed roster information on Philadelphia PCC cars. Books that served as excellent reference sources were *The Liberty Bell Route's 1000 Series Interurban Cars* edited by Randolph L. Kulp, *The Liberty Bell Route's Heavy Interurban Cars* edited by Randolph L. Kulp, *Lehigh Valley Transit Co. 1934-1953* by Benson W. Rohrbeck, *McGraw Electric Railway List August 1918*, *McGraw Electric Railway Directory 1924*, *Transit in the Triangle Volume I* by Blaine S. Hays and James A. Toman.

This book is dedicated to the author's daughter Kathleen May Ruggio who has been an inspiration to our family and friends.

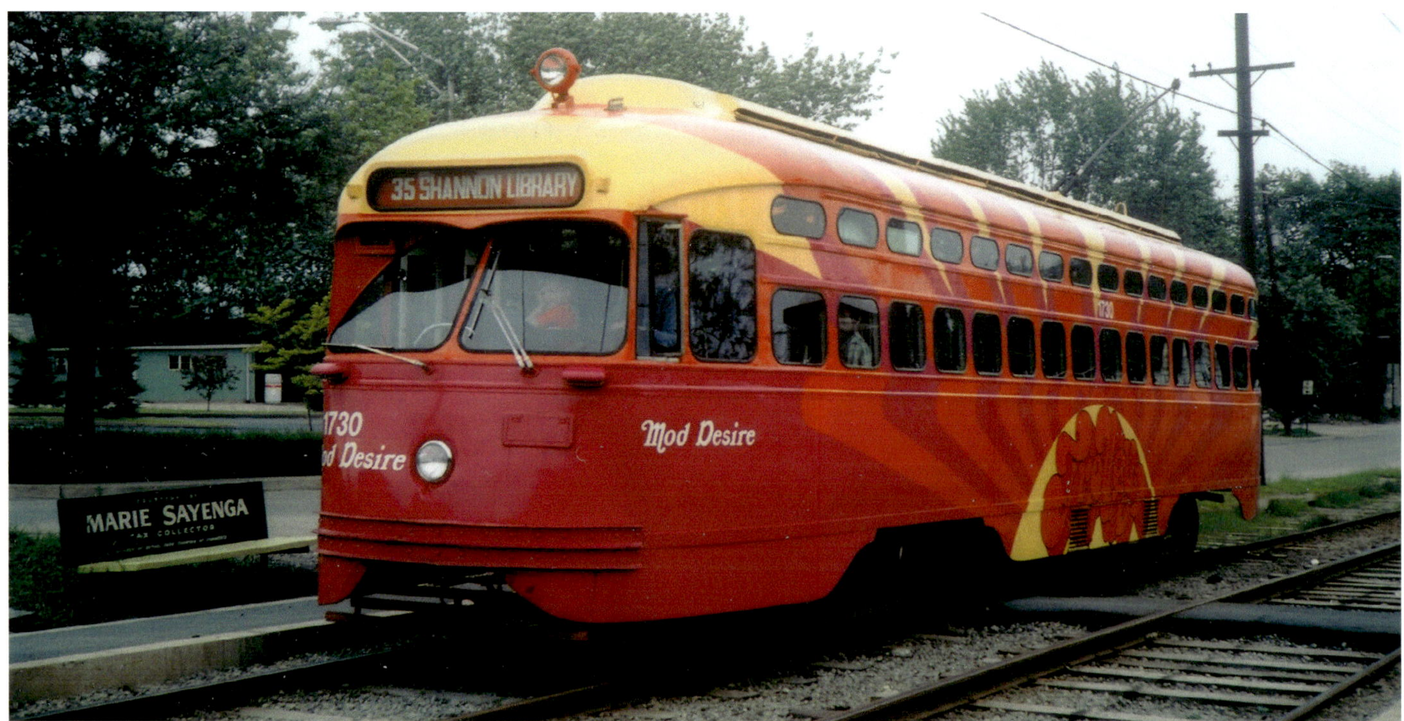

Port Authority Transit Route 35 PCC car No. 1730, in a psychedelic paint scheme, is handling a southbound trip to the community of Library in South Park Township on May 27, 1973. St. Louis Car Company delivered 100 of these cars numbered 1700-1799 between December 1948 and July 1949. Pittsburgh's 666 PCC cars, the second largest fleet in the United States (Chicago with 683 PCC cars had the largest) dwindled to three operable cars: 4004 (originally 1739), 4008 (originally 1709), and 4009 (originally 1700) on September 4, 1999, for the last day of revenue service on Route 47D (Drake Shuttle). There was a special excursion on September 5, 1999 to commemorate the end of PCC car service in Pittsburgh.

Introduction

Trolley cars, which are now known as light rail vehicles, still operate in Philadelphia, suburban Philadelphia, and Pittsburgh. According to the *McGraw Electric Railway Directory 1924*, in July 1923, Pennsylvania had 104 operating trolley companies, which was the most of any state in the United States. Pennsylvania, with 4,625 miles of track, ranked second in the United States. New York, with 5,427 miles of track ranked first. With 7,355 passenger motor cars, Pennsylvania ranked second behind New York which had 16,882 passenger motor cars. Pennsylvania had 12.7 percent of the 821 operating companies in the United States, 9.8 percent of the 47,283 miles of single track in the United States, and 9.8 percent of the 75,249 passenger motor cars in the United States.

The first girder rail for trolley cars was rolled by the Cambria Iron Company at Johnstown, Pennsylvania, in 1877. When the Fairmount Park Trolley Line in Philadelphia was opened over the new Strawberry Mansion Bridge across the Schuylkill River on June 13, 1897, it was the first park in the world to have a trolley car line located entirely within the park. One of the longest interurban trolley car tunnels ever built was the 4,750 foot long Laurel Line Tunnel built in 1904 at South Scranton, Pennsylvania. Johnstown, Pennsylvania, was the smallest city in the United States to place in service new modern Presidents' Conference Committee cars. Until Philadelphia's Route 62 (Darby–Yeadon) was combined with Route 13 on January 24, 1971, Route 62 was the shortest trolley car line in the United States. The first high speed electric commuter car was built in 1931 based on extensive wind tunnel testing for the Philadelphia & Western Railway.

Philadelphia Transportation Company, which since September 30, 1968 is operated by the Southeastern Pennsylvania Transportation Authority (SEPTA), is one of only two US transit systems that operates five major types of transit vehicles: commuter rail trains, subway elevated lines operating on standard gauge, trolley cars operating on a 5 foot 2.25 inches track gauge, electric trackless trolleys, and motor buses. The other is Boston's Massachusetts Bay Transportation Authority (MBTA) which also runs ferry boat service. In 2015, SEPTA operates 112 trolley cars on its five subway surface lines, eighteen Presidents' Conference Committee Cars that were rebuilt by Brookville Equipment Corporation and designated as PCCII cars on Route 15 Girard Avenue, twenty-nine cars on the Media and Sharon Hill Trolley Lines and twenty-six cars on the Norristown High Speed Line.

Pittsburgh Railways Company (PRC) up to the early 1960s had an incredible trolley car operation along private right of way, over high trestles, amazing grades, and miles of city streets with a track gauge of 5 foot 2.5 inches which is 6 inches wider than the standard gauge of 4 foot 8.5 inches. Port Authority Transit (PAT) acquired Pittsburgh Railways on March 1, 1964 and converted most of the system to bus operation. Suburban lines in the south suburbs were former trolley car lines that have been rehabilitated to accommodate light rail vehicles. The Beechview Line was reconstructed and operated through the Mount Washington Tunnel and crossed the Monongahela River on the Panhandle Bridge (former Pennsylvania Railroad bridge) which then led into the newly built downtown subway with four stations. The Overbrook Line was rebuilt along the original line's right of way completely double-tracked with continuously welded rail plus upgraded catenary and signaling and high-level platform ADA accessible stations. The Overbrook Line reopened on June 2, 2004, and PAT purchased twenty-eight additional light rail cars to support the line plus increase overall system capacity, and the fifty-five existing cars were completely rehabilitated as well.

In 2015, PAT operates three modern light rail lines with eighty-three modern light rail vehicles. The Red Line, formerly 42S, operates between South Hills Village and Downtown Pittsburgh via Beechview. The Blue Line, formerly 47L, operates from Library and merges with the Red Line at Washington Junction and splits again to follow the Overbrook Line and merges with the Red Line at South Hills Junction for Downtown Pittsburgh. The Blue Line –South Hills Village, formerly 47S, follows the Red Line to Willow Station where it follows the Blue Line – Library to downtown Pittsburgh.

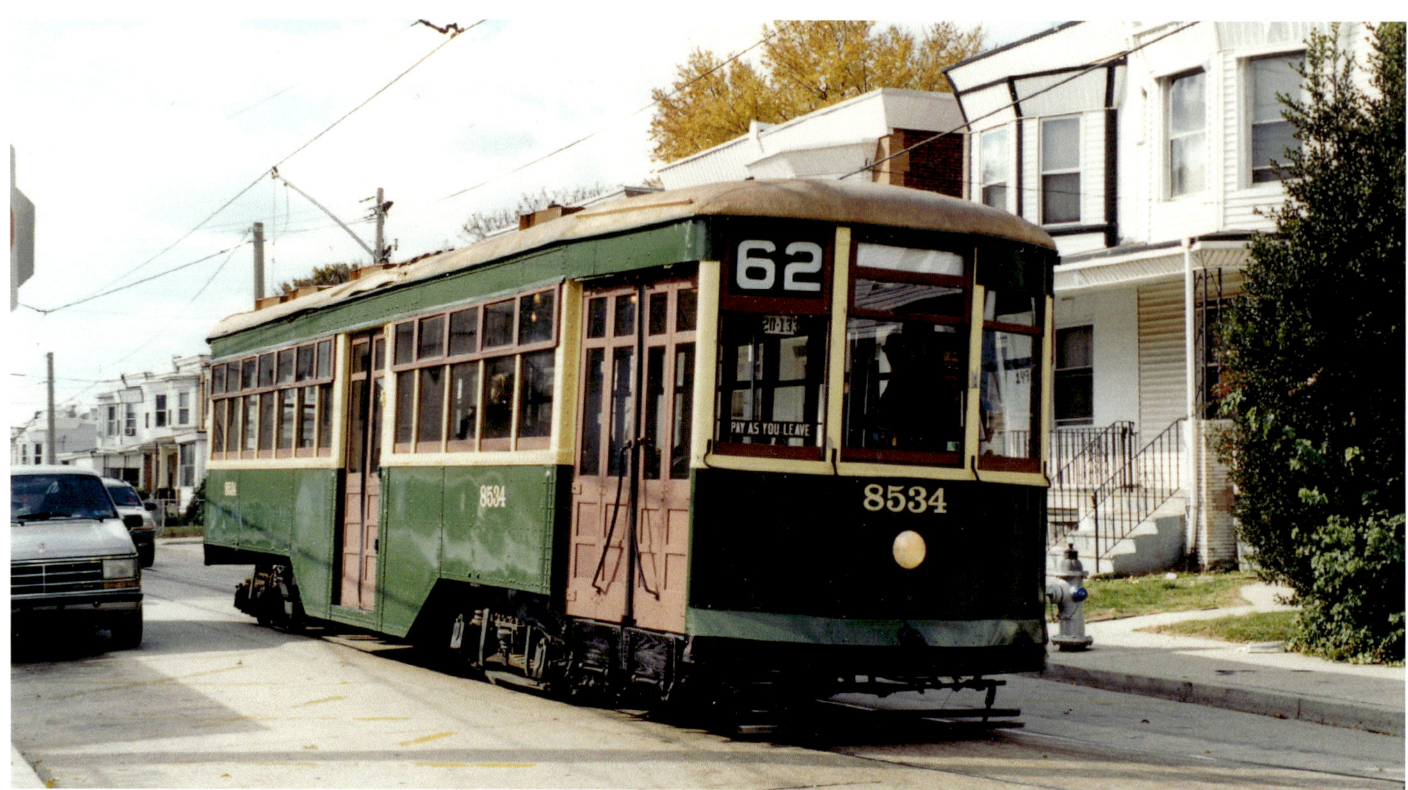

Peter Witt type trolley car No. 8534 is operating along SEPTA Route 62 for a rail excursion and has paused for a photo stop on 9th Street at Cedar Avenue in the borough of Darby in Delaware County southwest of downtown Philadelphia on November 5, 2000. The car was built by J. G. Brill Company and delivered in May 1926. It was remodeled in October 1940, sold to a private individual in March 1958, and is now on display at the Electric City Trolley Museum at Scranton, Pennsylvania.

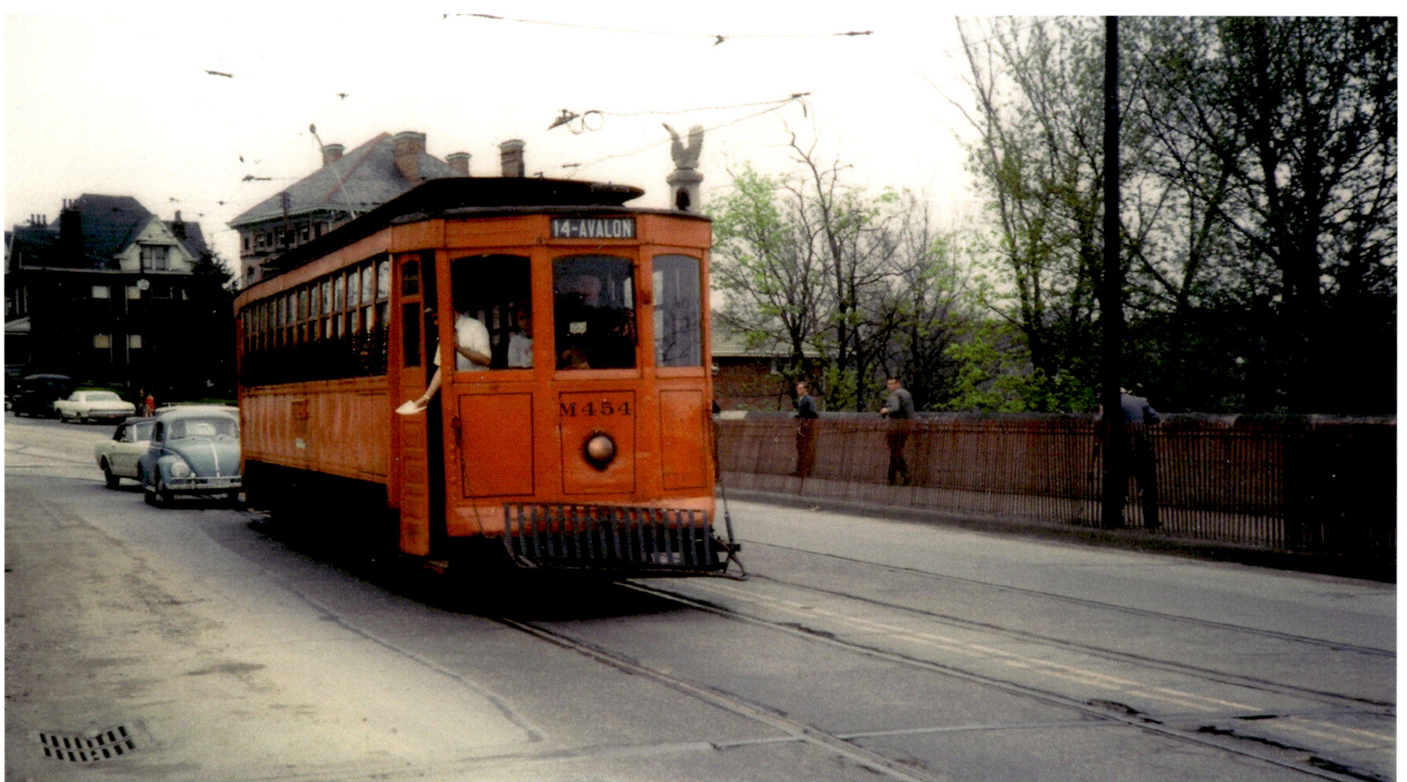

California Avenue west of Winhurst is the location of M454 operating on PAT Route 6/14 on April 30, 1966. This was originally Pittsburgh Railways Company car No. 4115 built by Pressed Steel Car Company in 1911 and later became a snow-scraper.

Chapter 1

Philadelphia Trolleys

The Philadelphia Traction Company opened Philadelphia's first electric trolley car line on December 15, 1892. Within five years all of the horse-drawn routes were converted to electric operation with the last horse-drawn operation on the Callowhill Street Line ending on January 15, 1897. Numerous trolley companies were merged into the Philadelphia Rapid Transit Company in 1902. The system peaked in 1911 with 3,399 trolley cars operating on eighty-six routes with 678 miles of track. Numbers were assigned to routes beginning October 15, 1911 when the 16th Street Line became Route 2.

A number of electric trolley company presidents formed a committee in 1929 to develop a new standardized streamlined trolley car which became known as the President's Conference Committee (PCC) car. PCC car production began in 1935, and the Philadelphia Rapid Transit Company (PRT) purchased forty-seven PCC cars in 1940. PRT and several smaller transit companies were merged into the Philadelphia Transportation Company (PTC) on January 1, 1940. PTC purchased additional PCC cars from the St. Louis Car Company. Route 59 (Castor Avenue) trolley car line was replaced by trackless trolleys on June 25, 1950. Even with the conversion of some of the trolley car lines to bus and trackless trolley operation, in 1954 PTC operated 1,513 trolley cars on forty-five lines. National City Lines obtained control of PTC in 1955.

The extension of the trolley car subway under the Schuylkill River opened on October 17, 1955 when eastbound PCC car No. 2631 entered the new 40th Street Portal at 4:55 a.m. Westbound trolley cars did not use the subway until November 7, 1955 when PCC car No. 2628 came through to 40th Street. Subway Surface Route 38 became a bus route on October 16, 1955. On December 25, 1955, buses took over Trolley Car Routes 5 (Frankford Terminal to South Philadelphia) and 33 (Arch Street), followed on January 29, 1956 by Route 48 (Fairmount–Arch Street), Route 52 (Chelten–Midvale), and Route 26 (Olney Avenue). Route 9 (Strawberry–4th & 5th) was combined into new Bus Route 48 on January 29, 1956. Route 3 (Frankford–Columbia Ave.) was replaced by buses on February 5, 1956. Buses took over Route 21 (North 17th & 18th) on March 25, 1956.

Crosstown east–west South Philadelphia Route 64 (Federal/Wharton) was converted to bus operation on April 25, 1956. The trolley tunnel under the Art Museum was abandoned with the conversion of Route 43 (Spring Garden) to bus operation on July 5, 1956. Route 6 (Glenside–Willow Grove) was converted to bus operation north of Cheltenham Avenue on June 8, 1958 with trolley car service remaining on the portion between Olney Avenue and City Line except on Sundays and early morning. Originally known as the Glenside Line, it was established in 1924 connecting Willow Grove Depot with City Line Avenue. In 1929 the line was extended to Broad and Olney. With trolleys discontinued north of City Line, the line was now known as Route 6 (Ogontz Avenue).

Only fourteen trolley car lines and 557 trolley cars remained by 1958. The opening of the surface of 8th Street between Market and Race Streets as part of the reconstruction of the 8th and Market subway station for the expansion of the Delaware River Port Authority's project to extend rail transit service to Lindenwold meant that PTC Route 47 became bus operation from Spring Garden Street south to its Wolf Street terminus in South Philadelphia. Route 47 trolley cars operated from Spring Garden Street to the northern terminus at 5th Street and Godrey Avenue. The Southeastern Pennsylvania Transportation Authority (SEPTA) took possession of PTC on September 30, 1968 for $47.9 million. On June 15, 1969, the northern section of Route 47 was converted to bus operation. A fire destroyed half of SEPTA's Woodland Depot along with sixty trolley cars and seven work cars in the early morning of October 23, 1975. Trolley Car Routes 11, 13, 34, and 36 operated out of Woodland Depot and service was severely disrupted for the Thursday morning rush hour. SEPTA purchased thirty PCC cars from the Toronto Transit Commission at a cost of $12,500 per car plus $1,300 shipping and $925 for any cars that were regauged.

Between 1980 and 1982, Kawasaki Heavy Industries built 112 new trolley cars known as light rail vehicles Nos. 9000-9111 for SEPTA Subway Surface Routes 10, 11, 13, 34, and 36. They were designed to negotiate the extremely tight curvature of Philadelphia's trackage that has a thirty-three foot radius in certain locations. The 2.8 mile Route 6, connecting Ogontz and Cheltenham via Ogontz Avenue to Broad and Olney, made its last run as a trolley line on January 11, 1986 with SEPTA operating buses the next day.

The 12.75 mile Route 23 connecting 10th and Bigler with Germantown Avenue and Bethlehem Pike began operation before 1887 from Germantown Depot to 8th and Dauphin Streets. On September 9, 1923, the line operated from Bethlehem Loop to Oregon Avenue via 10th and 11th Streets. Routes 20 and 23 were combined into Route 23 on December 29, 1957 and was designated the Germantown Avenue 11th and 12th Line. This line was converted to bus operation on February 21, 1992.

The 10.8 mile Route 50 was Philadelphia's first horse-drawn streetcar line, starting in 1858 on 5th and 6th streets from Montgomery to Morris Street. By 1913 the line operated from Fox Chase to 6th and Oregon. In 1956 the northern end of the line was cut back to Rising Sun and Knorr. Route 50 trolleys were replaced by buses on October 12, 1980.

The 4.4 mile Route 53 began operation before 1890 from 13th and Locust to Wayne and Johnson with an extension to Wayne and Carpenter in 1904. In 1929, 11th and Erie became the southbound terminal which was extended to 10th and Luzerne in 1930. Route 53 trolleys were replaced by buses on May 16, 1985.

The 7.45 mile Route 56 trolley line operated from 23rd and Venango to Torresdale and Cottman. In 1907 the line connected 2nd and Tioga with Pulaski and Hunting Park Avenues. The western terminus became 23rd and Venango in 1926. Torresdale and Cottman became the eastern terminus in 1928. Route 56 was converted to bus operation on June 14, 1992.

The 4.9 mile Route 60 trolley line operated from 35th and Allegheny to Richmond and Westmoreland. In 1906 the line began operation from Richmond and Allegheny to 17th and Allegheny. Route 60 was converted to bus operation on September 4, 1977.

Route 15 began operation as the Girard Avenue Line in 1895 from Richmond and Norris to 54th and Girard. It was later extended to 63rd and Girard, and in 1956 its eastern

loop became Richmond and Westmoreland Streets making Route 15 a 7.6 mile line. Beginning September 13, 1992, the line was temporarily converted to bus operation. Trolley service was restored on Route 15 on September 4, 2005 using eighteen PCCII cars completely rebuilt by Brookville Equipment Corporation. Because of the rebuilding of Interstate 95 necessitating replacement of track, a quarter mile of new track on Frankford Avenue from Girard Avenue to a new loop at Frankford and Delaware Avenues was placed in service on April 29, 2012. A shuttle bus operates from Front and Girard to the Richmond and Westmoreland Loop until the project is completed.

In 2015, along with Route 15, SEPTA operates five subway surface trolley car routes in Philadelphia. Subway Surface Route 10 started before 1887 operating from Belmont and Jefferson via Lancaster Avenue to Front and Walnut. On December 15, 1906, it began operating into the subway and was extended to 63rd and Malvern on June 20, 1926.

Subway Surface Route 11 was established before 1887 operating from 49th and Woodland to 9th and Main in Darby. It began operating into the subway on December 15, 1906.

Subway Surface Route 13 began as the Chester Avenue Line which was an extension of the Chestnut Street Line in 1907. On May 25, 1913, the two lines were consolidated operating from 9th and Main to Front and Chestnut. On September 9, 1956, the line was routed into the surface car subway.

Subway Surface Route 34, prior to 1890, operated from 25th and South Streets to 40th and Baltimore Avenue. On December 15, 1906, it began operating into the subway.

Subway Surface Route 36 was established on March 15, 1904 operating from Island Road and Elmwood Avenue to Paschall and Grays Ferry Avenue and was extended to 9th and Arch Streets on May 8, 1905. It was operated from Westinghouse Loop into the subway on November 6, 1955. Its western terminus was cut back to 94th Street on September 9, 1956; 88th and Eastwick on August 15, 1962; and 85th Street & Eastwick Avenue on January 5, 1966. Since April 26, 1975 Route 36 has terminated at Island Road and 80th Street.

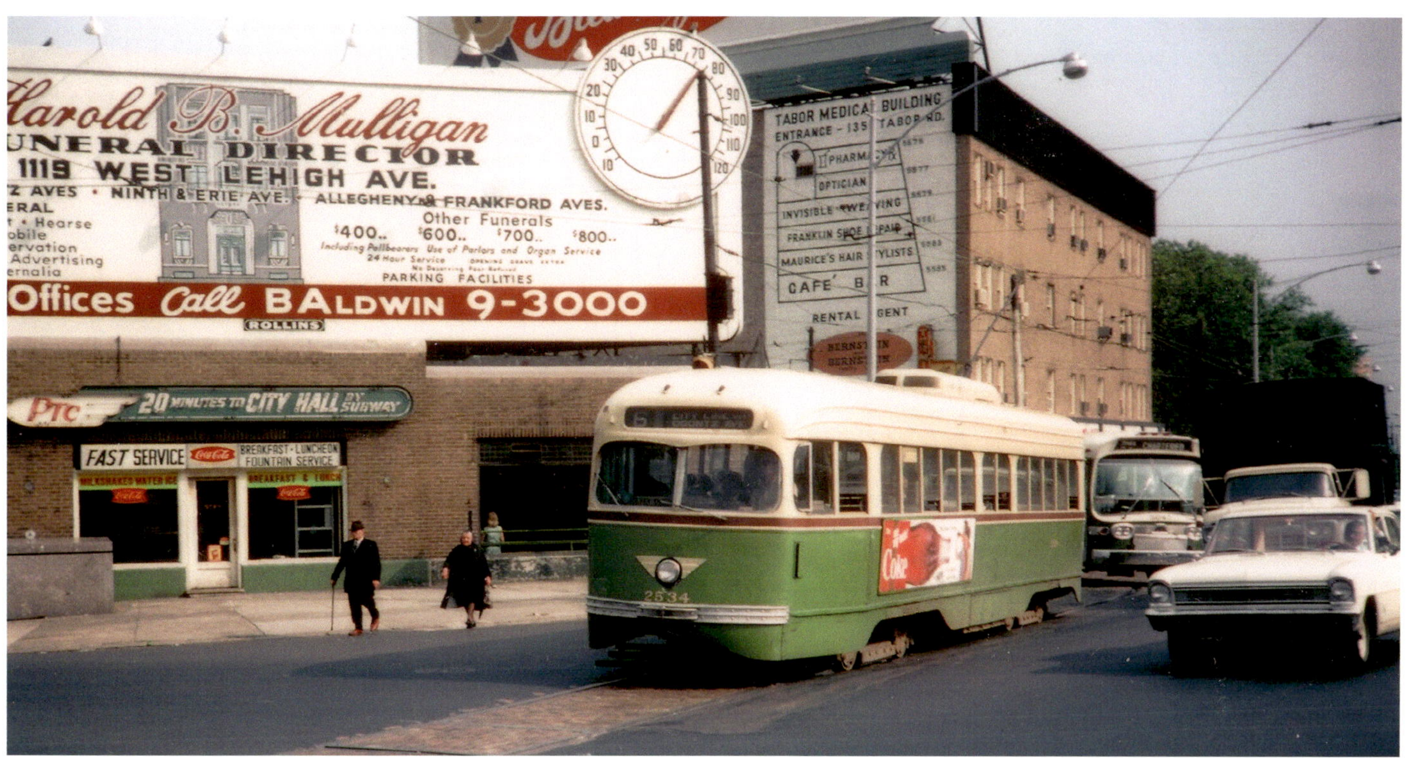

On May 31, 1968, PTC Route 6 PCC car No. 2534 is at Broad Street and Olney Avenue. This was one of eighty cars numbered 2501-2580 (each powered by four General Electric type 1198F3 motors) built by St. Louis Car Company in 1940-1941. Car No. 2534 was delivered in January 1941 and was scrapped in March 1982. On June 8, 1958, Route 6 was converted to bus operation north of Cheltenham Avenue to Willow Grove, and PCC car No. 2134 made the last run leaving Willow Grove at 5:13 a.m. that day.

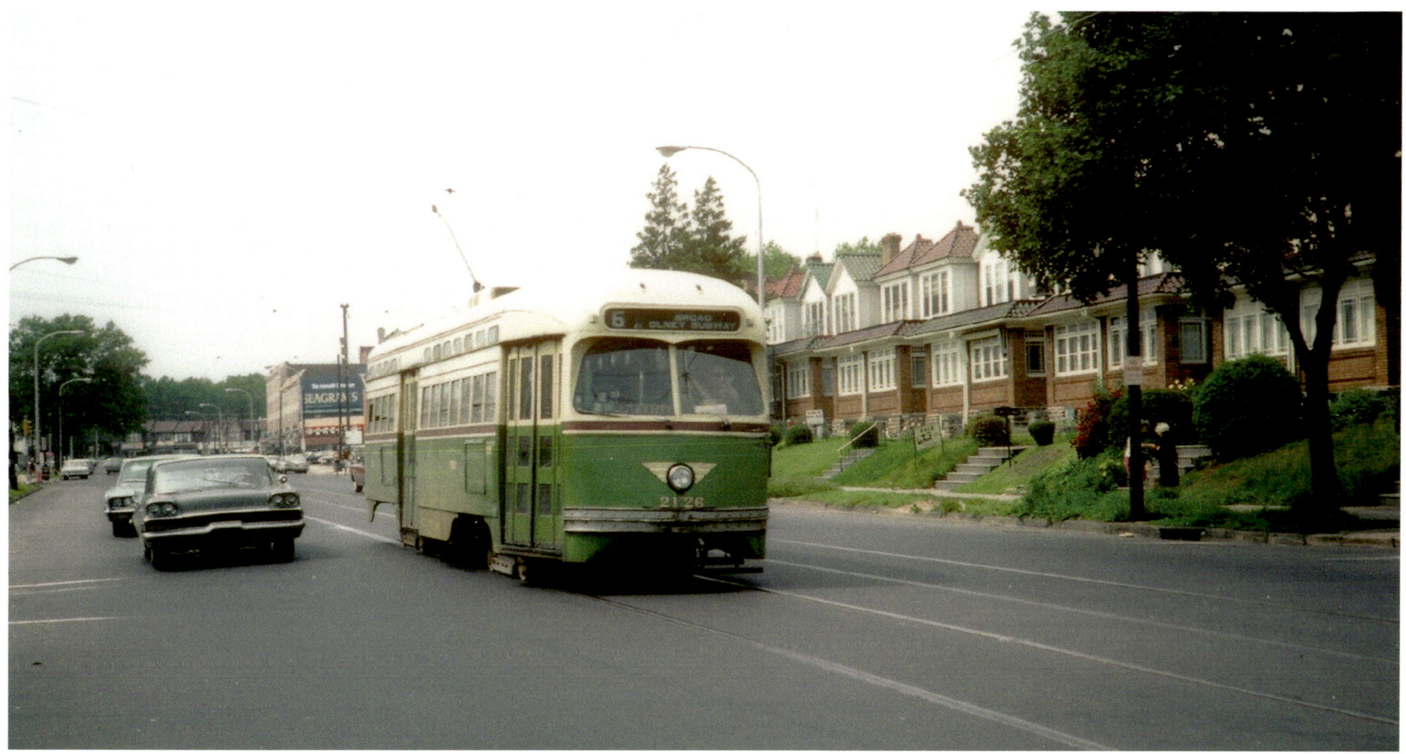

Southbound PTC Route 6 PCC car No. 2126 is on Ogontz Avenue ready to cross Andrews Avenue in the Ogontz neighborhood in upper north Philadelphia on May 31, 1968. This was one of fifty cars numbered 2091-2140 (each powered by four Westinghouse type 1432J motors) built by St. Louis Car Company in 1948. Car No. 2126 was delivered in September 1948, was overhauled by SEPTA in January 1982, and was sold to the San Francisco Municipal Railway for parts in October 1992.

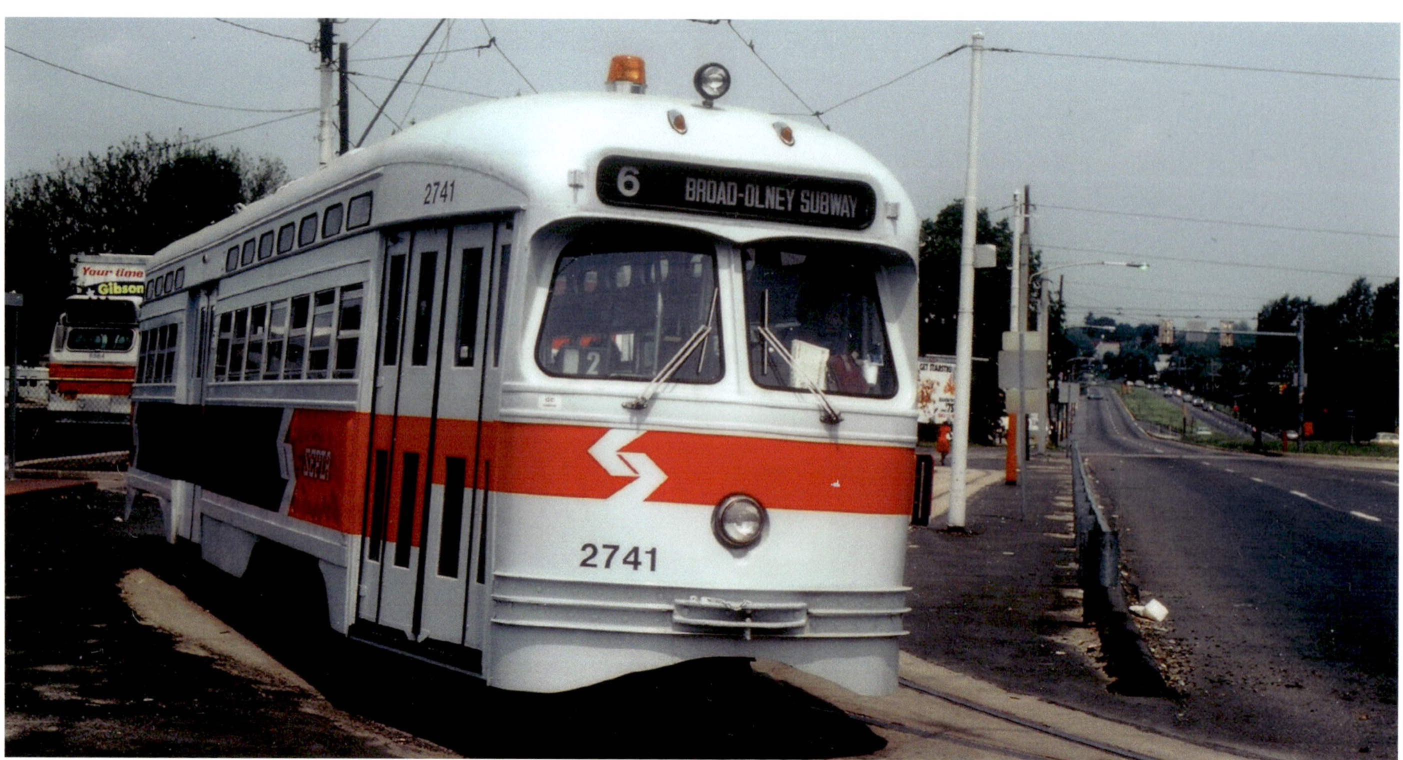

City Line Loop is the location of SEPTA Route 6 PCC car No. 2741 on May 26, 1984. This was one of seventy-five cars numbered 2726-2800 (each powered by four General Electric type 1220A motors) built by St. Louis Car Company in 1947. Car No. 2741 was delivered in March 1947, overhauled by SEPTA in May 1984, and rebuilt by Brookville Equipment Corporation as No. 2325 with delivery to SEPTA on April 14, 2004. Route 6 operated from City Line to Broad and Olney feeding passengers into the Broad Street Subway.

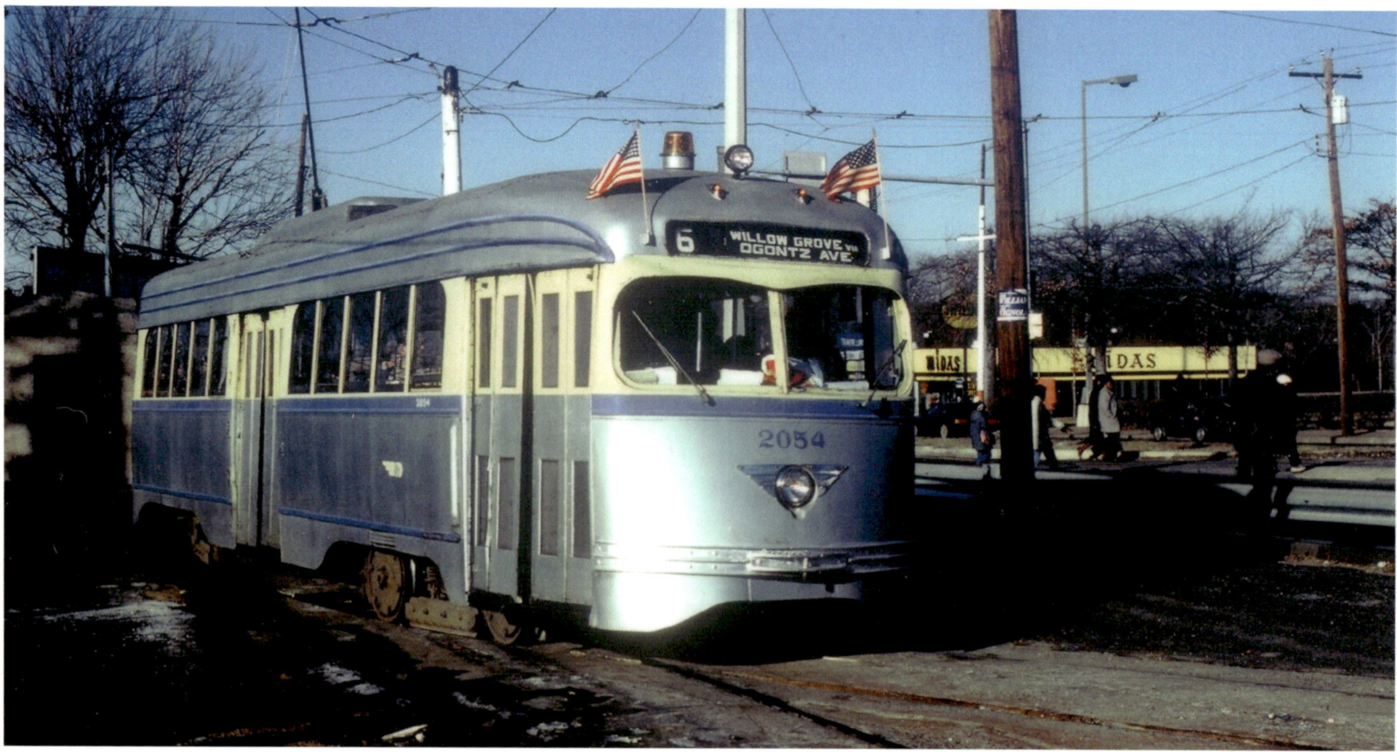

On January 11, 1986, the last day of trolley car service on Route 6 with SEPTA operating buses the next day, PCC car No. 2054 is at the City Line Loop for a photo stop on a rail excursion. This was one of fifty PCC cars numbered 2031-2080 (each powered by four Westinghouse type 1432D motors) built by St. Louis Car Company in 1941. Car No. 2054 was delivered in February 1941, painted in the original PTC silver and blue by SEPTA in 1978 and later sold to the Electric City Trolley Museum in Scranton, Pennsylvania.

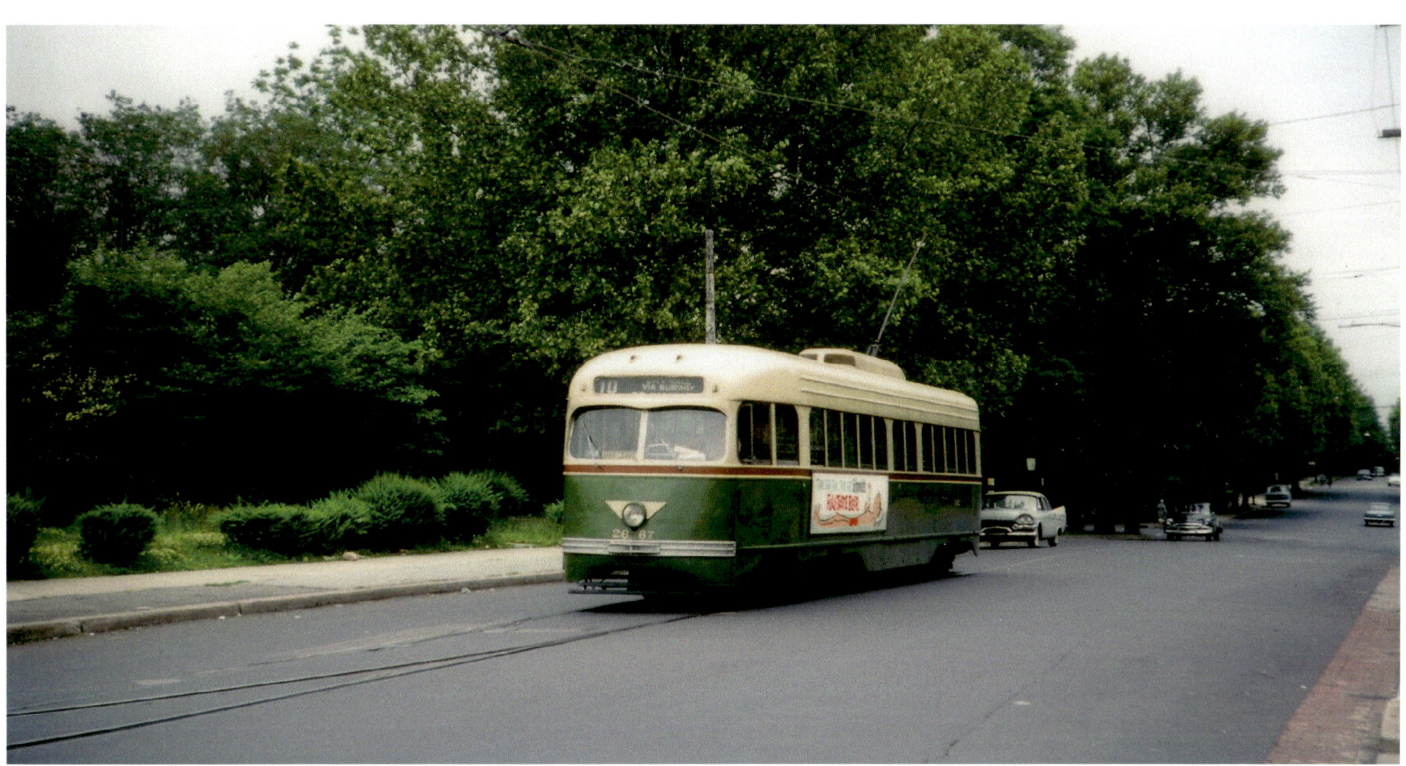

PTC Route 10 PCC car No. 2667 is near the 63rd Street and Malvern Avenue Loop in the Overbrook neighborhood of West Philadelphia on June 2, 1963. This was one of fifty-seven cars numbered 2624-2680 (powered by four Westinghouse type 1432D motors) built by St. Louis Car Company in 1942. Car No. 2667 was delivered in July 1942 and was scrapped in March 1982.

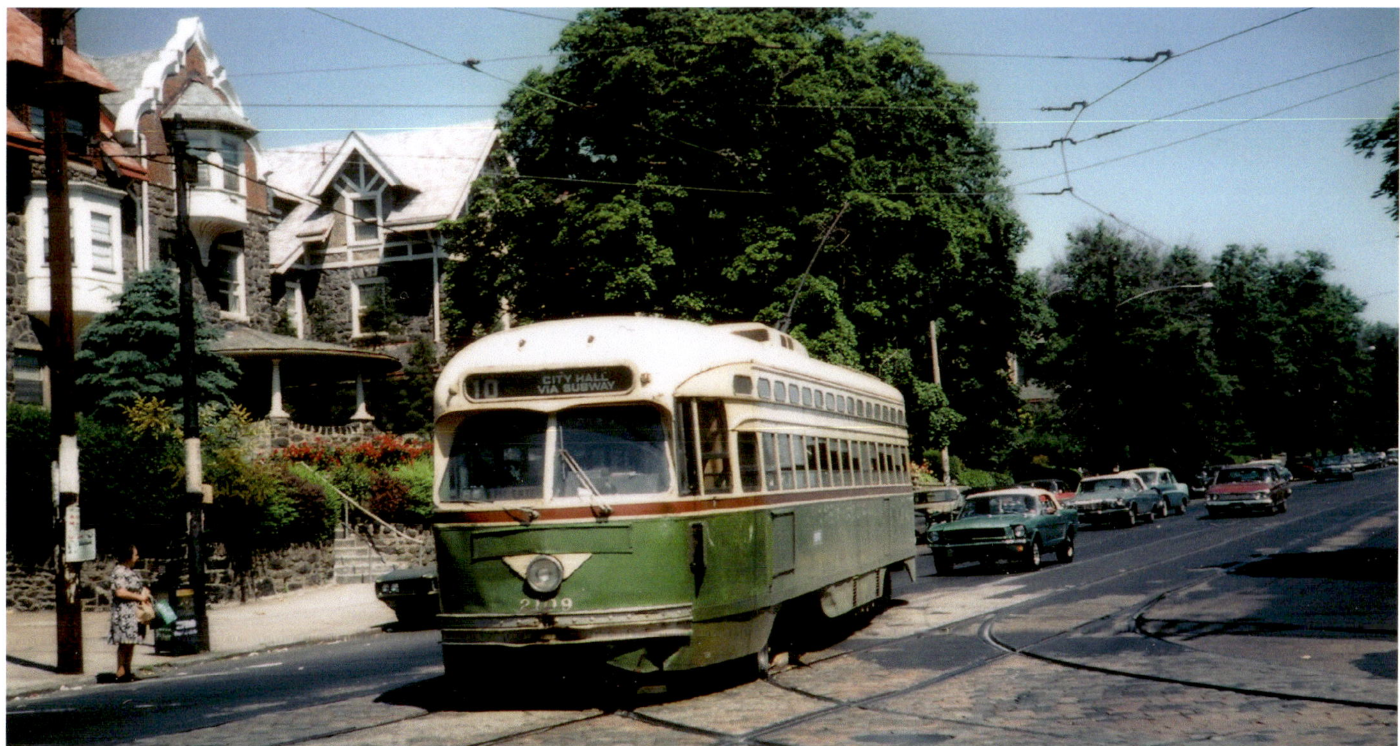

On May 31, 1969, SEPTA Route 10 PCC car No. 2109 is turning from the stately homes on 63rd Street onto Lansdowne Avenue heading for downtown Philadelphia. Car No. 2109 was delivered by St. Louis Car Company in August 1948, overhauled by SEPTA in August 1982, and sold in September 1995. When new the 2100 series PCC cars weighed 38,060 pounds, seated 49, had a trolley pole for current collection, had a maximum speed of forty-two miles per hour on a level surface, and cost $27,735 per car.

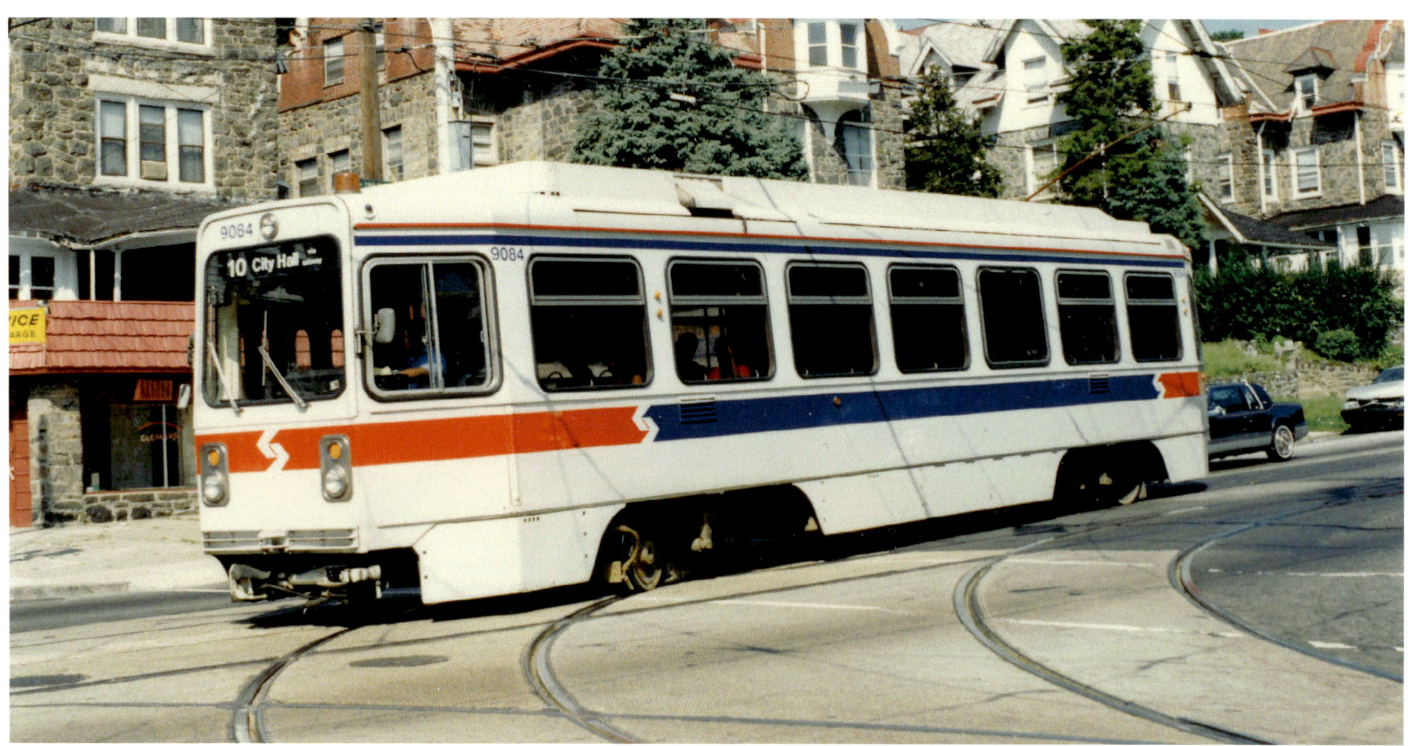

SEPTA Route 10 Kawasaki Heavy Industries car No. 9084 (delivered on October 23, 1981 and placed in revenue service on October 27, 1981) is on 63rd Street just starting the turn onto Lansdowne Avenue. The new single end Kawasaki cars weighed 57,882 pounds, seated fifty-one, had a trolley pole for power collection, had a maximum speed of fifty miles per hour on a level surface, and cost $186,000 per car. The 5.8 mile Subway Surface Route 10 operates in the underground subway and then through West Philadelphia to the 63rd and Malvern Loop.

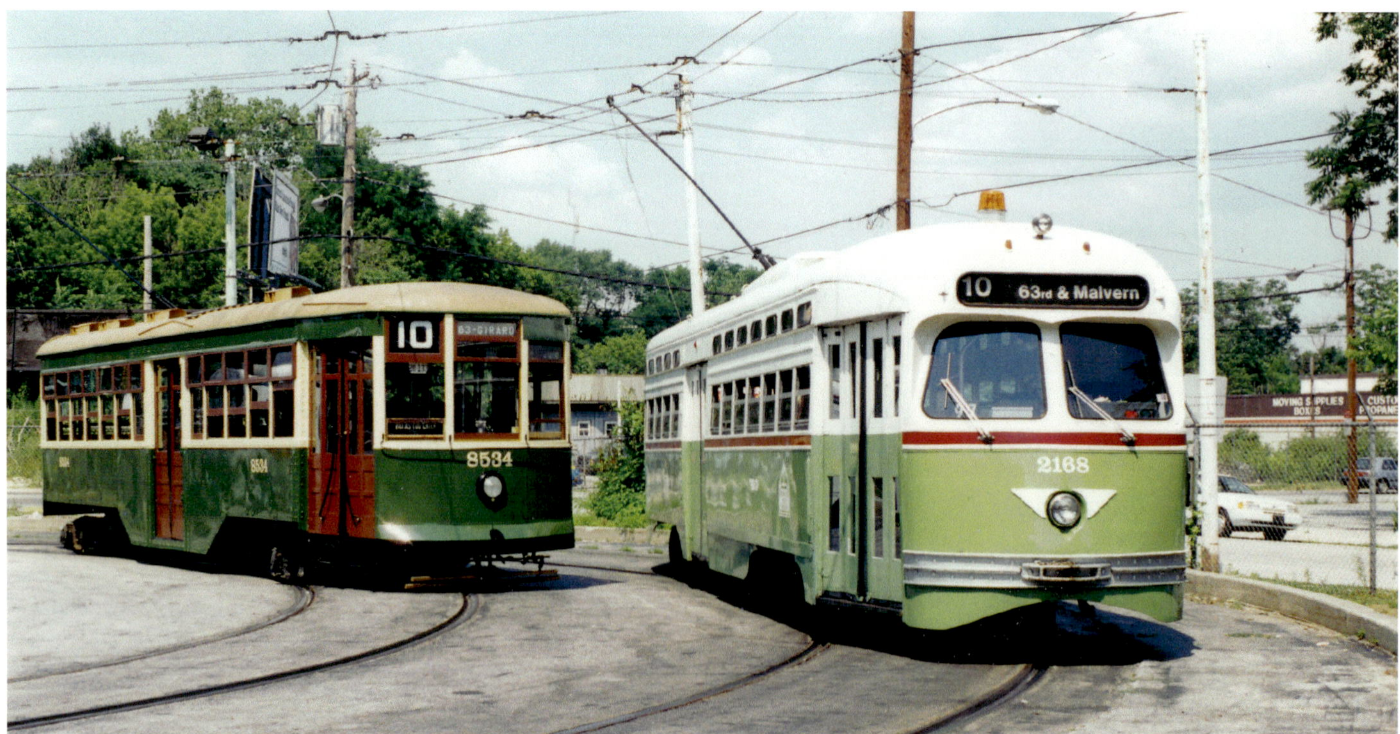

Vintage Peter Witt car No. 8534 and streamlined PCC car No. 2168 (one of sixty PCC cars numbered 2141-2200 built in 1948 by St. Louis Car Company and powered by four General Electric type 1220A motors) are at the 63rd Street and Malvern Avenue Loop of SEPTA Route 10 for a rail excursion photo stop on July 6, 1997. Car No. 2168 was delivered in July 1948, overhauled by SEPTA in January 1986, served on the Chestnut Hill trolley from 1992-1996, and was sold to the Baltimore Streetcar Museum where it arrived on June 21, 2005. Car No. 8534 was acquired by the Electric City Trolley Museum.

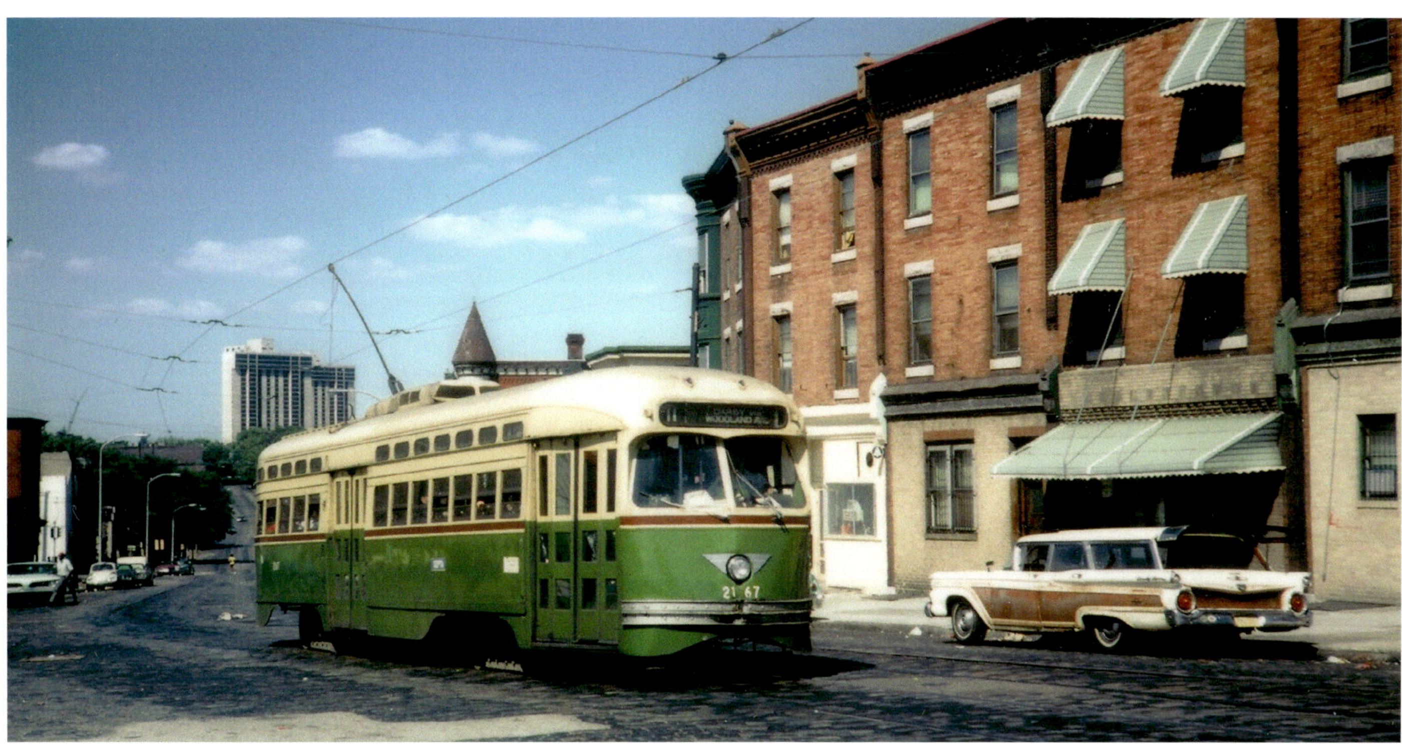

PTC Route 11 PCC car No. 2167 is on Woodland Avenue on May 30, 1970. This car was delivered by the St. Louis Car Company in June 1948 and was destroyed in the Woodland Depot fire of October 23, 1975. The 6.65 mile Subway Surface Route 11 operates in the underground subway and then through West Philadelphia to Darby in Delaware County.

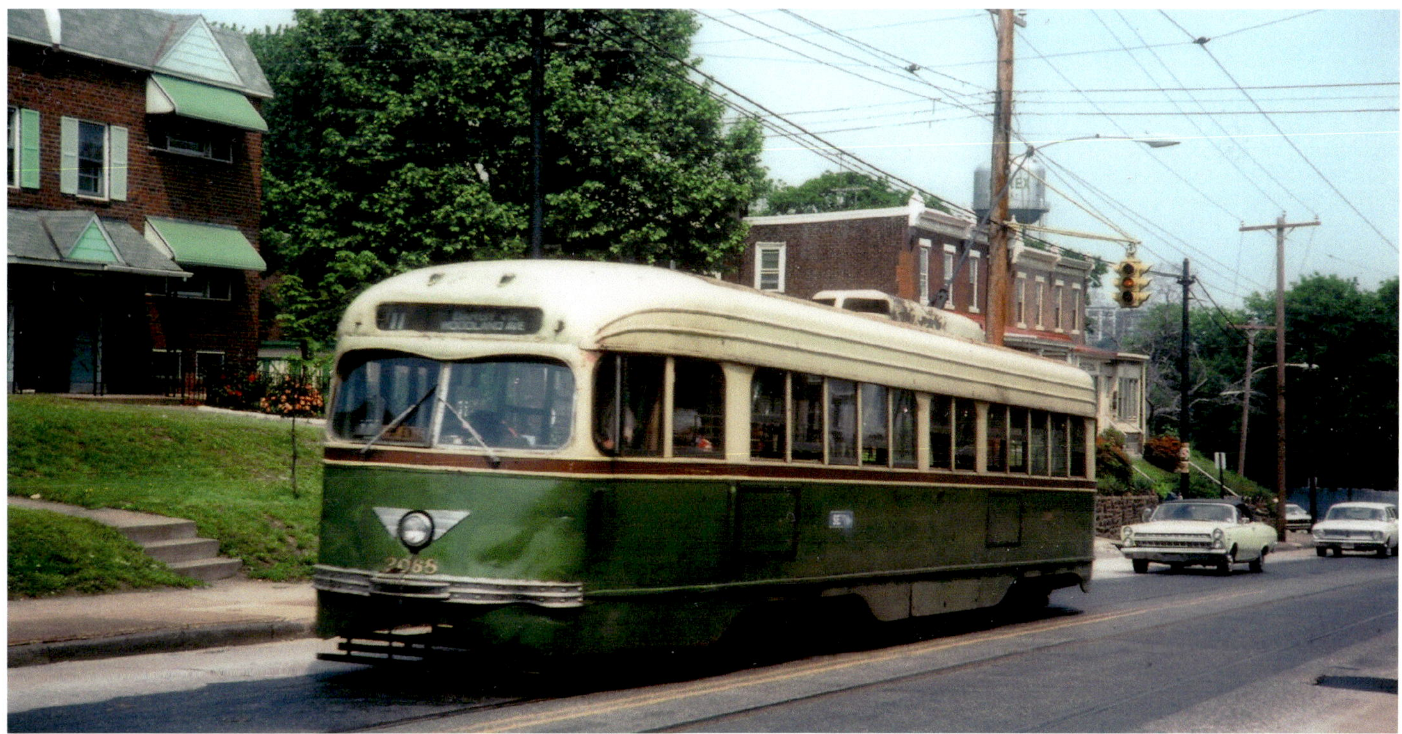

On May 24, 1975, SEPTA Route 11 PCC car No. 2068 is on Main Street passing through the borough of Darby. This was one of fifty cars numbered 2031-2080 built by St. Louis Car Company in 1941 and was powered by four Westinghouse type 1432 motors. Car No. 2068 was delivered in March 1941 and was destroyed in the Woodland Depot fire of October 23, 1975.

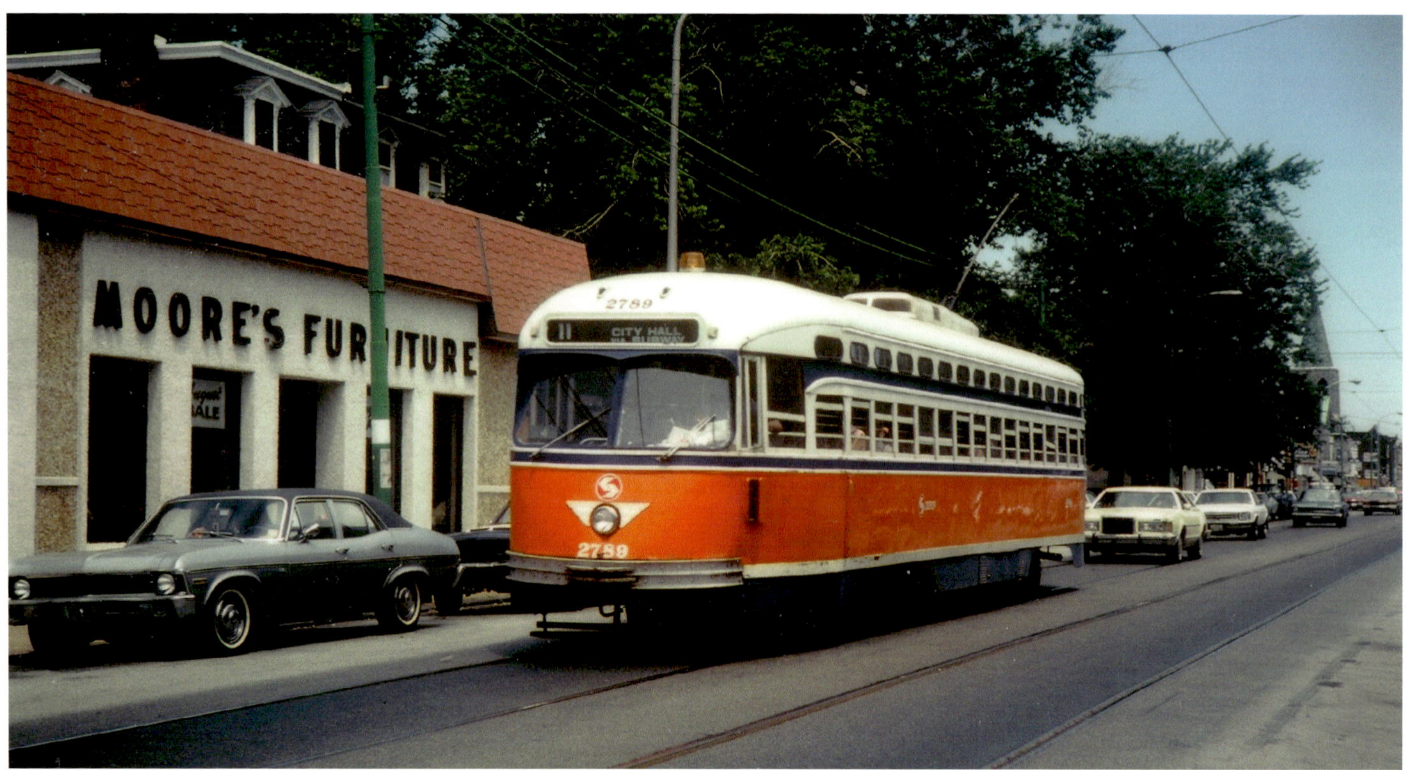

SEPTA Route 11 PCC car No. 2789 is on Woodland Avenue at Hobson Street on July 17, 1978. This car was delivered by St. Louis Car Company in April 1947 and was scrapped in 1983.

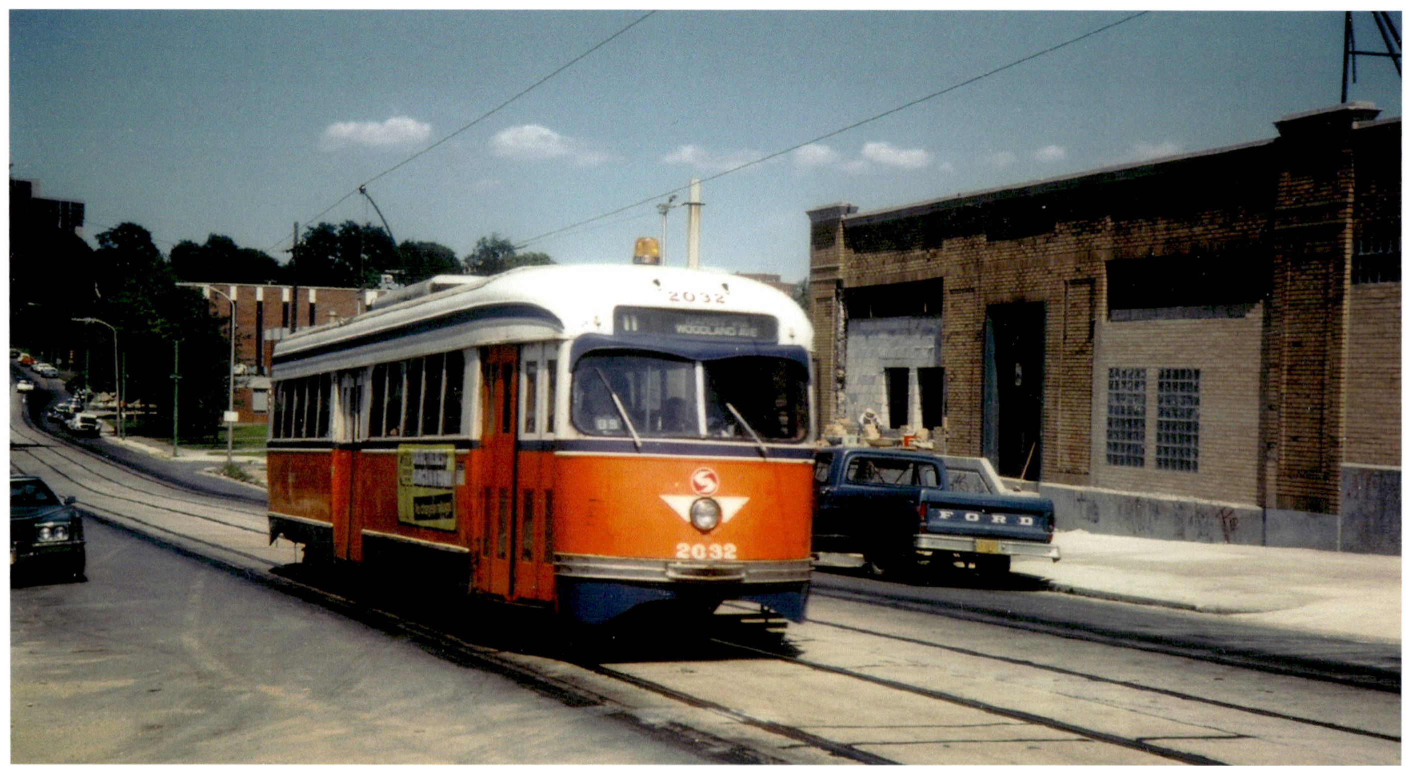

Woodland Avenue near 49th Street is the location of SEPTA Route 11 PCC car No. 2032 in this July 17, 1978 scene. This car was delivered by St. Louis Car Company in February 1941 and was scrapped in 1982.

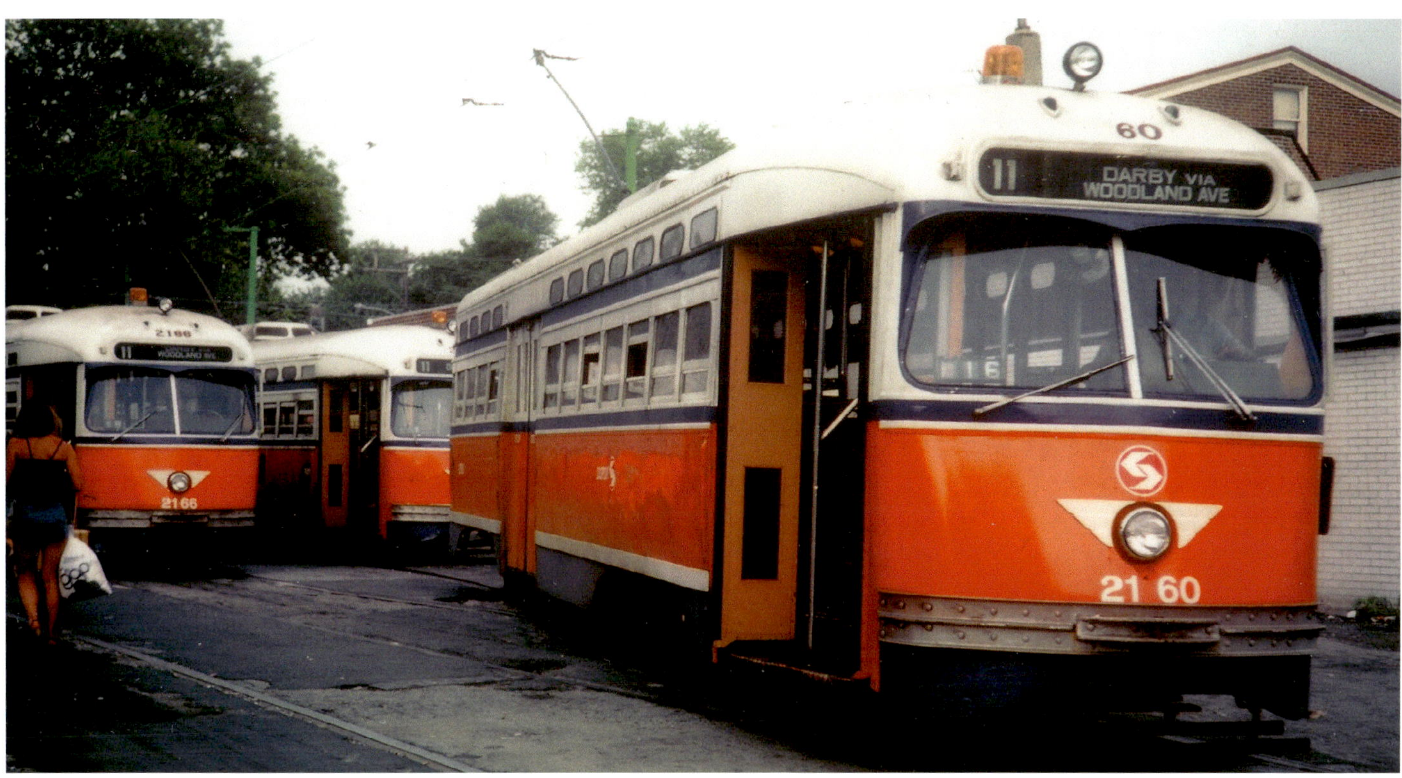

Darby Loop is the setting for three SEPTA Route 11 PCC cars headed by car No. 2160 on July 27, 1979. This car was delivered by St. Louis Car Company in June 1948, overhauled by SEPTA in January 1986, went to the Baltimore (Maryland) Streetcar Museum in 2006, later to Lancaster, Pennsylvania, for a proposed trolley car line, and later to the Warren (Pennsylvania) Car Company.

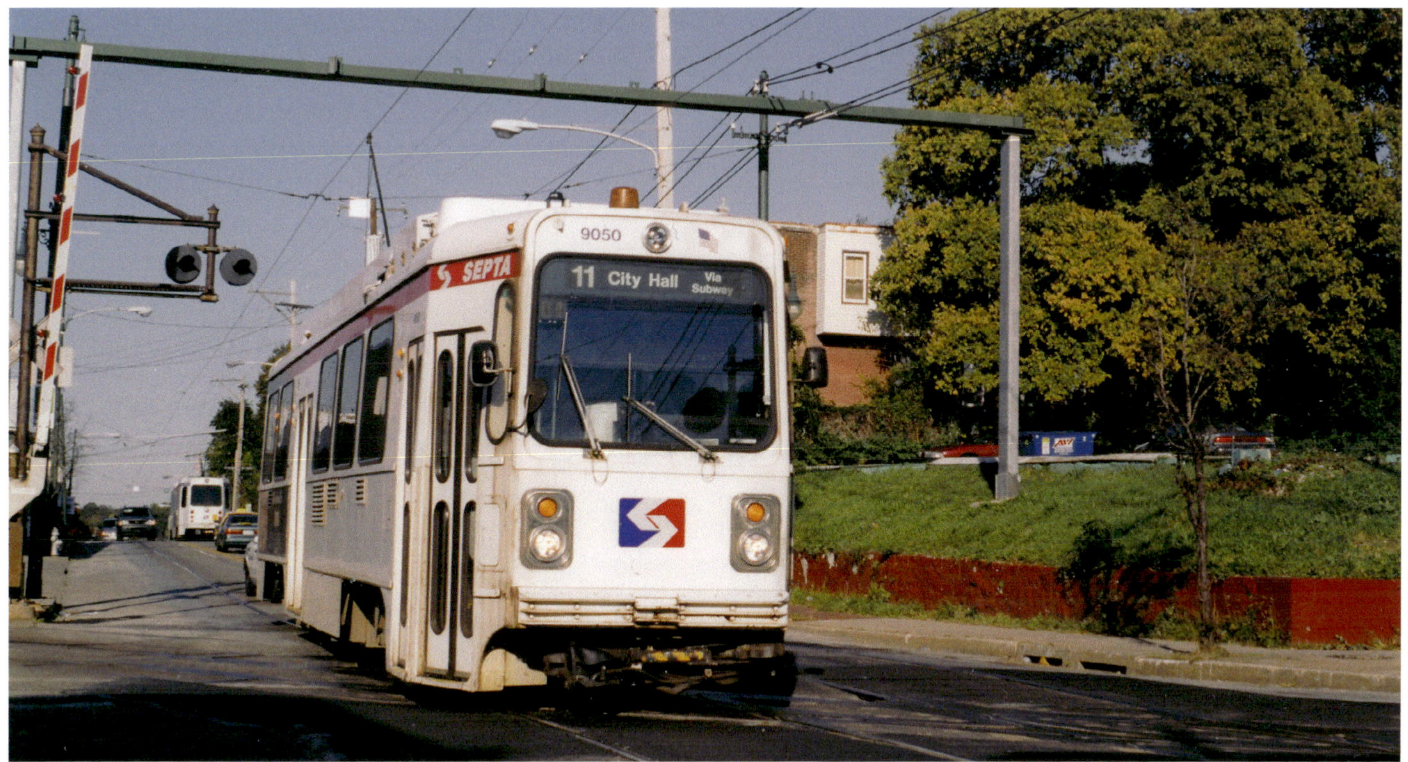

Eastbound for downtown Philadelphia, Kawasaki Heavy Industries Route 11 car No. 9050 (delivered on September 21, 1981 and placed on revenue service on October 2, 1981) is crossing the CSX Transportation railroad track on Main Street in Darby on October 15, 2006. The Kawasaki cars featured a stainless steel underframe, a rooftop air conditioning unit, an air suspension system for a smoother ride, and acceleration controls for smooth operation.

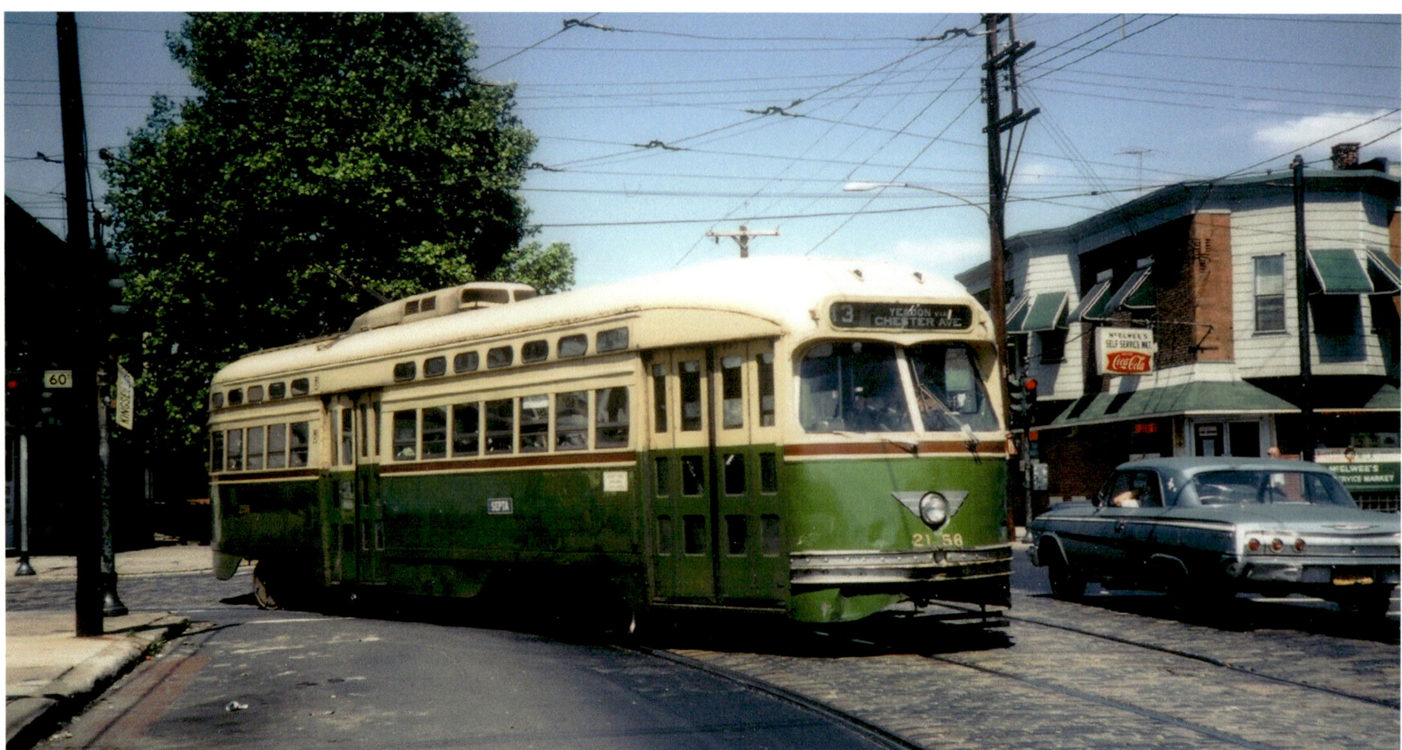

Westbound to Yeadon Loop, SEPTA Route 13 PCC car No. 2156 is turning from 60th Street onto Kingsessing Avenue in the Kingsessing neighborhood of southwest Philadelphia on May 30, 1970. This car was delivered by the St. Louis Car Company in June 1948, overhauled by SEPTA in September 1983, and was sold to Brookville Equipment Corporation in 2004. The 5.7 mile Subway Surface Route 13 operates in the underground subway and then through West Philadelphia to Yeadon in Delaware County.

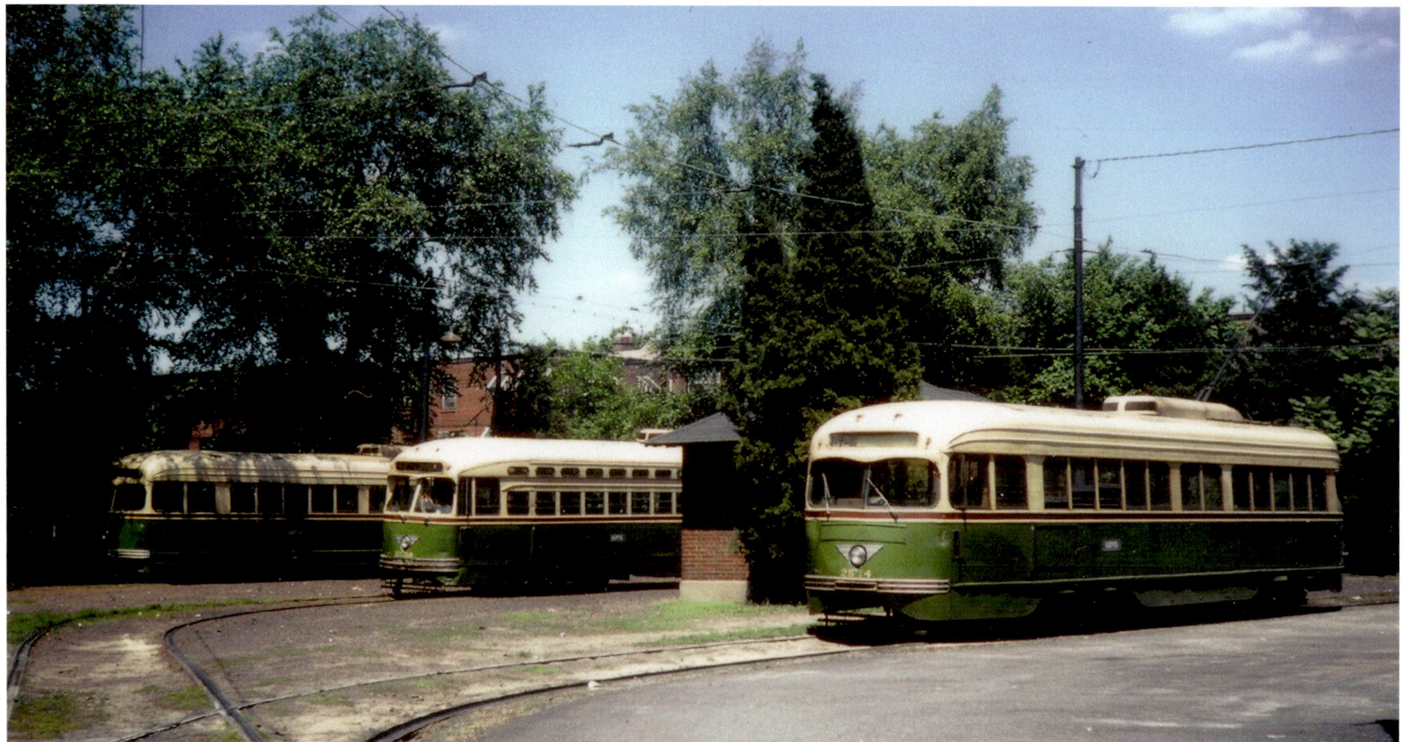

Yeadon Loop (in the borough of Yeadon in Delaware County, just outside of Philadelphia on May 30, 1970) is the location of SEPTA PCC cars (all built by St. Louis Car Company), from left to right, Route 13 car No. 2039 (delivered in February 1941 and destroyed in the Woodland Carbarn fire of October 1975), car No. 2156 (delivered in June 1948 and sold to Brookville Equipment Corporation in 2004), and Route 62 car No. 2514 (delivered in December 1940 and destroyed in the Woodland Depot fire of October 23, 1975).

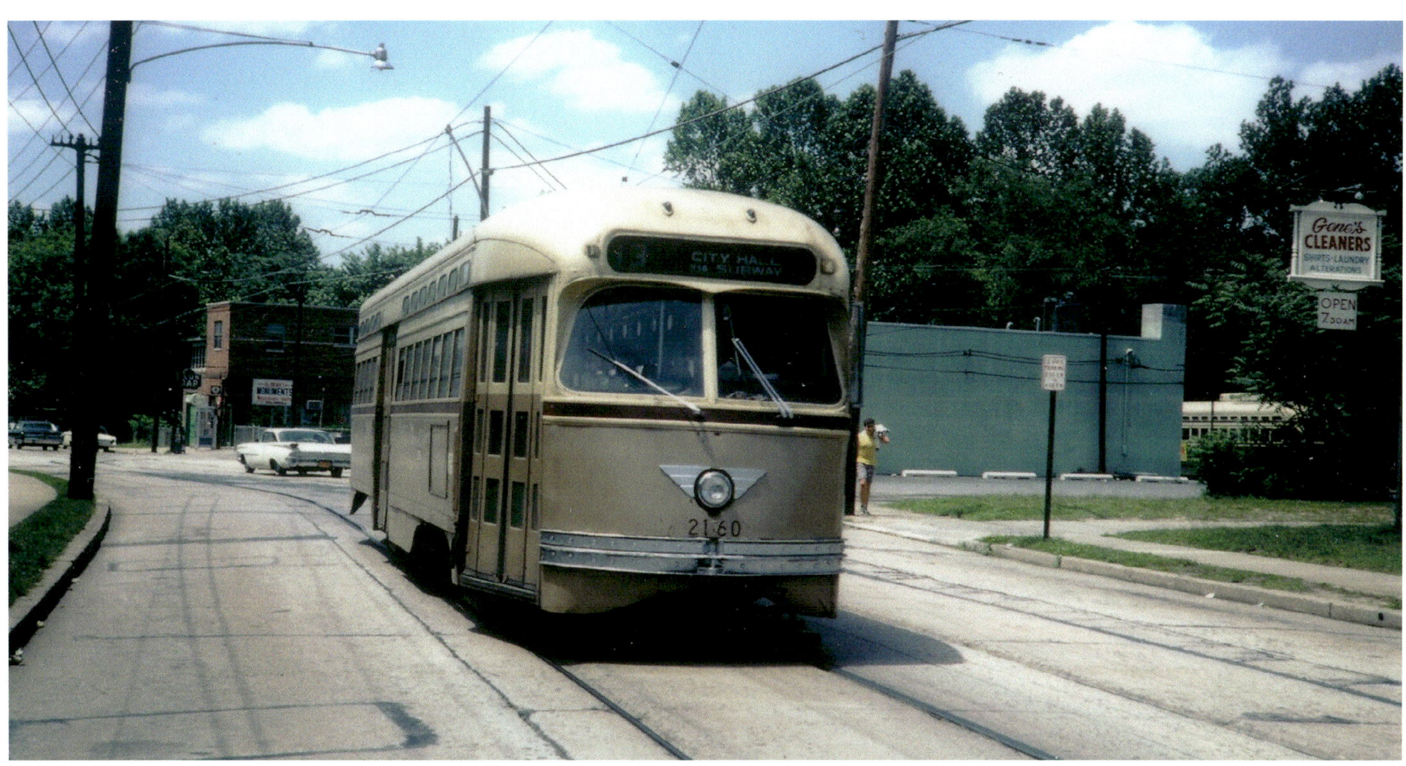

SEPTA Route 13 PCC car No. 2160 is just east of Yeadon Loop traveling along Chester Avenue heading for downtown Philadelphia on May 30, 1970.

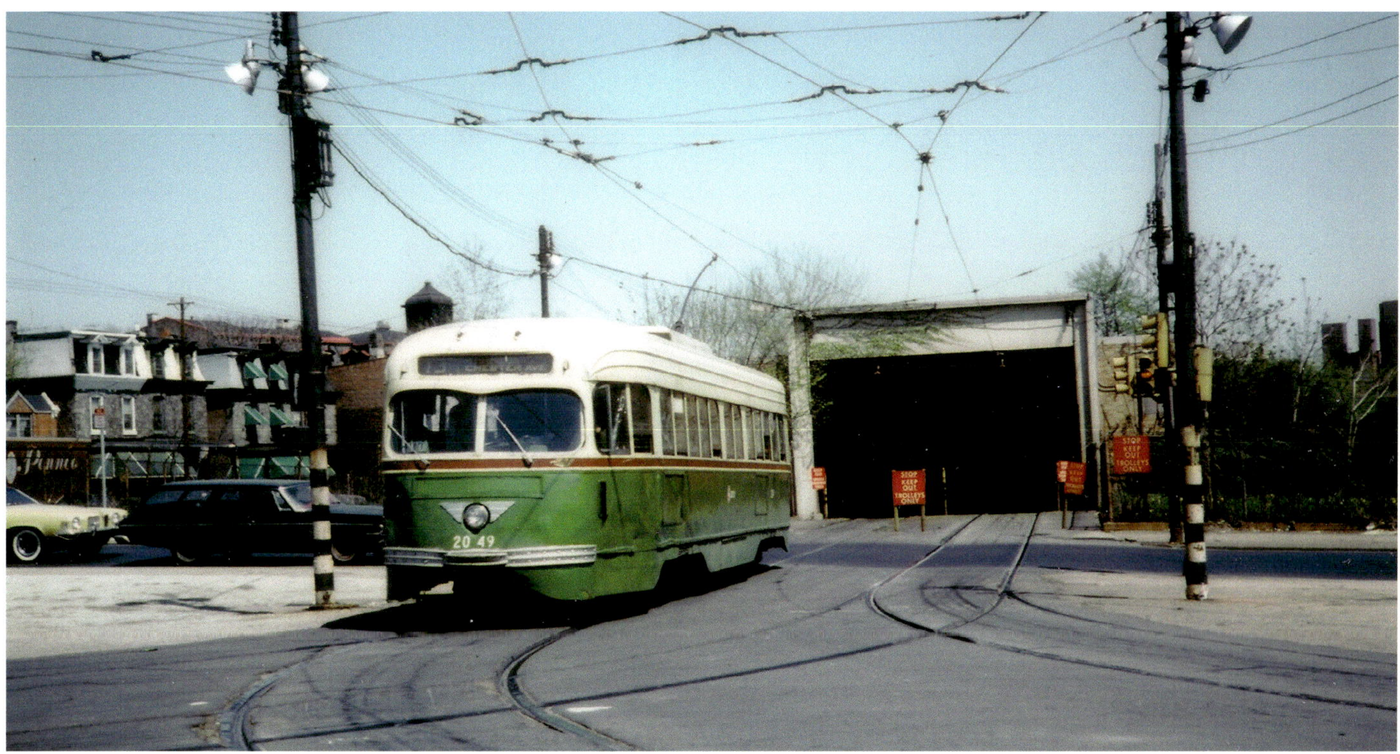

On April 20, 1973, SEPTA Route 13 PCC car No. 2049 has emerged from the 40th Street subway portal in the Spruce Hill neighborhood of the University City section of West Philadelphia. This car was delivered by St. Louis Car Company in February 1941 and was scrapped in 1978.

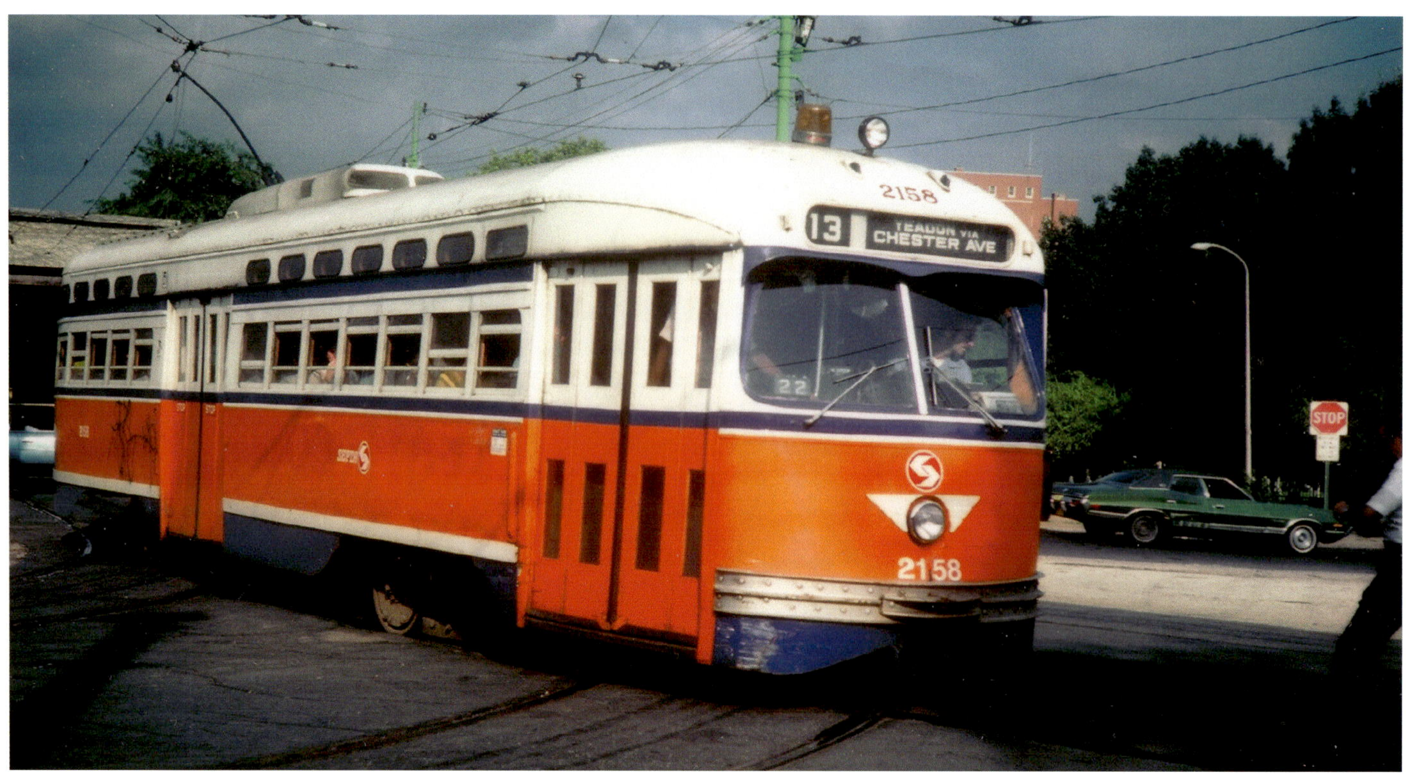

On July 27, 1979, SEPTA Route 13 PCC car No. 2158 is just west of the 40th Street subway portal handling a westbound trip to the Yeadon Loop. This car was delivered by St. Louis Car Company in June 1948, overhauled by SEPTA in June 1984, and went to Brookville Equipment Corporation on January 2, 2003 to be rebuilt into car No. 2335.

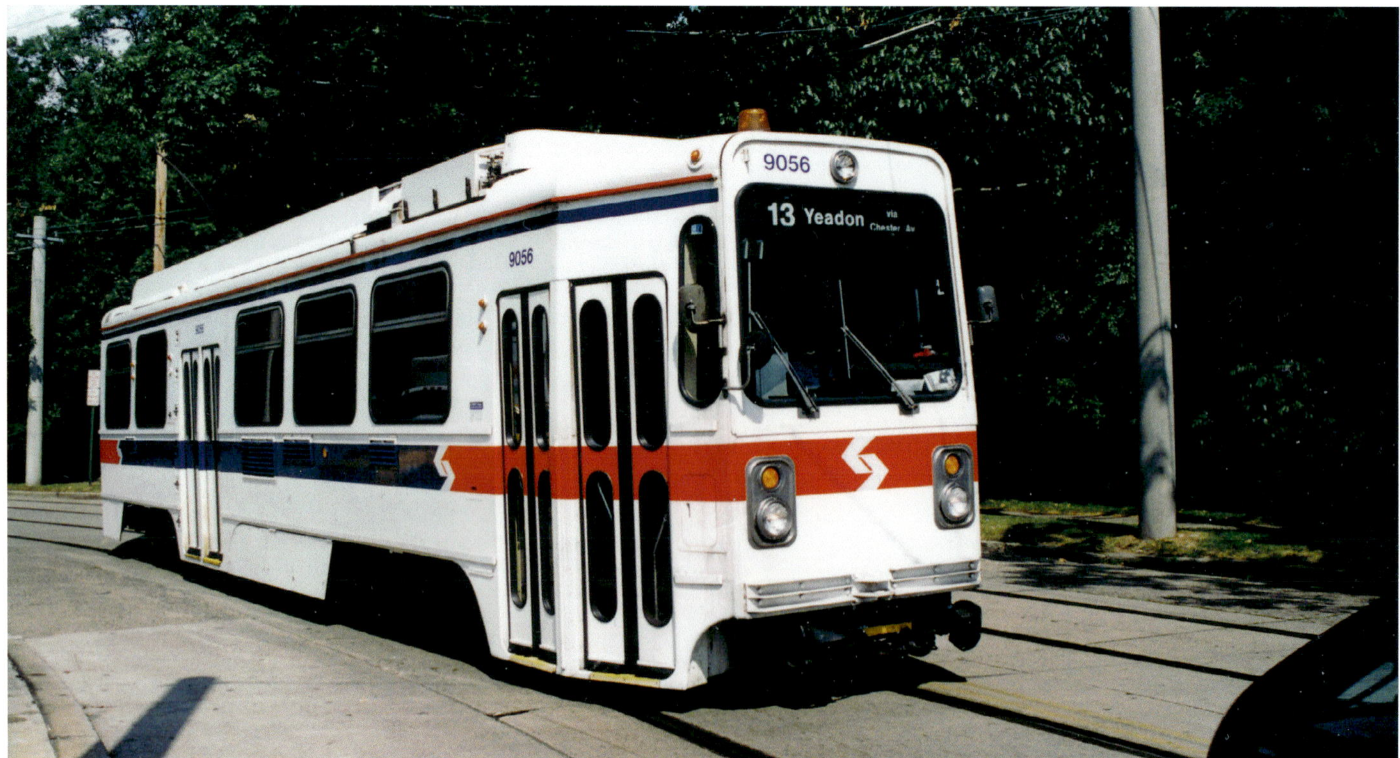

With Cobbs Creek Park on the south side of Chester Avenue, on July 31, 1998, SEPTA Route 13 Kawasaki Heavy Industries car No. 9056 (delivered September 30, 1981 and placed in revenue service on October 8, 1981) is approaching Church Lane for a westbound trip to Yeadon Loop. American suppliers for this car included Penn Machine for resilient wheels; Vapor Company for doors and door controls; Westinghouse Air Brake for compressor, air brake controls, disc brakes, and track brakes; and Westinghouse Electric for motors, gear boxes and controls.

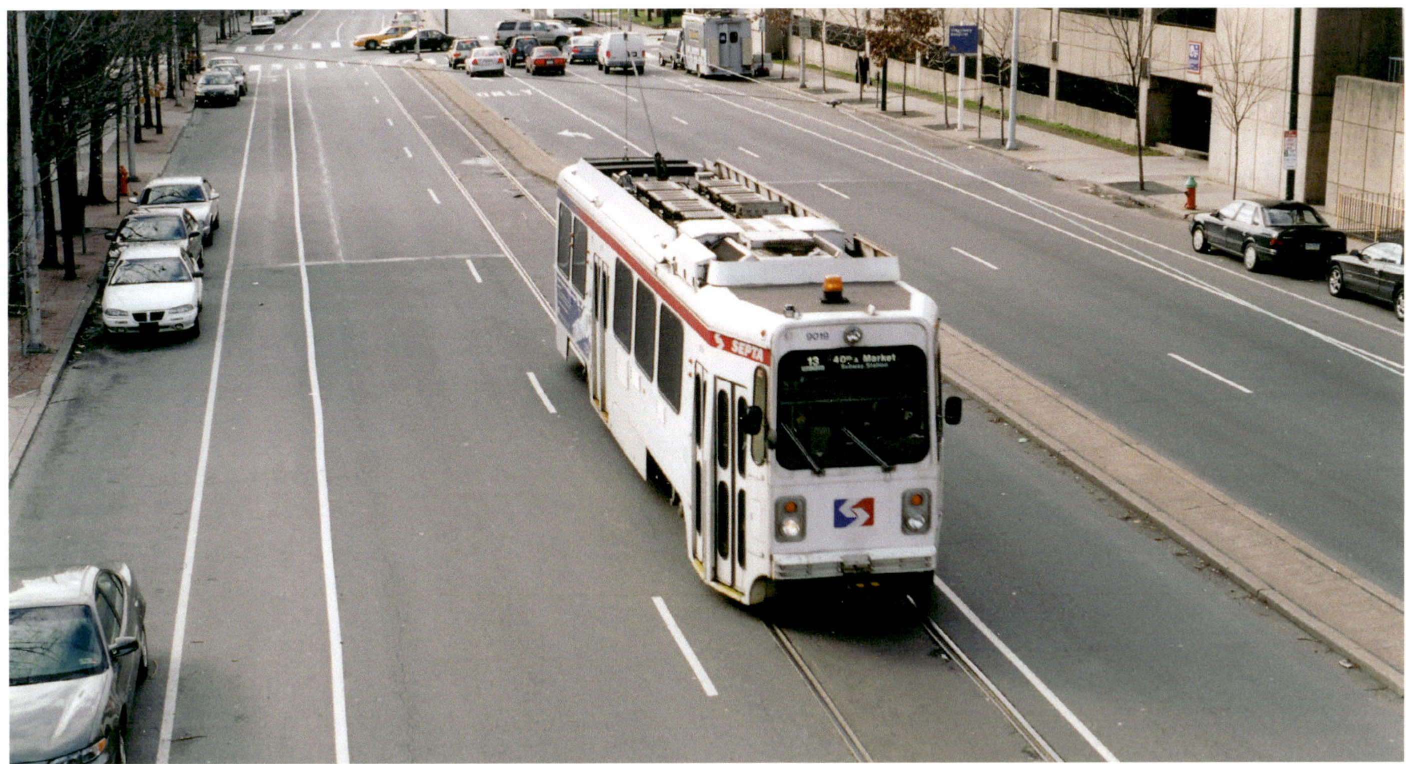

Northbound on 38th Street, SEPTA Route 13 Kawasaki Heavy Industries car No. 9019 is heading for 40th and Market Streets on a diversion routing on February 5, 2006. This diversion routing is used when the trolley car subway is closed for maintenance or emergency reasons.

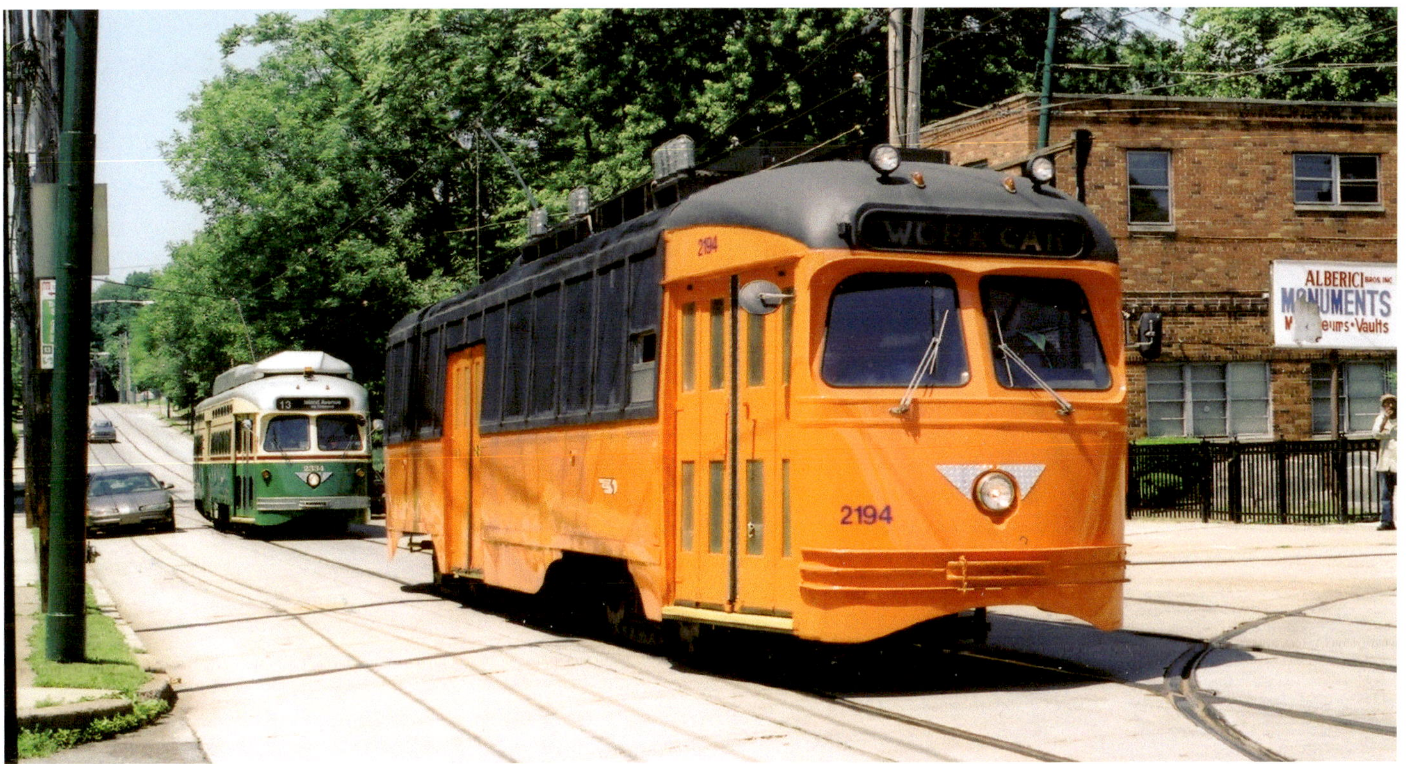

On a June 7, 2009 rail excursion, SEPTA work trolley PCC car No. 2194 (delivered in July 1948 and modified by SEPTA into an overhead line car in April 1988) followed by rebuilt PCCII car No. 2334 (originally car No. 2753 delivered in March 1947, overhauled by SEPTA in April 1985 and rebuilt by Brookville Equipment Corporation with delivery on September 24, 2004) are passing the Yeadon Loop eastbound on Chester Avenue near Callahan Avenue.

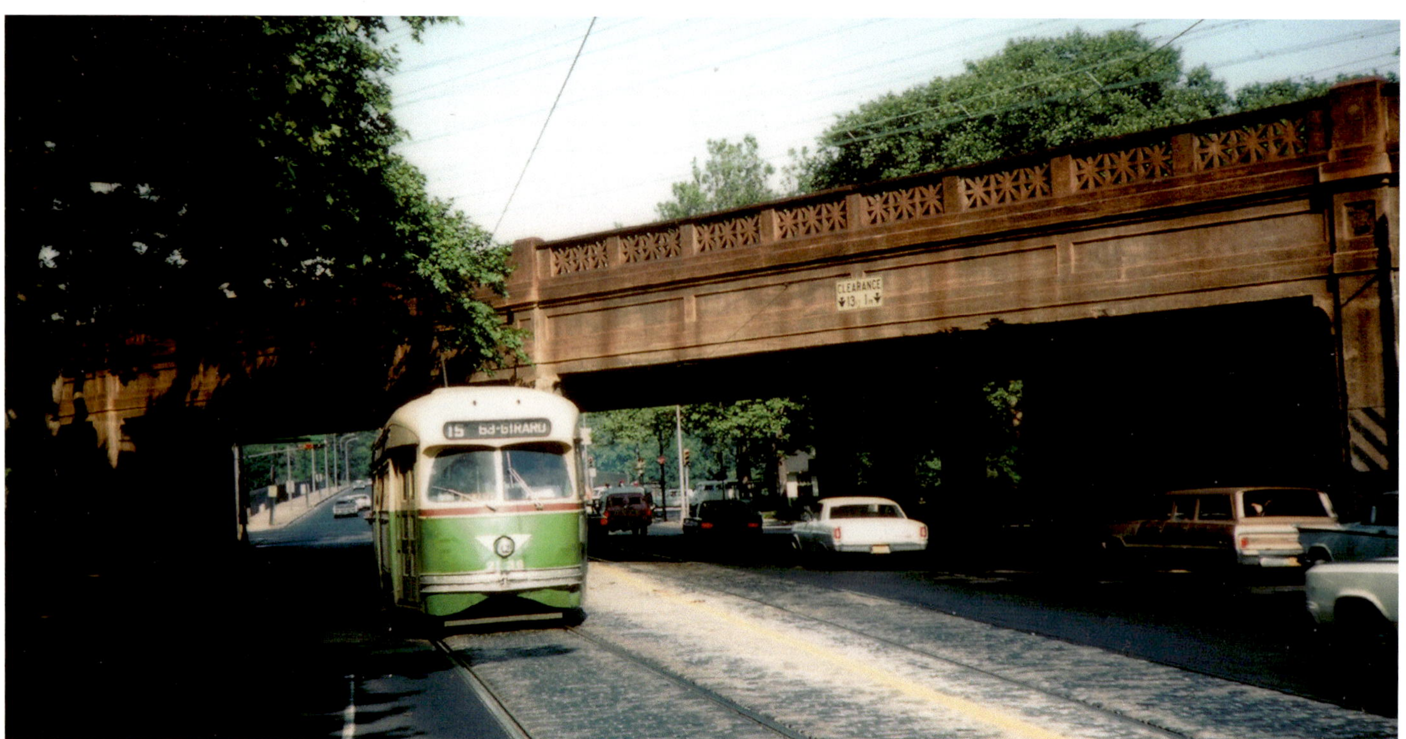

SEPTA Route 15 PCC car No. 2138 (delivered by St. Louis Car Company in September 1948, overhauled by SEPTA in May 1981, and sold to the San Francisco Municipal Railway in October 1992 and was renumbered 1057 with a Cincinnati paint scheme) is westbound on Girard Avenue near the Philadelphia Zoo on May 31, 1969. The former Philadelphia to New York mainline Pennsylvania Railroad Bridge is now used by Amtrak and SEPTA commuter trains.

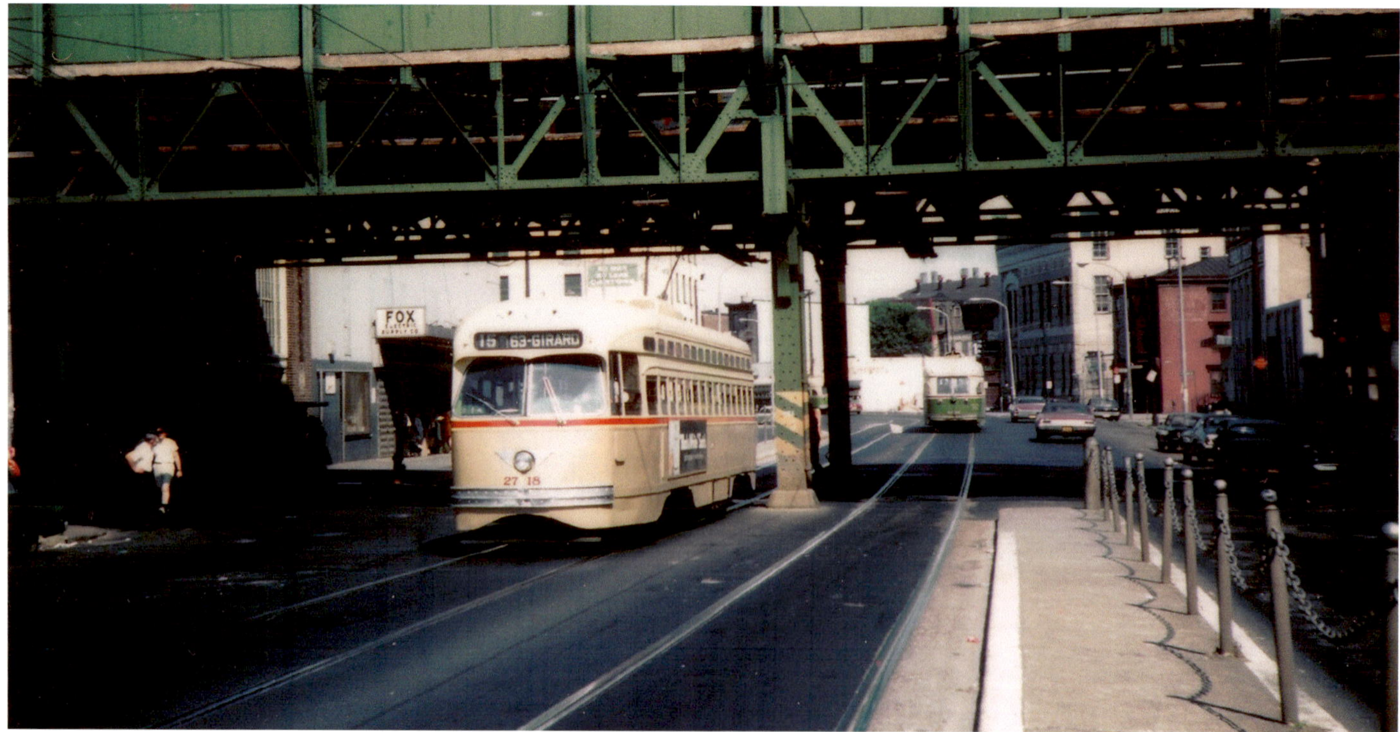

Crossing under the Frankford Elevated Station on Girard Avenue at Front Street on May 31, 1969, SEPTA Route 15 PCC car No. 2718 is handling a westbound trip to 63rd Street and Girard Avenue. This was one of twenty-five cars numbered 2701-2725 (each powered by four Westinghouse type 1432D motors) built by St. Louis Car Company in 1947. Car No. 2718 was delivered by the St. Louis Car Company in February 1947, and scrapped in 1979.

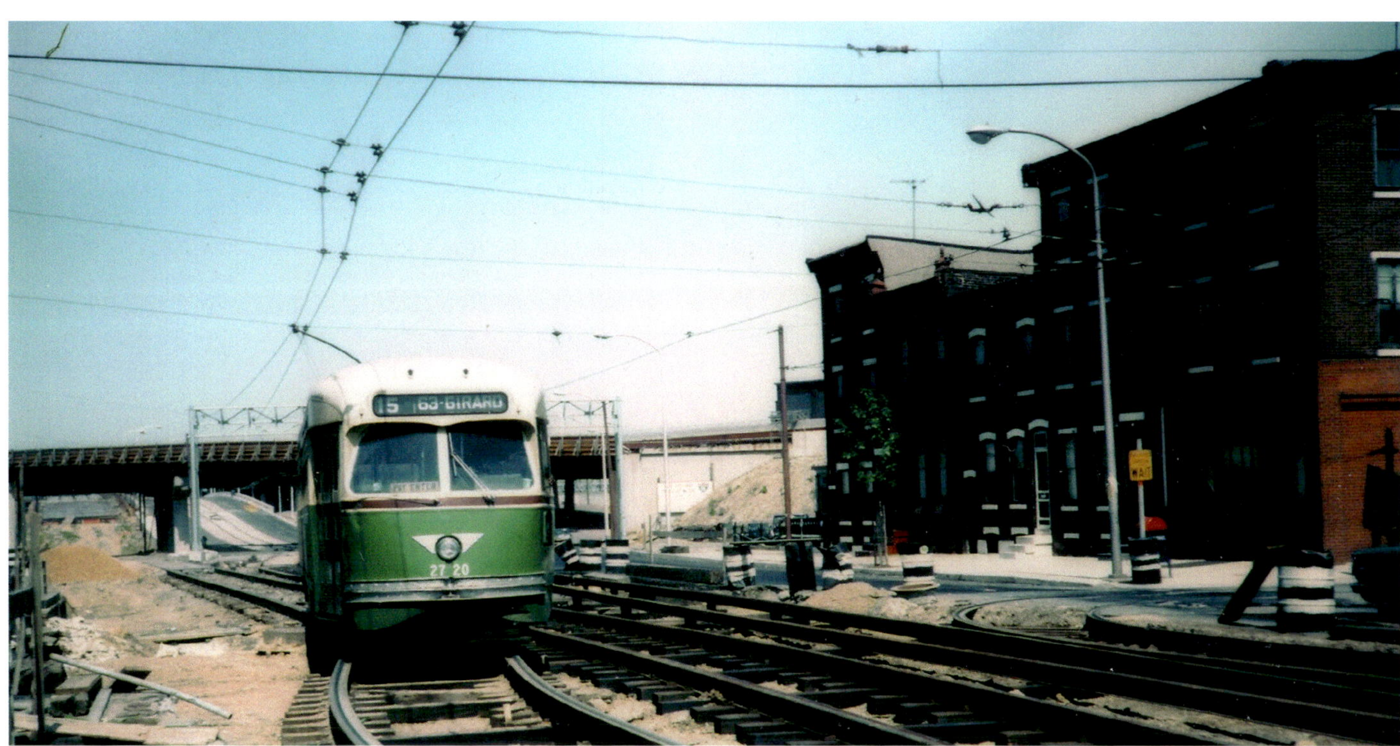

On May 31, 1969, SEPTA Route 15 PCC car 2720 is at a major track reconstruction project on Girard Avenue for the new bridge for Interstate 95 that was under construction in Philadelphia. This car was delivered by St. Louis Car Company in February 1947, overhauled by SEPTA in September 1982, and was sold in October 1994. Route 15 operated from 63rd and Girard to the Arsenal, but was cut back to Richmond and Allegheny Avenue on September 11, 1955 because of a new bridge being built on Richmond Street at Frankford Creek. A new loop was established at Richmond and Westmoreland on February 24, 1956.

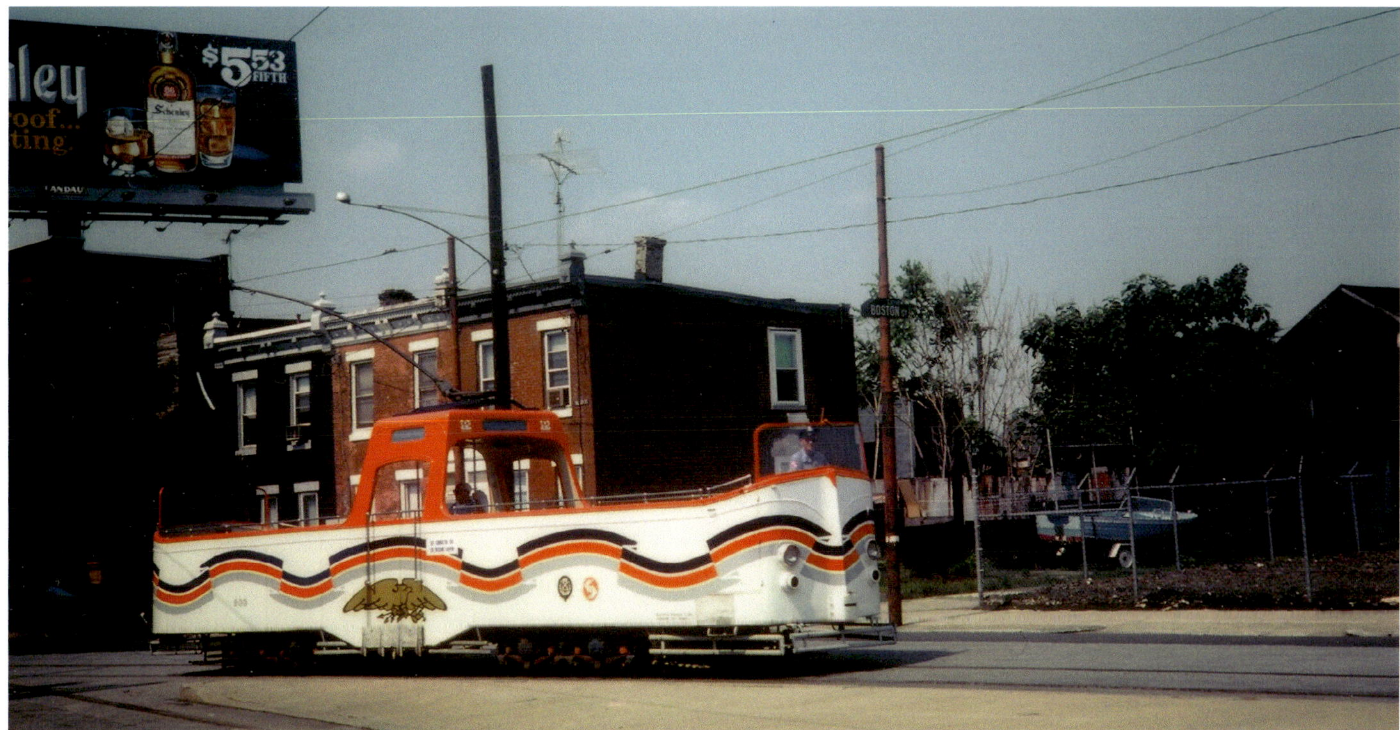

The Blackpool England "Boat Trolley" is at the Richmond and Cumberland Loop on August 6, 1977. SEPTA operated the Boat Trolley from 63rd Street to this loop during the summer of 1977. The Richmond and Cumberland Loop was used when Richmond Street was blocked by trucks that became stuck under the low bridge beneath the former Reading Railroad Port Richmond Yard that is now operated by Consolidated Rail Corporation.

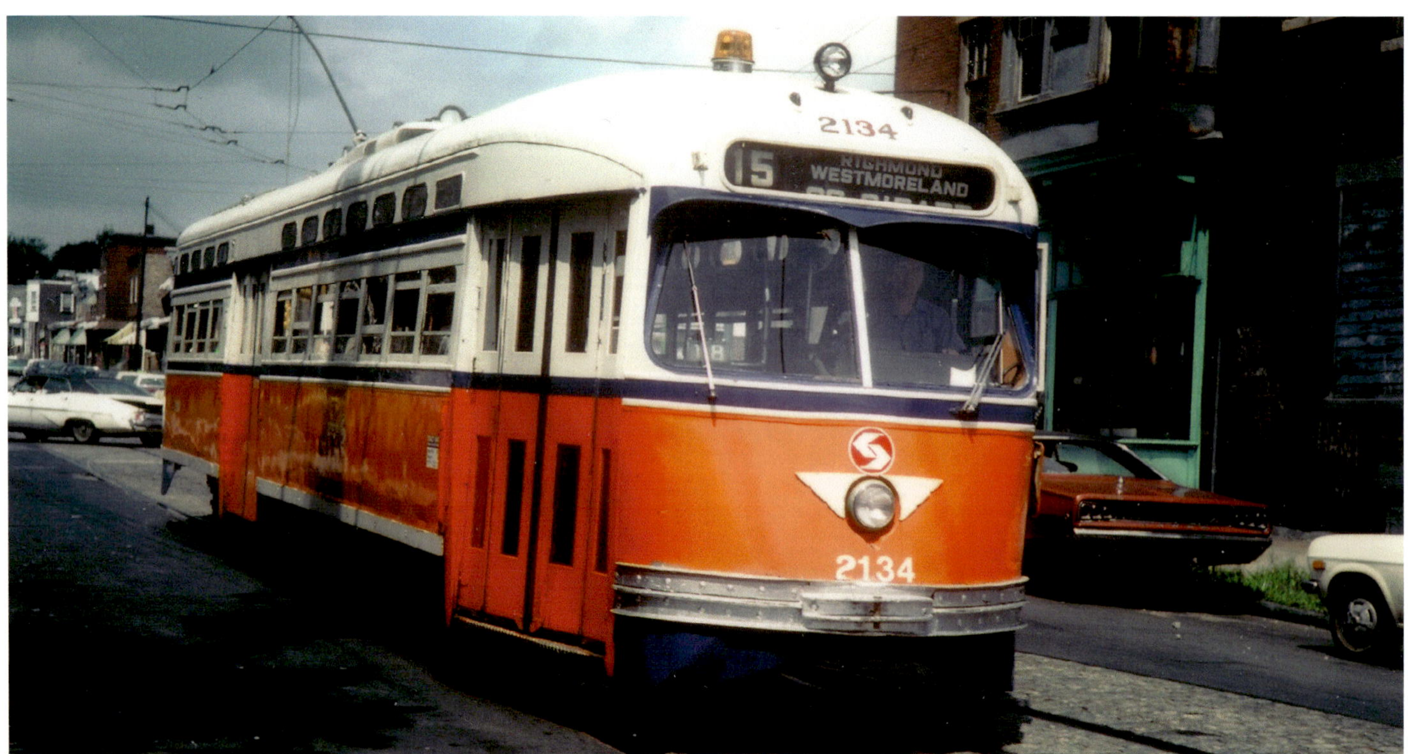

SEPTA Route 15 PCC car No. 2134 has turned from 63rd Street to Girard Avenue where the operator is awaiting departure time at the western end of the line on July 27, 1979. This car was delivered by the St. Louis Car Company in September 1948, overhauled by SEPTA in February 1983, and sold in 2003.

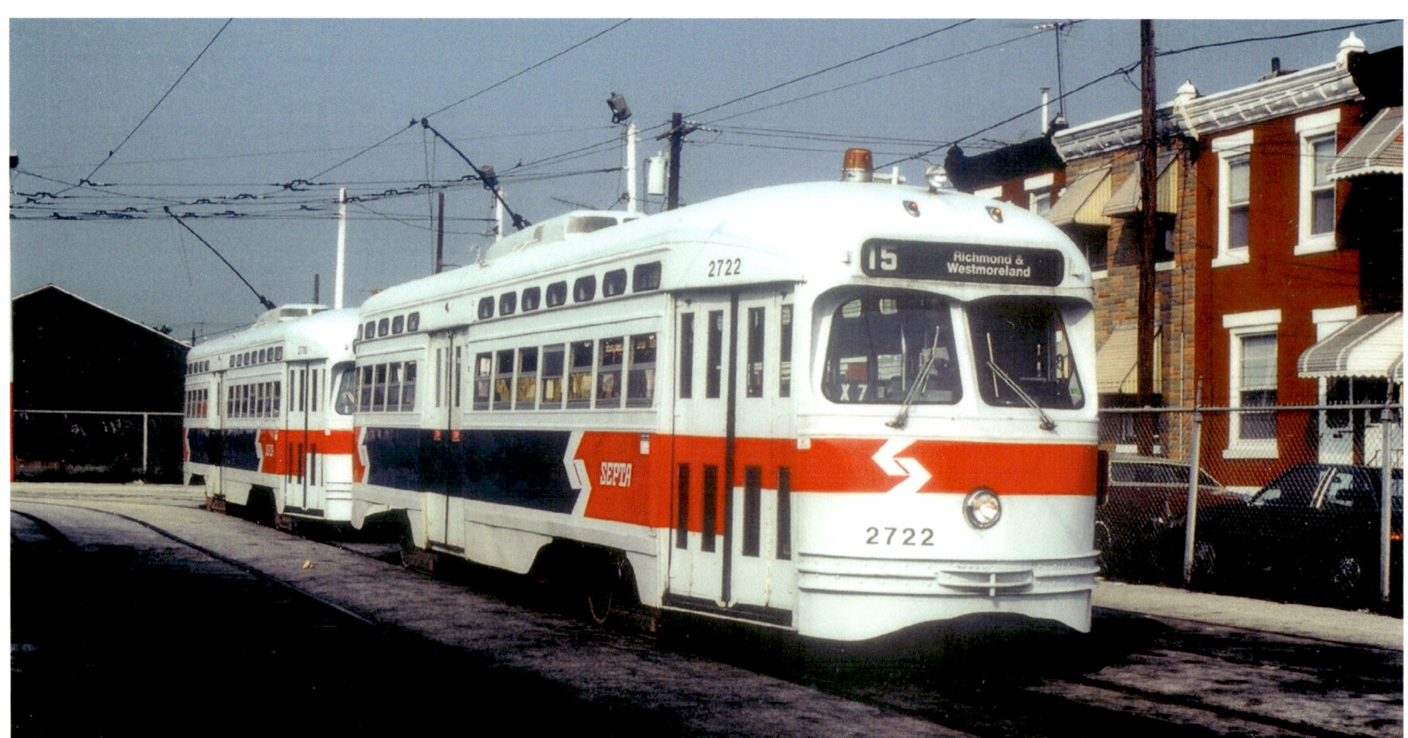

On August 6, 1984, the Richmond and Westmoreland Loop of SEPTA Route 15 is the location of St. Louis Car Company built PCC cars No. 2722 (delivered in March 1947, overhauled by SEPTA in May 1983, and sold in June 1995) and No. 2710 (delivered in February 1947, overhauled by SEPTA in June 1983, and sold in October 1994). A similar PCC car No. 2709 was acquired by the Seashore Trolley Museum in 1995.

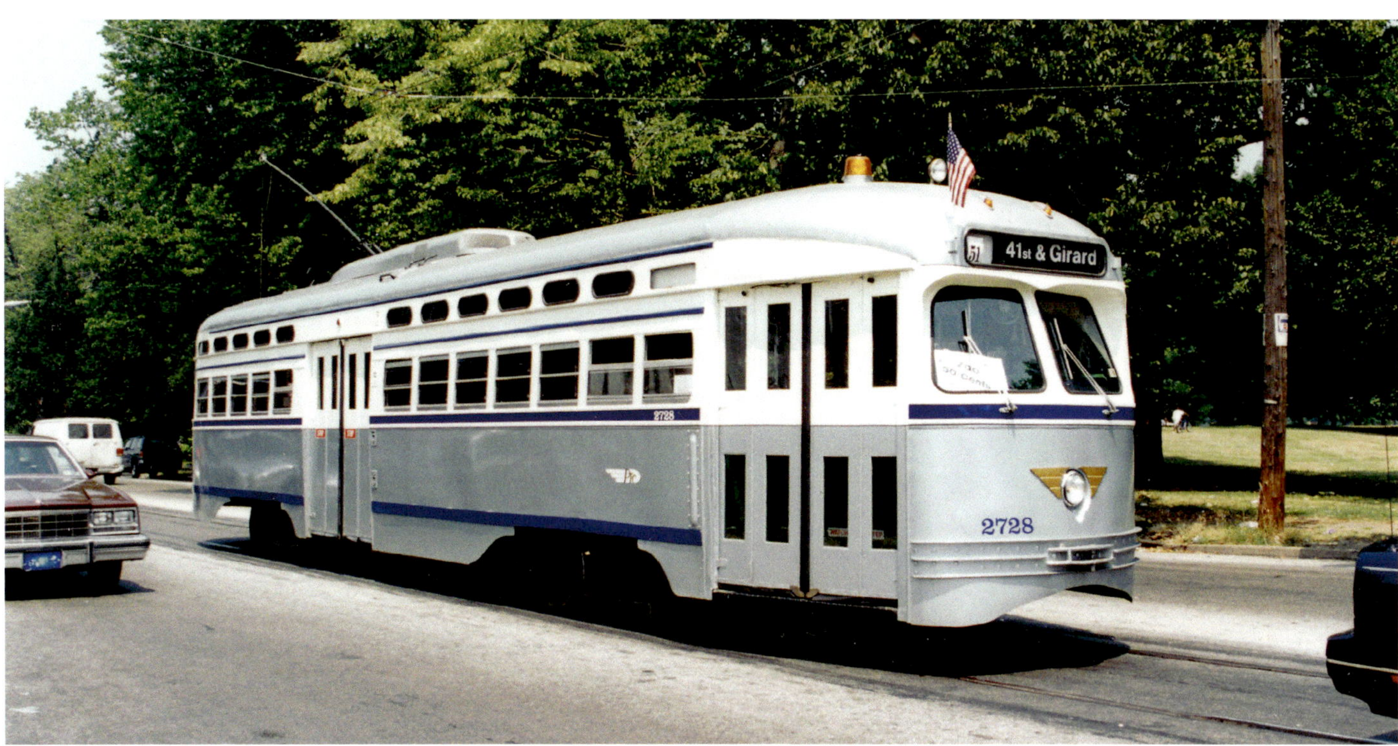

Parkside Avenue at 40th Street on a beautiful July 15, 1995 summer day finds SEPTA Route 51 PCC car No. 2728 (delivered in March 1947 by St. Louis Car Company, overhauled by SEPTA in May 1986, and painted silver and cream with blue trim in 1995). This line operated on 11th and 12th Street between Noble and Bainbridge Streets every twenty minutes on weekends with certain trips operating north to Girard Avenue and west past the zoo to the 41st and Parkside Loop. Route 51 Welcome Line operated from May 1995 to December 1995 during the summertime, as well as certain holidays.

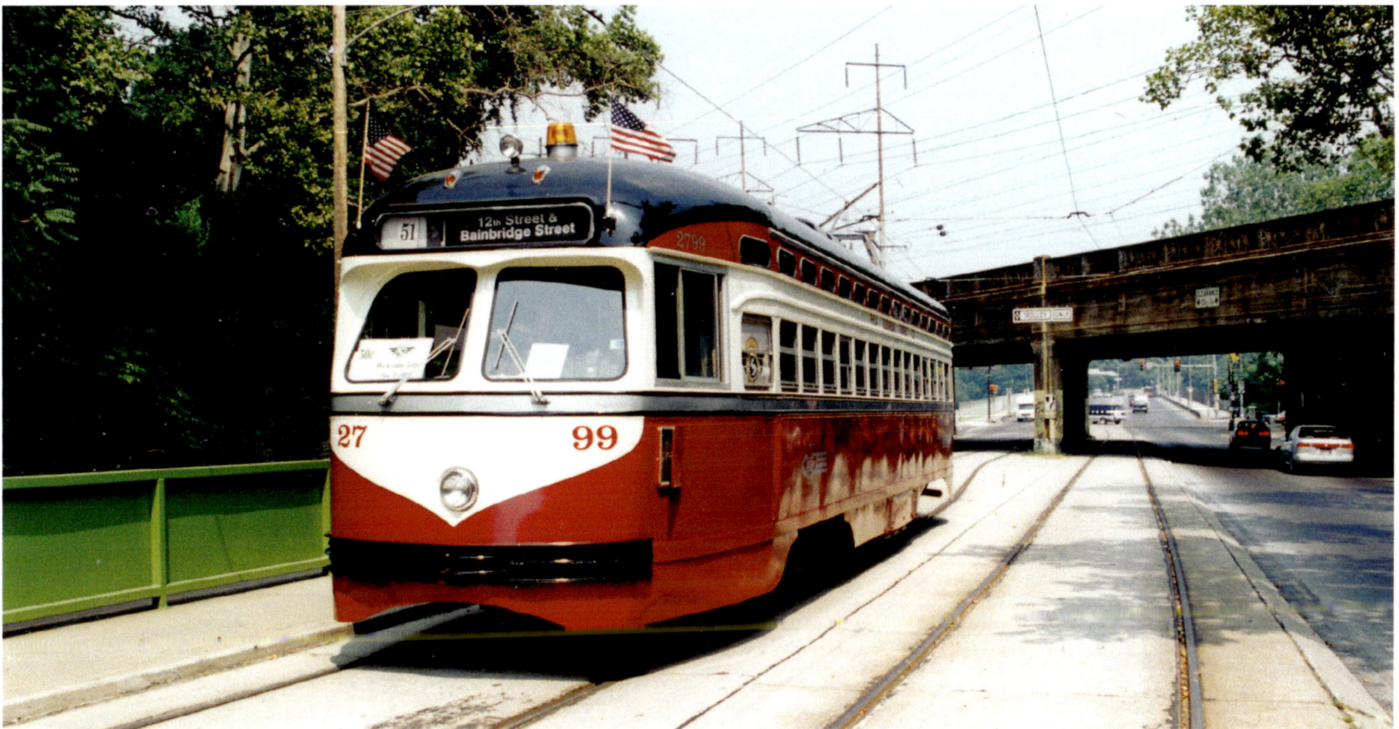

On July 15, 1995, SEPTA Route 51 Welcome Line PCC car No. 2799 (delivered by St. Louis Car Company in April 1947, overhauled by SEPTA in August 1985, and painted in the Philadelphia Suburban Transportation Company maroon and cream paint scheme) is westbound on Girard Avenue with the bridge of the former Pennsylvania Railroad mainline in the background. The Welcome Line was discontinued at the end of December 1995 due to budget cuts.

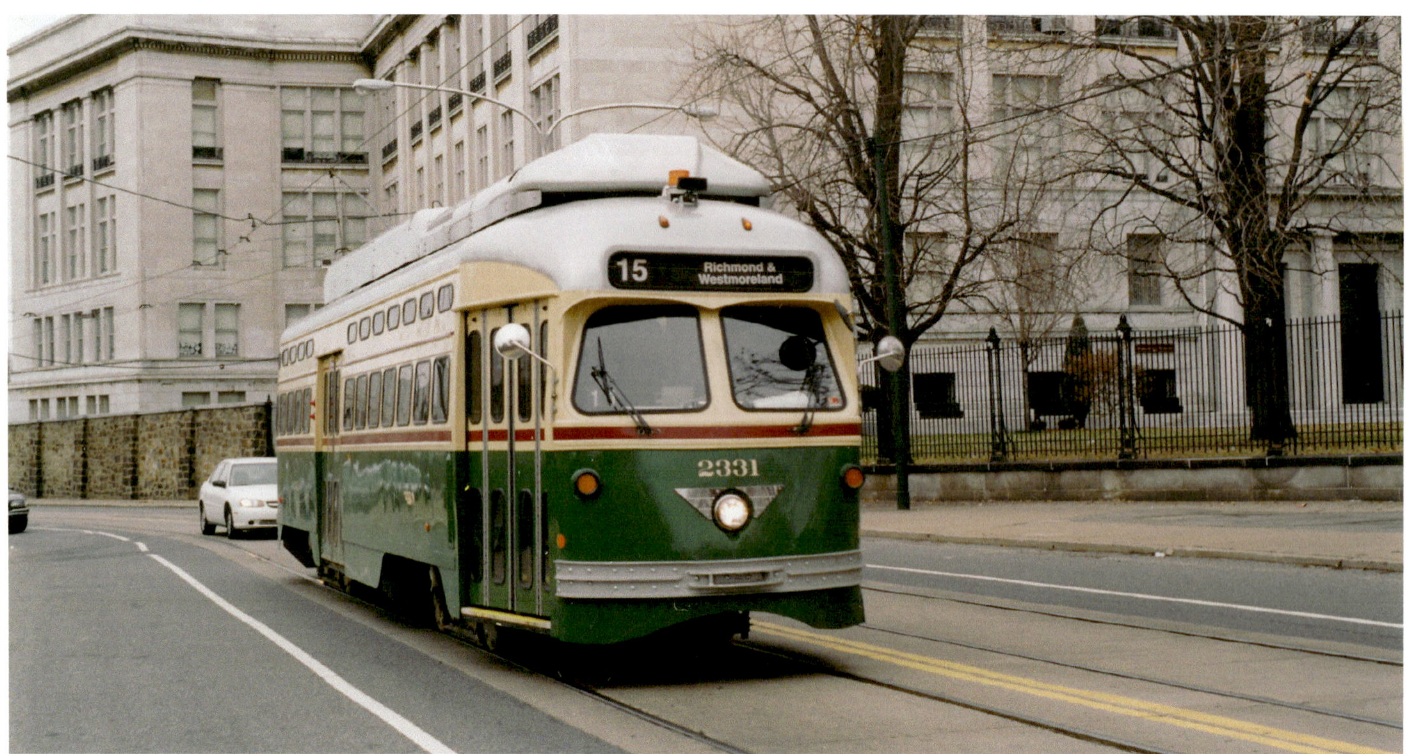

Eastbound SEPTA Route 15 PCC II car No. 2331 is on Girard Avenue at Corinthian Avenue on January 1, 2006 passing by Girard College. This car was originally car No. 2758 delivered by St. Louis Company in March 1947, overhauled by SEPTA in November 1985, and rebuilt by Brookville Equipment Corporation with delivery as car No. 2331 on July 30, 2004. Stephen Girard (1750-1831), who was successful in banking and international shipping, left the bulk of his fortune to establish Girard College which was founded in 1833.

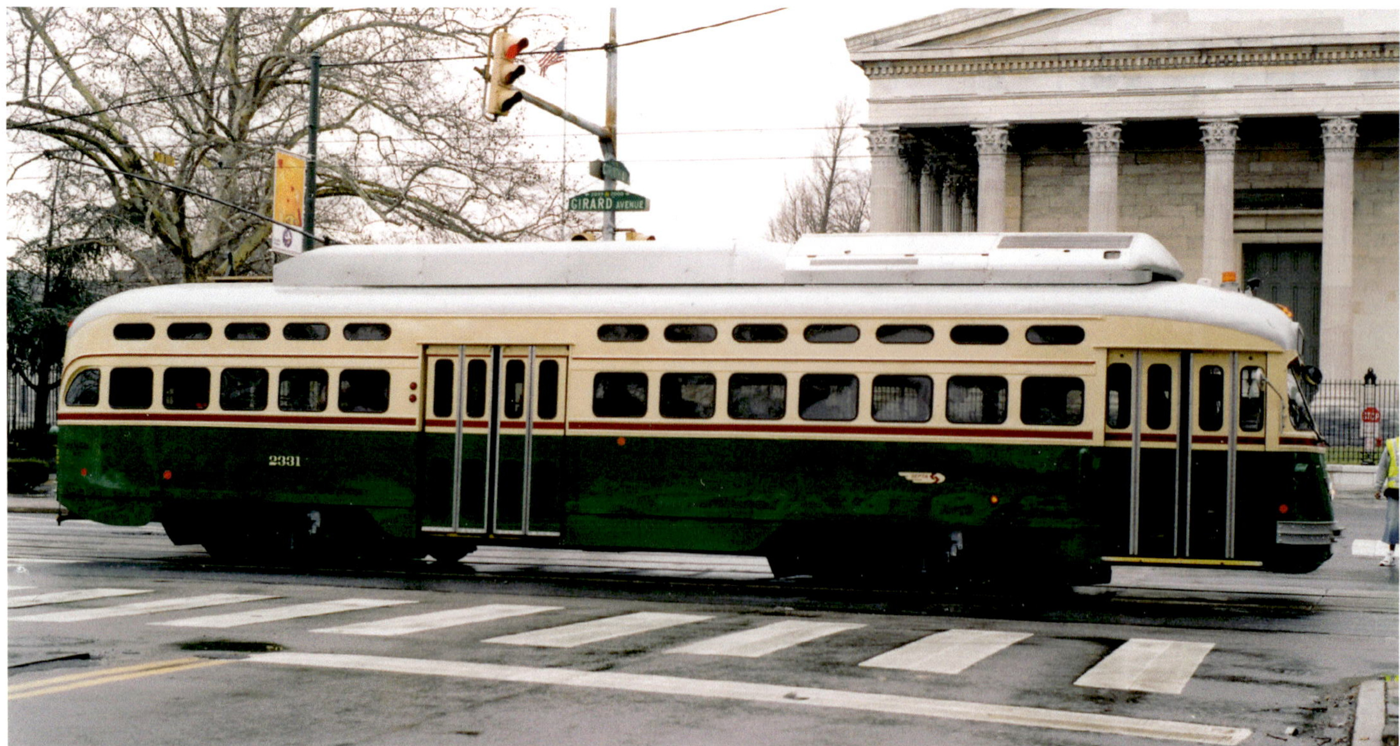

On February 4, 2006, Route 15 PCCII car No. 2331 is on Girard Avenue at Corinthian Avenue with the nineteenth century American Greek-Revival architecture Founder's Hall at Girard College in the background. College founder Stephen Girard specified in his will the dimensions, plan of the building, and required an architectural competition for the building's design which was won by architect Thomas Ustick Walter. The building was completed in 1847.

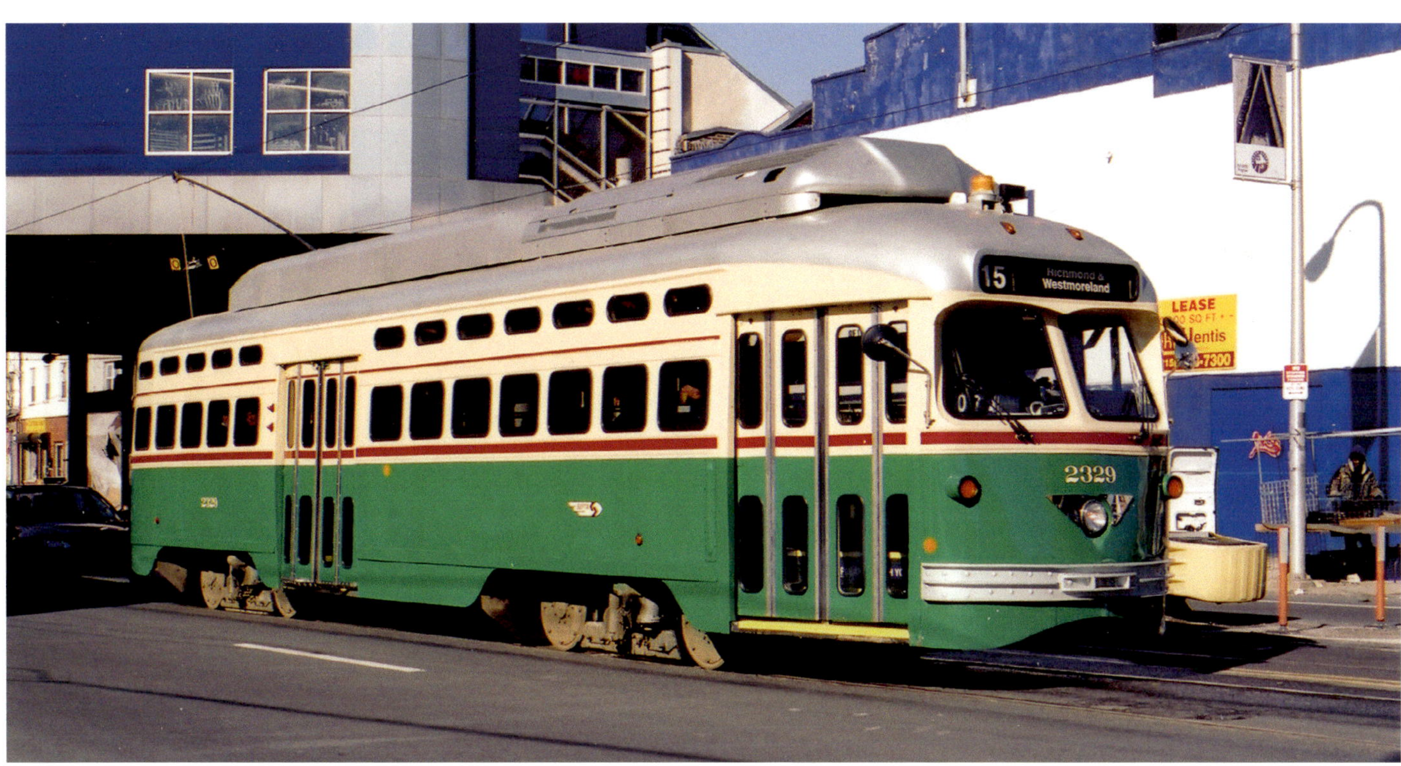

On February 3, 2007, SEPTA Route 15 PCCII car No. 2329 has crossed Front Street under the Girard Avenue Station of the Frankford Elevated Line and is eastbound on Girard Avenue heading for the Richmond and Westmoreland Loop. This car was originally No. 2182 delivered by St. Louis Car Company in July 1948, overhauled by SEPTA in April 1986, and rebuilt by Brookville Equipment Corporation with delivery on June 23, 2004.

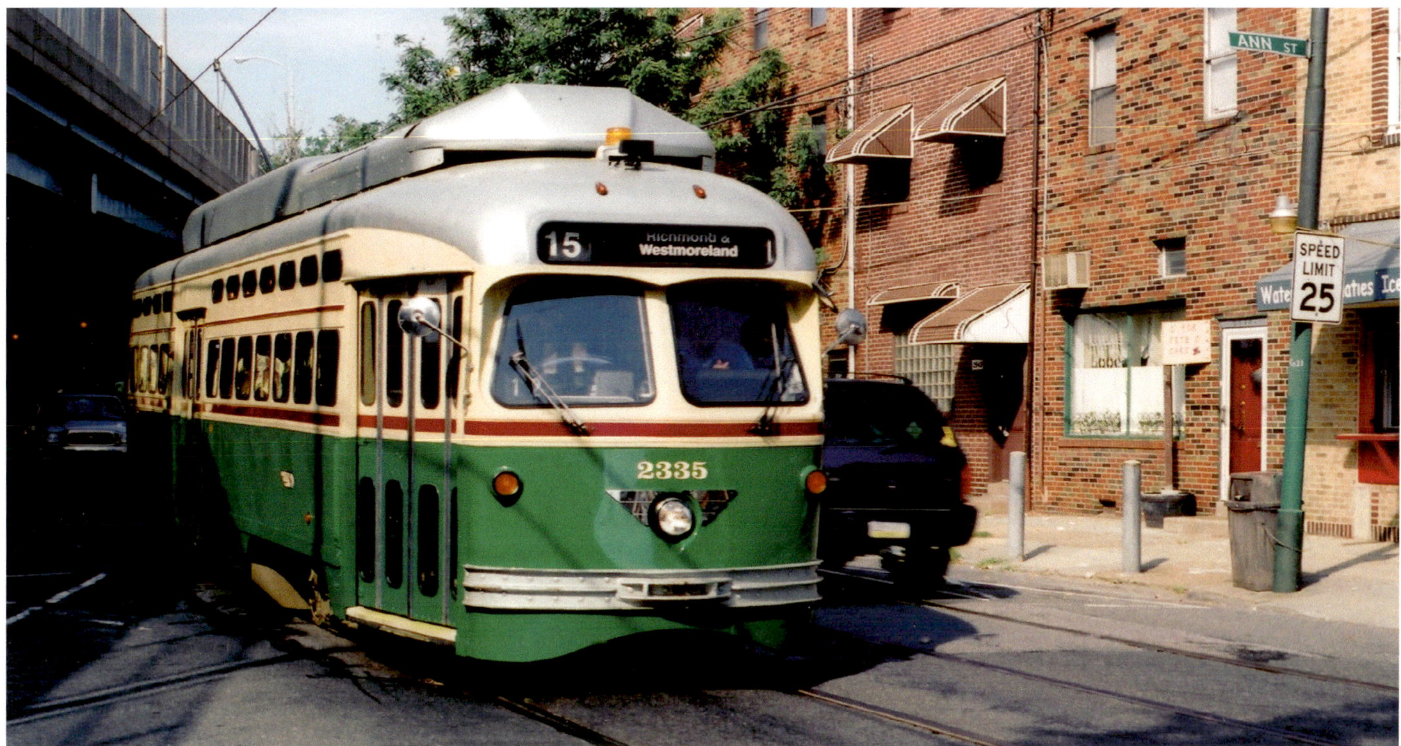

Having crossed under the Interstate 95 Bridge, SEPTA Route 15 PCCII car No. 2335, on August 6, 2010, is eastbound on Richmond Street at Ann Street in the Fishtown neighborhood of Philadelphia. This was originally car No. 2158, which was rebuilt by Brookville Equipment Corporation, with delivery on October 19, 2004. Northeast of downtown, Fishtown was once the center of the shad fishing industry on the Delaware River. This working class neighborhood in recent years has attracted an influx of artists and professionals.

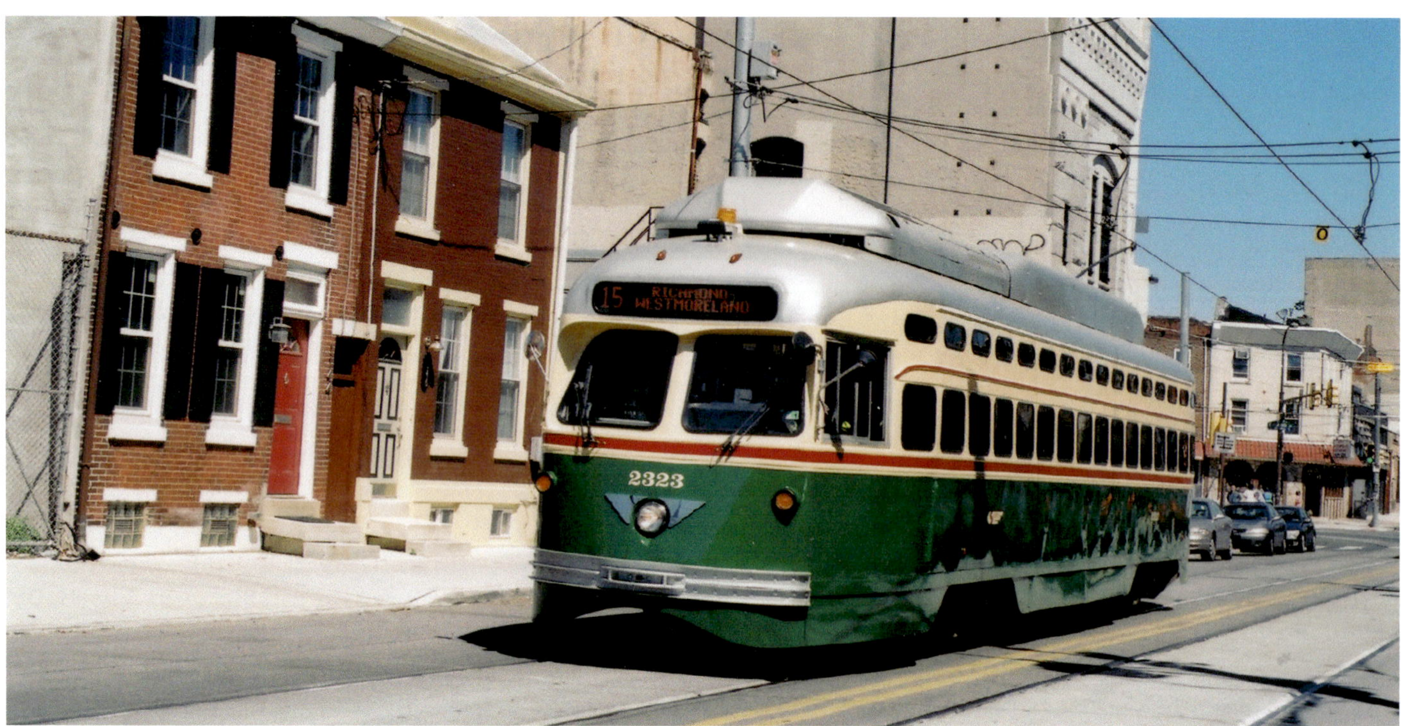

Because of the reconstruction of Interstate 95 in Philadelphia, SEPTA installed new trackage on Frankford Avenue from Girard Avenue to a loop on Delaware Avenue. Route 15 PCCII car No. 2323 is on this new trackage on Frankford Avenue south of Girard Avenue on April 29, 2012. This was originally car No. 2798 that was delivered by St. Louis Car Company in April 1947, overhauled by SEPTA in September 1985, and was rebuilt by Brookville Equipment Corporation with delivery as car No. 2323 on March 11, 2004.

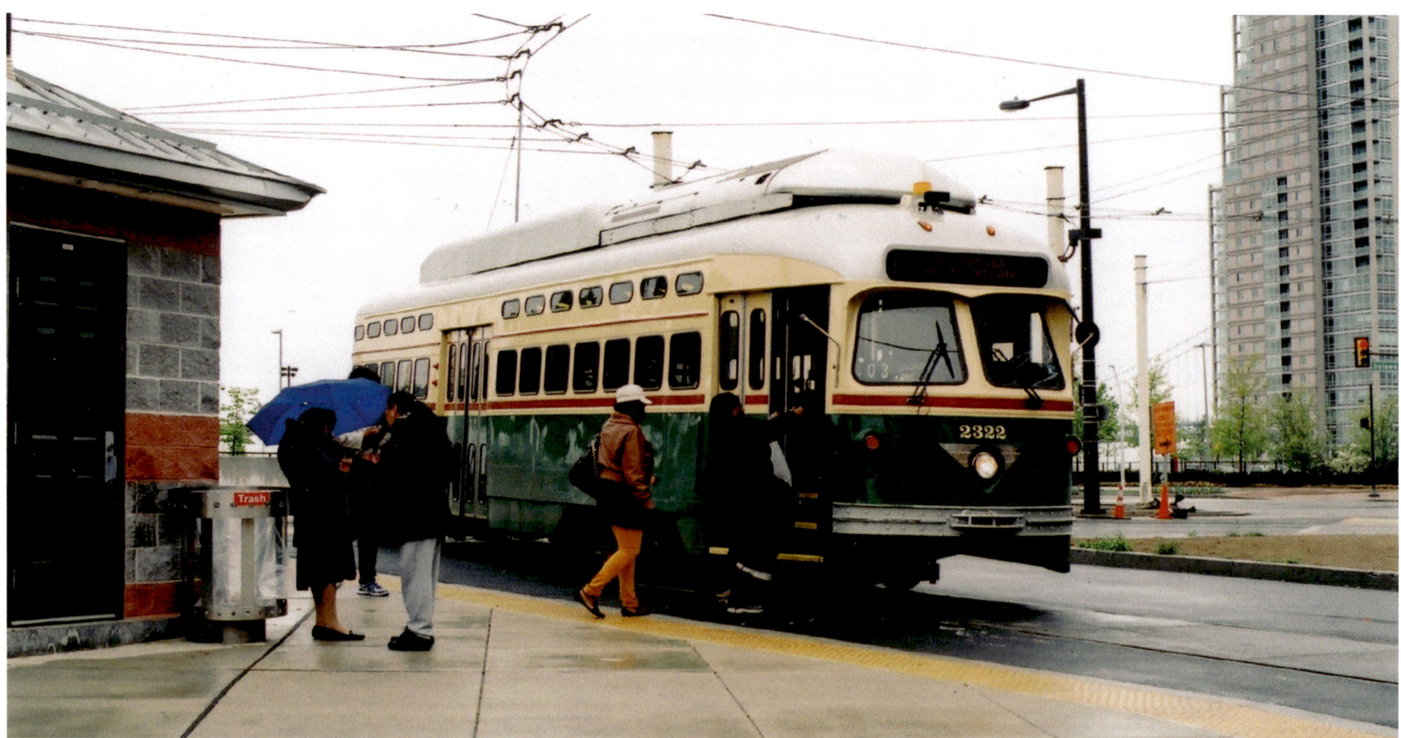

On April 29, 2013, SEPTA Route 15 PCCII car No. 2322 is loading passengers at the Frankford and Delaware Avenue Loop. This was originally car No. 2770 delivered by St. Louis Car Company in April 1947, overhauled by SEPTA in May 1985, and rebuilt by Brookville Equipment Corporation with delivery on January 29, 2004. Until the reconstruction of Interstate 95 in that part of Philadelphia is completed, Route 15 will operate from this loop via Frankford Avenue and Girard Avenue to its western terminus at 63rd and Girard Avenue.

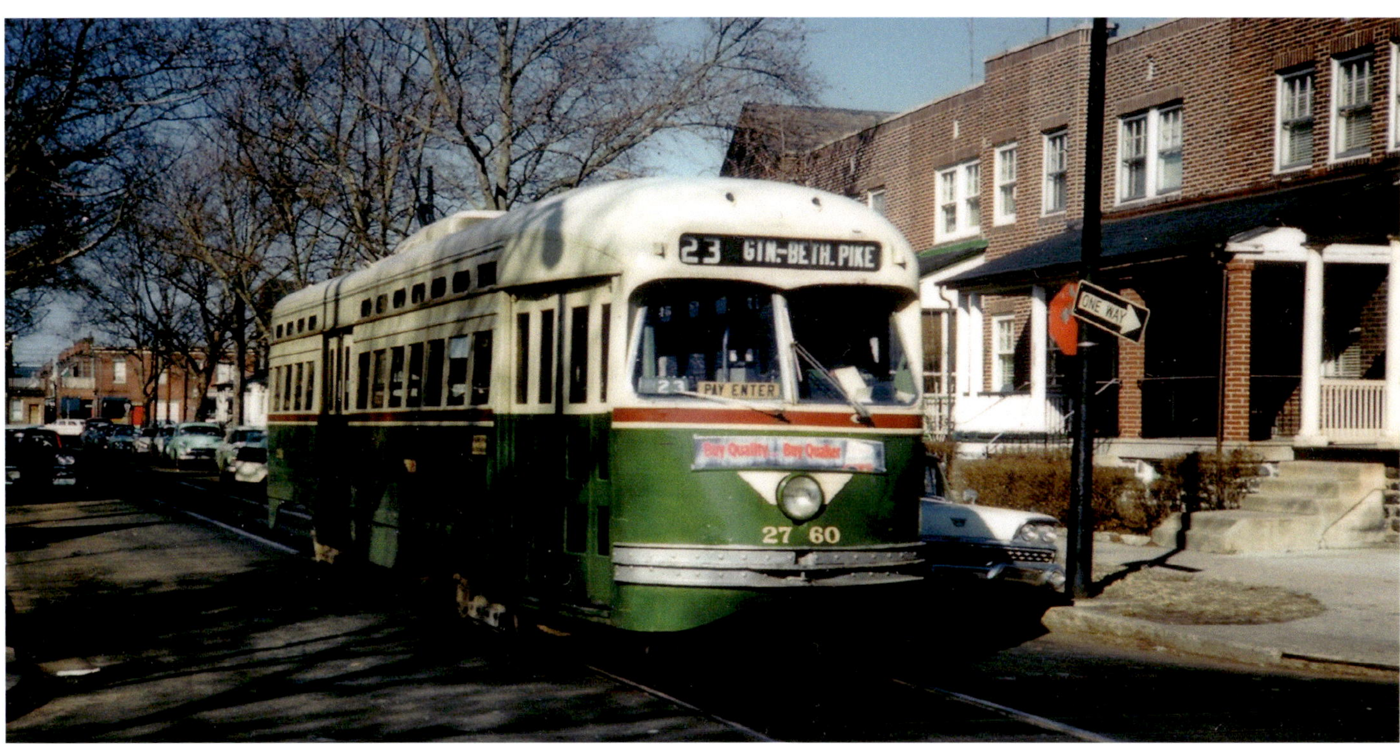

On March 4, 1962, PTC Route 23 PCC car No. 2760 is at the 10th and Bigler Streets southern terminus in South Philadelphia. This car was delivered by St. Louis Car Company in March 1947, overhauled by SEPTA in February 1984, and sold in October 1996. On May 11, 1947, eighty-five new 2700 series PCC cars were assigned to Germantown Depot for Route 23.

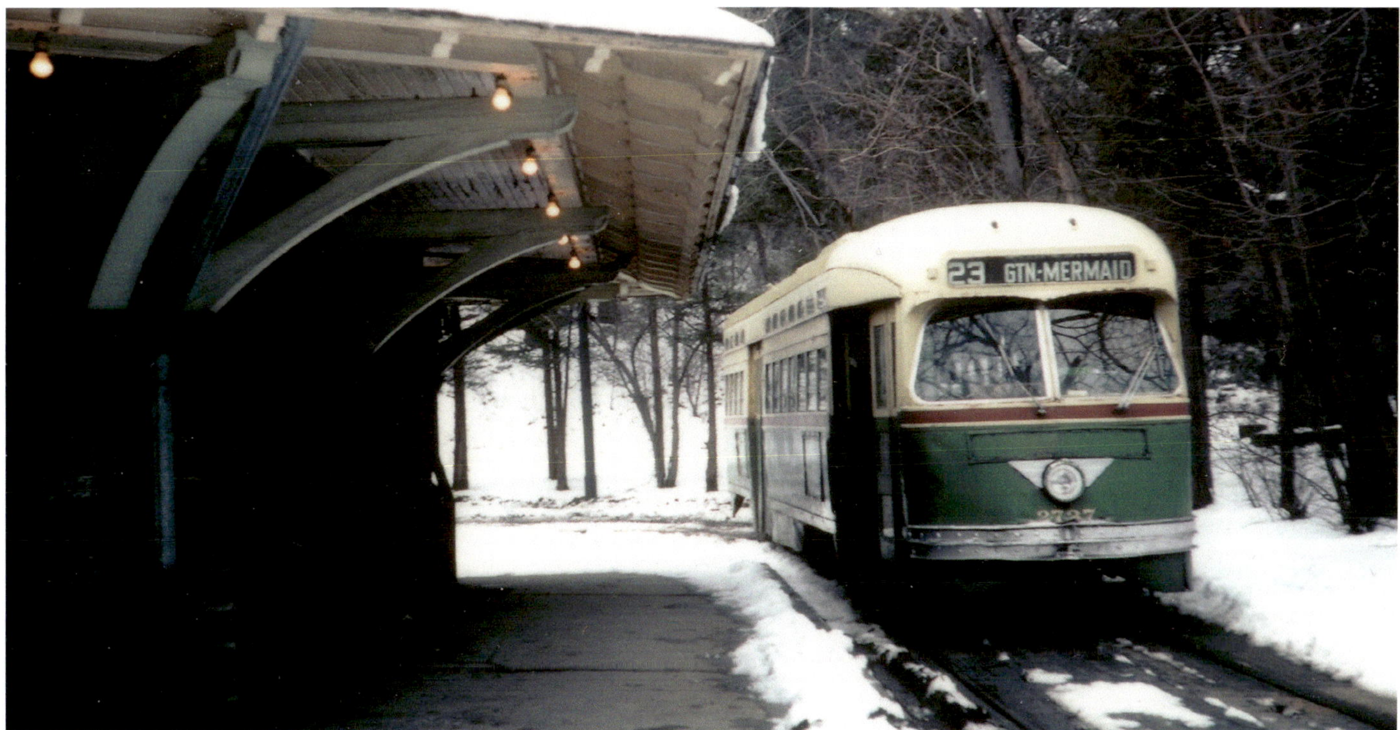

Germantown and Mermaid Lane Loop is the location of SEPTA Route 23 PCC car No. 2737 on February 22, 1969. This car was delivered by St. Louis Car Company in March 1947, overhauled by SEPTA in October 1983, and sold to the New Orleans Regional Transit Authority in December 1994 with the body scrapped in March 1997. In its final years of operation, Route 23 had a number of short turn loops including Germantown & Gorgas, Germantown & Venango (later moved to Germantown & Ontario; both were the cutback to get to Luzerne Depot), 10th & Susquehanna, 12th & Bainbridge, and 12th & Snyder.

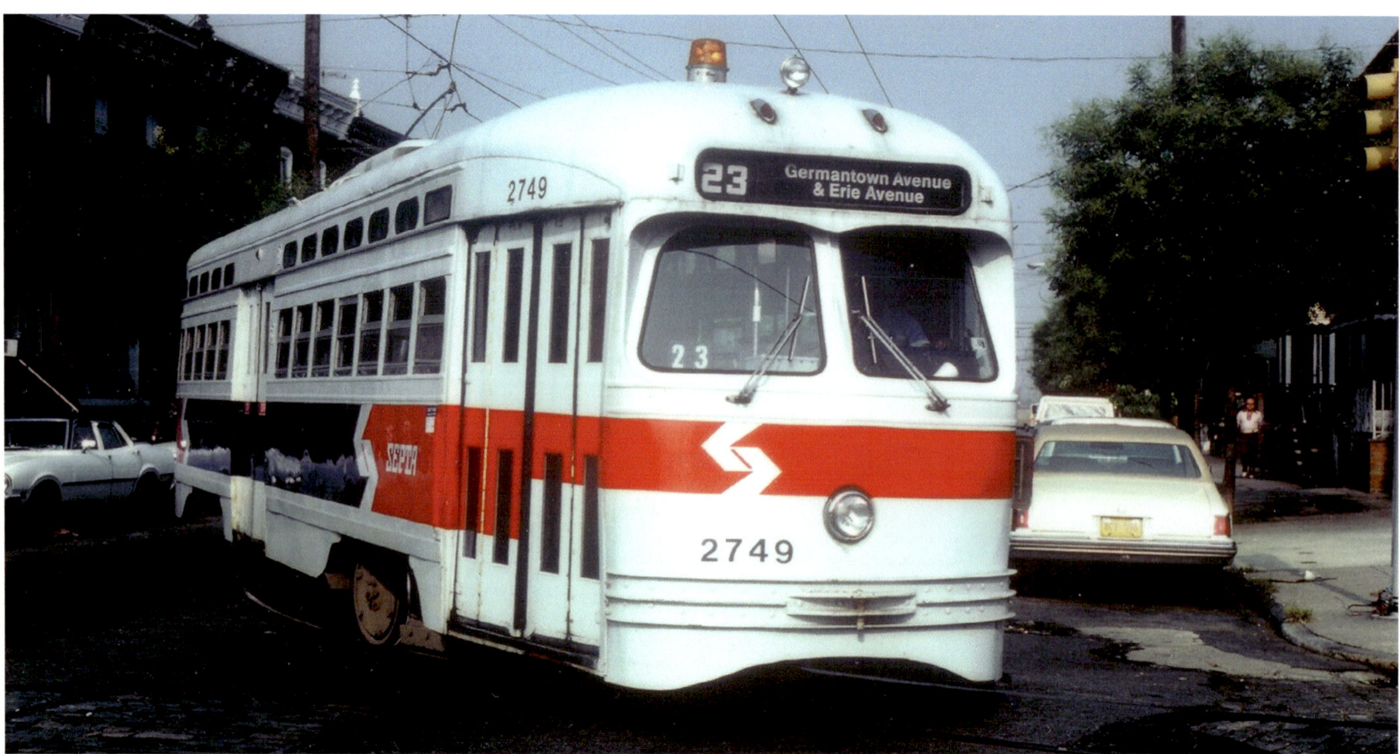

SEPTA Route 23 PCC car No. 2749 is turning from Snyder Avenue onto 11th Street in South Philadelphia for a northbound trip in August 1985. This car was delivered by St. Louis Car Company in March 1947, overhauled by SEPTA in November 1983, and sold to the New Orleans Regional Transit Authority in December 1994. The double wire on Snyder Avenue is for trackless trolley Route 79, which was converted to bus operation on July 1, 2003.

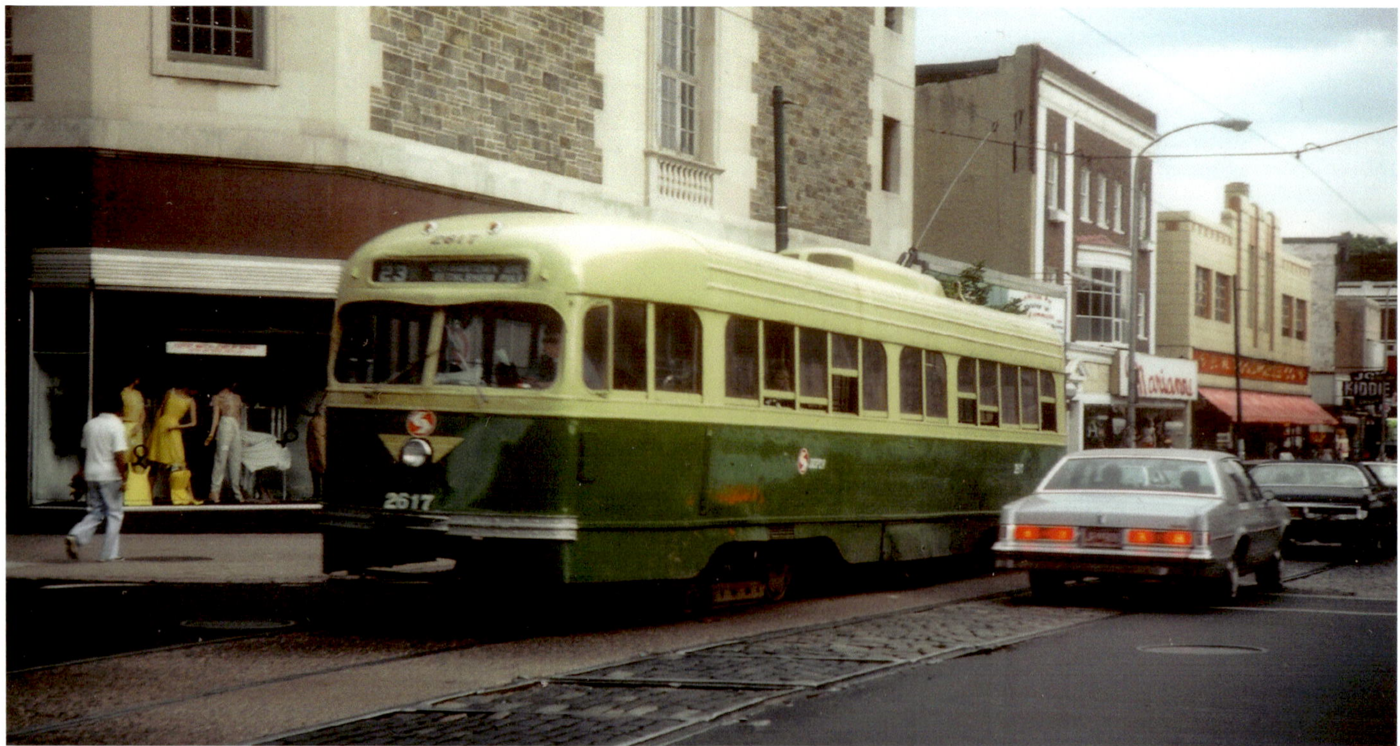

On June 20, 1980, SEPTA Route 23 PCC car No. 2617 (delivered by St. Louis Car Company in June 1942 and was scrapped in 1982) is on Germantown Avenue crossing Chelten Avenue in the Germantown neighborhood of northwest Philadelphia, for a northbound trip to the Germantown–Bethlehem Loop. Route 23, Philadelphia's longest trolley car line, traversed every kind of neighborhood from picturesque Chestnut Hill to urban areas of challenge, working class districts, and everything in between.

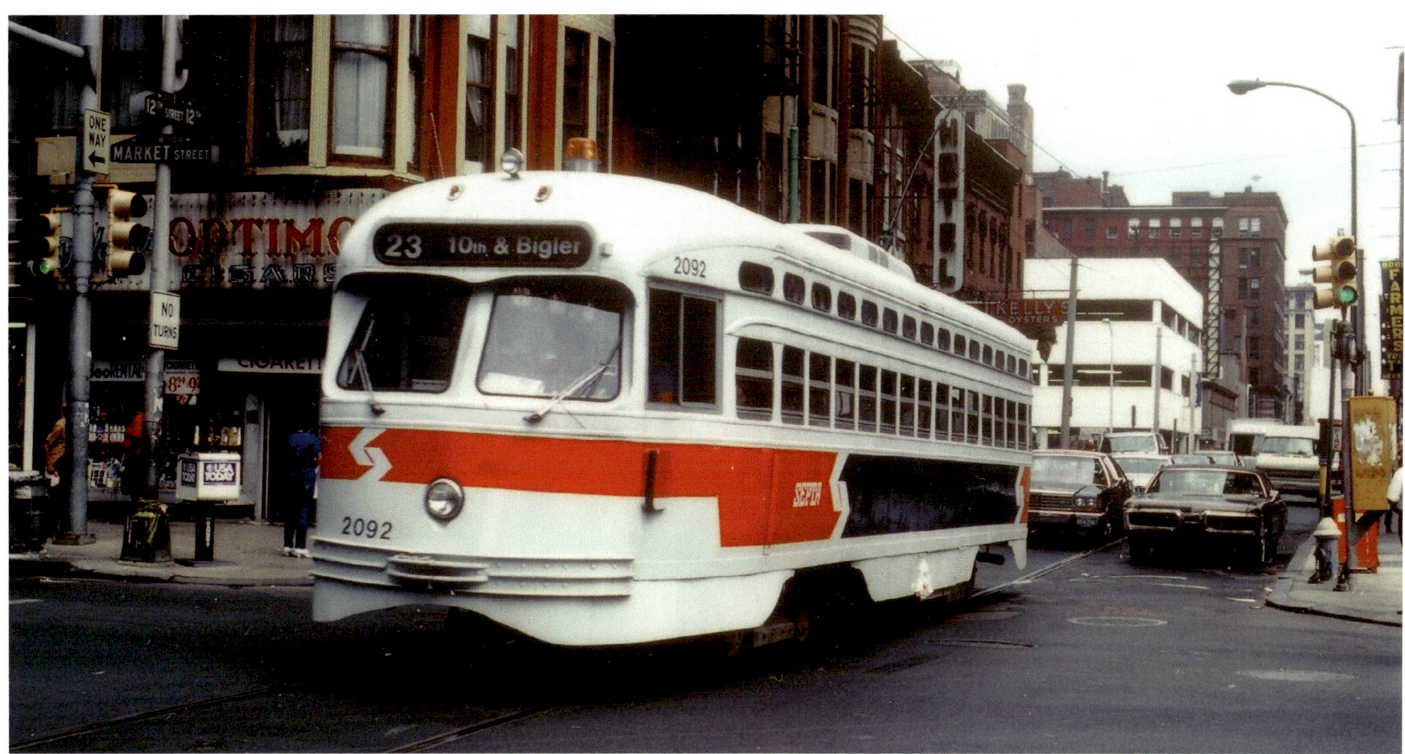

SEPTA Route 23 PCC car No. 2092 is southbound on 12th Street crossing Market Street in center city Philadelphia in August 1985. This car was delivered by St. Louis Car Company in August 1948, overhauled by SEPTA in March 1982, and was sold to Brookville Equipment Company in 2004.

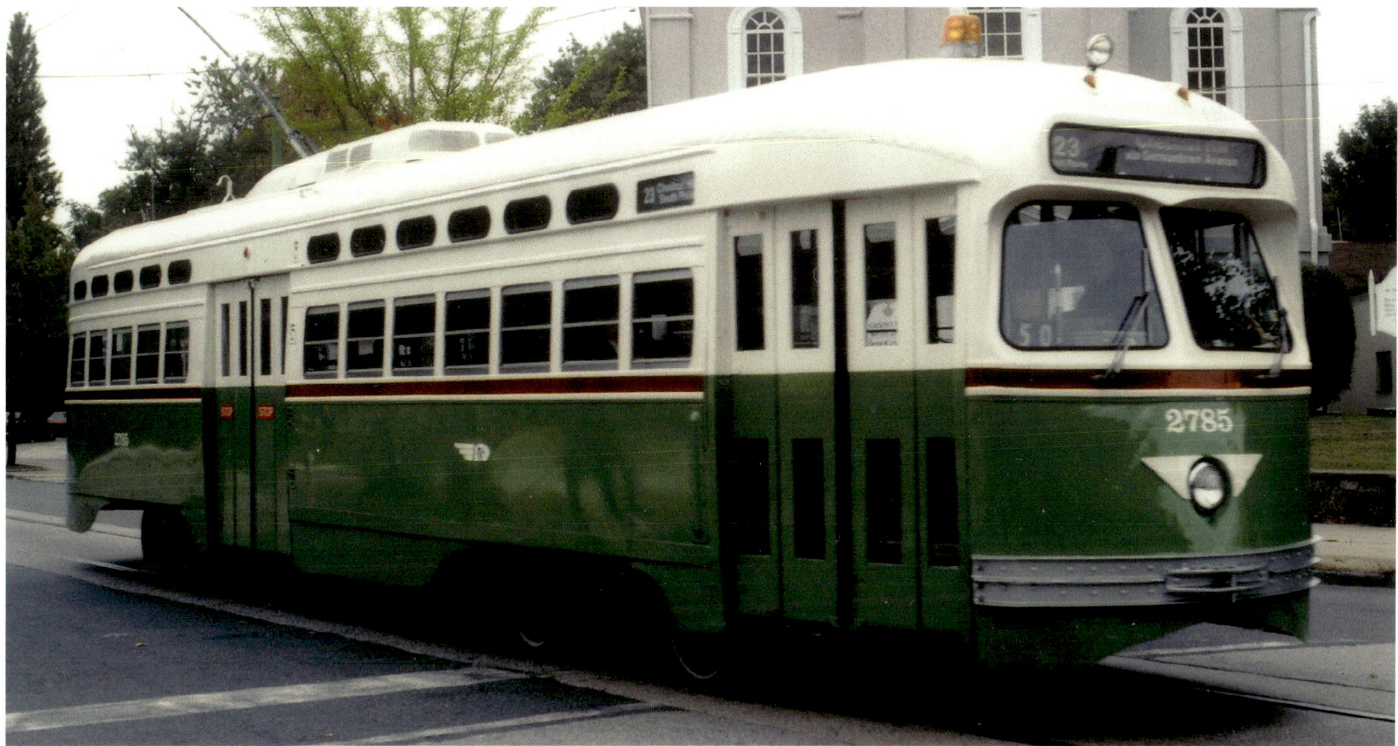

Bethlehem Pike at Germantown is the location of SEPTA PCC Car No. 2785 on October 4, 1992. This car was delivered by St. Louis Car Company in April 1947, overhauled by SEPTA in August 1986, was the Chestnut Hill trolley from 1992 to 1996, in 2005 was sold to Glen Echo Park in Maryland, and in 2010 was sold to the San Diego Vintage Trolley and renumbered 533.

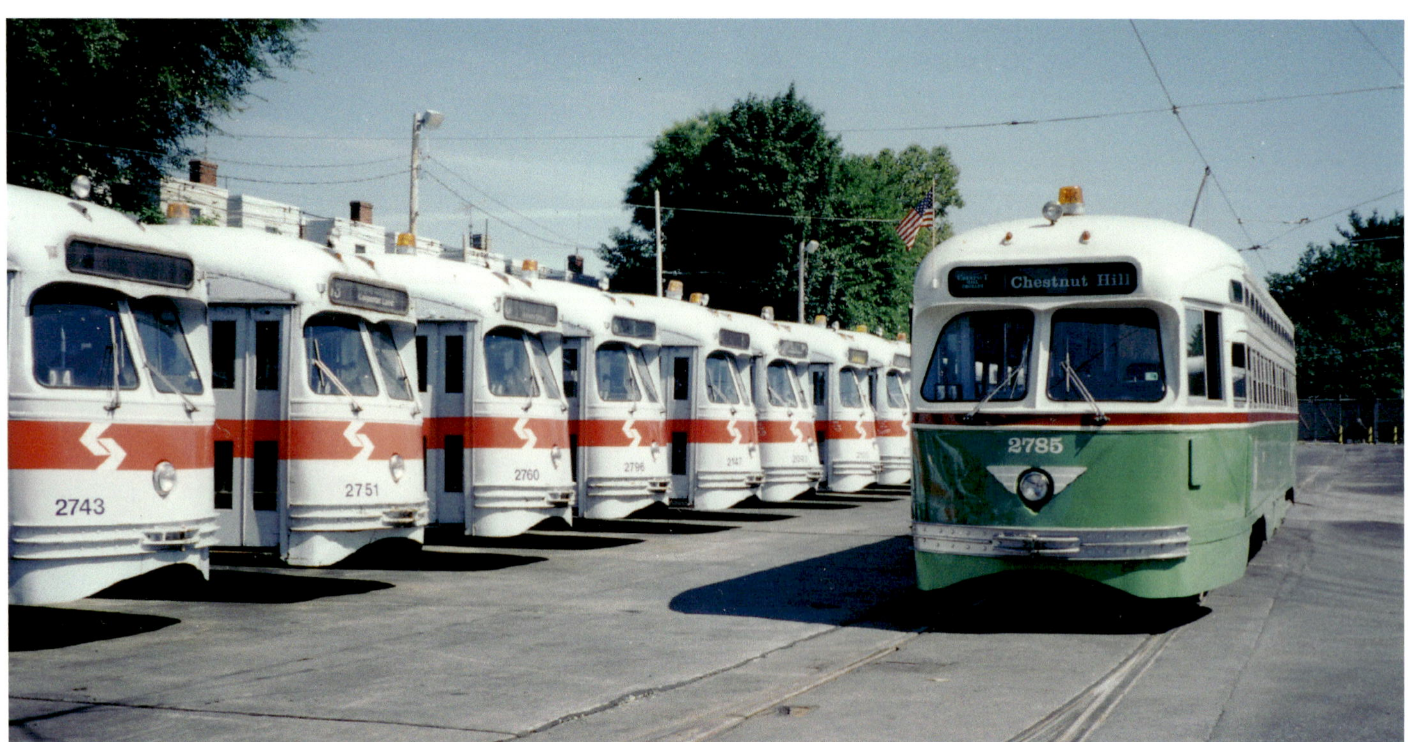

On August 22, 1993, SEPTA PCC car 2785 is passing a lineup of out of service PCC cars at Germantown Depot on a Chestnut Hill Trolley trip. The Chestnut Hill Trolley operated every twenty minutes between 10 a.m. and 6 p.m. on weekends except holidays from September 1992 to June 15, 1996 on a two mile section of the northern end of Route 23 from Chestnut Hill to Gorgas Lane. On the left, PCC car No. 2743 (delivered by St. Louis Car Company in March 1947, and overhauled by SEPTA in May 1984) was out of service and was acquired by the Rockhill Trolley Museum in May 1994. It was regauged from Philadelphia's 5 foot 2.25 inches broad gauge to the museum's 4 foot 8.5 inches standard gauge which required 600 hours of volunteer work during the winter of 1997-1998.

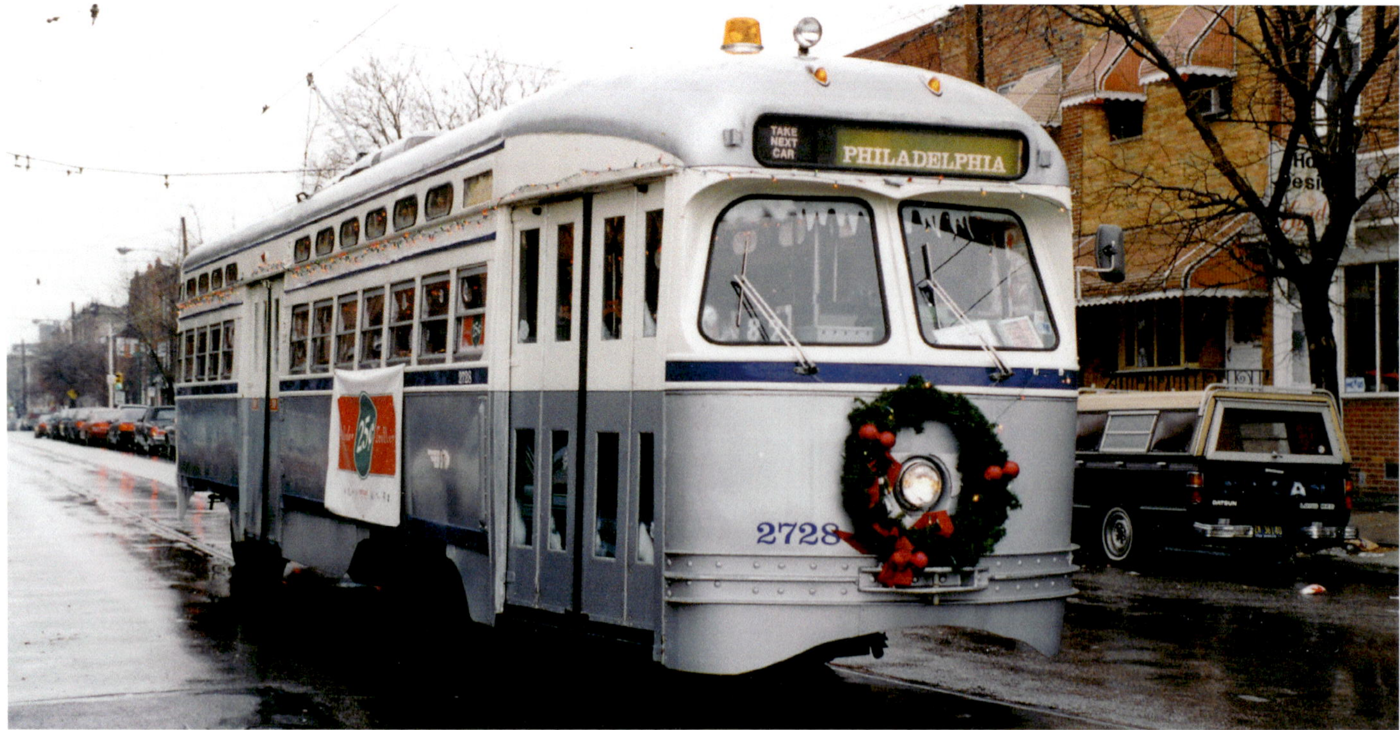

The SEPTA "Holiday Trolley" PCC car No. 2728, painted in silver and cream with blue striping is on Snyder Avenue ready to turn north on 11th Street on December 27, 1997. SEPTA provided free rides on vintage trolleys on 11th and 12th Streets every twenty minutes on weekdays from 10:30 a.m. to 7:30 p.m. and weekends from 10 a.m. to 5 p.m. from November 29 to December 29, 1996.

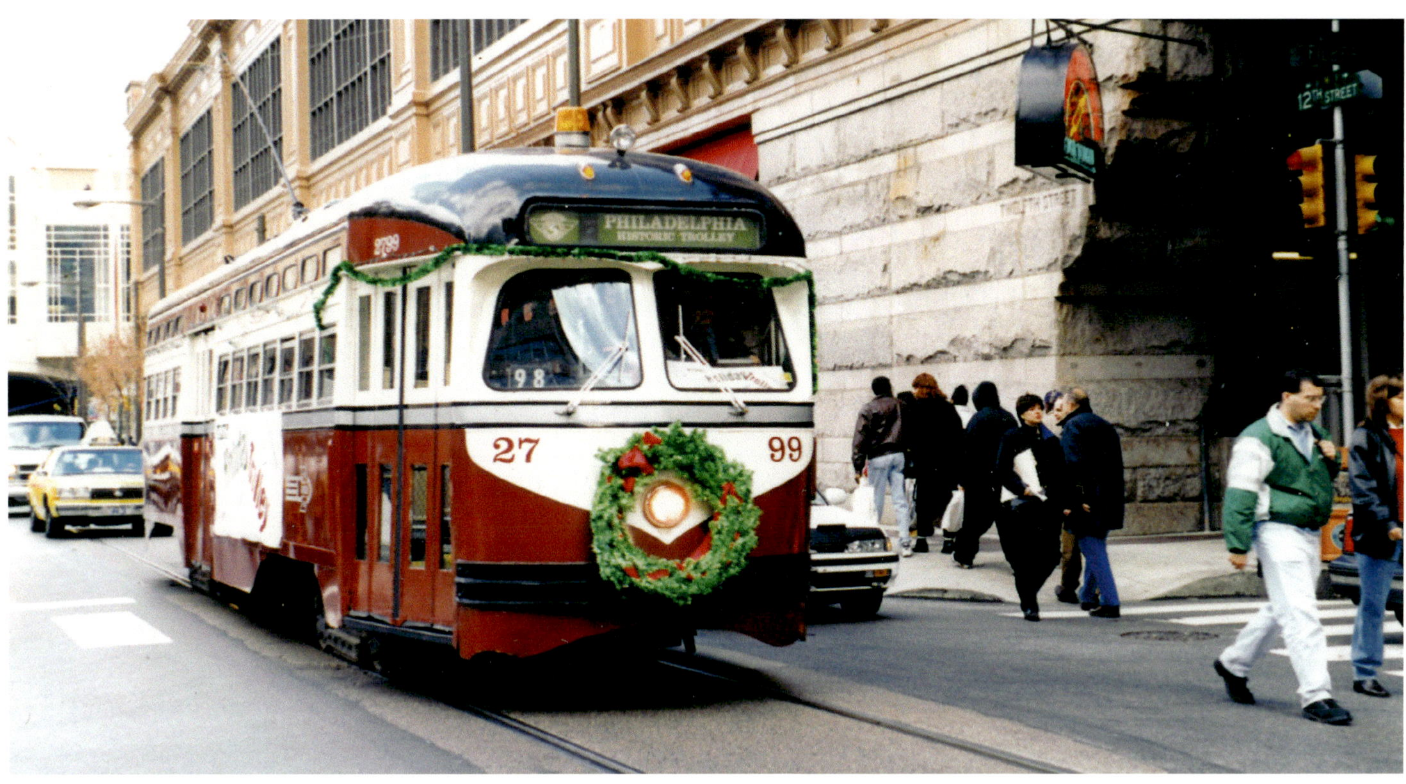

Southbound SEPTA PCC car No. 2799 is on 12th Street crossing Filbert Street for a "Holiday Trolley" run on November 27, 1998.

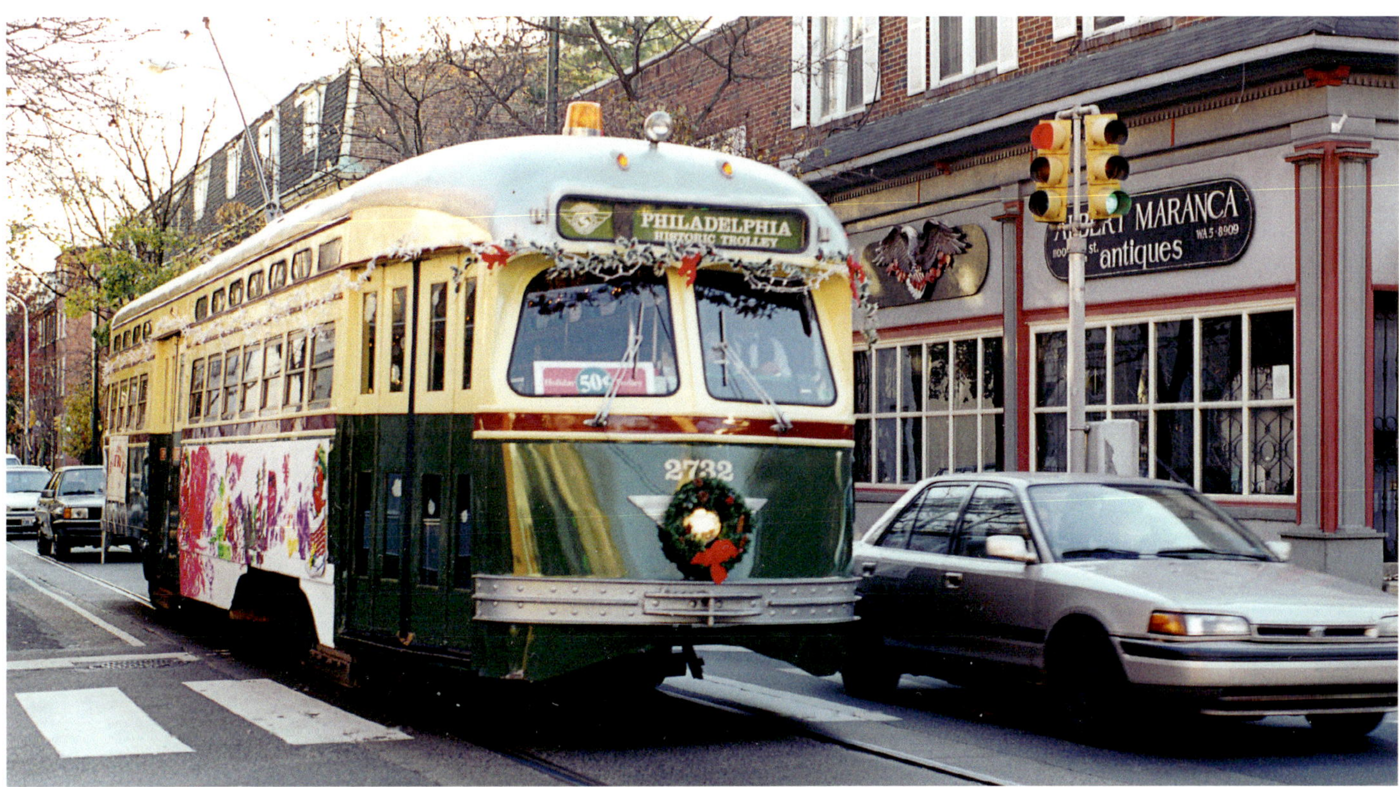

SEPTA "Holiday Trolley" PCC car No. 2732 is southbound on 12th Street ready to cross Pine Street on November 24, 2000. The historic holiday trolley operated from November 24 to December 31, 2000, Thursdays through Sundays, between 10 a.m. and 5 p.m. on 11th and 12th Streets every twenty minutes for a 50 cents cash fare. This car was delivered by St. Louis Car Company in March 1947, overhauled by SEPTA in February 1985, painted green and cream with a grey roof and a red stripe below the windows in 1995, sold to Glen Echo Park in Maryland in 2005, and in 2012 was sold to General Machine & Tool Company in Cheverly, Maryland.

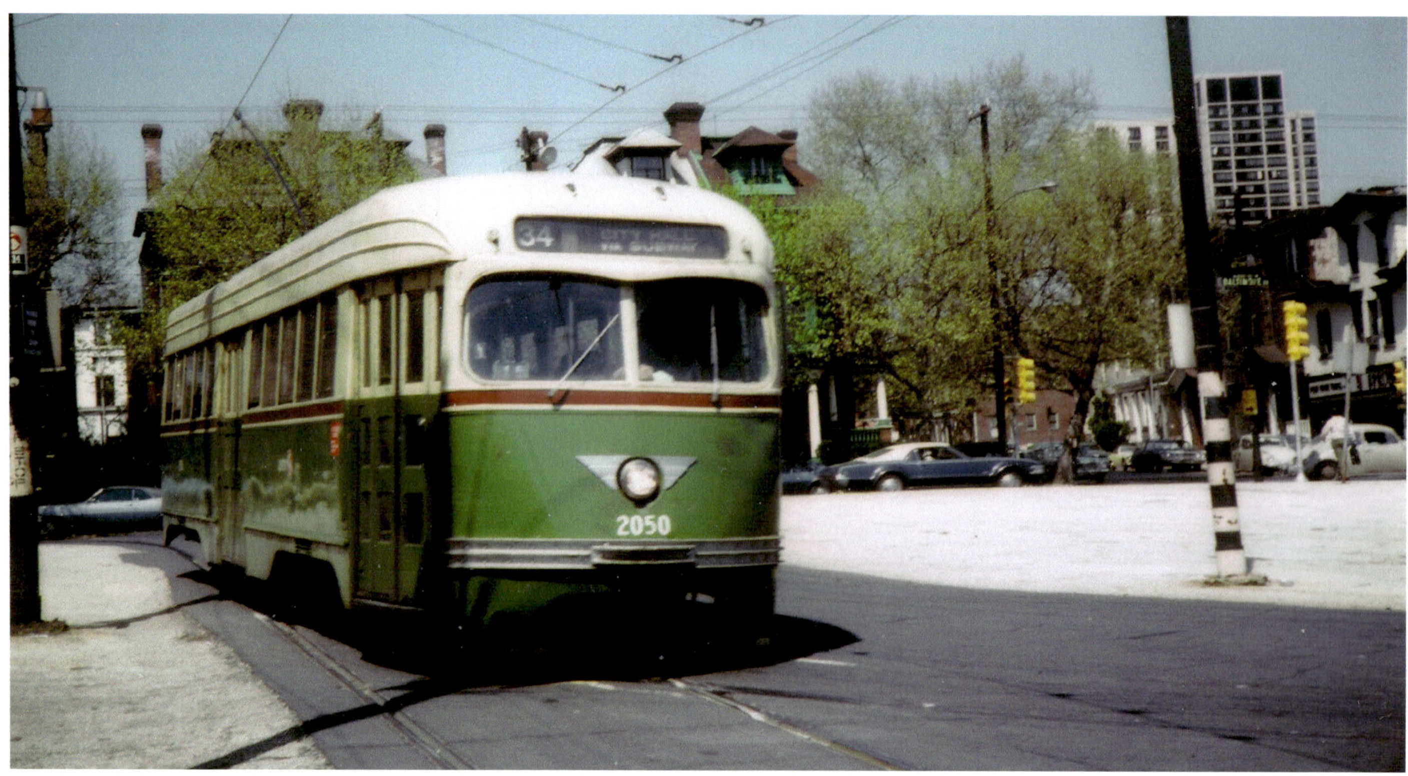

On a sunny April 20, 1973, SEPTA Route 34 PCC car No. 2050 is ready to turn into the subway at the 40th Street portal for a trip to City Hall. This car was delivered by St. Louis Car Company in February 1941 and was scrapped in 1982. The 5.05 mile Subway Surface Route 34 operates in the underground subway and then through West Philadelphia.

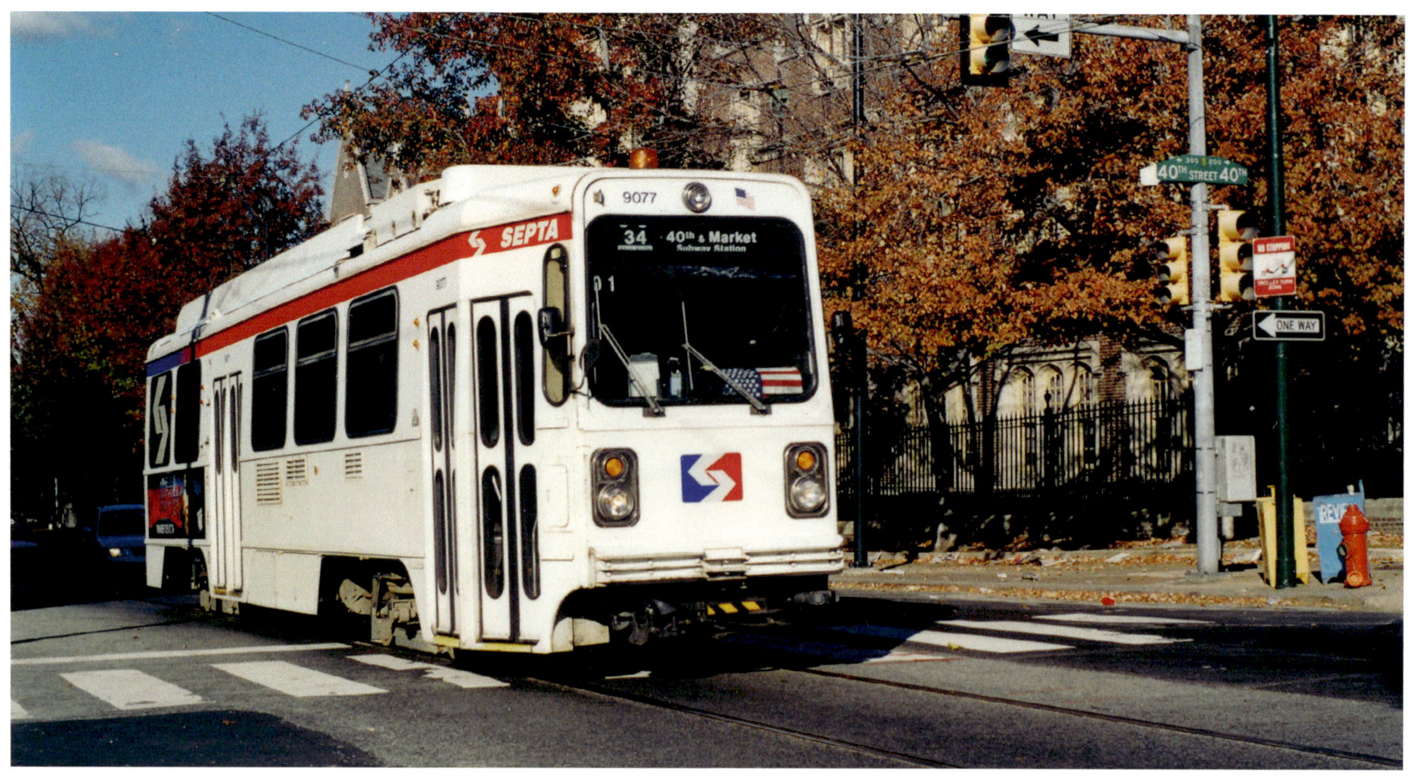

In the University City district of West Philadelphia on October 28, 2001, SEPTA Route 34 Kawasaki Heavy Industries car No. 9077 (delivered on October 1, 1982 and placed in revenue service on November 2, 1982) is eastbound on Spruce Street ready to cross 40th Street along the diversion route used when the trolley subway is closed.

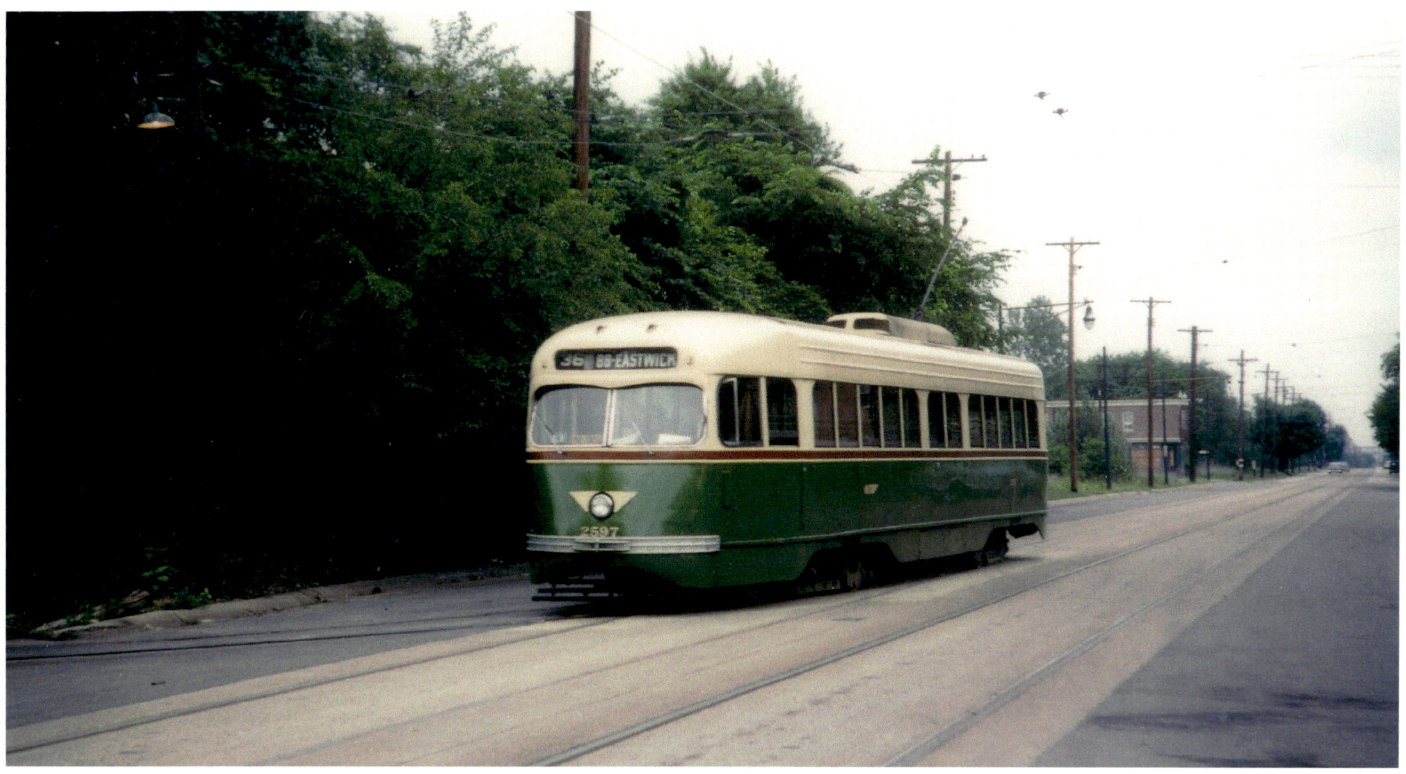

PTC Route 36 PCC car No. 2597 is on Eastwick Avenue near 88th Street in the Eastwick neighborhood located in Southwest Philadelphia on June 2, 1963. This was one of 43 PCC cars numbered 2581-2623 (powered by four General Electric type 1198 motors) built by St. Louis Car Company in 1942. Car No. 2597 was delivered in June 1942 and scrapped in May 1972. The 8.1 mile Subway Surface Route 36 operates in the underground subway and then through Southwest Philadelphia.

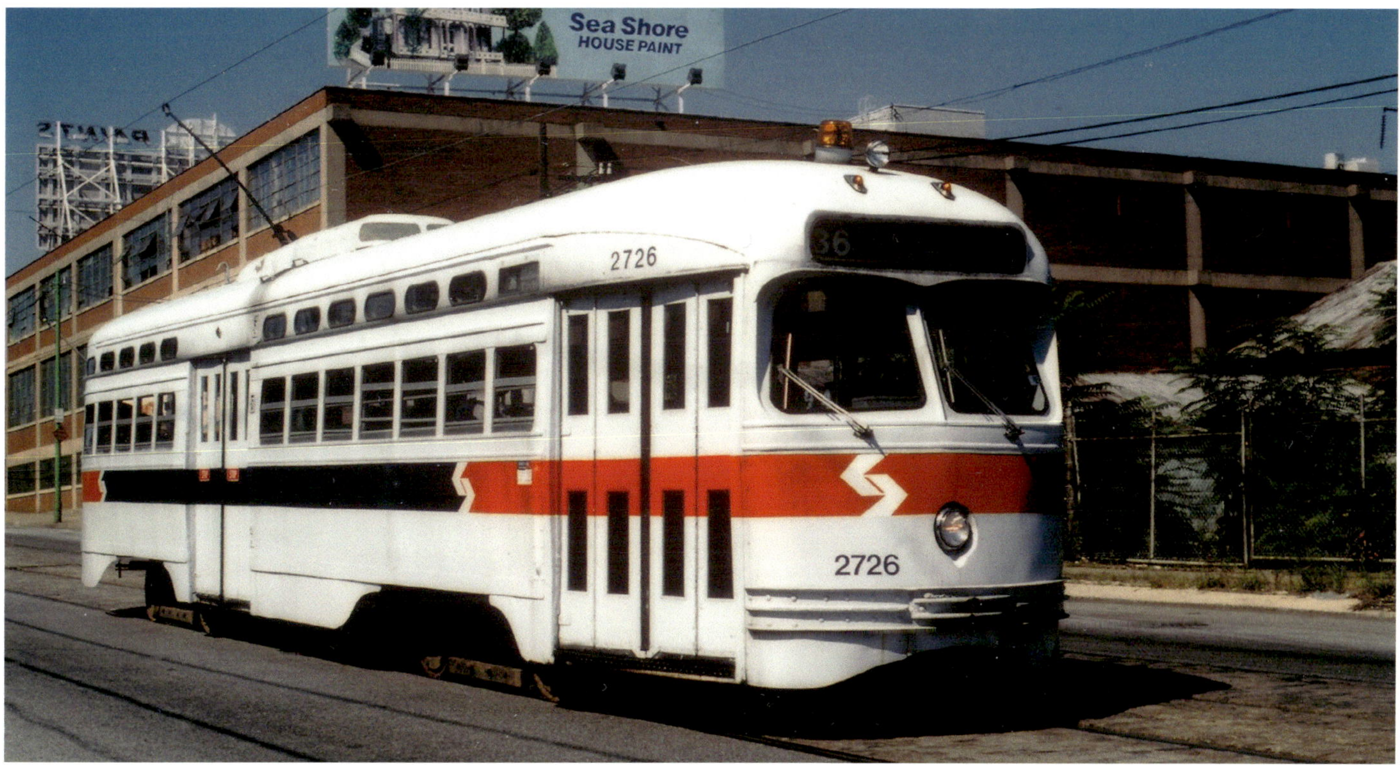

On August 7, 1994, SEPTA PCC car No. 2726 is on Elmwood Avenue at 59th Street operating on a rail excursion along Route 36 in the Elmwood neighborhood of southwest Philadelphia. This car was delivered by St. Louis Car Company in March 1947, overhauled by SEPTA in April 1987, and rebuilt by Brookville Equipment Corporation as car No. 2328 with delivery on May 27, 2004.

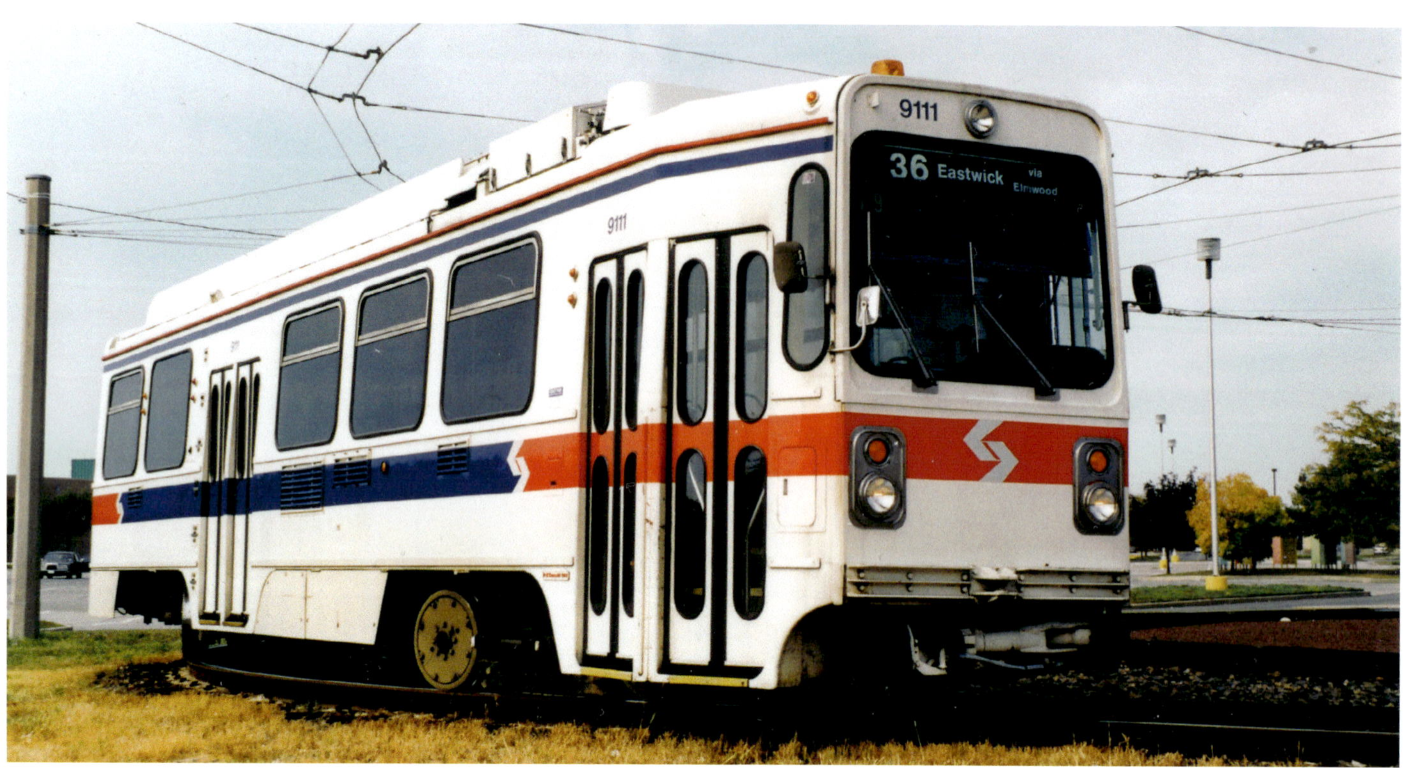

SEPTA Route 36 Kawasaki Heavy Industries car No. 9111 (delivered on March 15, 1982 and placed in revenue service on March 22, 1982) is at the Island Road and 80th Street terminus of the line on October 4, 1997.

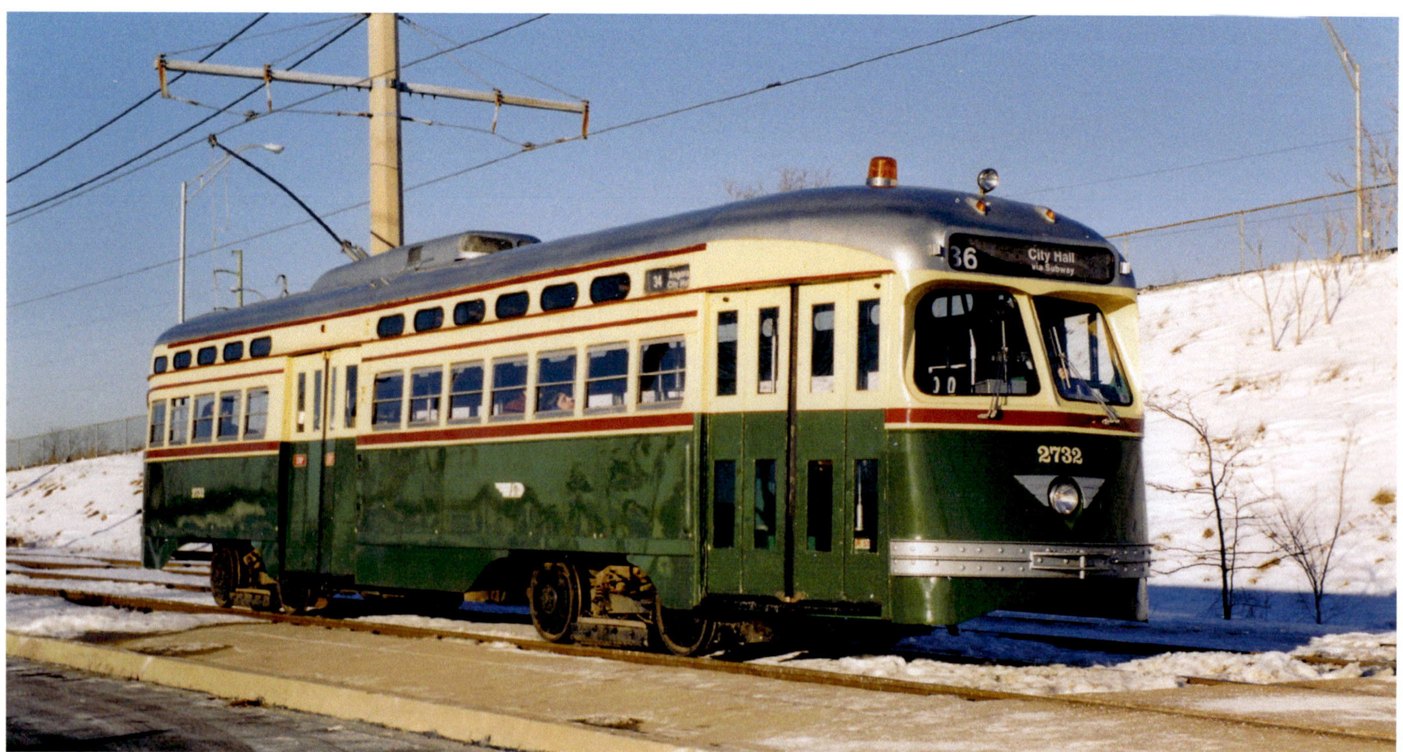

With a light covering of snow on the ground, SEPTA PCC car No. 2732 is at the Island Road and 80th Street terminus of Route 36 on January 29, 2000. This was once Route 37 which operated to Chester but following a fiery collision on August 28, 1946 between a trolley car and truck which destroyed the Crum Creek Bridge, the line was cut back to the Westinghouse (plant) Loop at Lester. Routes 36 and 37 were combined into Route 36 operating between Center City and Westinghouse Loop on November 6, 1955. Service was cut back to 94th Street and Eastwick Avenue on September 9, 1956; cut back to 88th Street and Eastwick Avenue on August 15, 1962; and cut back to 85th Street and Eastwick Avenue on January 5, 1966. Since April 26, 1975, Route 36 has terminated at Island Road and 80th Street.

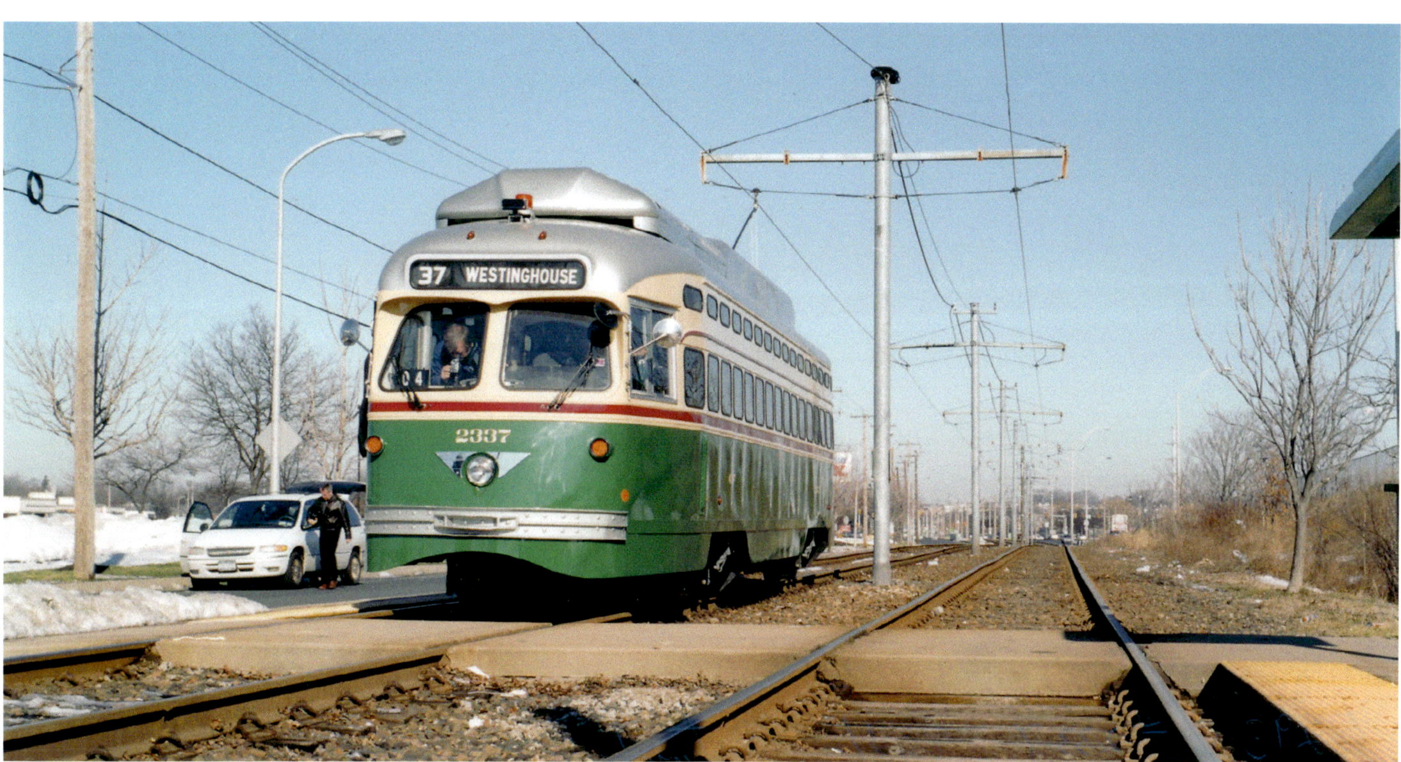

On February 5, 2005, SEPTA rebuilt PCCII car No. 2337 is on Island Road near the 80th Street terminus of Route 36 on a rail excursion with Route 37 Westinghouse on the destination sign that has not been possible since September 8, 1956. This was originally car No. 2783 delivered by St. Louis Car Company in April 1947, overhauled by SEPTA in February 1986, and rebuilt by Brookville Equipment Corporation with delivery on November 23, 2004.

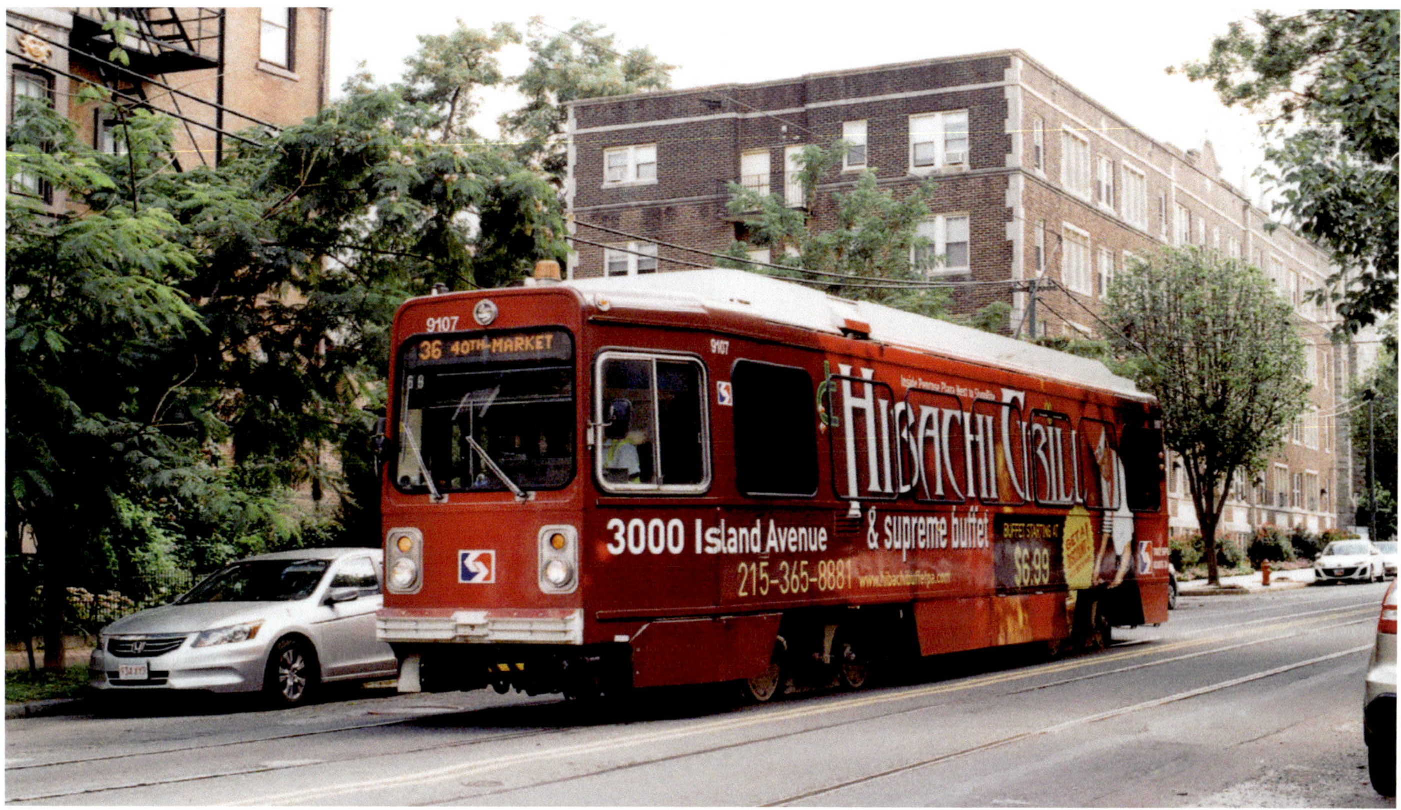

SEPTA Route 36 Kawasaki Heavy Industries car No. 9107 (delivered on March 17, 1982 and placed in revenue service on March 22, 1982) is on 42nd Street at Baltimore Avenue in the University City section of West Philadelphia on August 15, 2014.

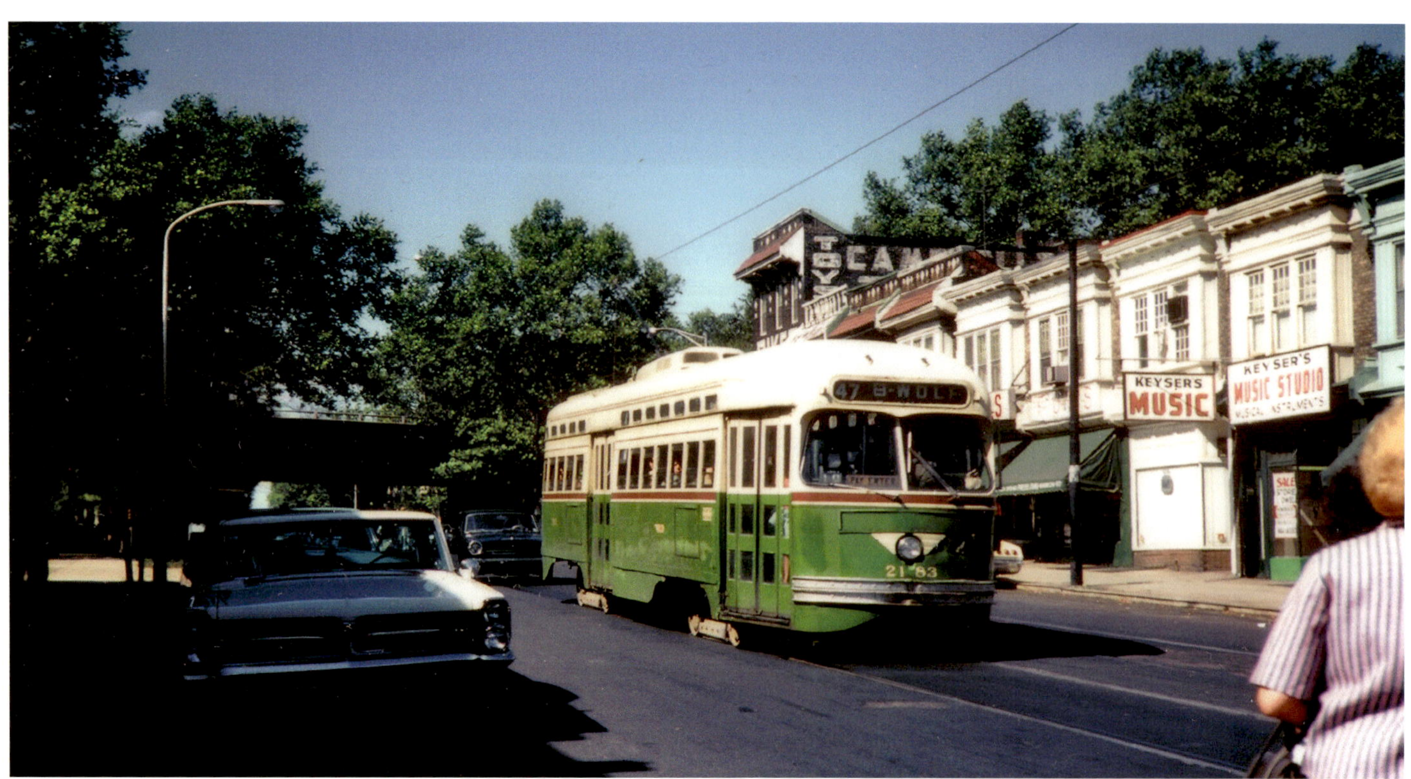

On July 22, 1966, PTC Route 47 PCC car No. 2183 is on 5th Street, north of Wyoming Avenue, in the Feltonville neighborhood of North Philadelphia. This car was delivered by St. Louis Car Company in July 1948, was overhauled by SEPTA in August 1983, and was later sold to the New Orleans Regional Transit Authority.

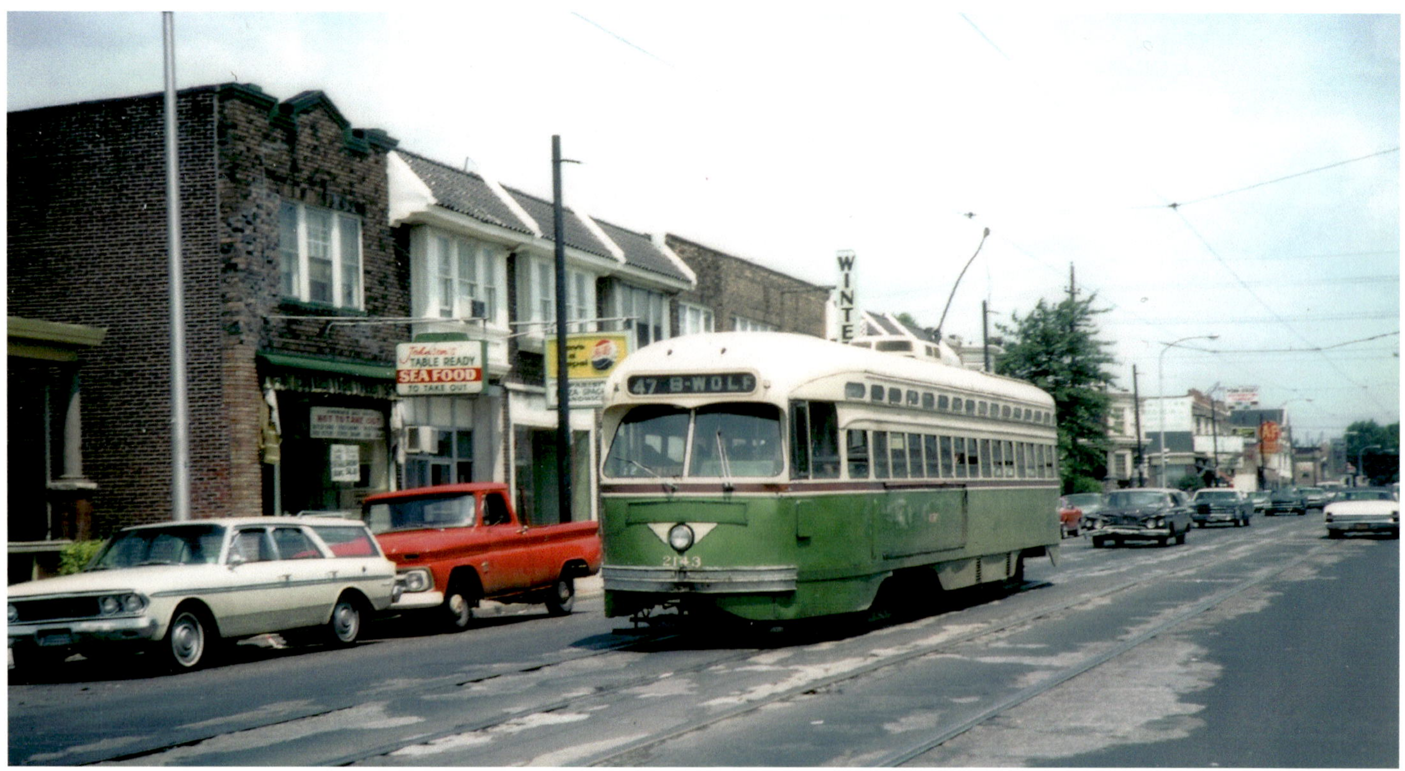

Traversing 5th Street between Lindley Avenue and Duncannon Avenue in the Feltonville neighborhood of Philadelphia, PTC Route 47 PCC car No. 2143 is southbound heading for 8th and Wolf Street on May 31, 1968. This car was delivered by St. Louis Car Company in June 1948, was overhauled by SEPTA in July 1985, and was sold to Brookville Equipment Corporation in 2004. Route 47 was a busy north–south line from 5th and Godfrey in the northern part of Philadelphia to 8th and Wolf in South Philadelphia.

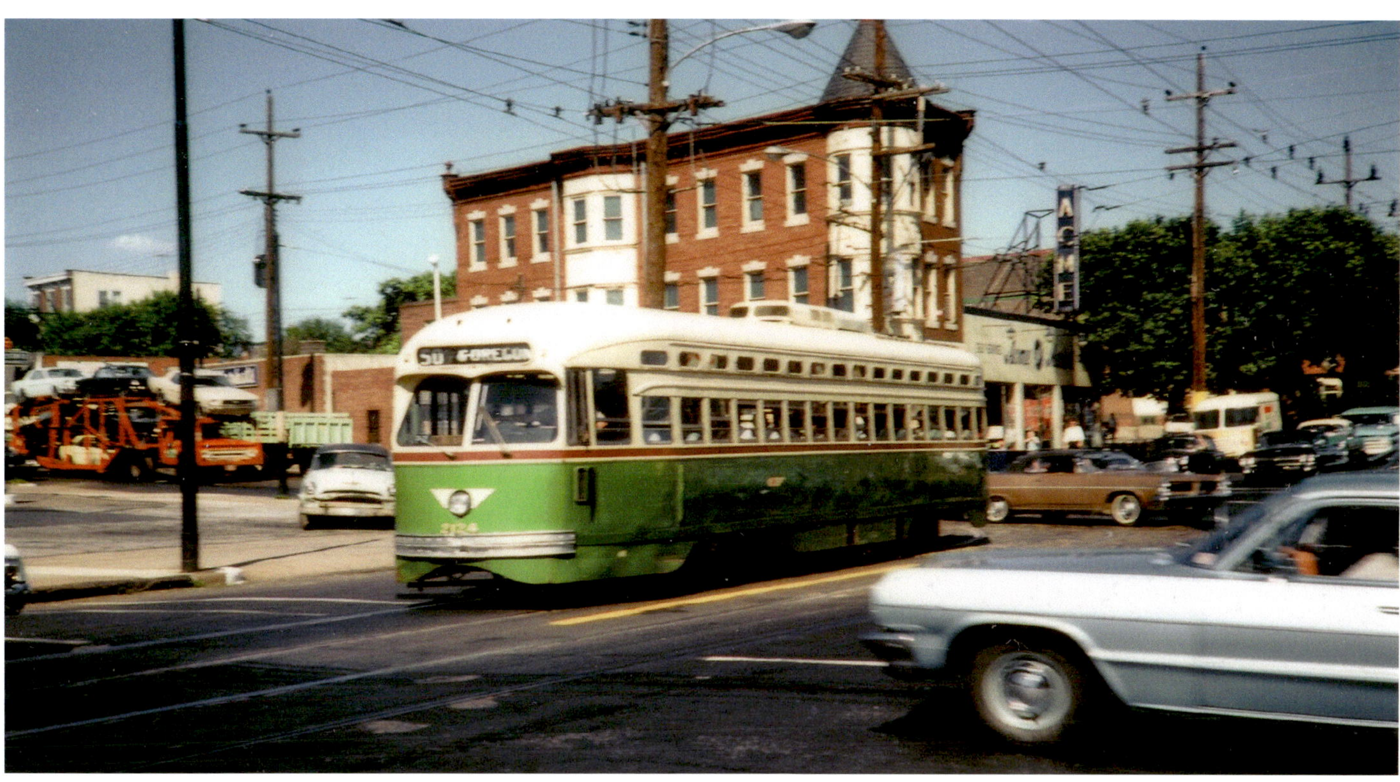

PTC Route 50 PCC car No. 2124 is on Wyoming Avenue at Rising Sun Avenue on July 22, 1966, where the double overhead wire is for trackless trolley Route 75. This car was delivered by St. Louis Car Company in August 1948 and was overhauled by SEPTA on August 1980. In October 1992, it was sold to the San Francisco Municipal Railway and became No. 1058 in a Chicago paint scheme.

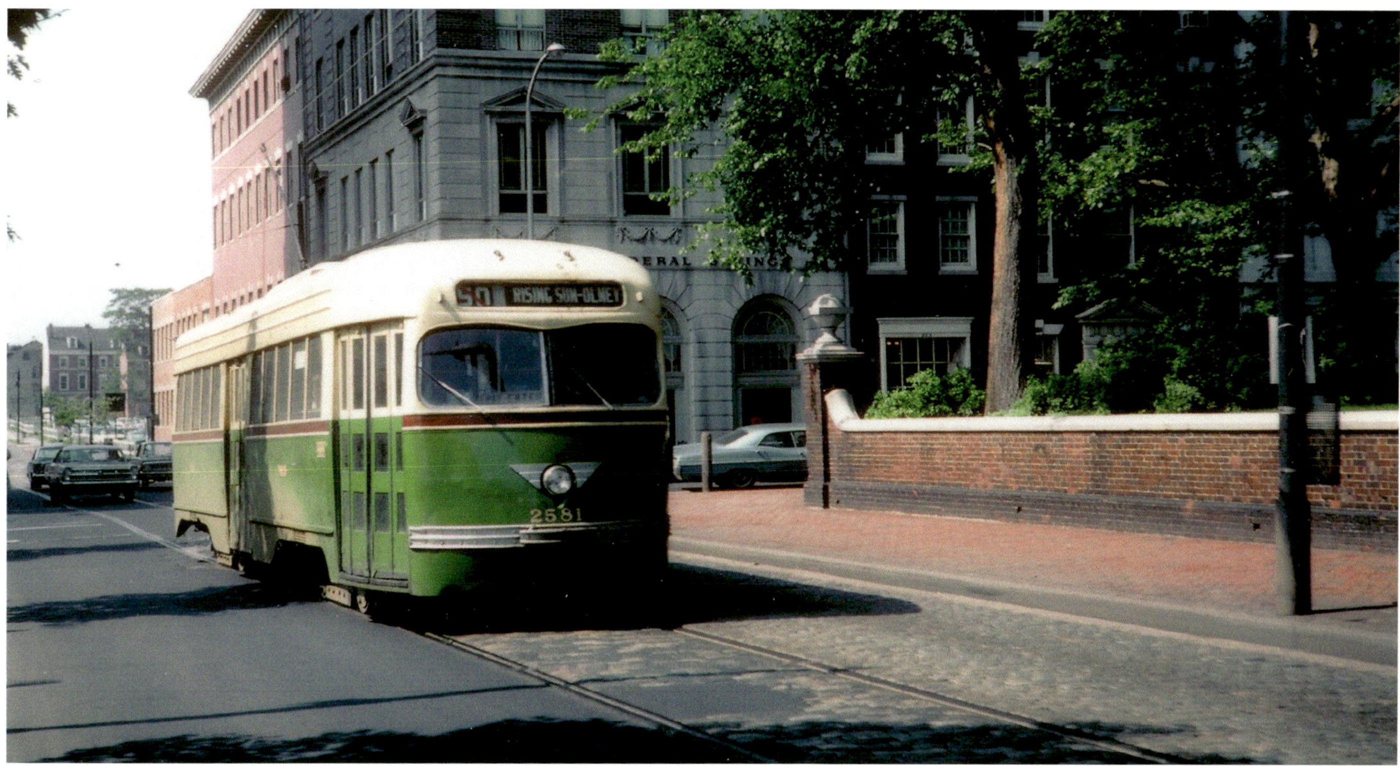

On May 31, 1968, PTC Route 50 PCC car No. 2581 is on 5th Street at Walnut Street in the historic district of downtown Philadelphia. This car was delivered by St. Louis Car Company in May 1942 and was scrapped in 1979. Route 50 connected Rising Sun and Knorr in the Lawndale neighborhood of Philadelphia to 7th and Oregon with some trips to 4th and Ritner in South Philadelphia.

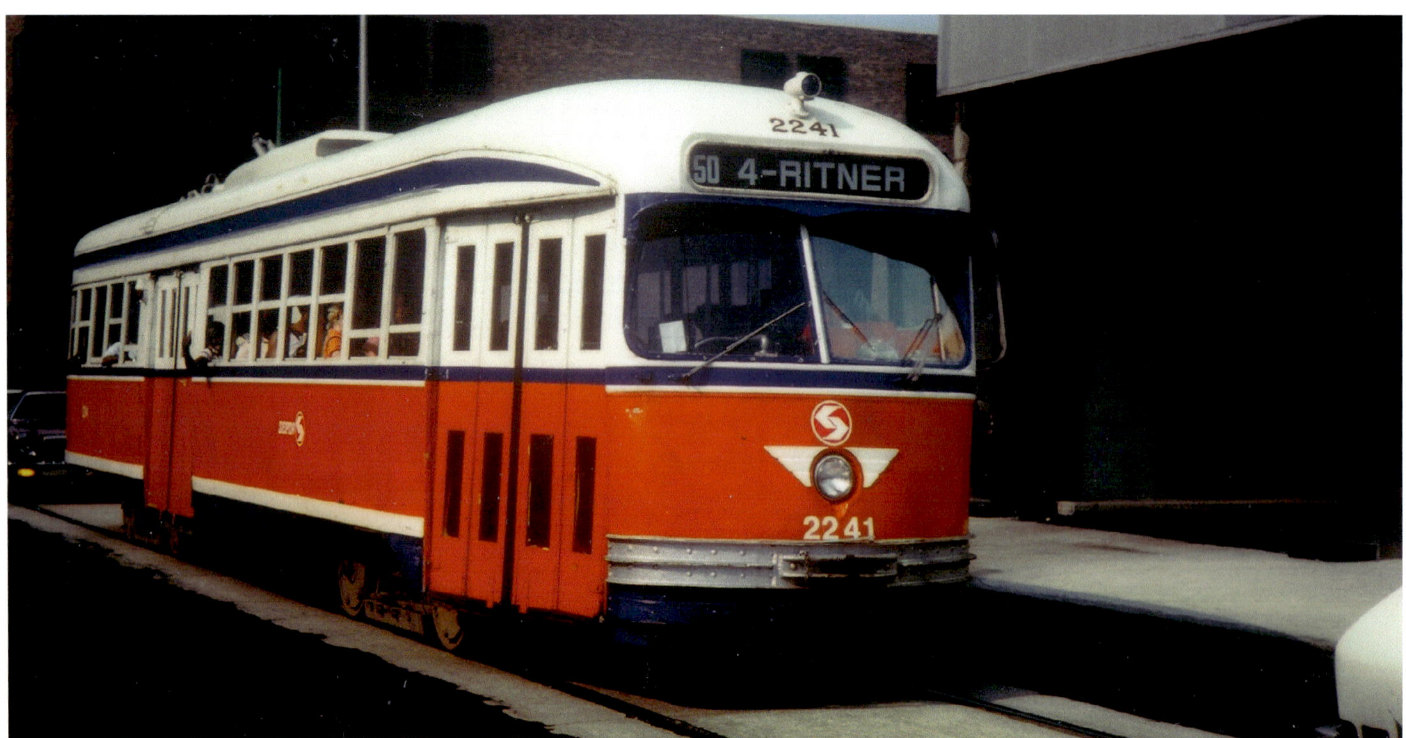

SEPTA Route 50 PCC car No. 2241 is on 4th Street near Market Street for a south bound trip to 4th and Ritner Streets on July 19, 1978. This was one of eleven PCC cars acquired by SEPTA from the Toronto Transit Commission (TTC) in 1976 and were renumbered 2240-2250. These cars (each powered by four Westinghouse type 1432J motors) were built by St. Louis Car Company as part of number series 501-585 and 725-799 for the Kansas City Public Service Company (KCPS) in 1946 and thirty were sold to the (TTC) in 1957 where they were renumbered 4750-4779. Car No. 2241 was originally KCPS No. 535, later TTC No. 4751, and was scrapped in 1983.

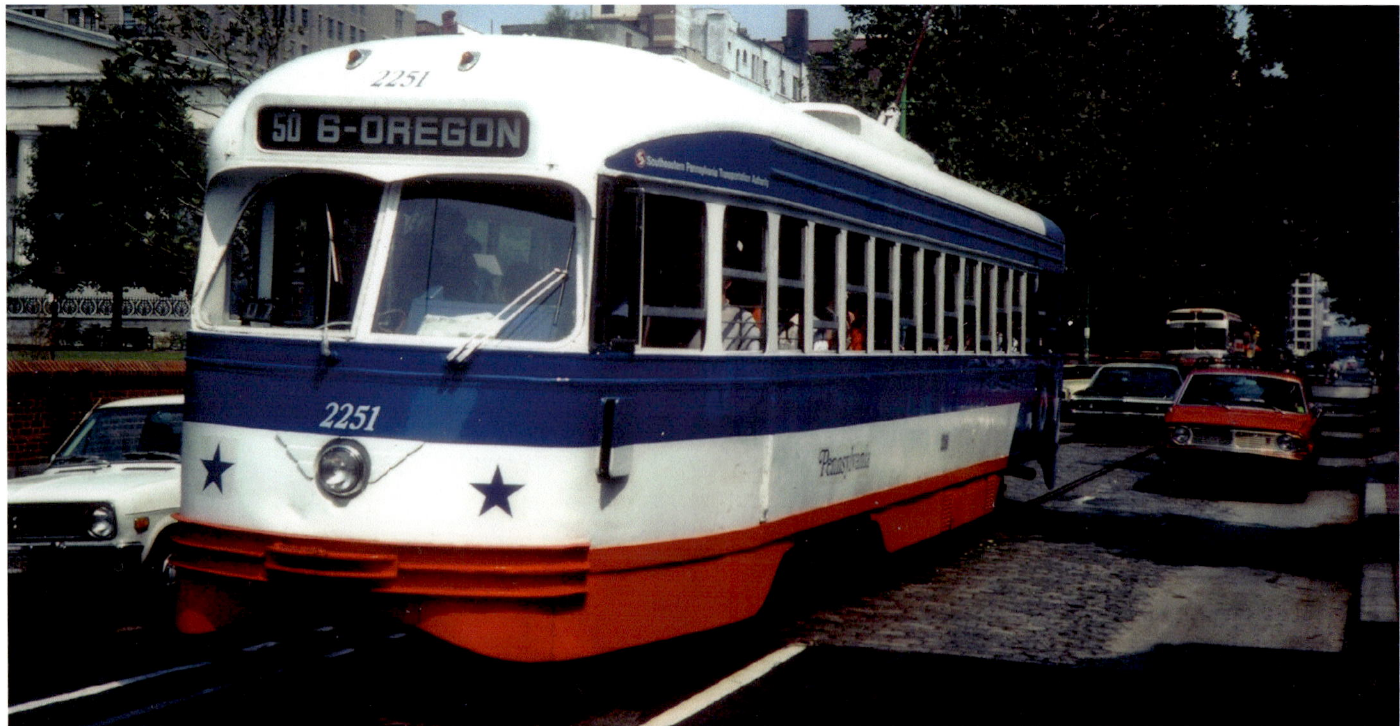

In a bicentennial paint scheme, SEPTA Route 50 PCC car No. 2251 is on 4th at Walnut Streets on August 14, 1976. This was one of forty PCC cars (each powered by four Westinghouse type 1432J motors) built by St. Louis Car Company as part of number series 725-799 in 1946 for KCPS, acquired by PTC in 1954, and they were renumbered 2251-2290. Car No. 2251 was originally KCPS No. 787, rebuilt by PTC in February 1955 and was scrapped in March 1982.

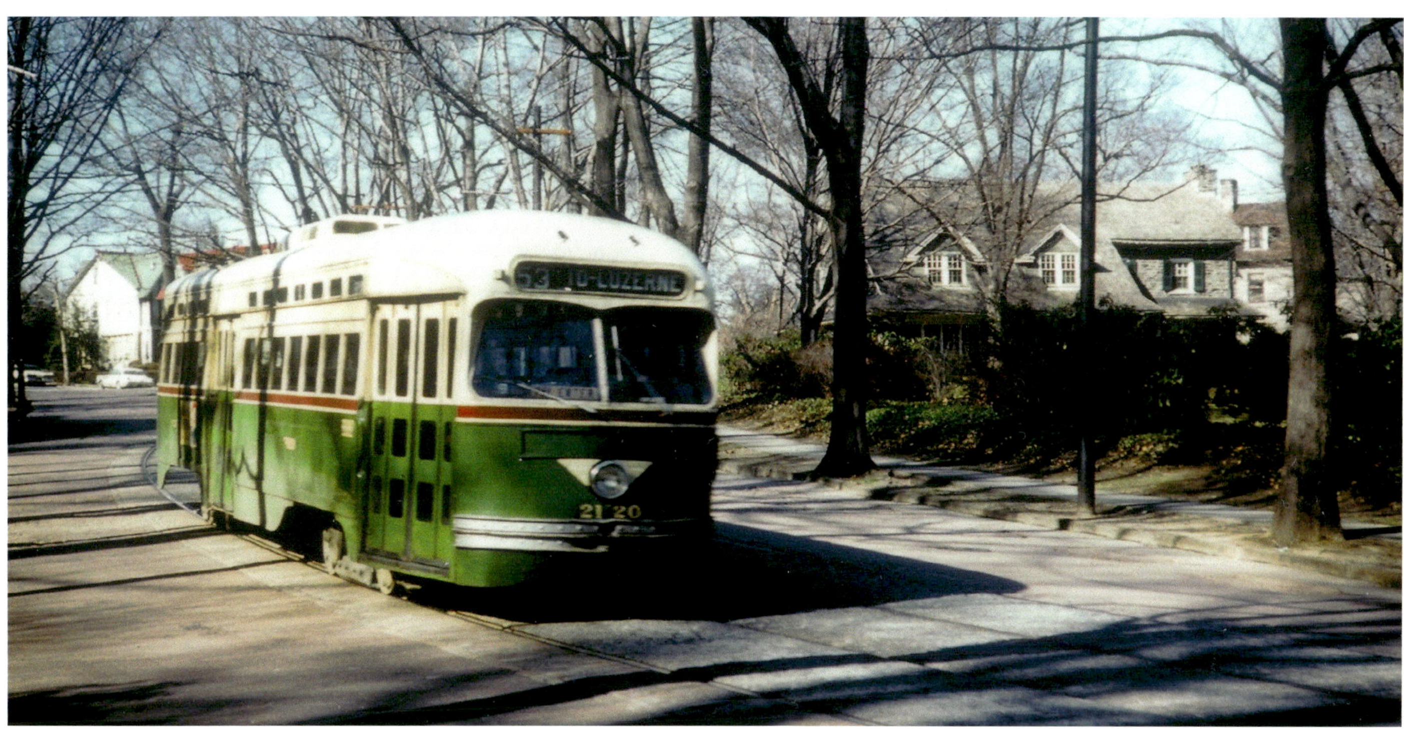

On April 2, 1961, PTC Route 53 PCC car No. 2120 is quickly making its way along tree-lined Wayne Avenue in the West Mount Airy neighborhood of Northwest Philadelphia. This car was delivered in August 1948 by St. Louis Car Company, overhauled by SEPTA in December 1981, and is now at Kenosha Area Transit in Kenosha, Wisconsin. Route 53 was a light feeder line in Germantown.

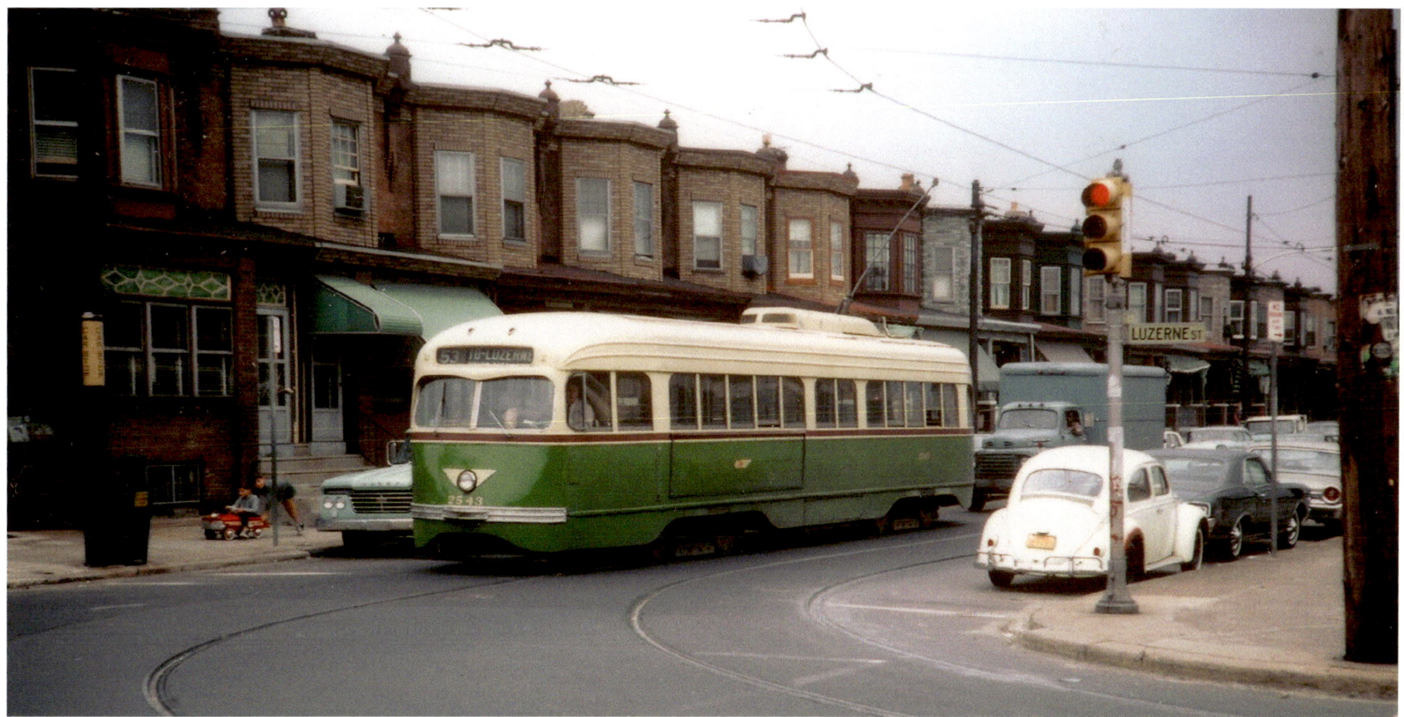

PTC Route 53 PCC car No. 2543 is on 10th Street, ready to turn onto Luzerne Street at its terminus in the Hunting Park neighborhood of North Philadelphia, on April 27, 1968. This car was delivered by St. Louis Car Company in January 1941 and was scrapped in 1977.

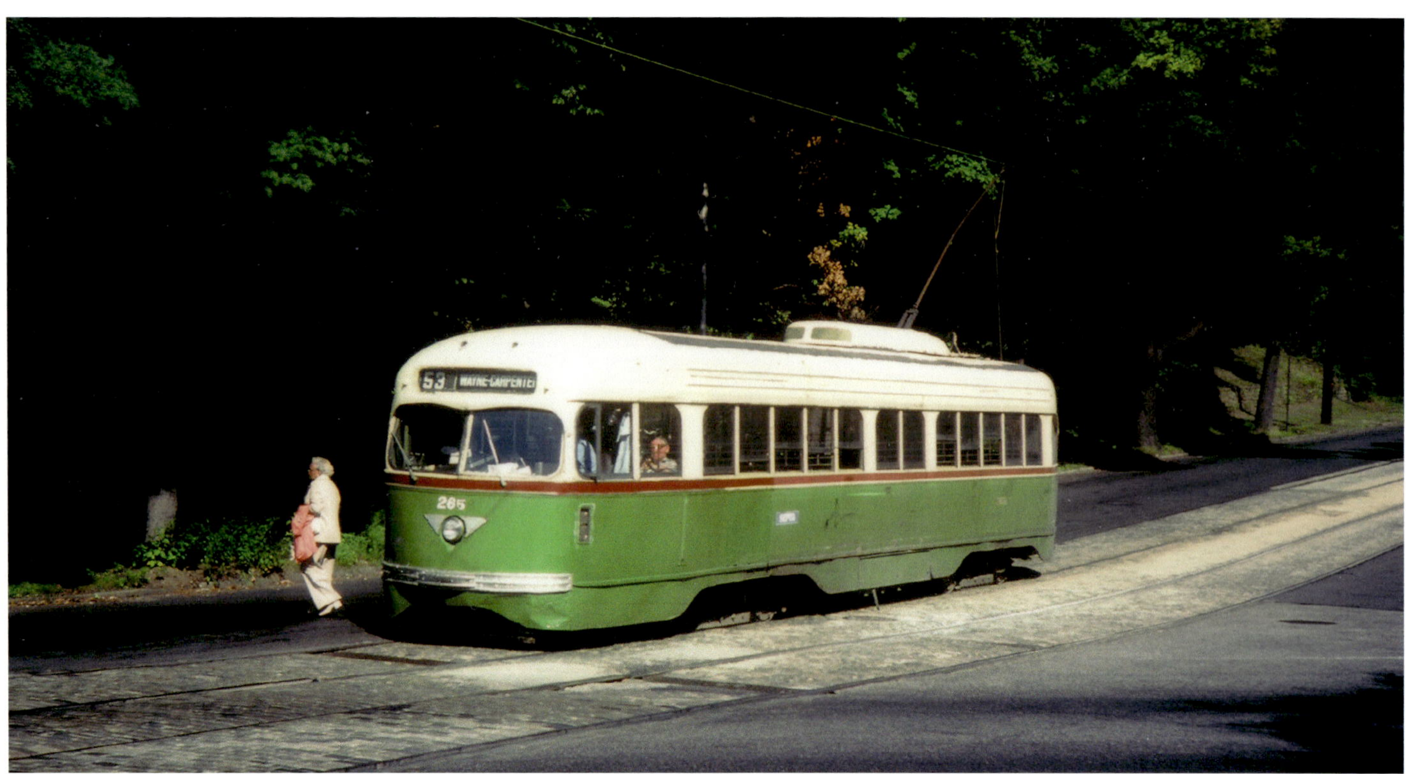

SEPTA Route 53 PCC car No. 2656 is on Wayne Avenue at scenic Lincoln Drive on July 27, 1977. This car was delivered in July 1942 and was scrapped in 1978.

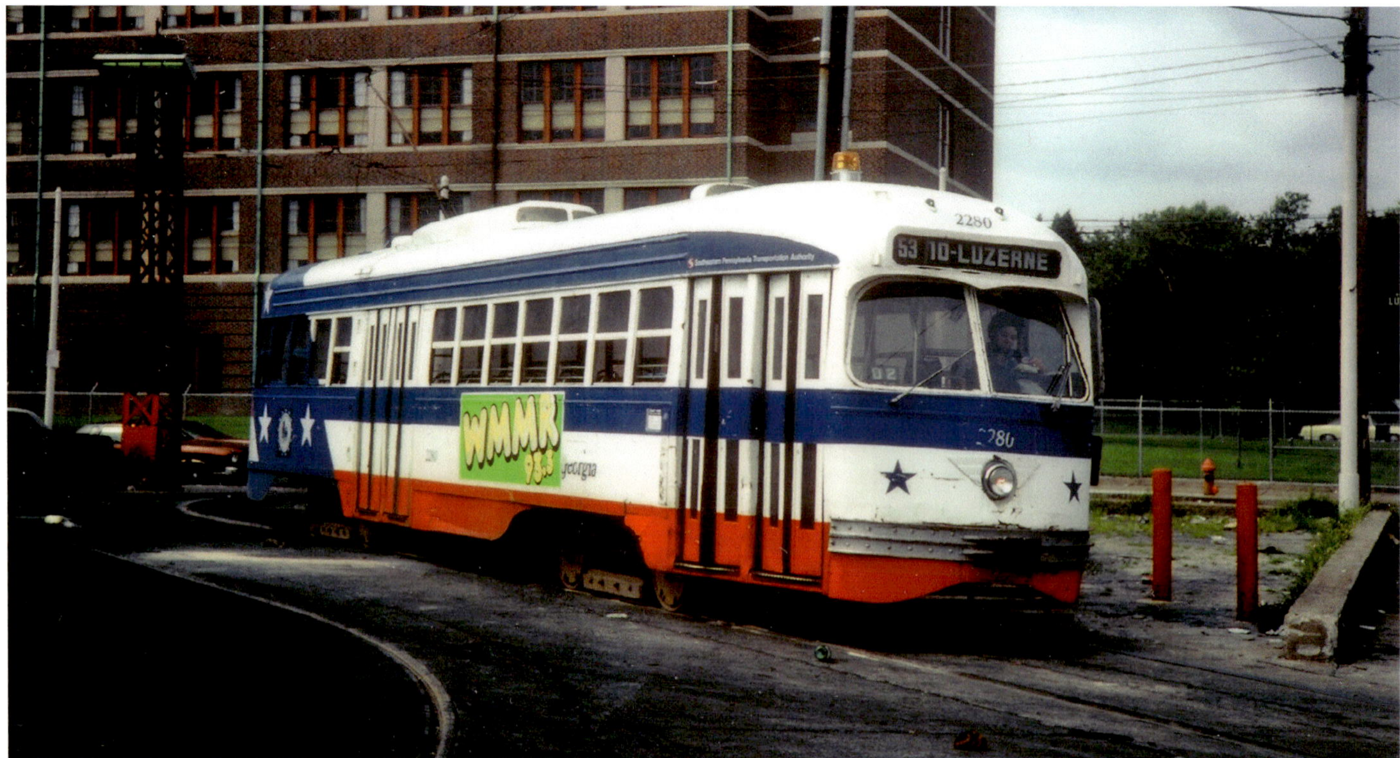

On July 27, 1979, SEPTA Route 53 PCC car No. 2280 (car No. 748 acquired from KCPS in June 1955 and scrapped in 1982) is at the 10th and Luzerne Loop at the Luzerne Depot on July 27, 1979. Philadelphia's Luzerne Depot, when opened in 1913, was the largest precast concrete structure in the world, with space for 355 trolleys, and room for 115 more in the outside adjacent yard.

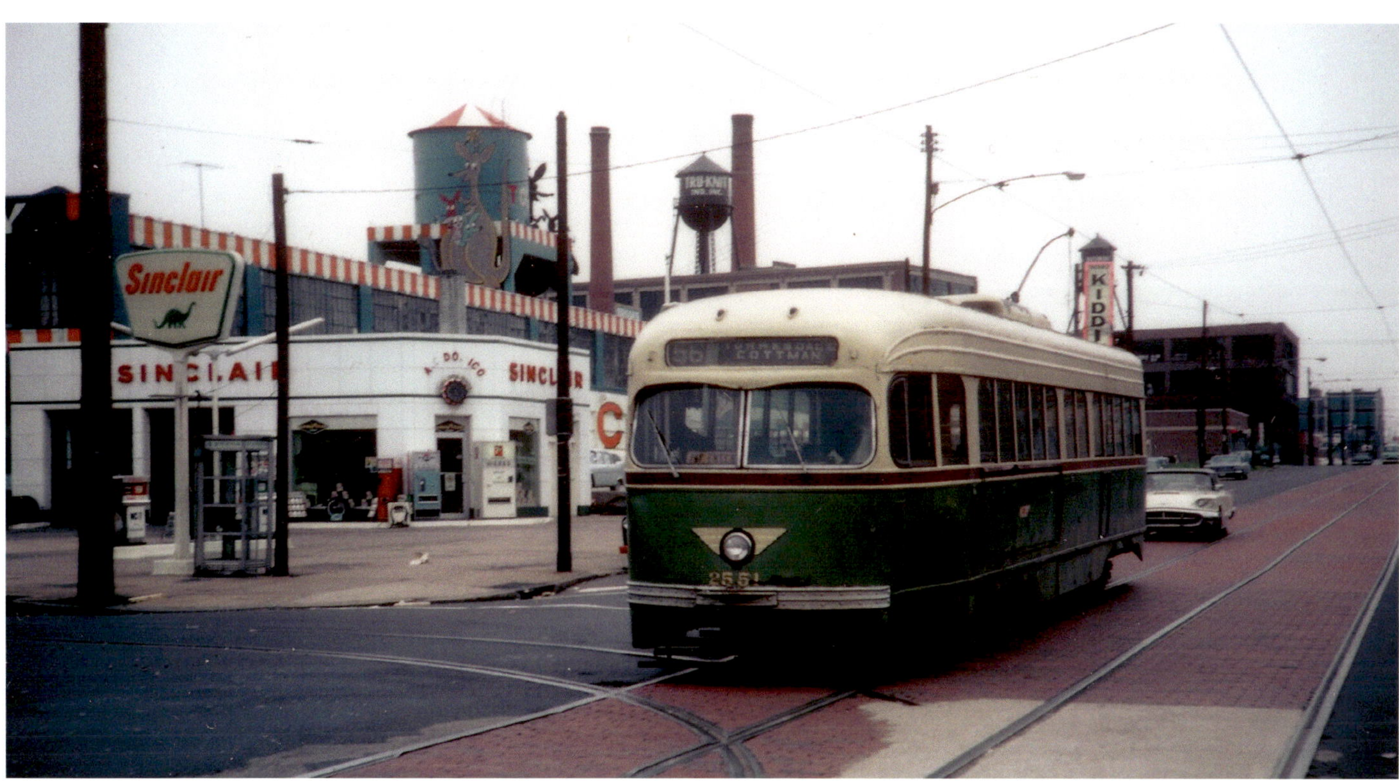

Erie Avenue at O Street just west of Kensington Avenue is the location of PTC Route 56 PCC car No. 2551 on April 27, 1968. Time was running out for PTC as SEPTA took over PTC on September 30, 1968. This car was delivered in January 1941 and was destroyed in the Woodland Depot fire of October 23, 1975. Route 56 was a long crosstown line connecting Torresdale and Cottman with 23rd and Venango at the Budd plant.

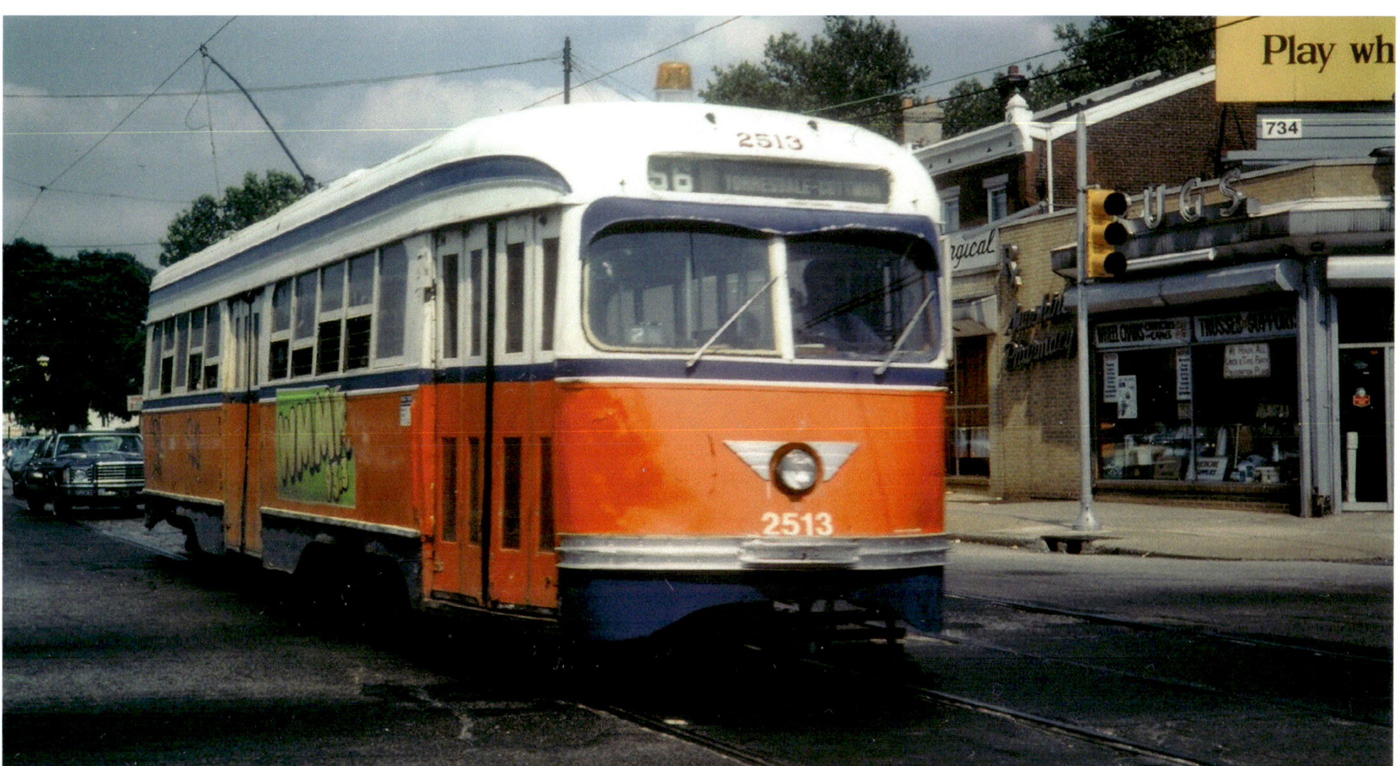

On a summer June 19, 1980, SEPTA Route 56 PCC car No. 2513 is on Torresdale Avenue at Robins Avenue in the Wissinoming neighborhood of Northeast Philadelphia. This car was delivered in December 1940 and was scrapped in March 1982.

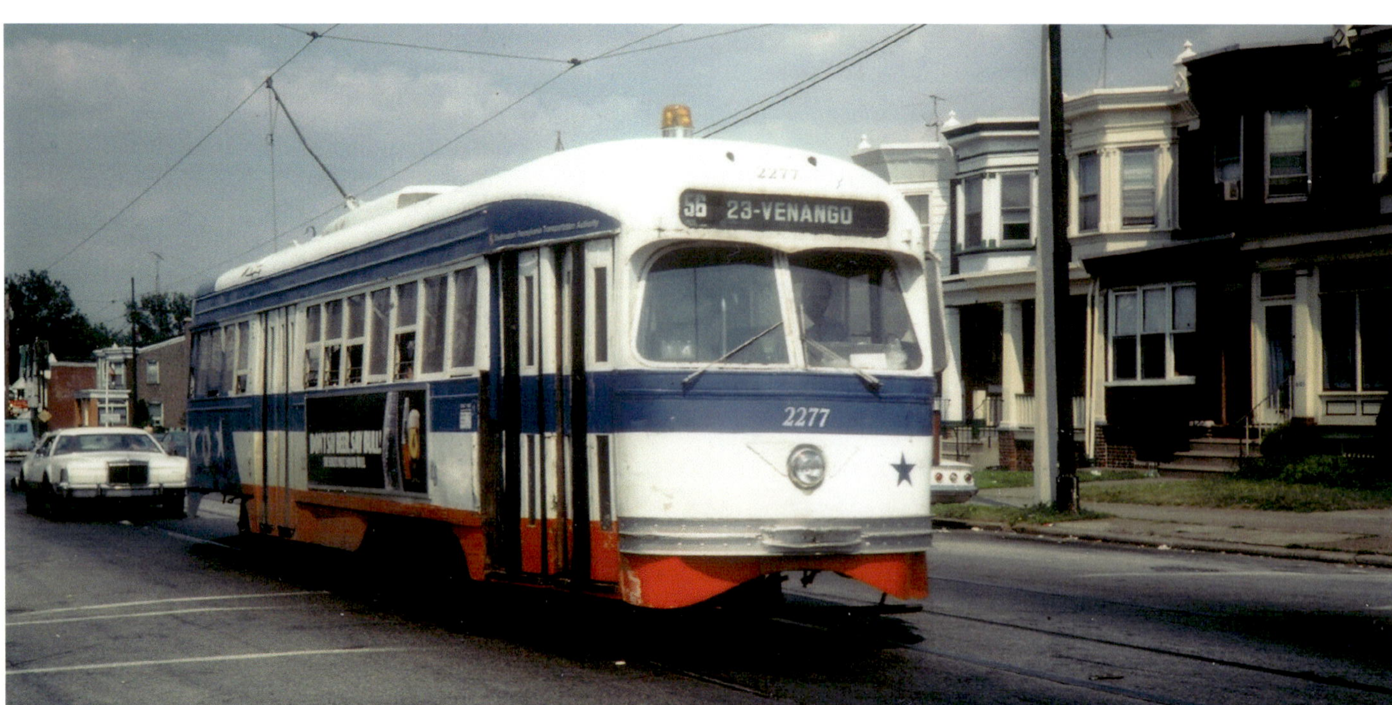

On June 19, 1980, SEPTA Route 56 PCC car No. 2277 is on Torresdale Avenue at Benner Street two blocks east of Robbins Avenue in the Wissinoming neighborhood of Philadelphia. Car No. 2277 was originally KCPS No. 729, was acquired by PTC in May 1955, and was scrapped in 1983.

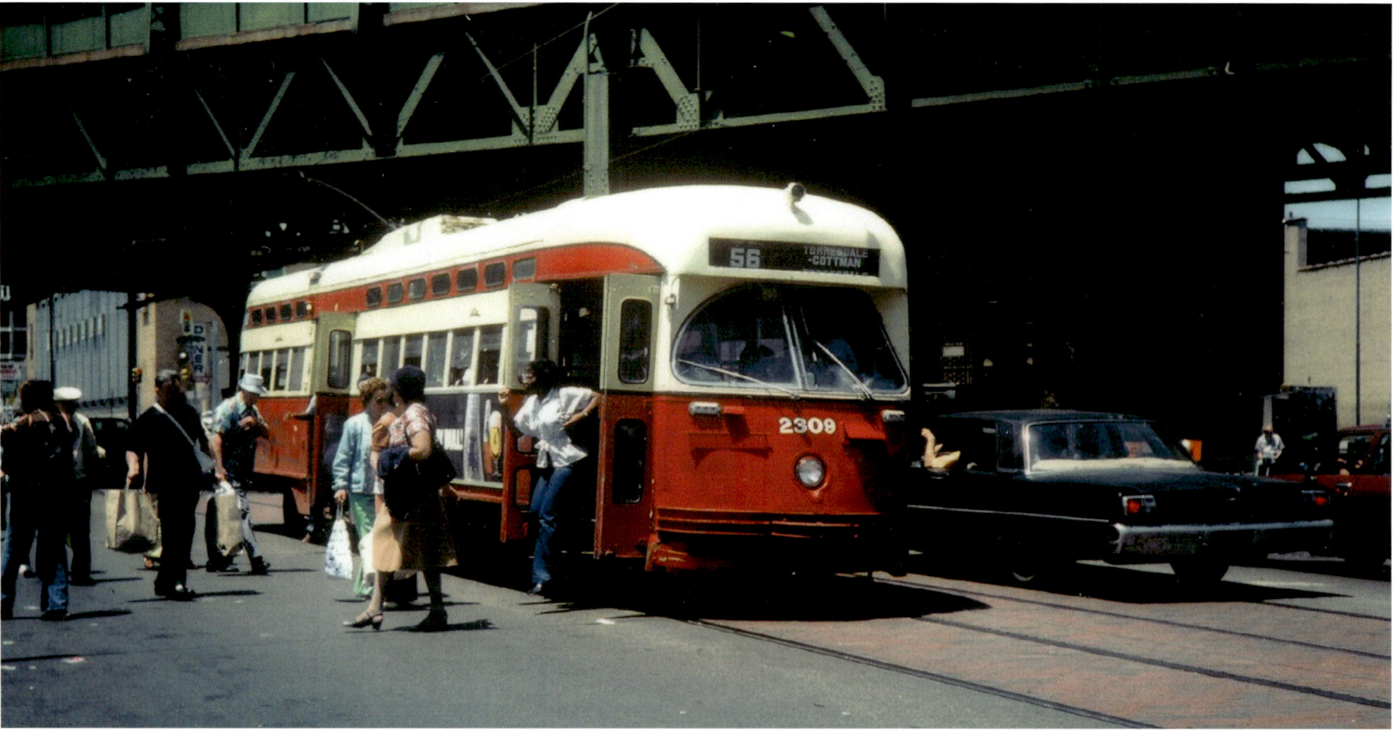

Torresdale Avenue at Kensington Avenue under the Frankford Elevated Line is the location of SEPTA Route 56 PCC car No. 2309 at this busy transfer point on June 21, 1980. This was one of nineteen PCC cars, acquired from the TTC by SEPTA during 1976, which were renumbered 2300-2318. The cars were built by Pullman Standard Manufacturing Company (each powered by four Westinghouse type 1432 motors) for the Birmingham Electric Company (BEC) which became Birmingham Transit Company (BTC) in 1951 as part of number series 800-847 in 1946-1947. These cars were sold to the Toronto Transit Commission (TTC) in 1952 and were consecutively renumbered 4700-4747. Car No. 2309 (ex BTC 828 and later ex TTC No. 4727) was scrapped in August 1981.

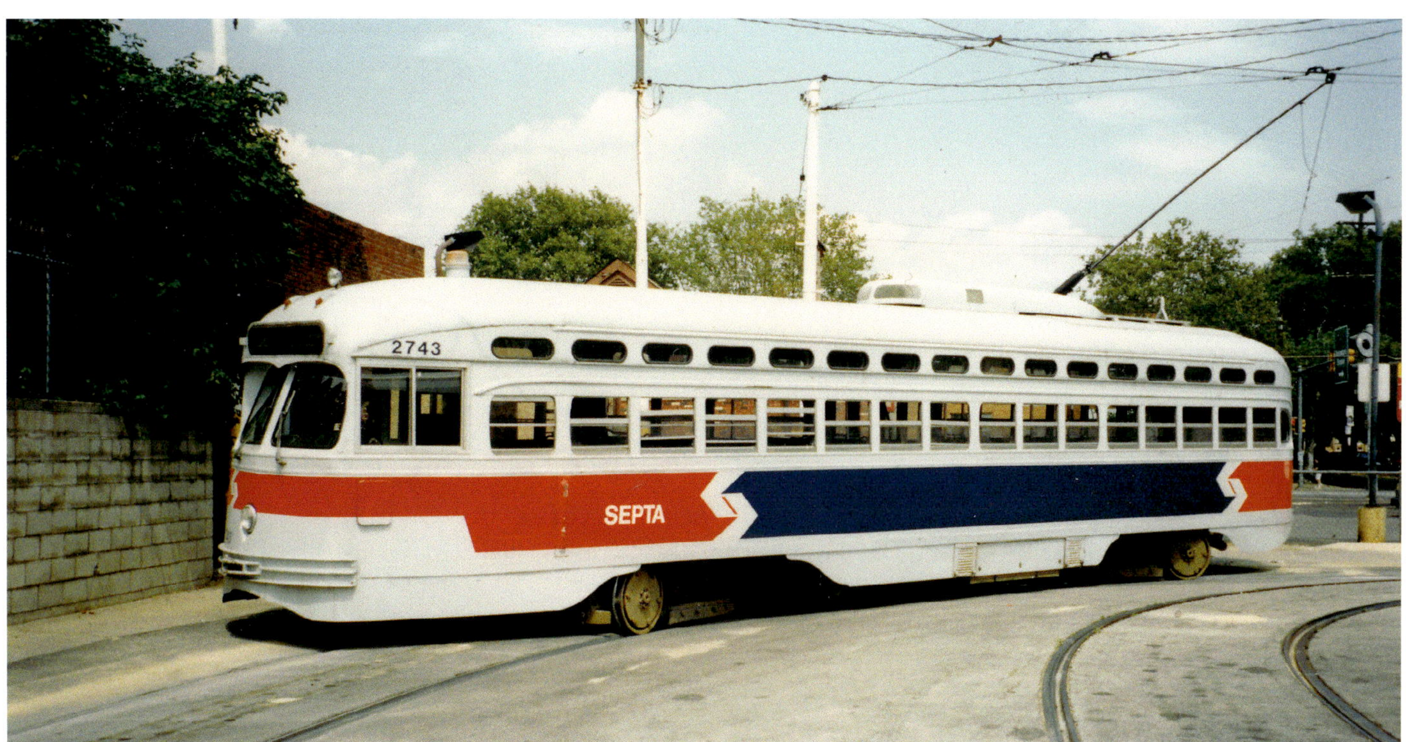

SEPTA Route 56 PCC car No. 2743 is at the Torresdale and Cottman Loop on August 5, 1991. This car is shown on page 32 when it was stored outside off the tracks at Germantown Depot.

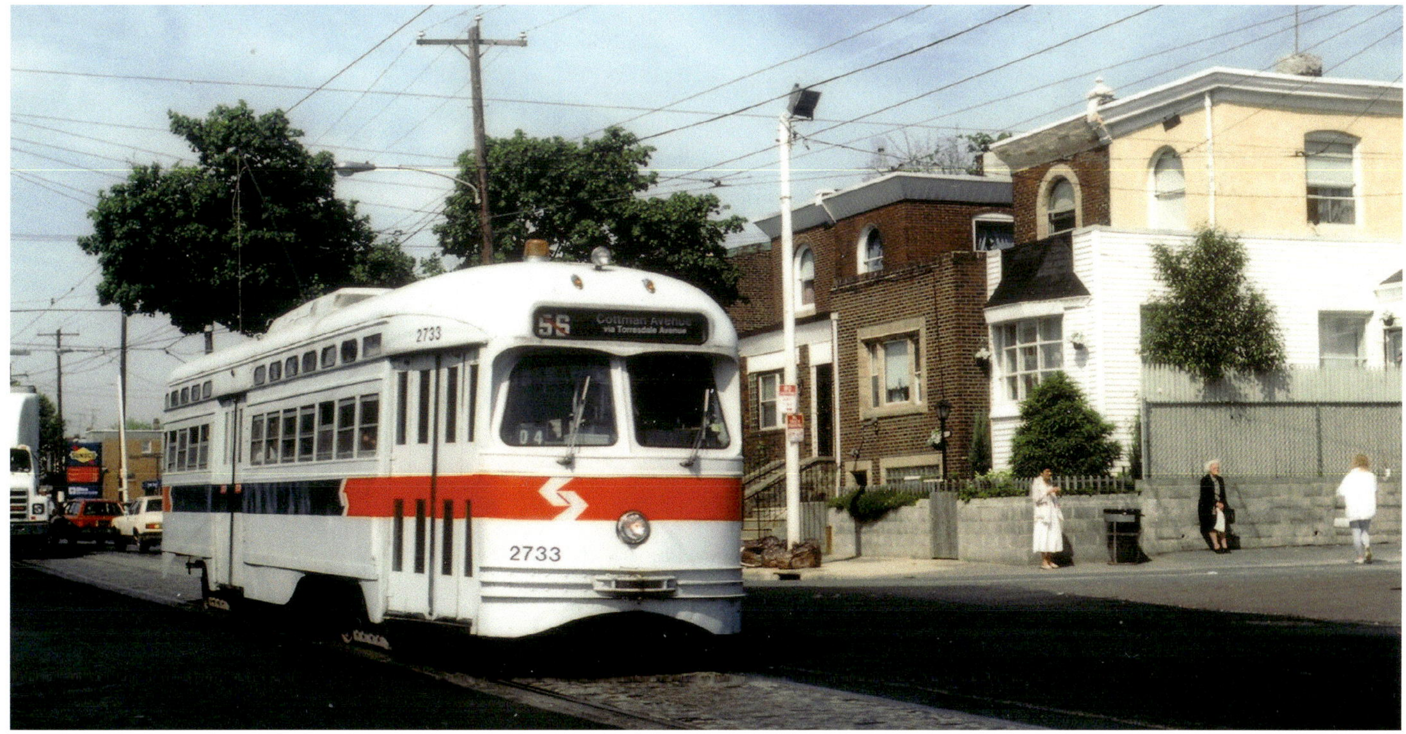

On May 29, 1992, SEPTA Route 56 PCC car No. 2733 is on Torresdale Avenue ready to turn into the loop at Cottman Avenue in the Tacony neighborhood of Northeast Philadelphia. This car was delivered by St. Louis Car Company in March 1947, went into service on Route 23 on May 11, 1947, overhauled by SEPTA in October 1986, and in September 1995 was placed at the SEPTA Transit Museum in the SEPTA headquarters building located at 1234 Market Street in Philadelphia which has displays on Philadelphia's transit history.

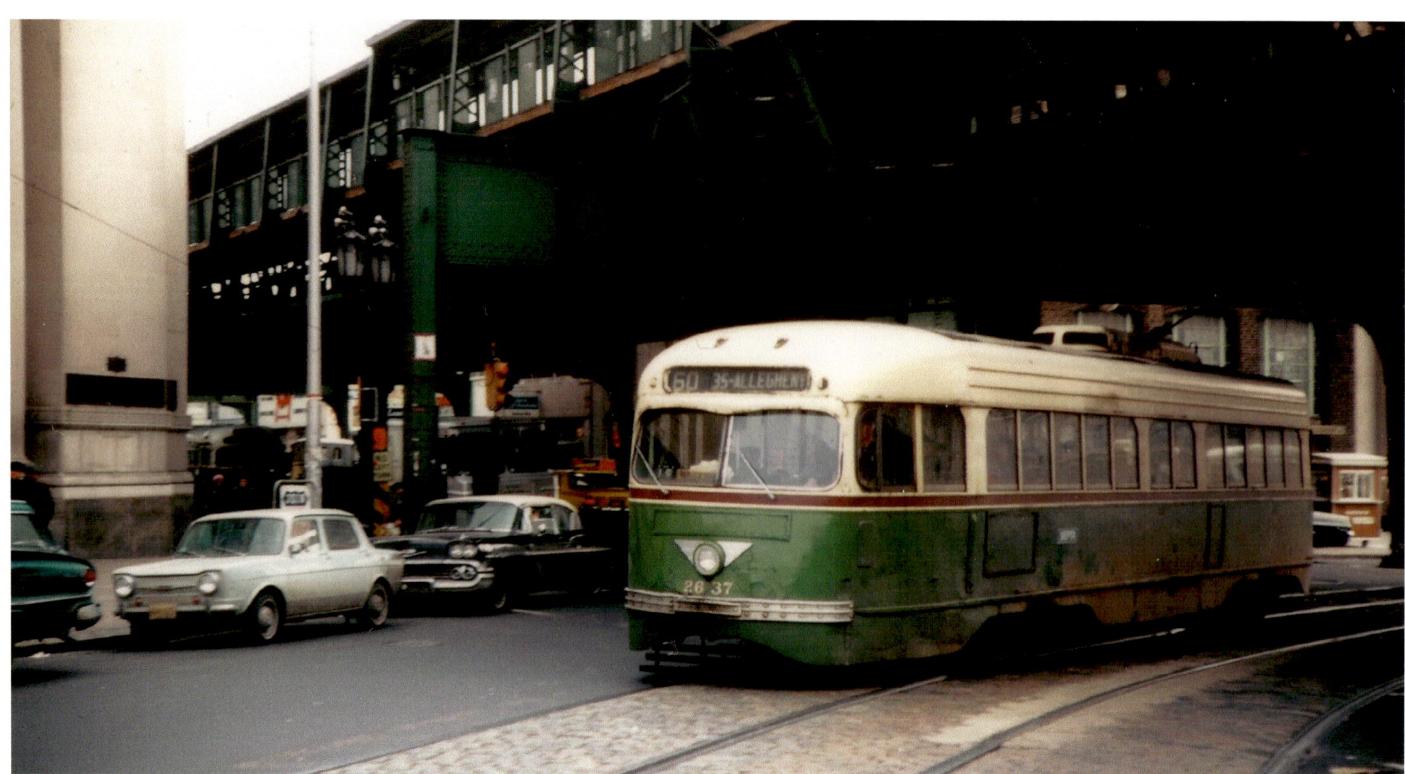

Westbound for 35th and Allegheny Avenue, SEPTA Route 60 PCC car No. 2637 is on Allegheny Avenue at Kensington Avenue passing under the Frankford Elevated Line on February 28, 1969. This car was delivered in July 1942 by St. Louis Car Company and was scrapped in March 1982. Route 60 was a crosstown line linking Richmond and Westmoreland with 35th and Allegheny.

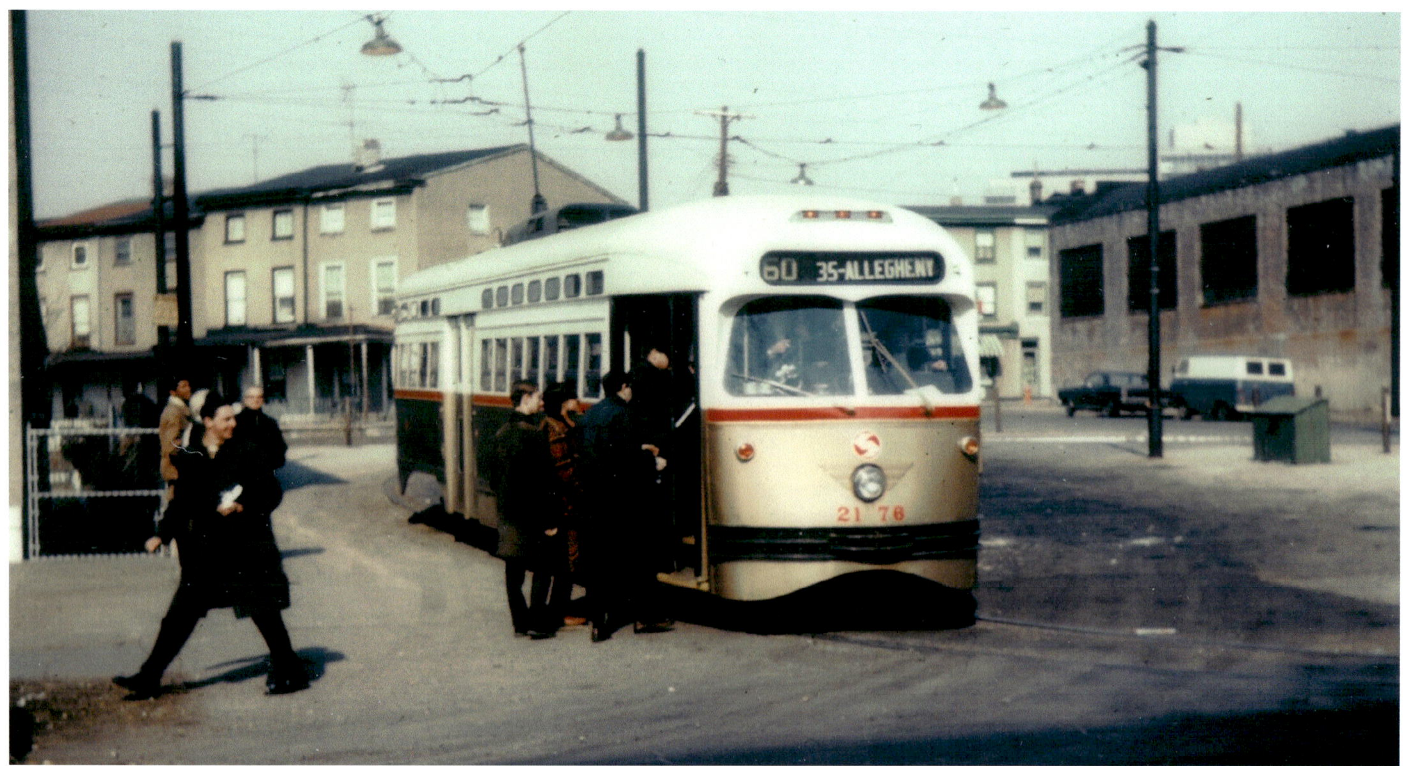

SEPTA Route 60 PCC car No. 2176 is loading passengers at the 35th and Allegheny Loop on May 30, 1970. St. Louis Car Company delivered this car in July 1948, and it was destroyed in the Woodland Depot fire of October 23, 1975.

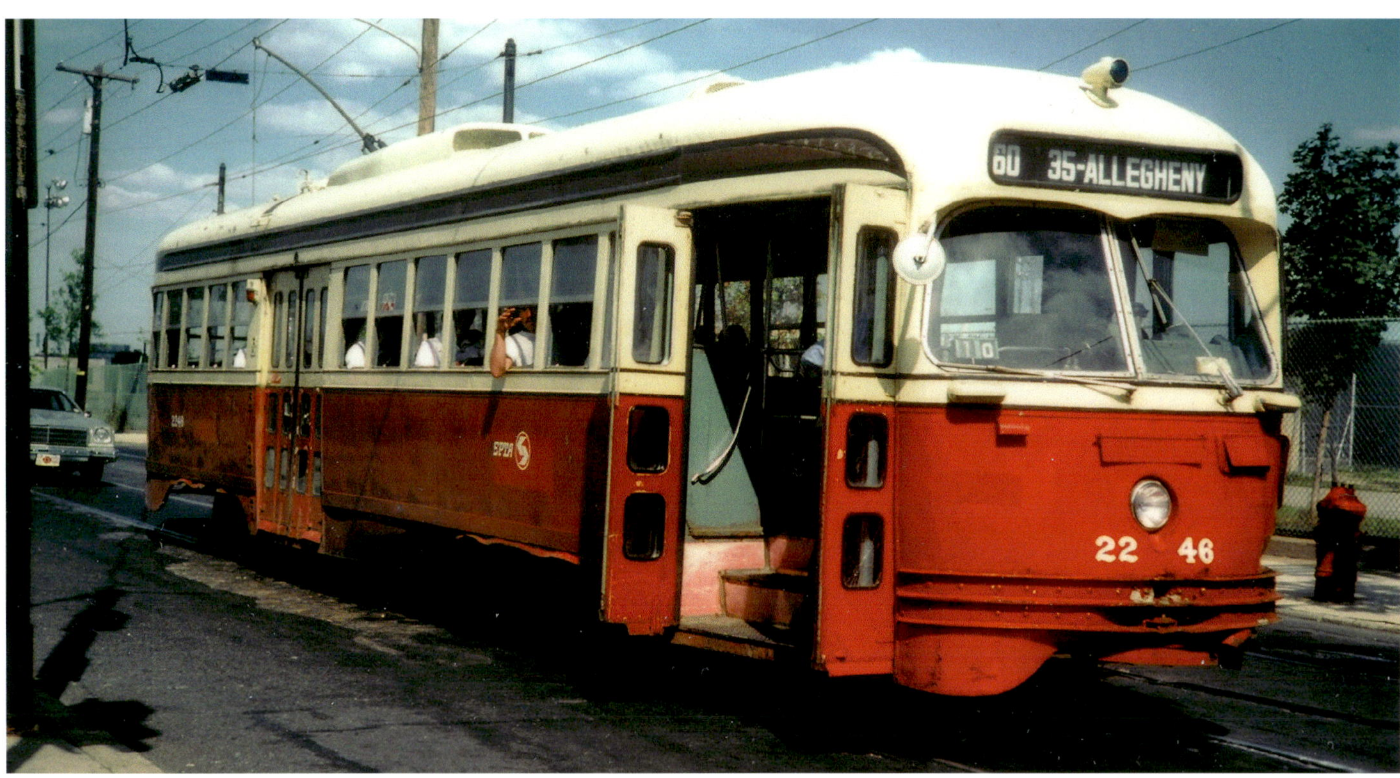

On July 28, 1977, SEPTA Route 60 PCC car No. 2246 is on Richmond Street at Allegheny Avenue for a passenger stop. This car was built as No. 771 by the St. Louis Car Company for the KCPS in 1946 and was sold to the TTC in 1957 and became car No. 4765. It was acquired by SEPTA in March 1976 becoming car No. 2246 and was scrapped in 1982.

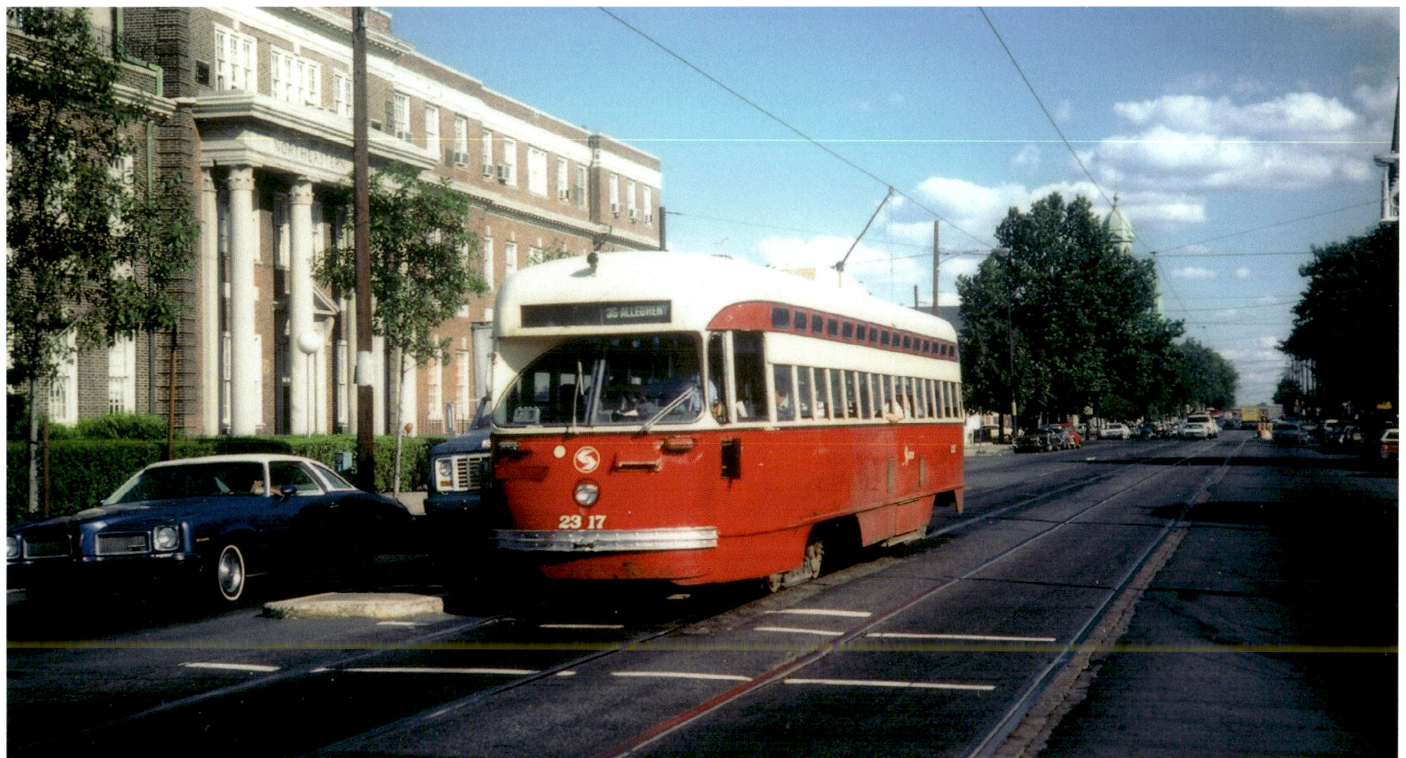

SEPTA Route 60 PCC car No. 2317 is on Allegheny Avenue at Tulip Street with the Northeastern Hospital on the left in the Port Richmond neighborhood of Philadelphia on July 29, 1977. This car was built by Pullman Standard Manufacturing Company as car No. 844 for Birmingham Electric Company (BEC), which became Birmingham Transit Company (BTC) in 1951 and was sold to the TTC in 1952, and became No. 4744. It was acquired by SEPTA in March 1976 becoming car No. 2317 and was scrapped in February 1982.

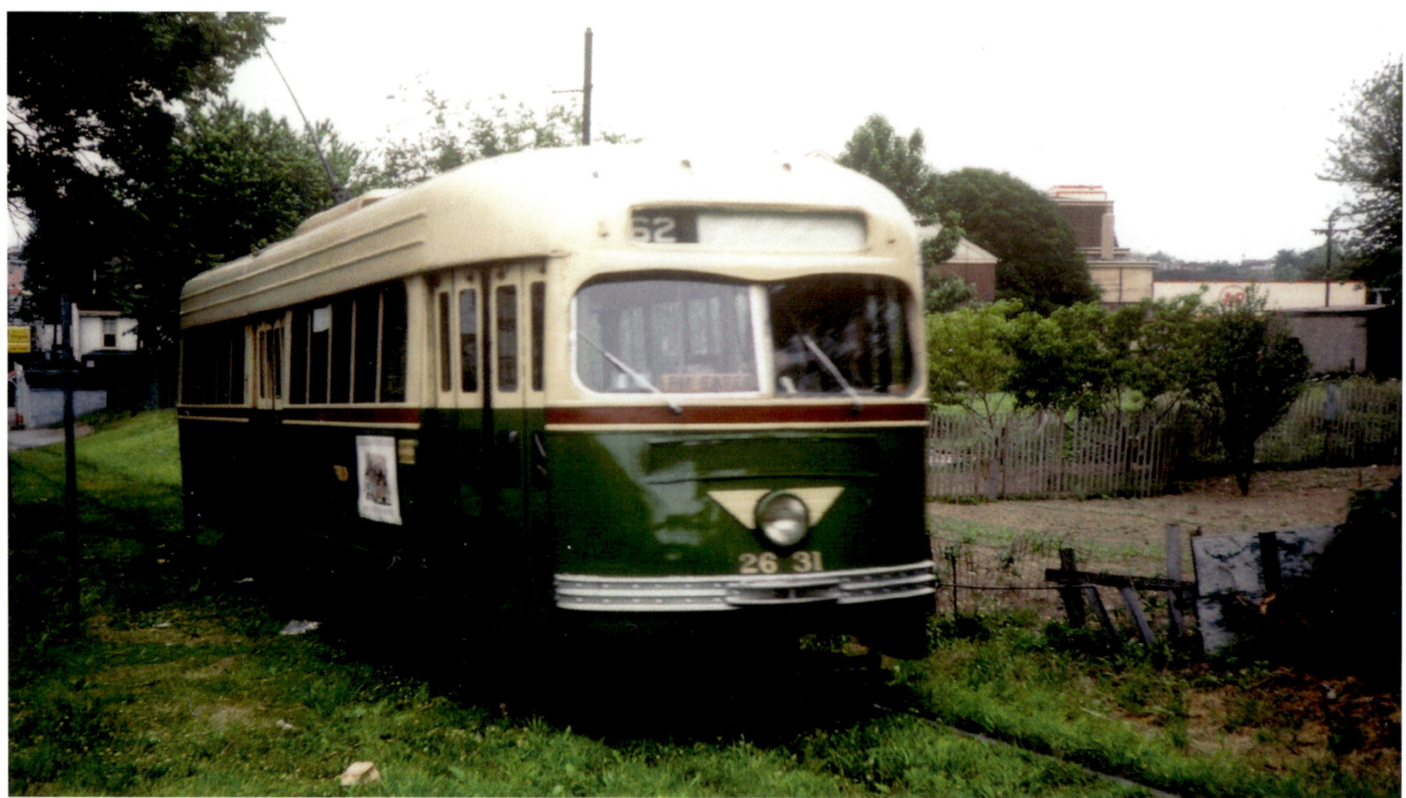

PTC Route 62 PCC car No. 2631 is on a private right of way near the Darby terminus on June 2, 1963. This was a short shuttle route between Darby and Yeadon Boroughs. Car No. 2631 was delivered by the St. Louis Car Company in June 1942 and was scrapped in 1977.

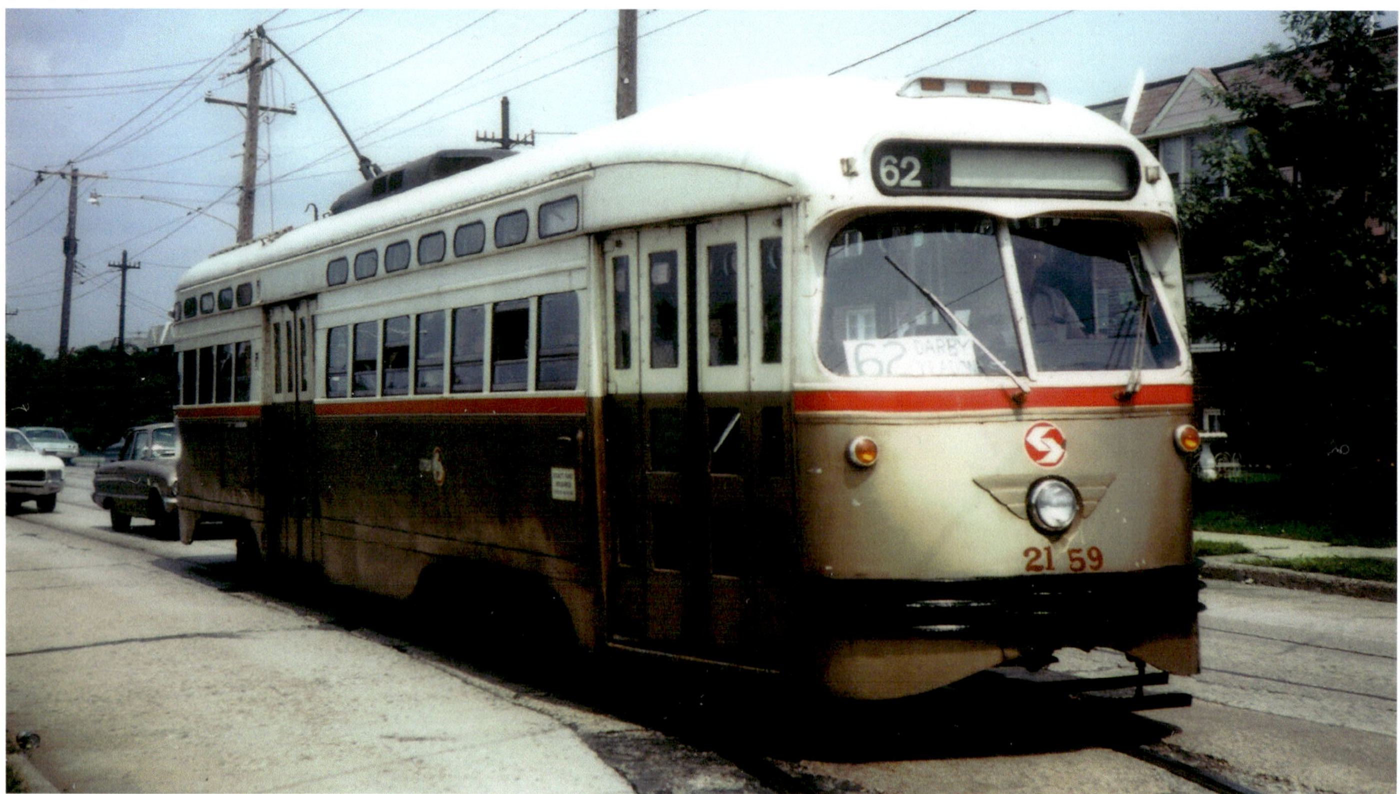

On June 25, 1972, SEPTA Route 62 PCC car No. 2159 is on Chester Avenue at Cedar Avenue in the borough of Yeadon for a photo stop on a rail excursion. Route 62 service ended on January 24, 1971, and was replaced by a weekday rush hour-only extension of the Route 13 trolley. Route 62 was a short shuttle between Yeadon and Darby.

Chapter 2

Suburban Philadelphia Trolleys

On December 17, 1898, the Philadelphia & West Chester Traction Company began trolley car service from 69th Street Terminal to West Chester. The Ardmore & Llanerch Street Railway opened the line to Ardmore from 69th Street Terminal on May 29, 1902. Trolley service from 69th Street Terminal to Clifton Heights by the Philadelphia & Garrettford Street Railway began on March 15, 1906 and reached Sharon Hill on August 1, 1917. Media was connected to the 69th Street Terminal by trolley on April 1, 1913. These trolley lines had a track gauge of 5 foot 2.25 inches and became the Philadelphia Suburban Transportation Company (PSTC), officially incorporated on April 13, 1936. During 1937, it became known as the Red Arrow. State highway work to widen West Chester Pike that would have cost PSTC $375,000 to realign tracks resulted in the conversion of the West Chester Line to bus operation on June 4, 1954, with rush hour trolley car service to Westgate Hills remaining until August 23, 1958. Buses replaced trolley cars on the Ardmore Line on December 30, 1966.

The standard gauge 4 foot 8.5 inches Philadelphia & Western Railway (P & W) rail line opened a from 69th Street Terminal via Villanova to Strafford on May 22, 1907 followed by a line from Villanova Junction to Norristown on August 26, 1912. The Lehigh Valley Transit Company (LVTC) began regular service on December 12, 1912 from Allentown to 69th Street Terminal using the P & W Line from Norristown to 69th Street Terminal. Effective with the new schedules issued on September 26, 1949, LVTC ended through service from Allentown to 69th Street Terminal; however, it continued to operate from Allentown to Norristown until buses took over on September 6, 1951. The P & W became part of the PSTC on December 31, 1953. The Strafford Line from Villanova Junction to Strafford was converted to bus operation on March 23, 1956.

On January 31, 1964, PSTC placed in regular service two luxurious commuter trains known as *Liberty Liners*. Car Nos. 801 and 802 became the *Valley Forge* and car Nos. 803 and 804 became the *Independence Hall*. These had been purchased from the abandoned Chicago North Shore & Milwaukee Railroad and were extensively refurbished. The Ardmore Trolley Car Line of PSTC was abandoned on December 29, 1966. The Southeastern Pennsylvania Transportation Authority (SEPTA) took over PSTC on January 29, 1970. Trackage remained on the two mile section of West Chester Pike from Llanerch to 69th Street to connect the Media and Sharon Hill Lines with the Llanerch Carbarn until it was removed in December 1971 when SEPTA opened new shop facilities for the trolleys at the Market-Frankford Subway Elevated shops at 69th Street.

Kawasaki Heavy Industries of Kobe, Japan, the prime contractor for Nissho Iwai American Corp., built twenty-nine double ended cars Nos. 100-128 for the Media and Sharon Hill Lines. Car 100 was the first new car for suburban service on the Media Line on November 4, 1980. On the Red Arrow Division, October 15, 1982 was the official final day for the older trolley cars; however, a number of the older cars were used until all of the operators had been qualified to operate the new cars. Beginning April 11, 1994, the Norristown to 69th Street Line was operated by twenty-six new cars built by Asea Brown Boveri. Under SEPTA the Norristown to 69th Street Line became Route 100 and later Norristown High Speed Line, Media Line became Route 101, and Sharon Hill Line became Route 102.

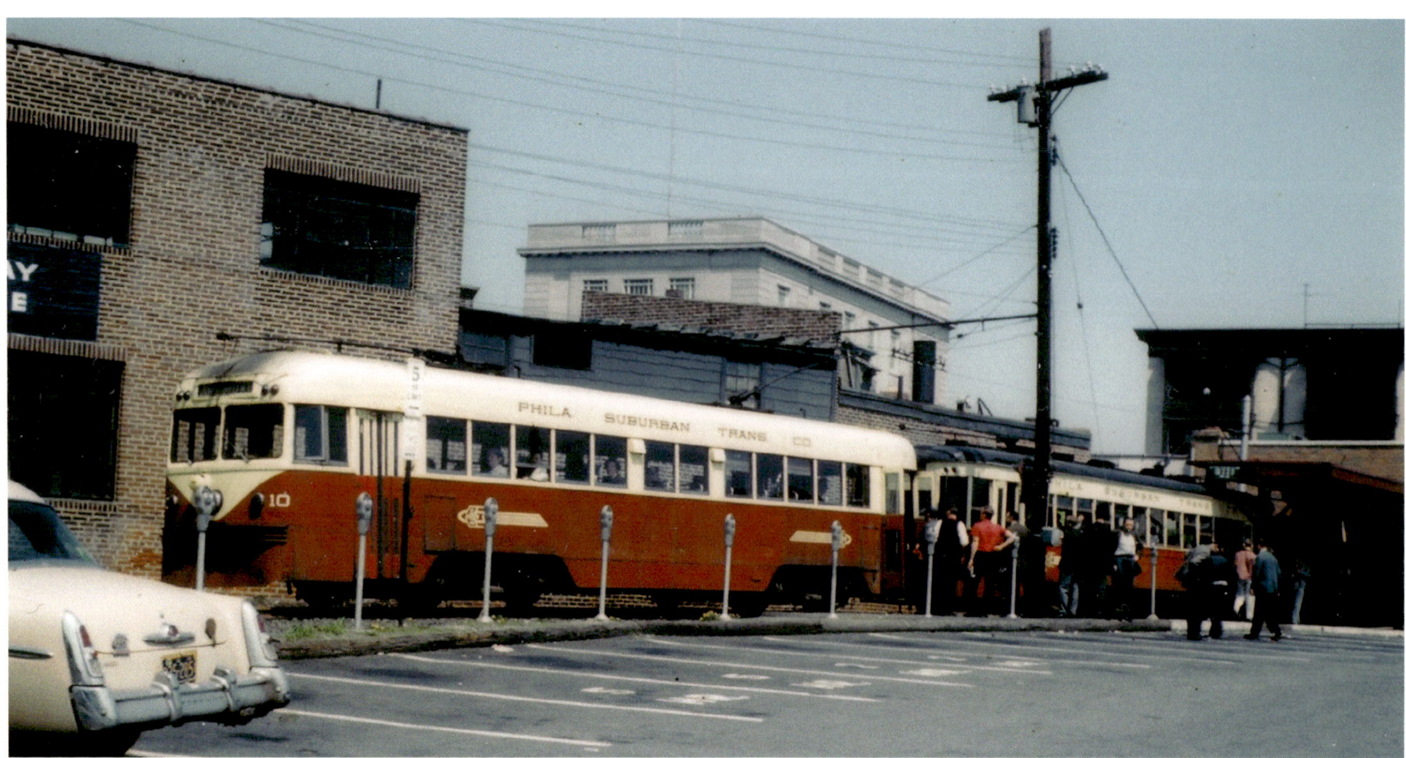

Philadelphia Suburban Transportation Company (PSTC) "Brilliner" car No. 10 (one of eleven cars Nos. 1-10 built by J. G Brill Company in 1941 seating fifty-eight, weighing 42,350 pounds, and powered by four Westinghouse type 1433 motors) and an 80 series Brill car are at the Ardmore terminus of the Ardmore Line on April 24, 1960.

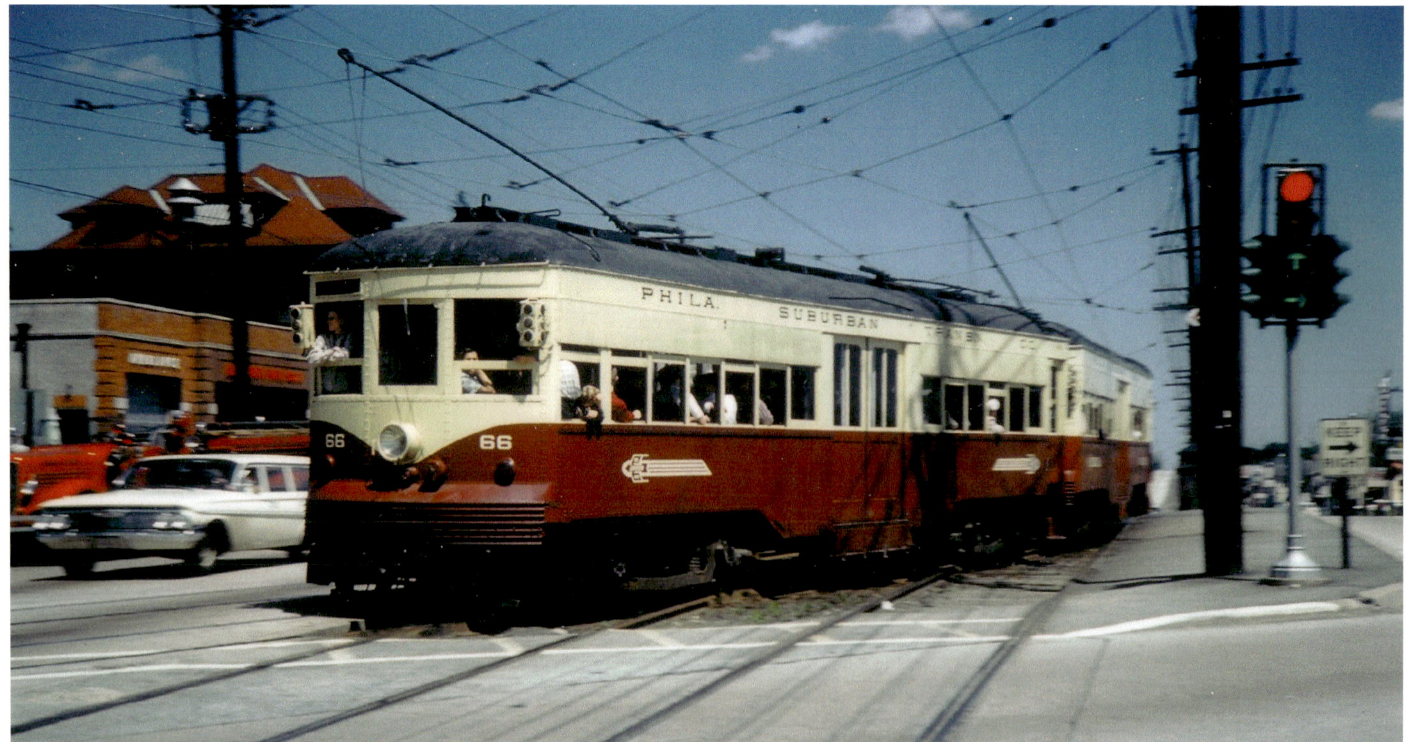

On June 4, 1961, PSTC center door cars Nos. 76 and 66 are turning from Darby Road onto West Chester Pike. These were two of twelve cars Nos. 65-76 built by J. G. Brill Company in 1926 powered by four General Electric type 203L motors, seating sixty-two, and weighing 59,280 pounds. Car Nos. 66 and 73 were acquired by the Pennsylvania Trolley Museum near Washington, Pennsylvania, in 1970 and it enables the operation of two car trains just like PSTC had done during peak periods.

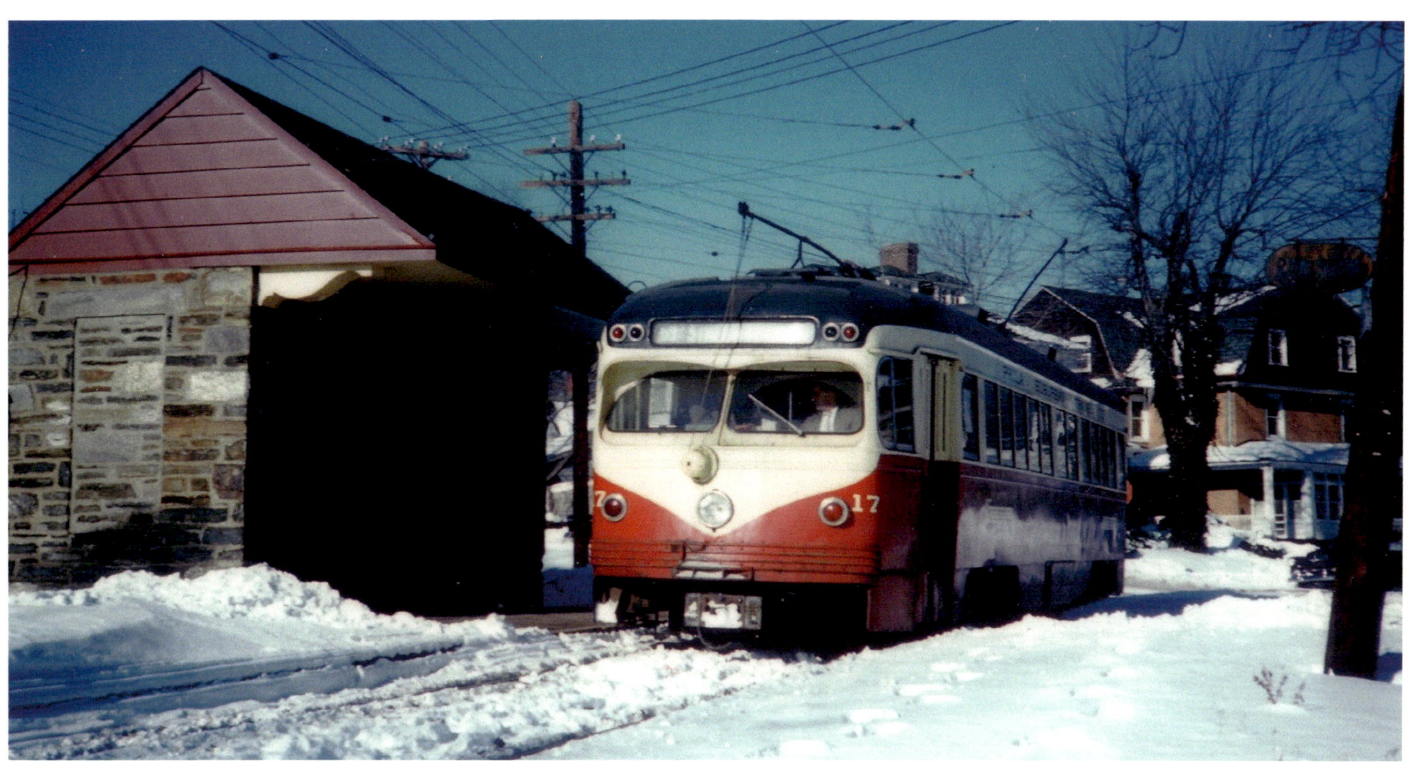

On January 29, 1961, PSTC car No. 17 is at County Line Road on the Ardmore Line. This was one of fourteen cars Nos. 11-24 built by St. Louis Car Company in 1949 powered by four Westinghouse type 1433 motors. Costing $46,000 each, the 50.4 foot long cars featured two way radio (enabling the operator to talk with the dispatcher eliminating stops at phone booths) and remote controlled automatic couplers. The cars, delivered on flatcars to the PSTC siding, were rolled down a temporary track that had been built up to the flat cars.

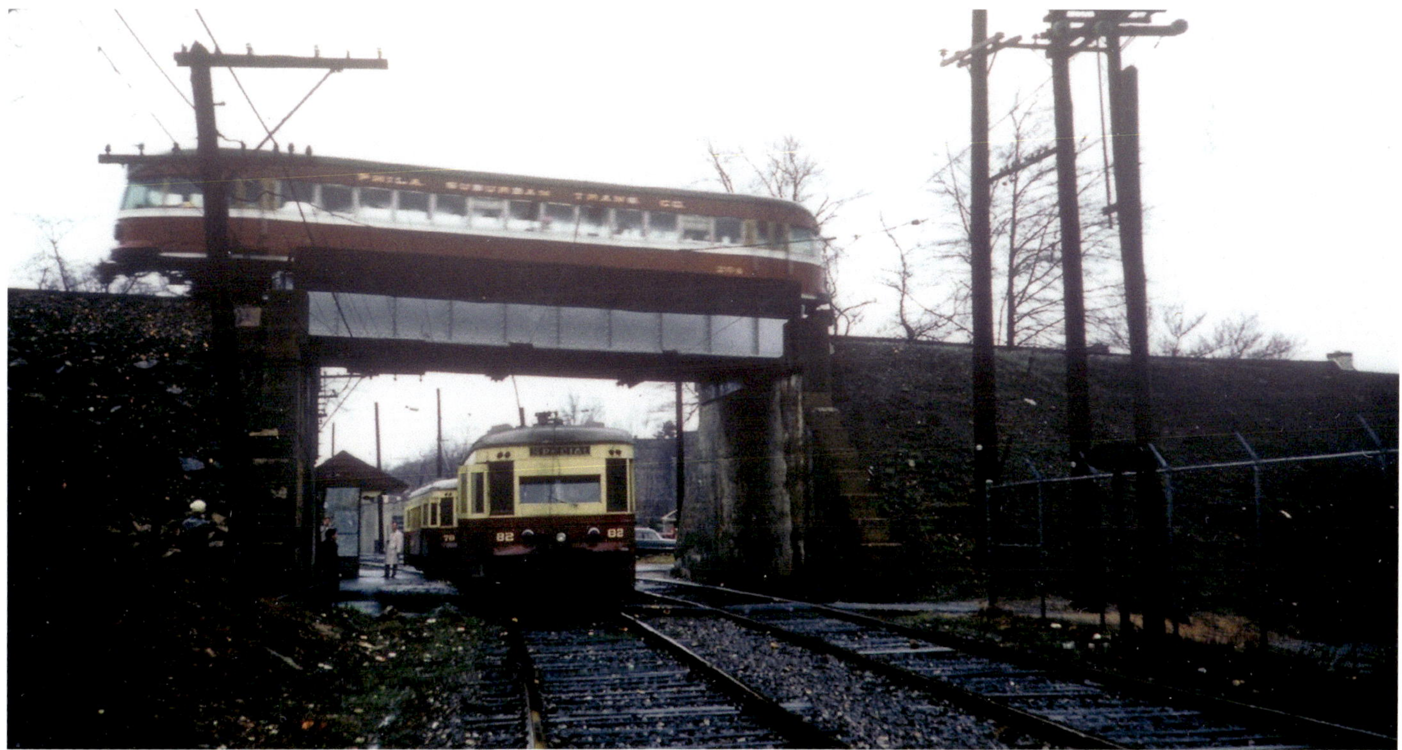

PSTC 80 series Brill cars Nos. 82 and 78 (two of ten cars Nos. 77-86 built by J. G. Brill Company in 1932 powered by four General Electric type 301B motors) are on the Ardmore Line at Ardmore Junction on a rail excursion. PSTC "Bullet" type car No. 206 is on the bridge of the former Norristown Line of the Philadelphia & Western Railway on April 1, 1962. Car #206 was converted into a "pickle car" to apply an anti-icing brine solution onto the line's electrified third rail. Car #206, was retired in 1995, and was acquired by the Electric City Trolley Museum.

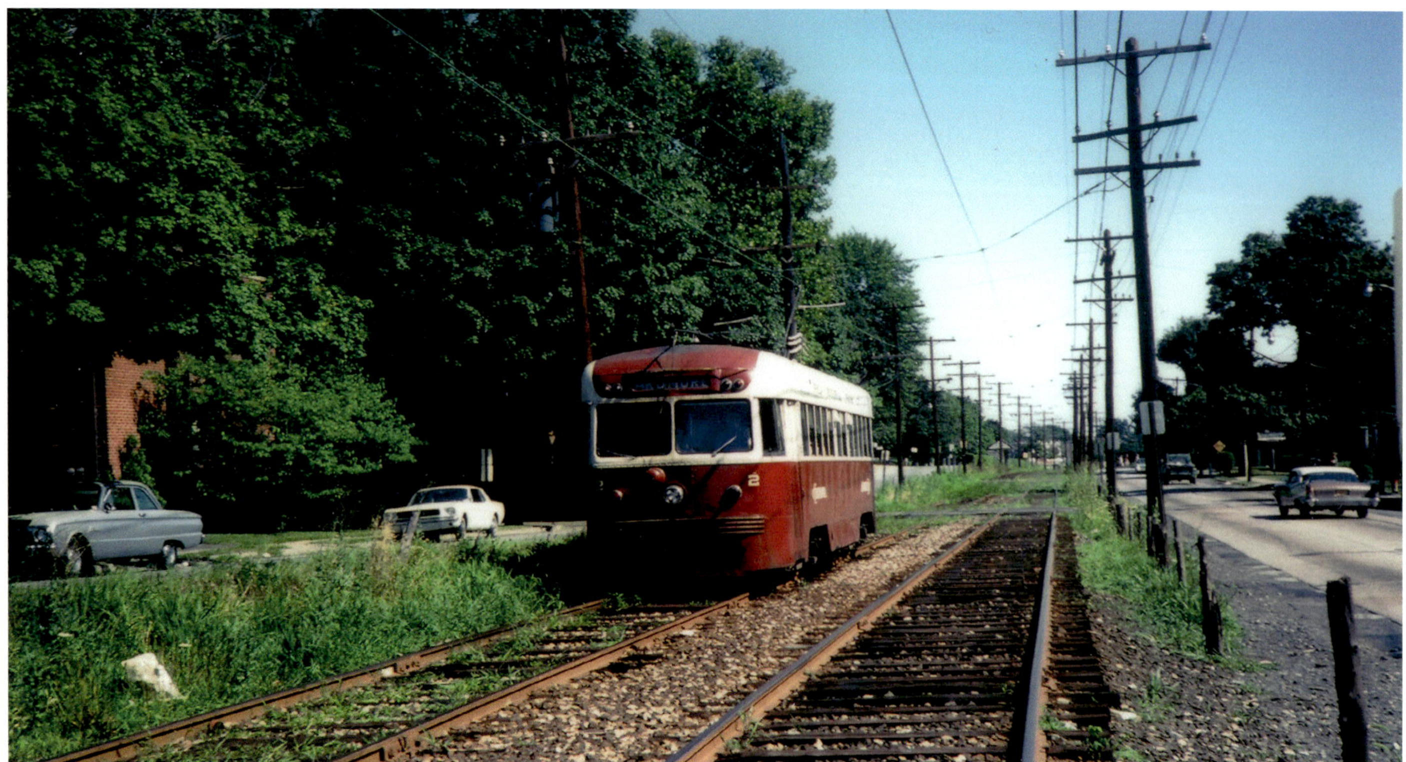

On July 22, 1966, PSTC "Brilliner" car No. 2 is on center-of-the-road private right of way of Darby Road south of Eagle Road along the Ardmore Line in the Oakmont section of Haverford Township.

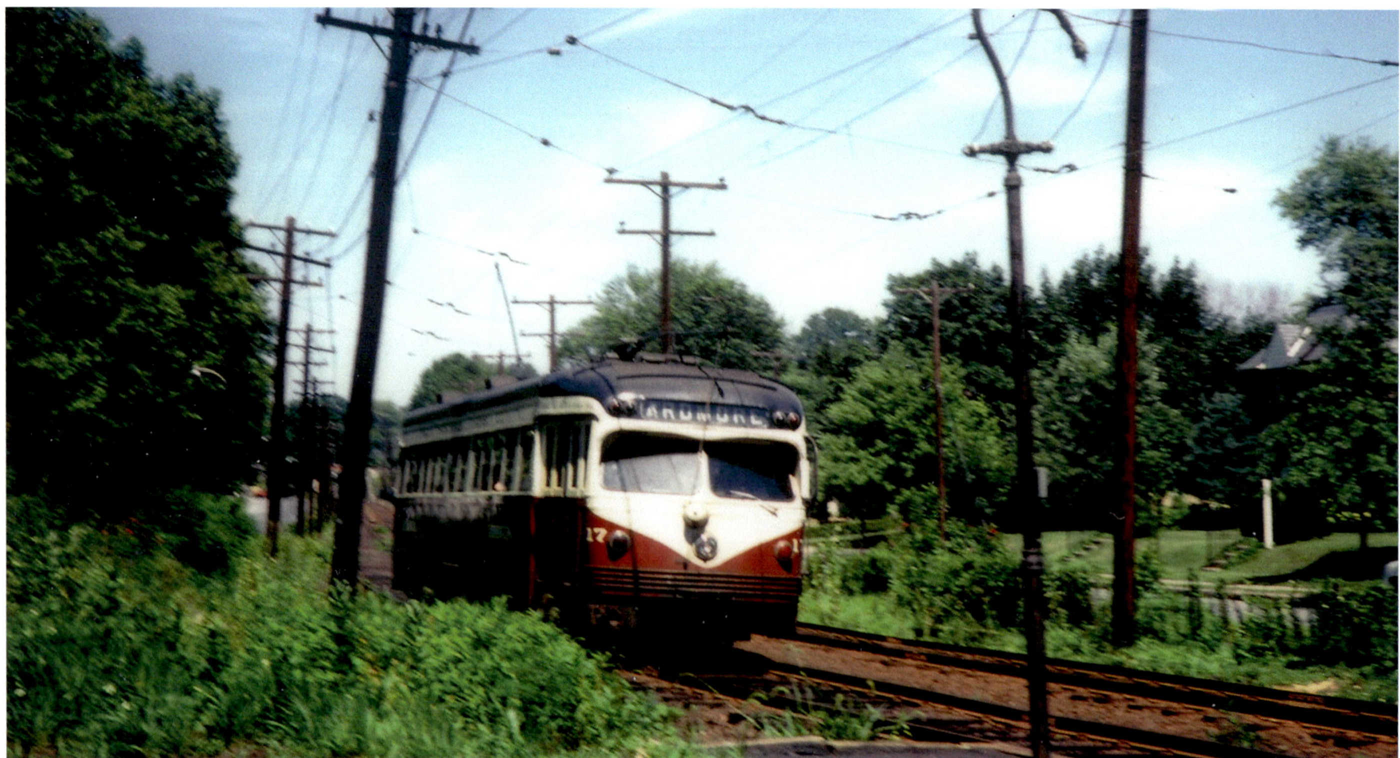

PSTC car No. 17 is on Hathaway Lane at Merwood Lane for a run on the Ardmore Line on July 22, 1966. The Ardmore Trolley Car Line was abandoned on December 29, 1966 with cars Nos. 20 and 13 operating in multiple unit leaving 69th Street Terminal at 11:30 p.m. and operated to County Line Road in Ardmore, as the rest of the line to Ardmore Terminal had been out of service since December 24th due to heavy snow and ice. Cars Nos. 86 and 83 on a rail excursion returned to 69th Street Terminal after 2 a.m. December 30, 1966, ending trolley car service on the Ardmore Line.

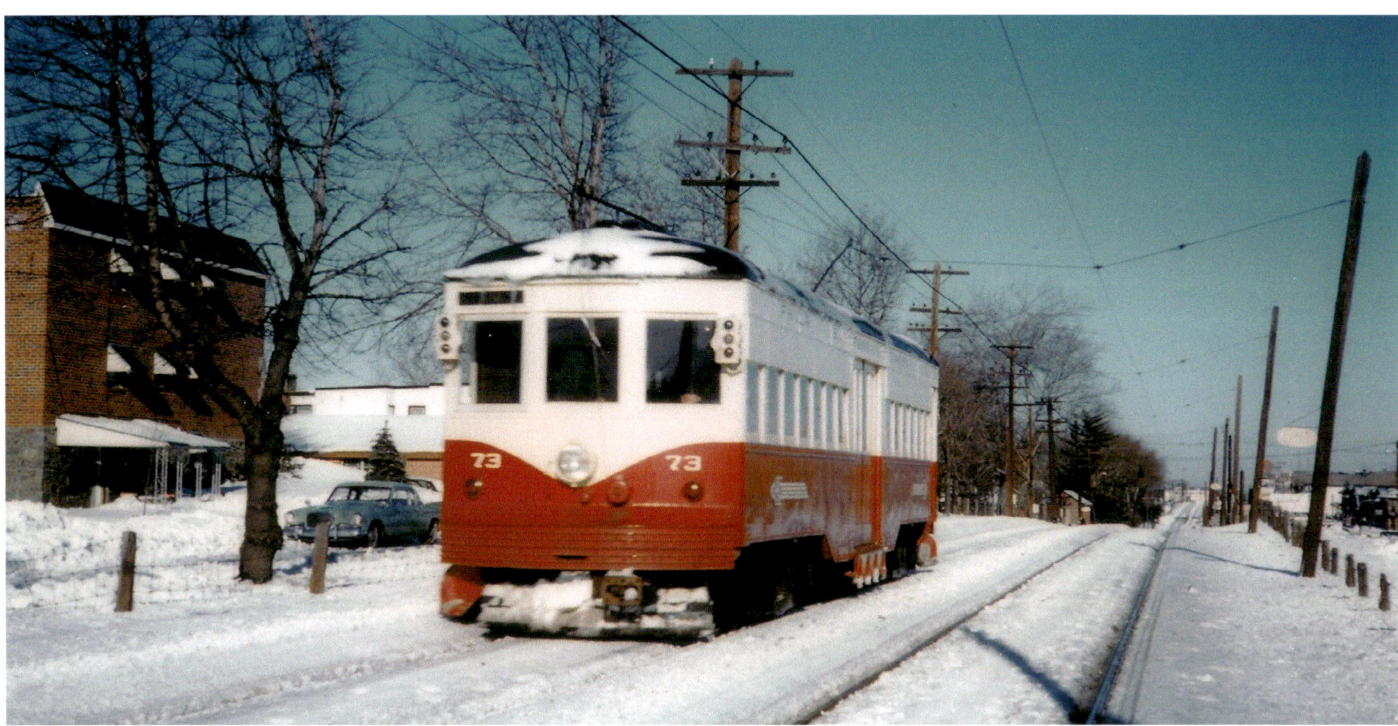

Following a winter snowstorm, PSTC center-door car No. 73 is westbound on Garrett Road between Hilltop Road and Beverly Hills station stop in the Beverly Hills neighborhood of Upper Darby Township on February 5, 1961. The Media and Sharon Hill Lines share trackage between 69th Street terminal and Drexel Hill Junction. Car No. 73 was refurbished in 1972 by SEPTA. It was used in Media to promote the "Media Town Fair." The regular trolley car would turn back at the edge of the business district and passengers would transfer to car No. 73 for the trip down State Street to downtown Media. The Pennsylvania Trolley Museum acquired car No. 73 in 1990.

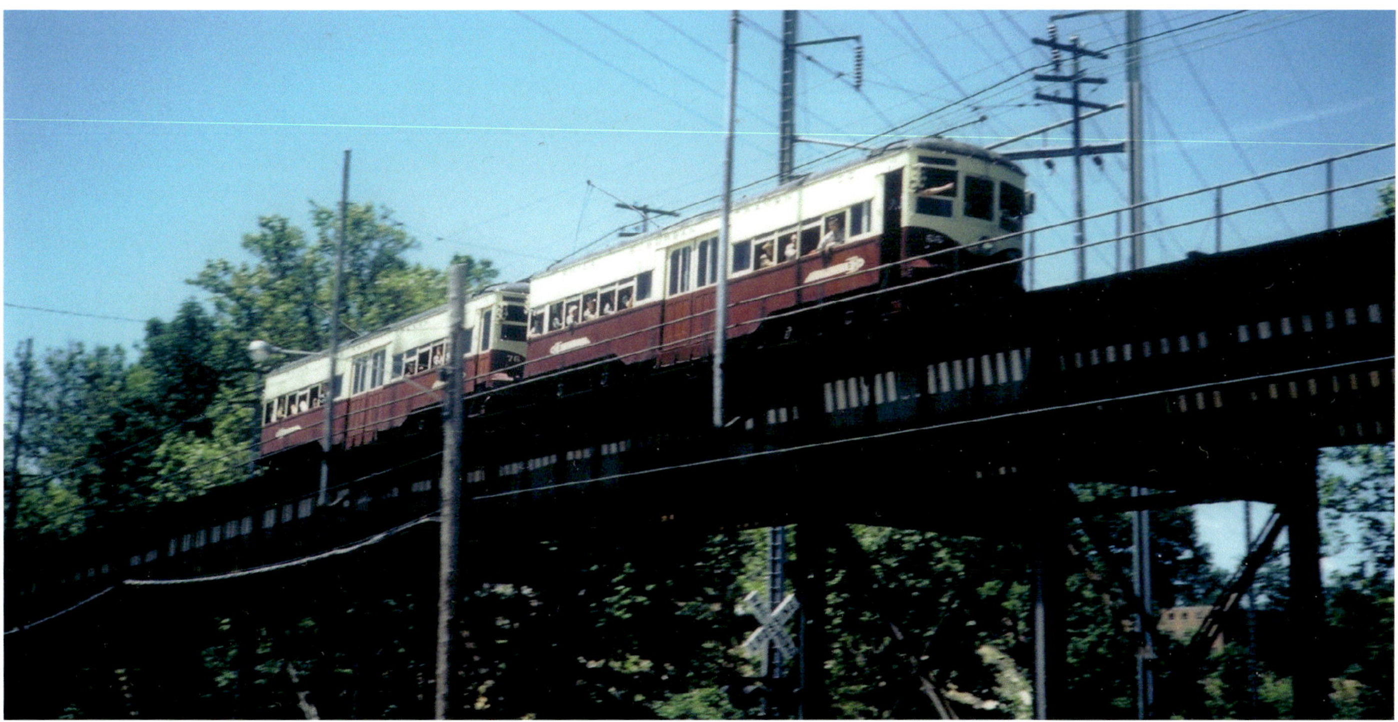

On June 4, 1961 PSTC center-door cars Nos. 76 and 66 are on the Garrett Road trestle over the Pennsylvania Railroad's Newtown Square branch (originally the Philadelphia & Delaware County Railroad in 1888 and leased to the Pennsylvania Railroad in 1894) and Naylor's Run in Upper Darby Township. Competition from the Philadelphia & West Chester Traction Company trolleys ended the Pennsylvania Railroad's passenger service on this line in 1908.

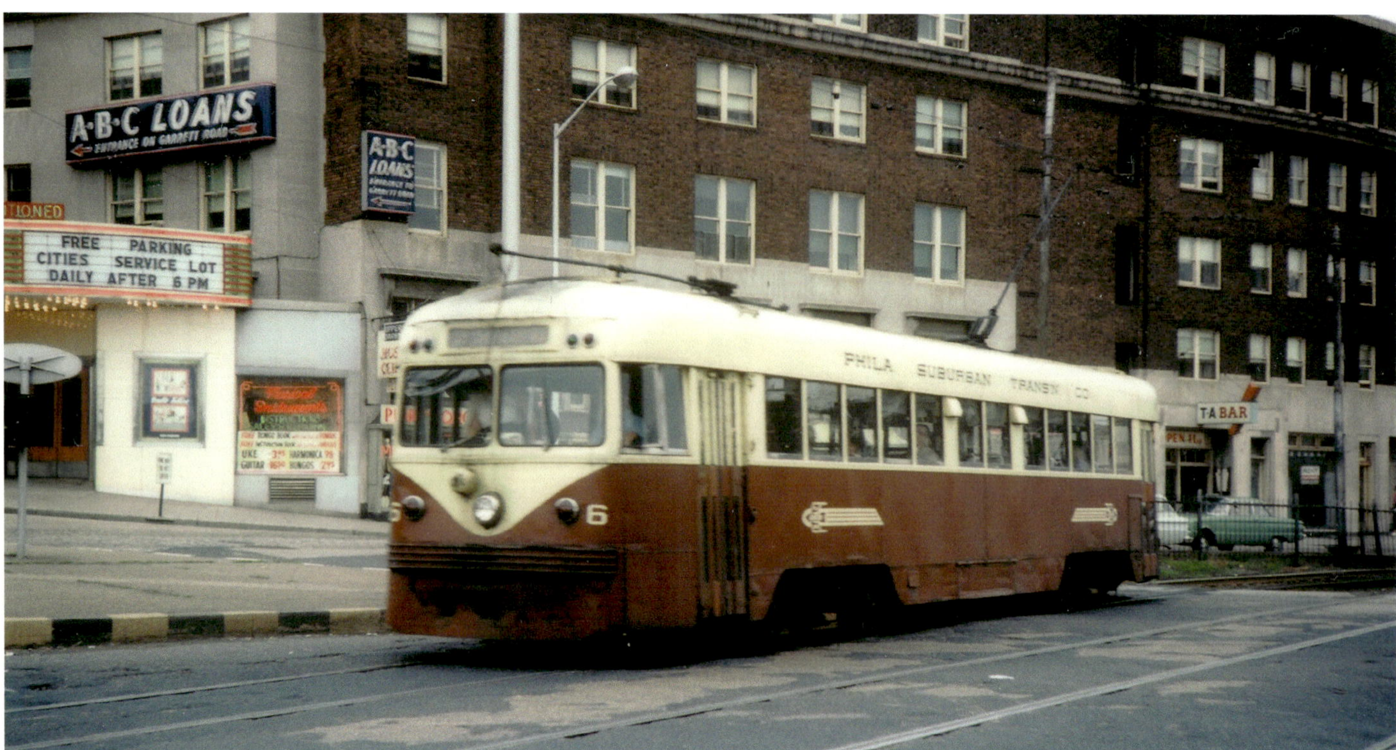

PSTC "Brilliner" car No. 6 is coming into the 69th Street Terminal on June 2, 1963. Just west of the Philadelphia city line, 69th Street Terminal (located in Upper Darby Township) is a major transfer point. It is the eastern terminus of the Media and Sharon Hill trolley car lines, the Norristown Line, and numerous bus routes where passengers can transfer to the western terminus of the Market Frankford Subway Elevated Line.

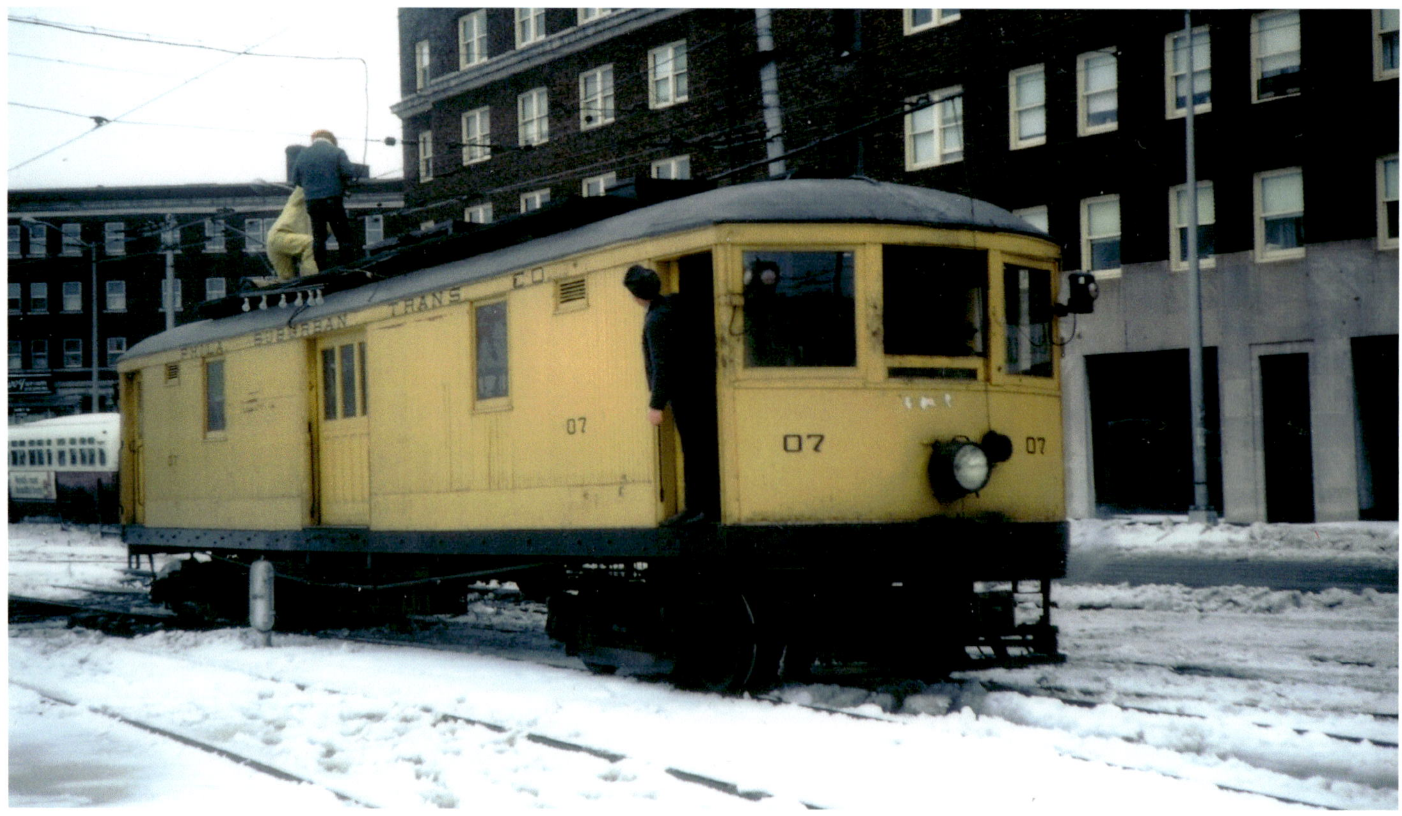

On December 26, 1969, PSTC work car No. 07 is working on the overhead wire near 69th Street. This was built by Jewett Car Company in 1911 as milk car No. 07 and was later converted to a line car to handle the work on the overhead wire.

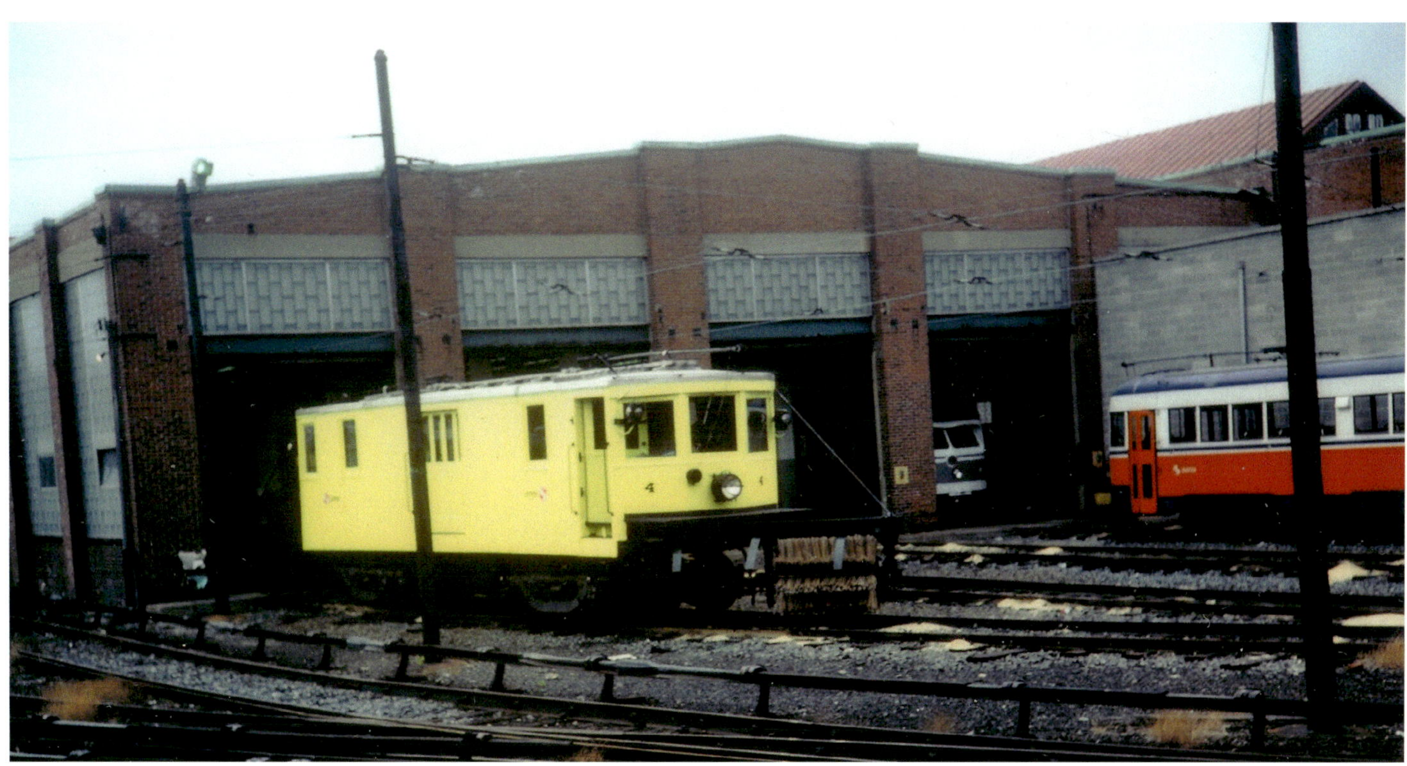

On November 24, 1979, SEPTA snow sweeper car No. 4 is at the 69th Street yard. Car No. 4 was built by the McGuire-Cummings Manufacturing Company for the Philadelphia and West Chester Traction Company in 1922 after a severe winter that hit the region in January 1922. It was acquired by the Pennsylvania Trolley Museum in 1988.

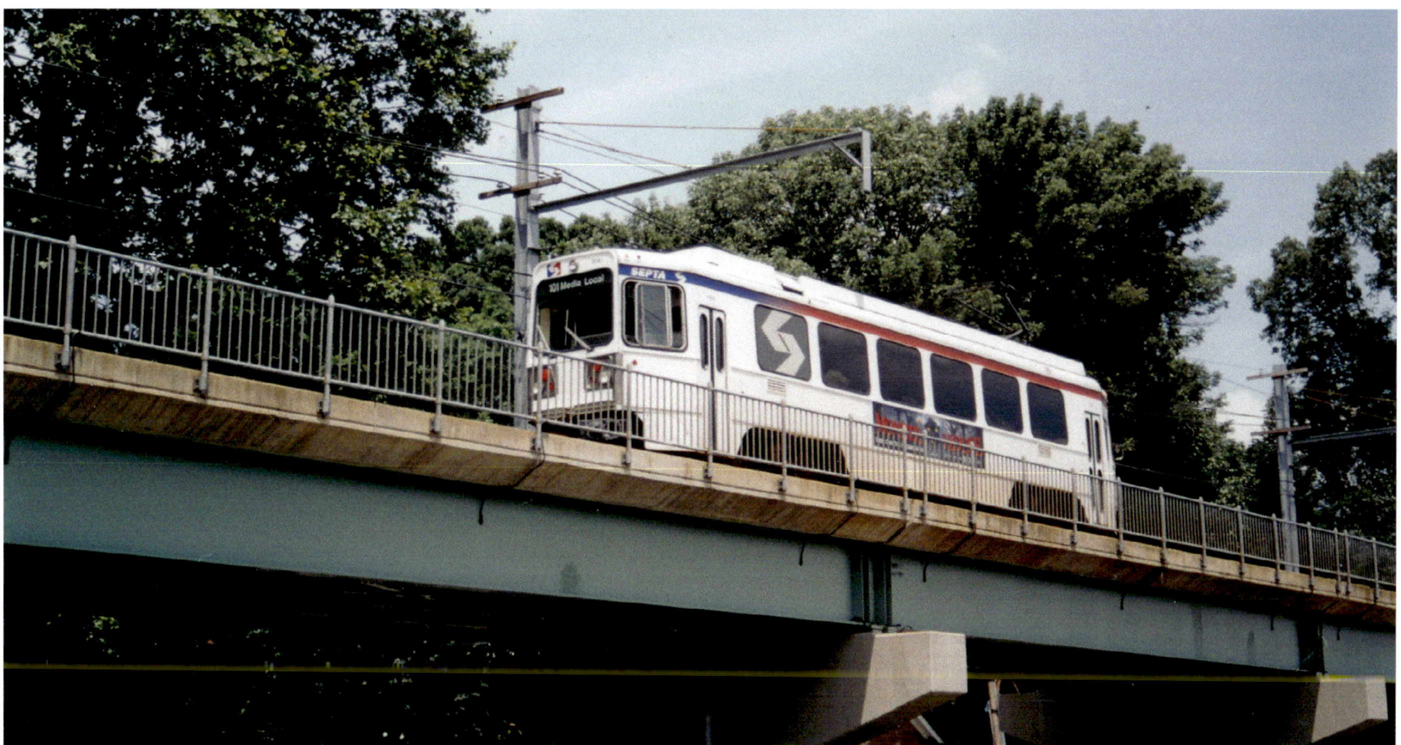

Kawasaki Heavy Industries car No. 104 (delivered on December 4, 1982 and placed in revenue service on December 22, 1982) is swiftly passing over the Garrett Road trestle, over the abandoned right of way of the Pennsylvania Railroad's Newtown branch, on July 7, 2006. This was one of twenty-nine doubled ended cars Nos. 100-128 that weighed 60,043 pounds, seated fifty passengers, had a maximum speed of sixty-two miles per hour on a level surface, had a pantograph for power collection, and cost $486,000 per car. Under Consolidated Rail Corporation, the trackage of the Newtown Square branch was removed by 1985.

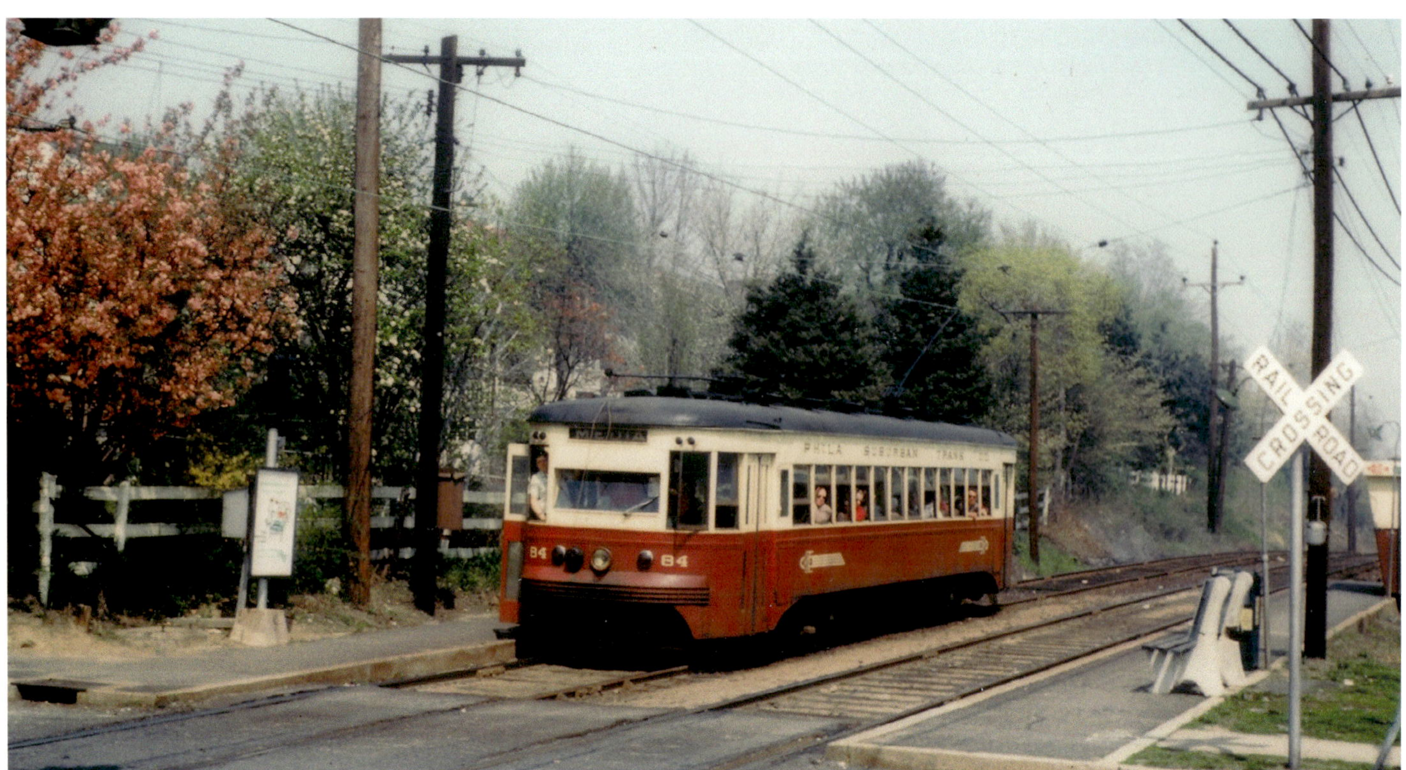

On April 24, 1960, 80 series Brill car No. 84 is at the Drexelbrook stop on the Media Line. Drexelbrook is a community within the Drexel Hill section of Upper Darby Township that encompasses 1,223 homes in ninety Federal style buildings (square or rectangular configuration featuring columns and molding that are narrow and simple) with recreational areas that include playgrounds and walking areas.

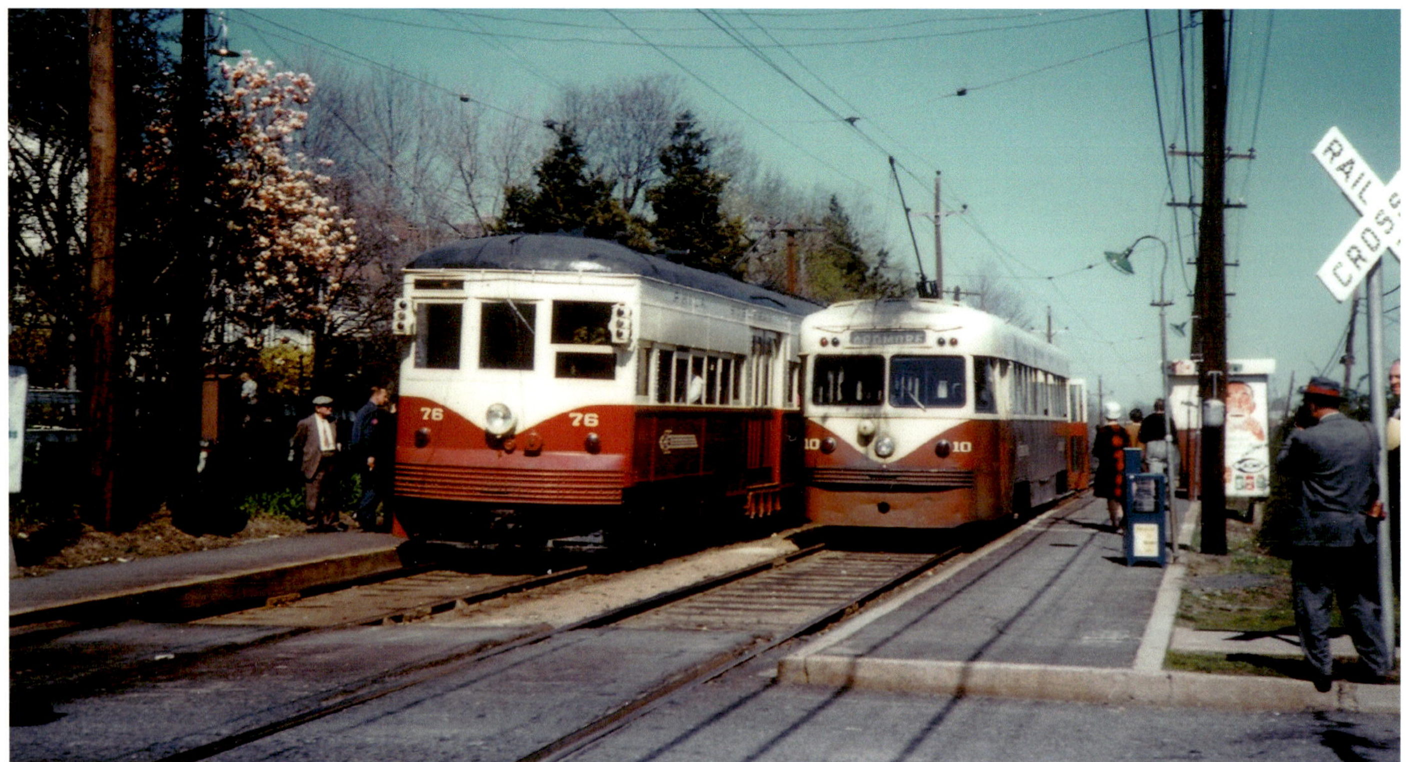

Center-door car No. 76 passes "Brilliner" car No. 10 at the Media Line's Drexelbrook stop on April 23, 1961. Car No. 10 was scrapped as a result of extensive damage due to a head on collision on the Media Line on July 23, 1963. With the arrival of more modern trolley cars, the remaining center-door cars were used in rush hour service, school trips, rail excursions, and winter operation to keep the lines clear of snow. Car #76 was retired in 1976, and was acquired by the Electric City Trolley Museum.

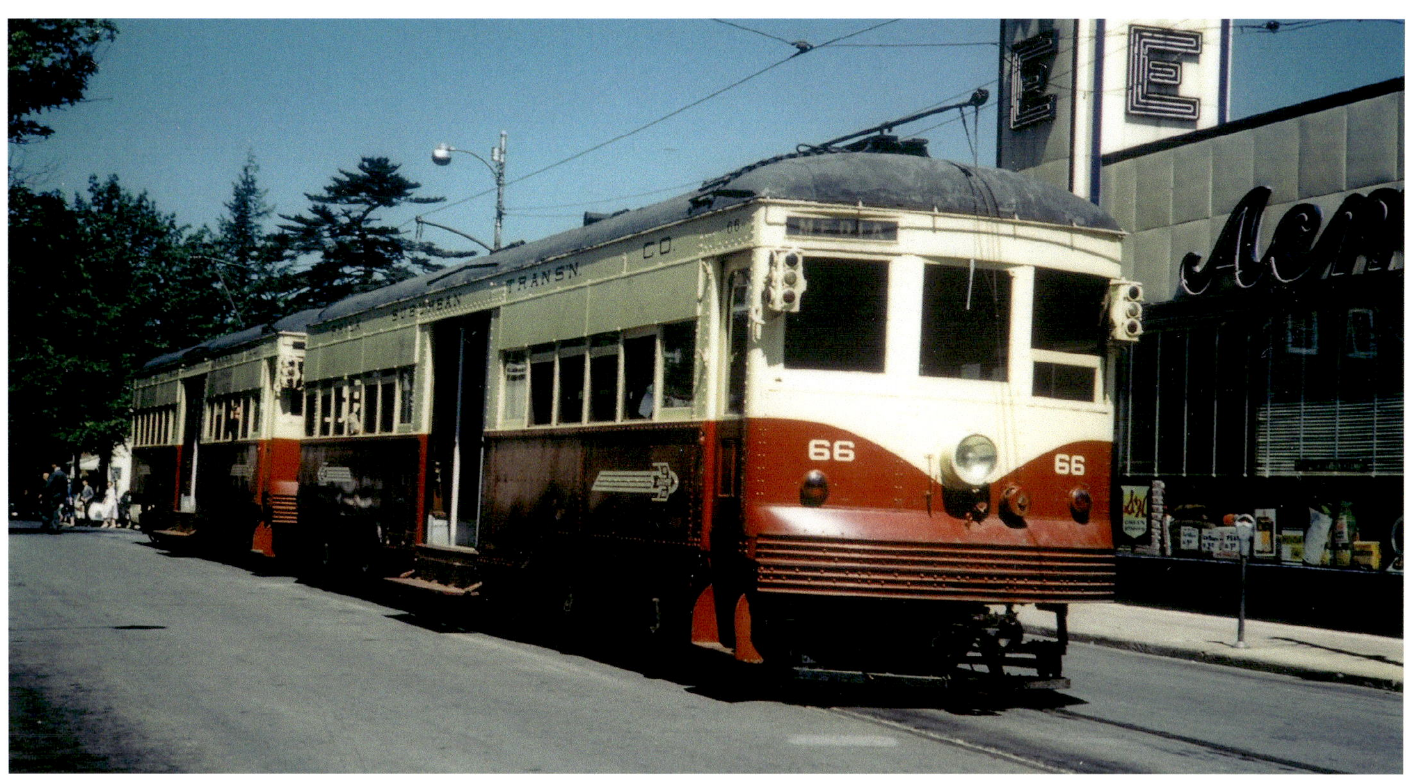

On June 4, 1961, PSTC center-door cars Nos. 76 and 66 are at the end of the Media Line on State Street just west of Orange Street in the borough of Media that is the county seat of Delaware County west of Philadelphia. ACME Markets Inc. no longer has the store shown on the right side of the picture; however, it has a store on Baltimore Avenue near the Providence Road trolley car station in Media.

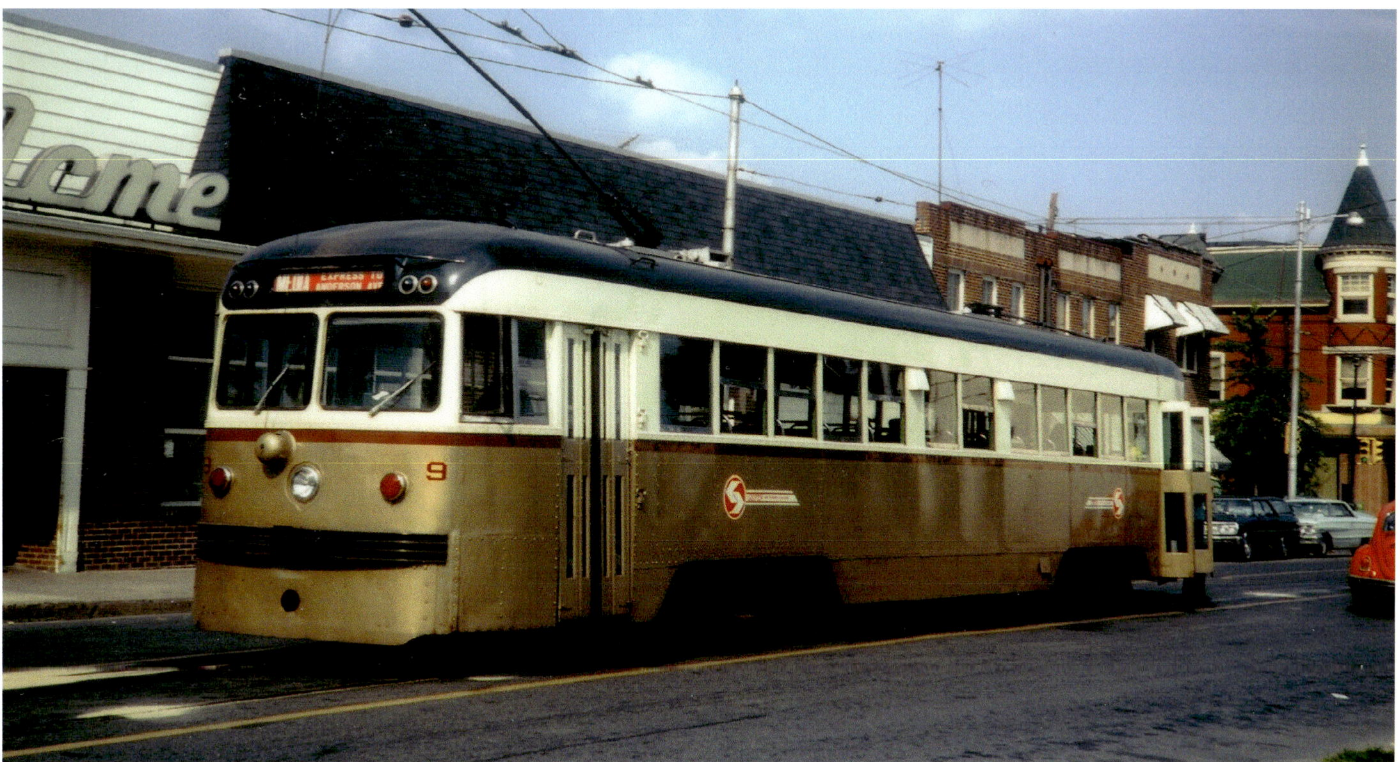

SEPTA "Brilliner" car No. 9 is on State Street just west of Orange Street on the Media Line in Media on July 16, 1970. Car #9 is one of the last ten cars built by the J. G. Brill Company of Philadelphia. It has been acquired by the Electric City Trolley Museum. The Brilliner was a last-ditch attempt by Brill to match the PCC car, a design developed by other industry suppliers and transit companies working together to improve the trolley car and win back riders.

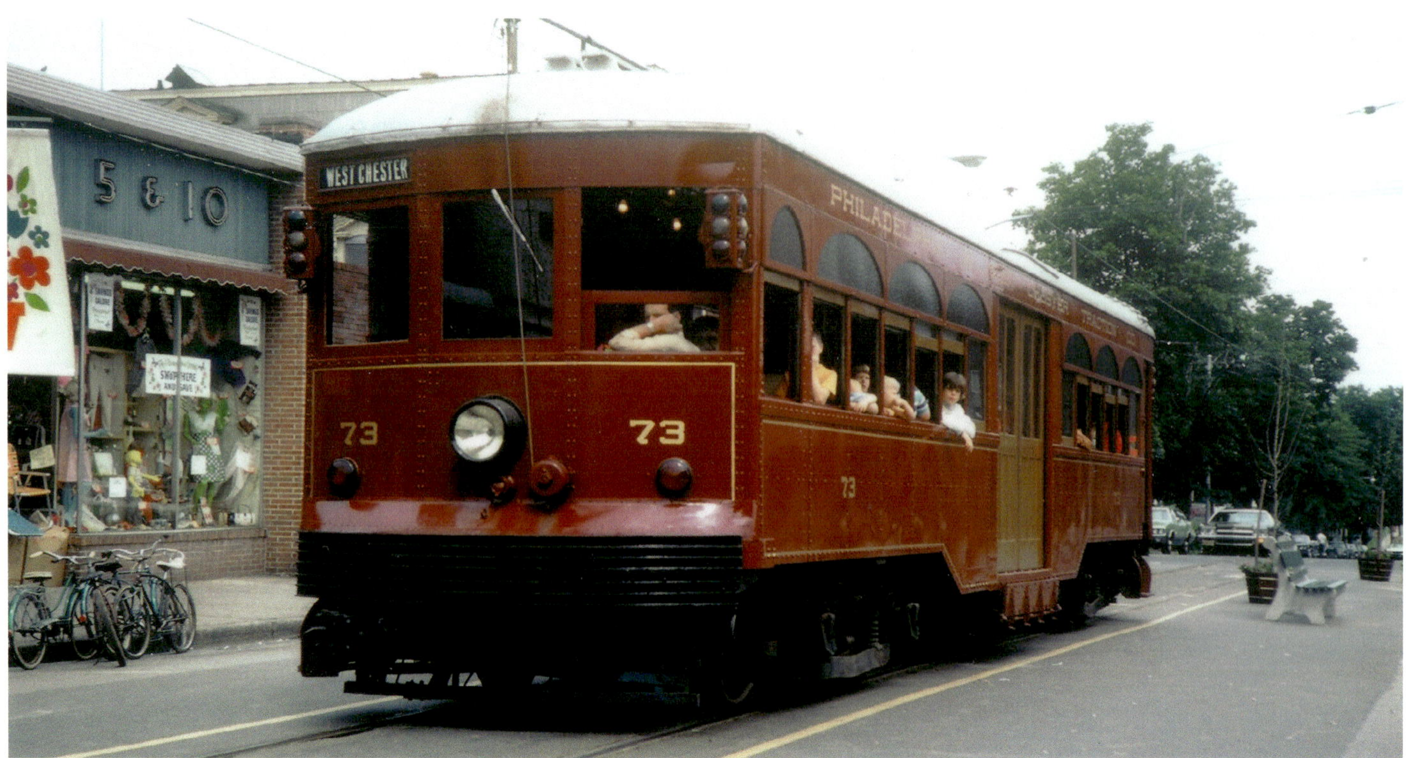

On June 24, 1972, SEPTA center-door car No. 73 is on State Street at Monroe Street in Media operating a special shuttle from that point to the end of the line just beyond Orange Street. This portion of State Street was closed to motor vehicles but open to pedestrians and the shuttle trolley for the "Media Town Fair" which featured sidewalk sales, civic displays and musical entertainment.

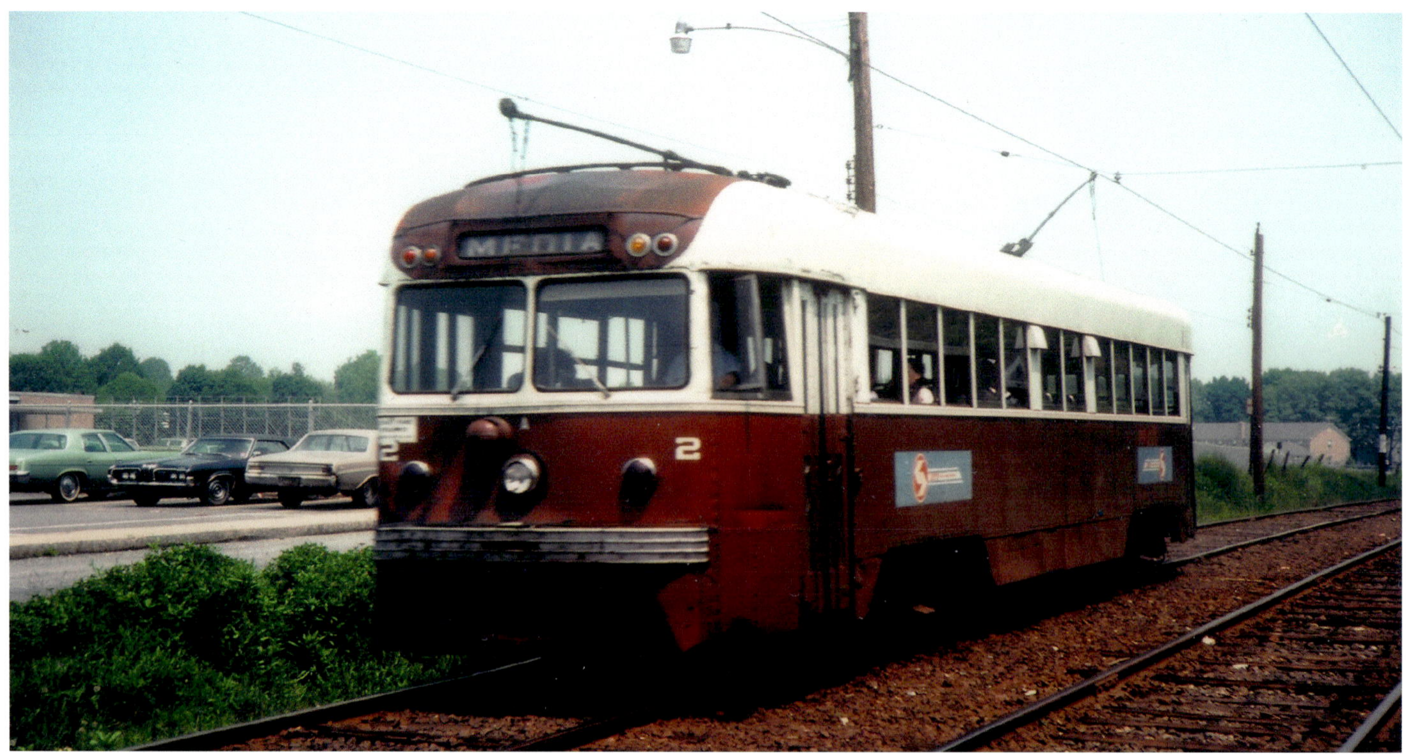

"Brilliner" car No. 2 is approaching Leamy Avenue in Springfield Township, Delaware County, on its westbound trip to Media on May 24, 1975. The Media Line features street running, private right of way, side of the road right of way, and traverses scenic wooded areas that make it a pleasure to ride.

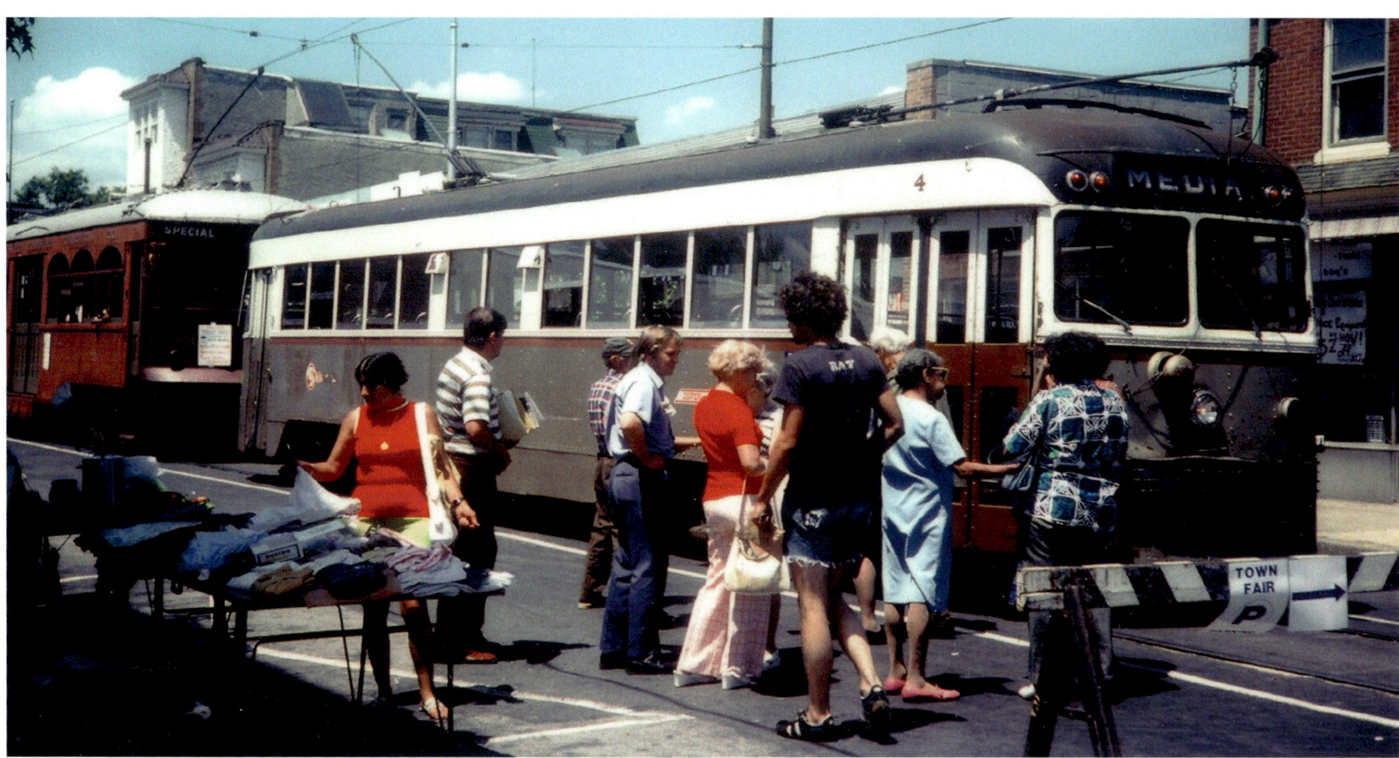

On July 28, 1977, passengers are waiting to board "Brilliner" car No. 4 on State Street at Monroe Street during the Media Town Fair. With State Street in Media closed to motor vehicles from Monroe Street to Orange Street, passengers used center-door car No. 73 shown on the left to reach the end of the line just beyond Orange Street. For the July 28 to July 30, 1977 "Media Town Fair," rides on car No. 73 cost 10 cents, and senior citizens rode free.

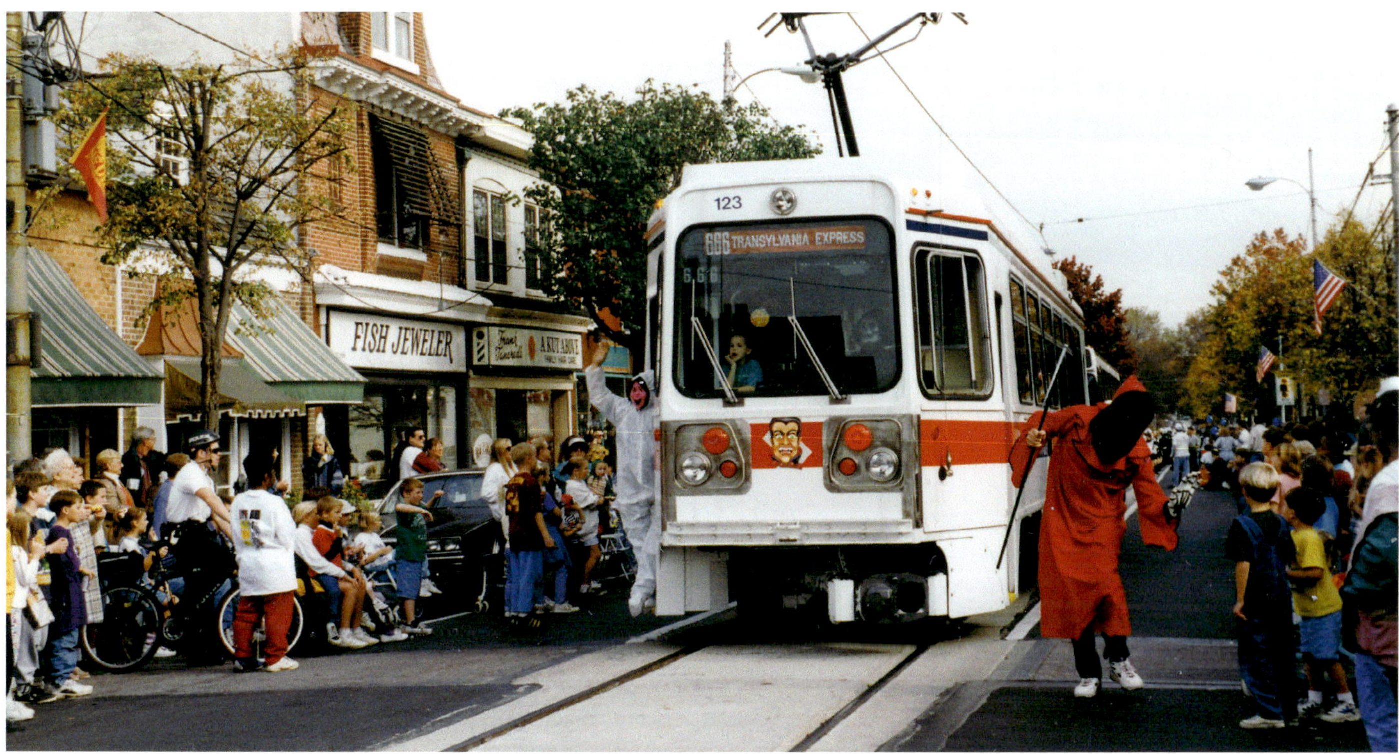

A crowd greets Kawasaki Heavy Industries car No. 123 (delivered on August 27, 1982 and placed in revenue service on September 23, 1982) decorated for Halloween with an unusual destination sign on October 26, 1996 on State Street at Edgemont Streets in Media. American suppliers for this double end car included Penn Machine for resilient wheels; Vapor Company for doors and door controls; Westinghouse Air Brake for compressor, air brake controls, disc brakes and track brakes; and Westinghouse Electric for motors, gear boxes, and controls.

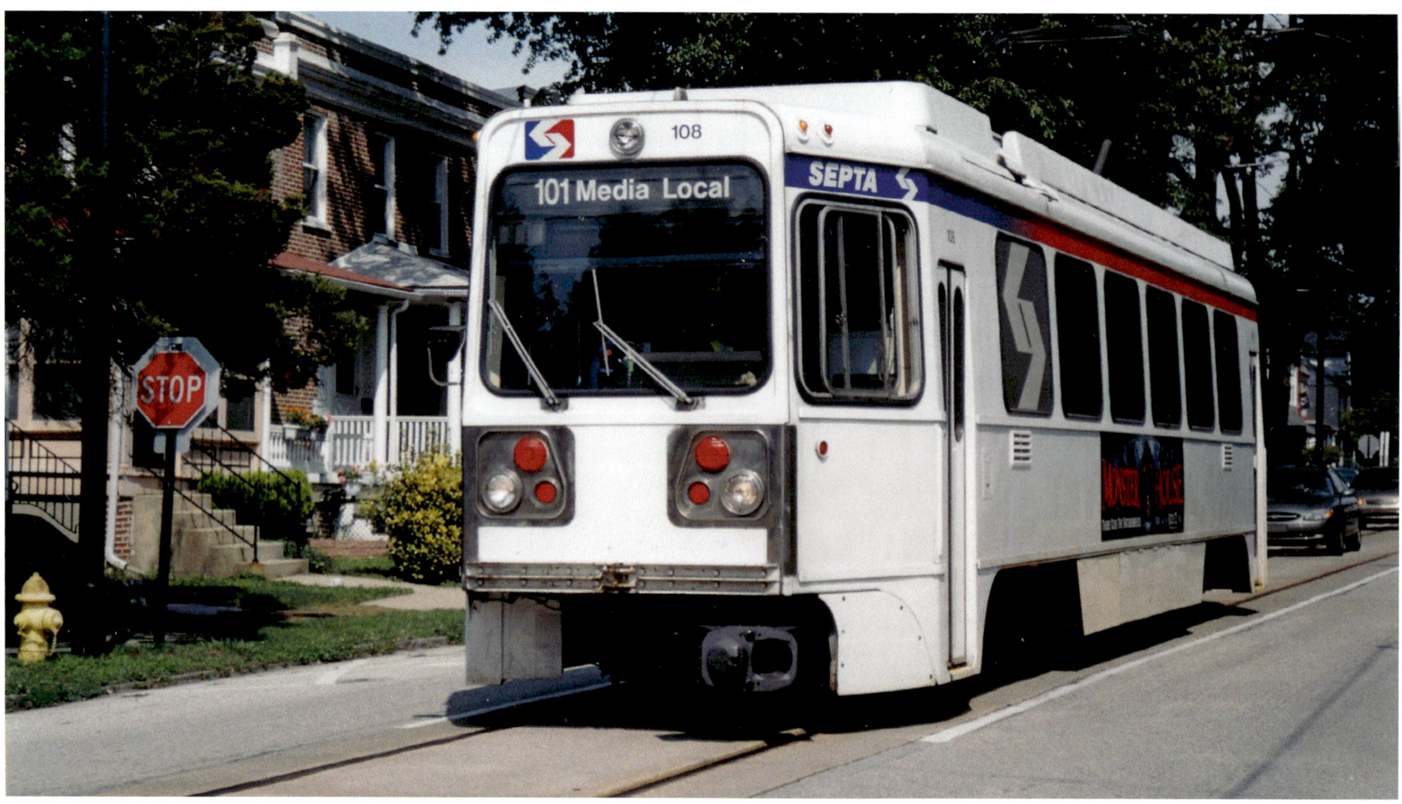

On a beautiful July 7, 2006, SEPTA Kawasaki Heavy Industries car No. 108 (delivered on August 27, 1981 and placed in revenue service on November 2, 1981) is on State Street at Radnor Street in Media.

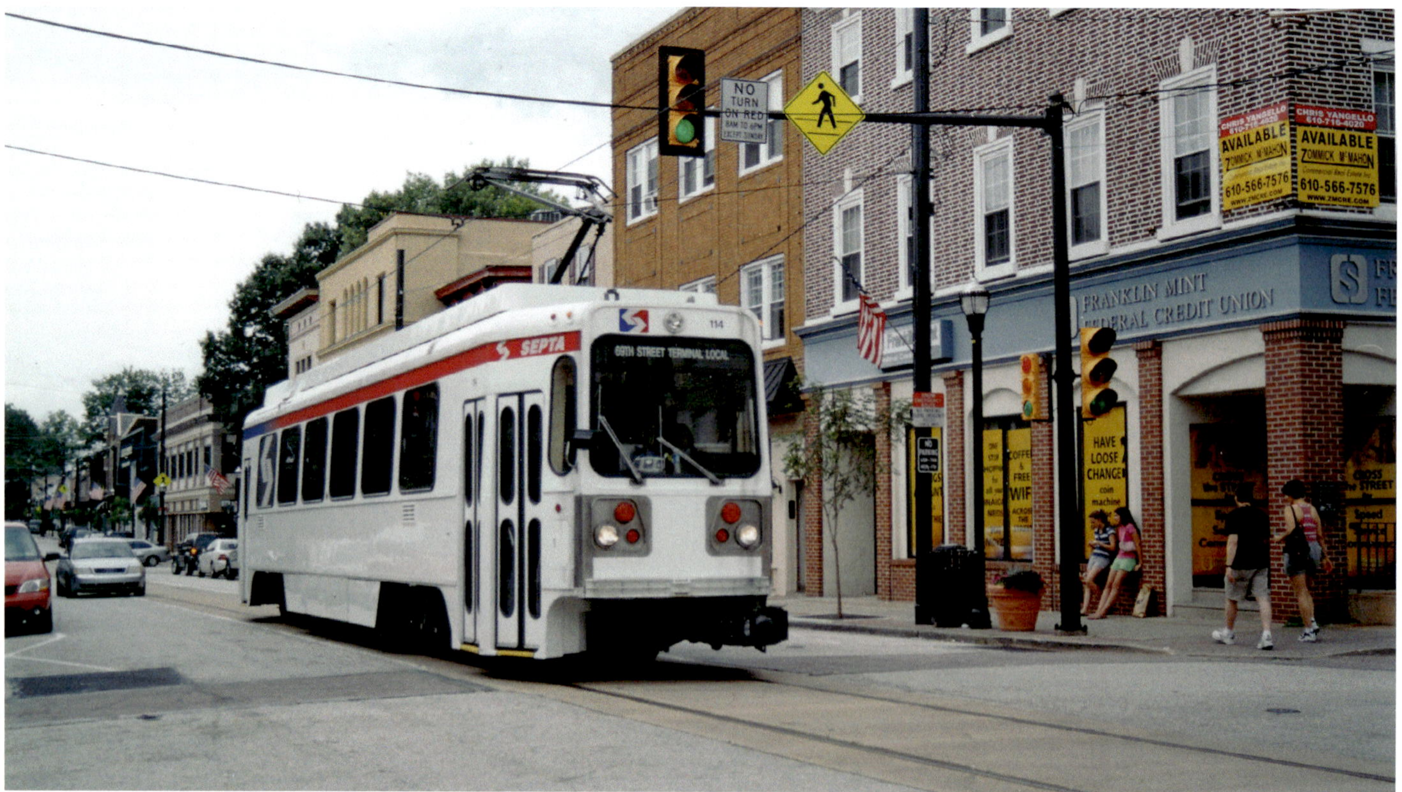

Passing through downtown Media on July 8, 2006, SEPTA Kawasaki Heavy Industries car No. 114 (delivered on August 4, 1982 and placed in revenue service on August 13, 1982) is on State Street at Olive Street making an eastbound trip to 69th Street Terminal.

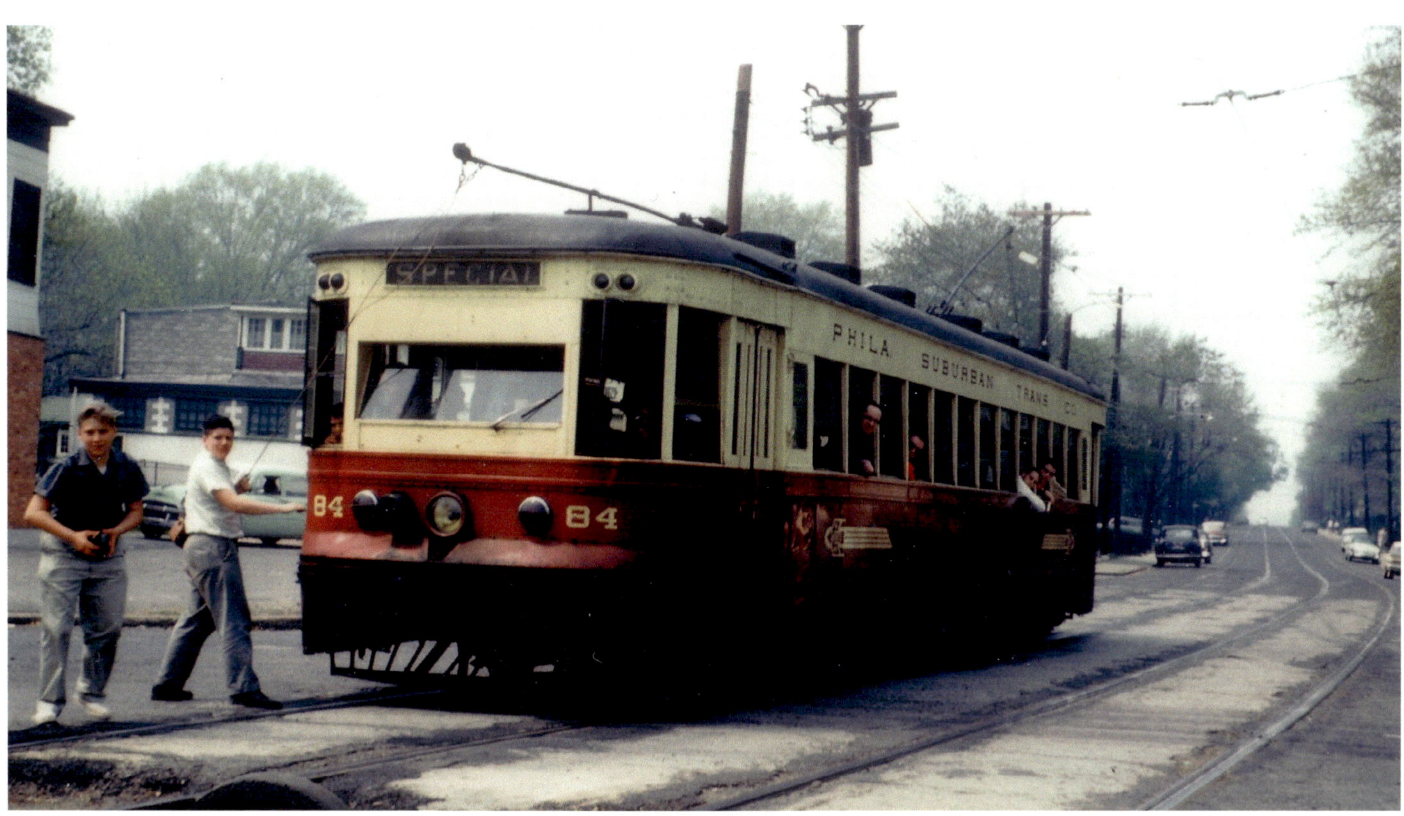

On April 24, 1960, PSTC 80 series Brill car No. 84 is on Woodlawn Avenue at North Street for a photo stop on a rail excursion trip to Sharon Hill.

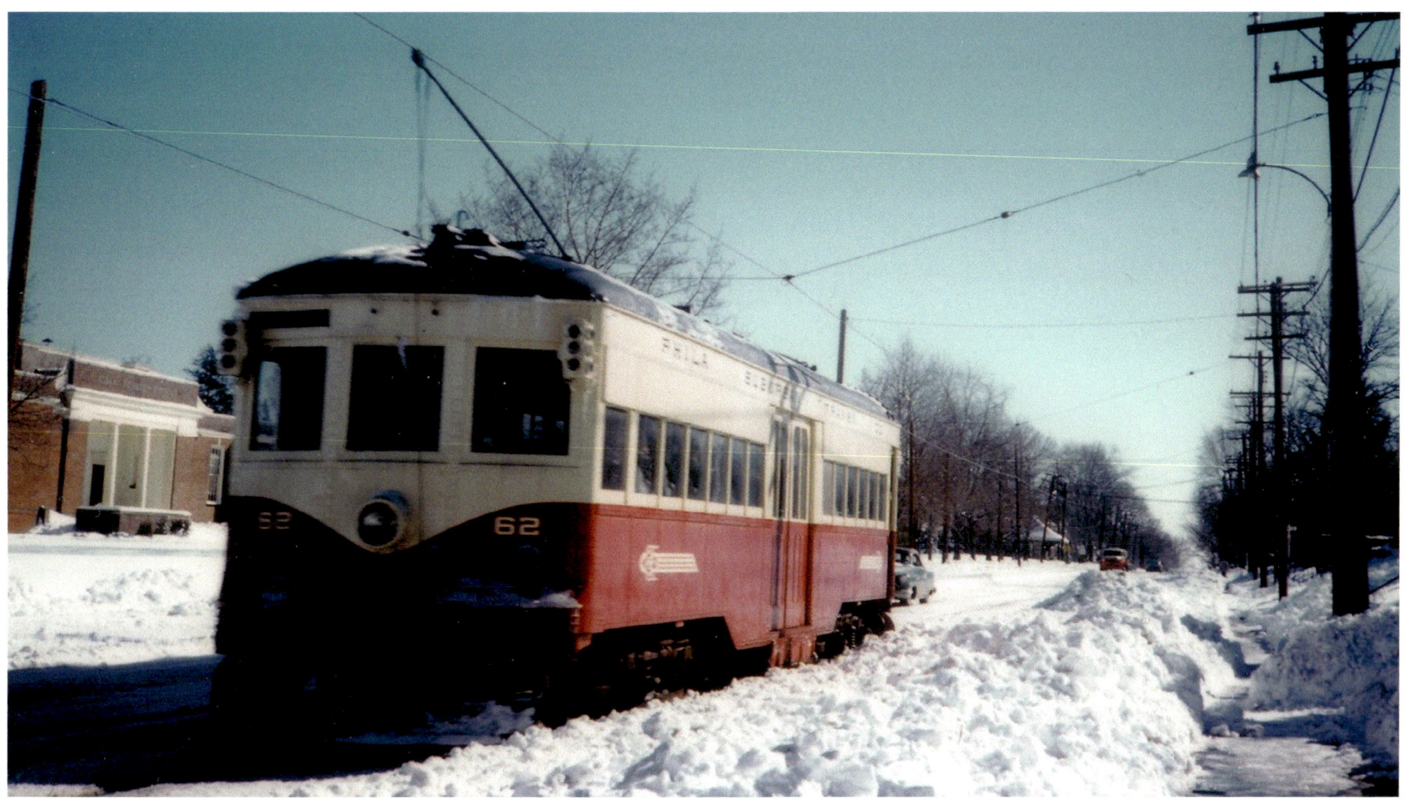

To get through the heavy winter snow, PSTC center-door car No. 62 is southbound on Woodlawn Avenue at Shisler Avenue in the borough of Aldan on February 5, 1961 for a trip to Sharon Hill. The heavy vintage center-door cars were pressed into service that Sunday to literally push through the snow.

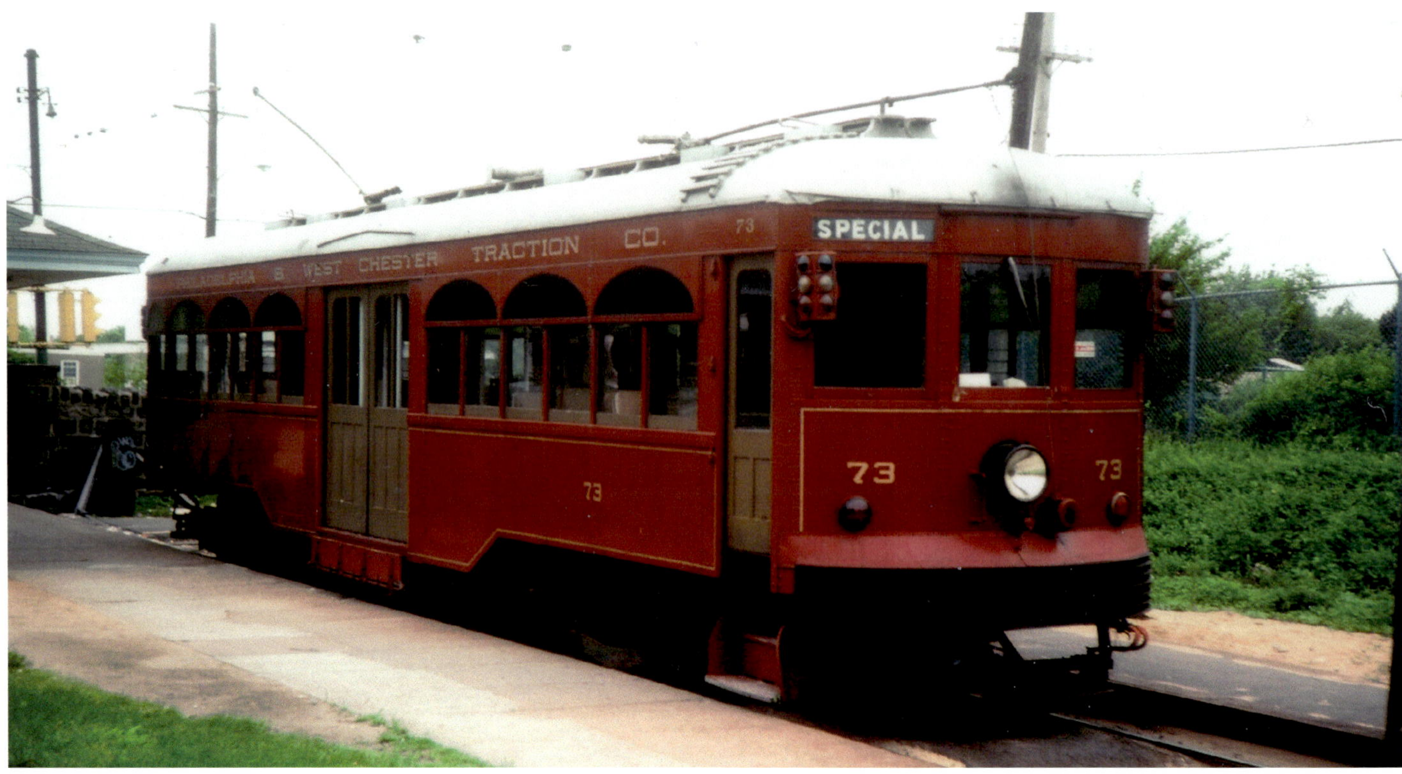

On May 25, 1975, SEPTA center-door car No. 73 is at the Chester Pike terminus of the Sharon Hill Line. In addition to the trolley line, the borough of Sharon Hill is connected to Philadelphia by the SEPTA Wilmington/Newark Regional Rail Line plus SEPTA provides local bus service.

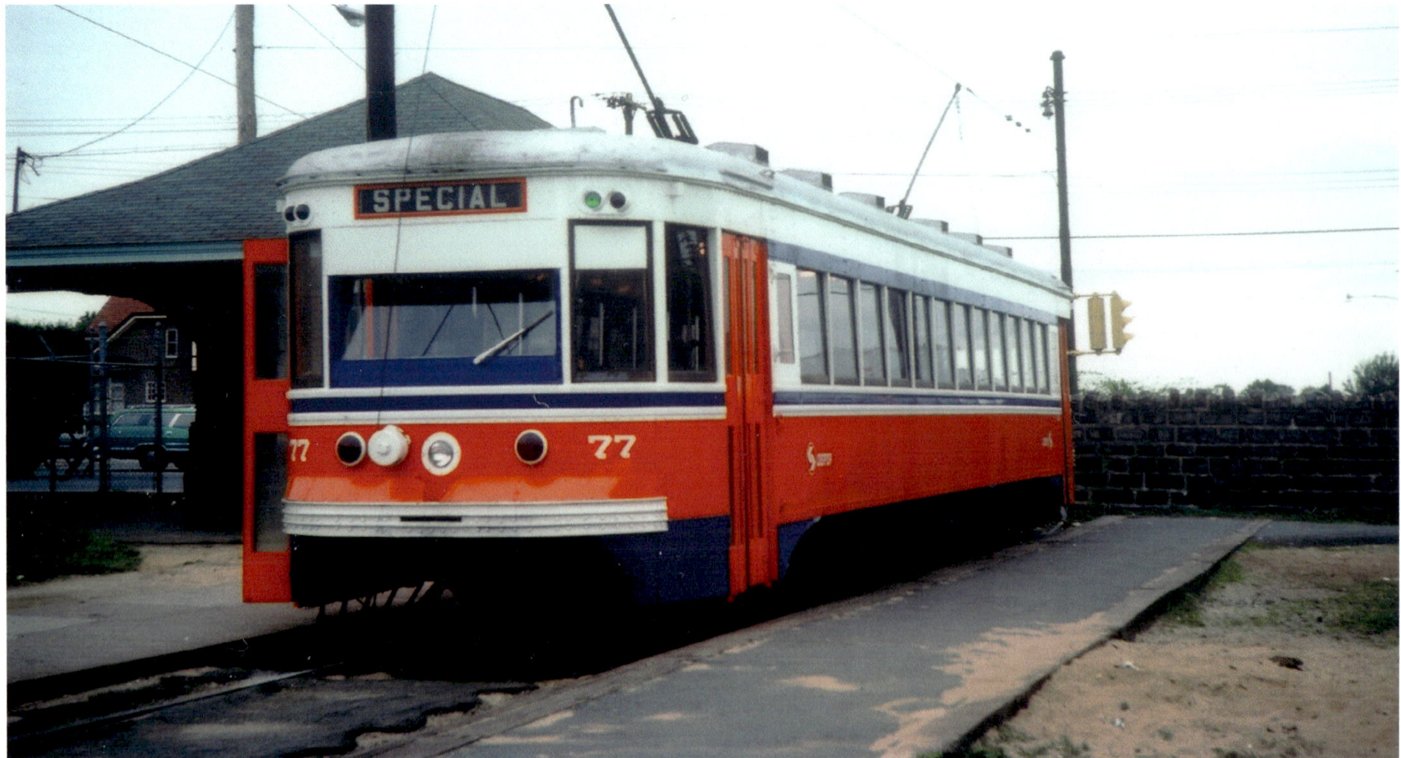

The classy stone station at Sharon Hill is the terminal for the Sharon Hill Line where 80 series Brill car No. 77 is on a May 25, 1975 rail excursion. Beyond the stone wall is Chester Pike.

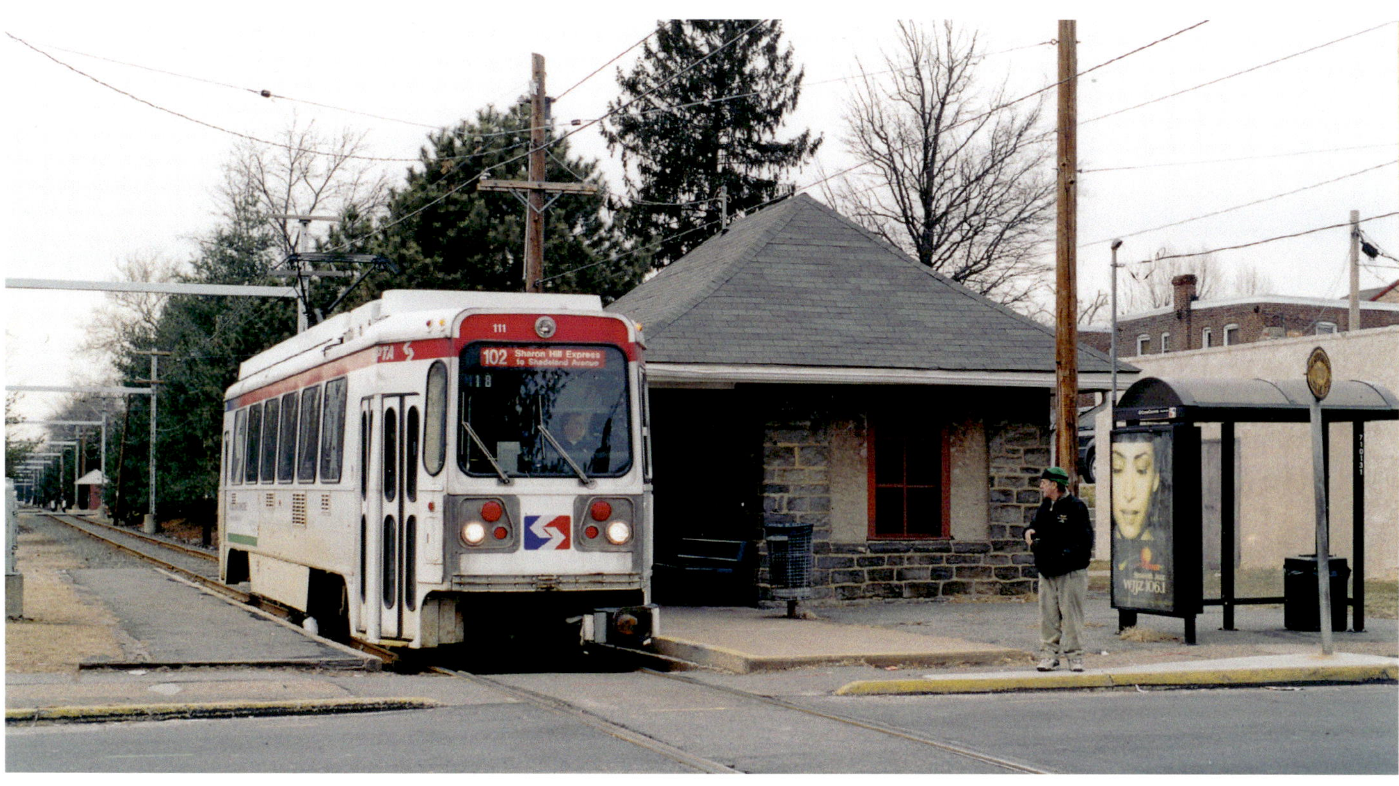

On February 26, 2004, SEPTA Route 102 Kawasaki Heavy Industries car No. 111 (delivered on December 30, 1981 and placed in revenue service on January 21, 1982) is ready to cross MacDade Boulevard in the borough of Collingdale heading south to Sharon Hill. The bus shelter is for SEPTA Bus Route 113 which operates east to Darby and the 69th Street Terminal and west to Chester and the Tri State Mall in the state of Delaware.

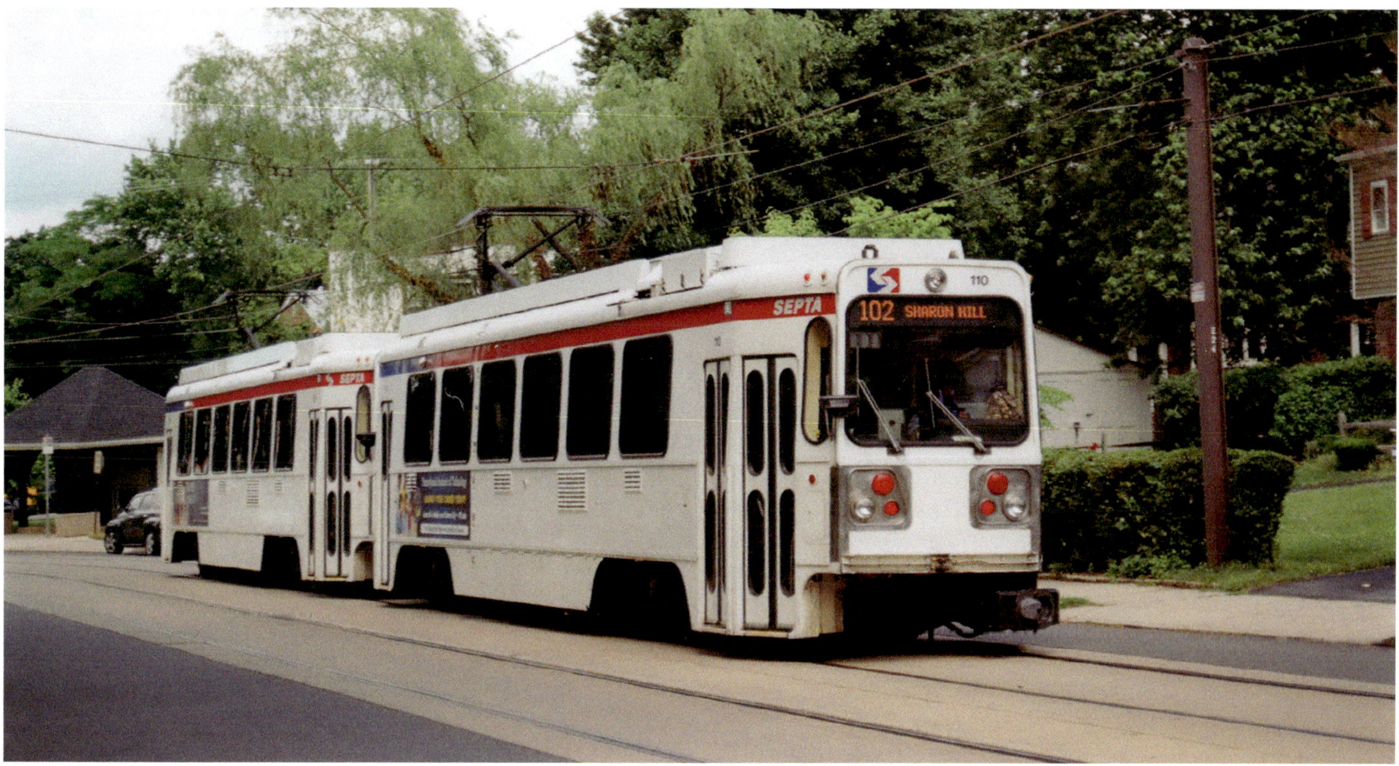

A two car train of SEPTA Route 102 Kawasaki Heavy Industries cars Nos. 119 (delivered on August 20, 1982 and placed in regular service on March 27, 1982) and 110 (delivered on August 25, 1981 and placed in regular service on November 12, 1981) are northbound on Woodlawn Avenue at Priscilla Lane near the Clifton Aldan station of the Media/Elwin Regional Rail Line on June 5, 2014.

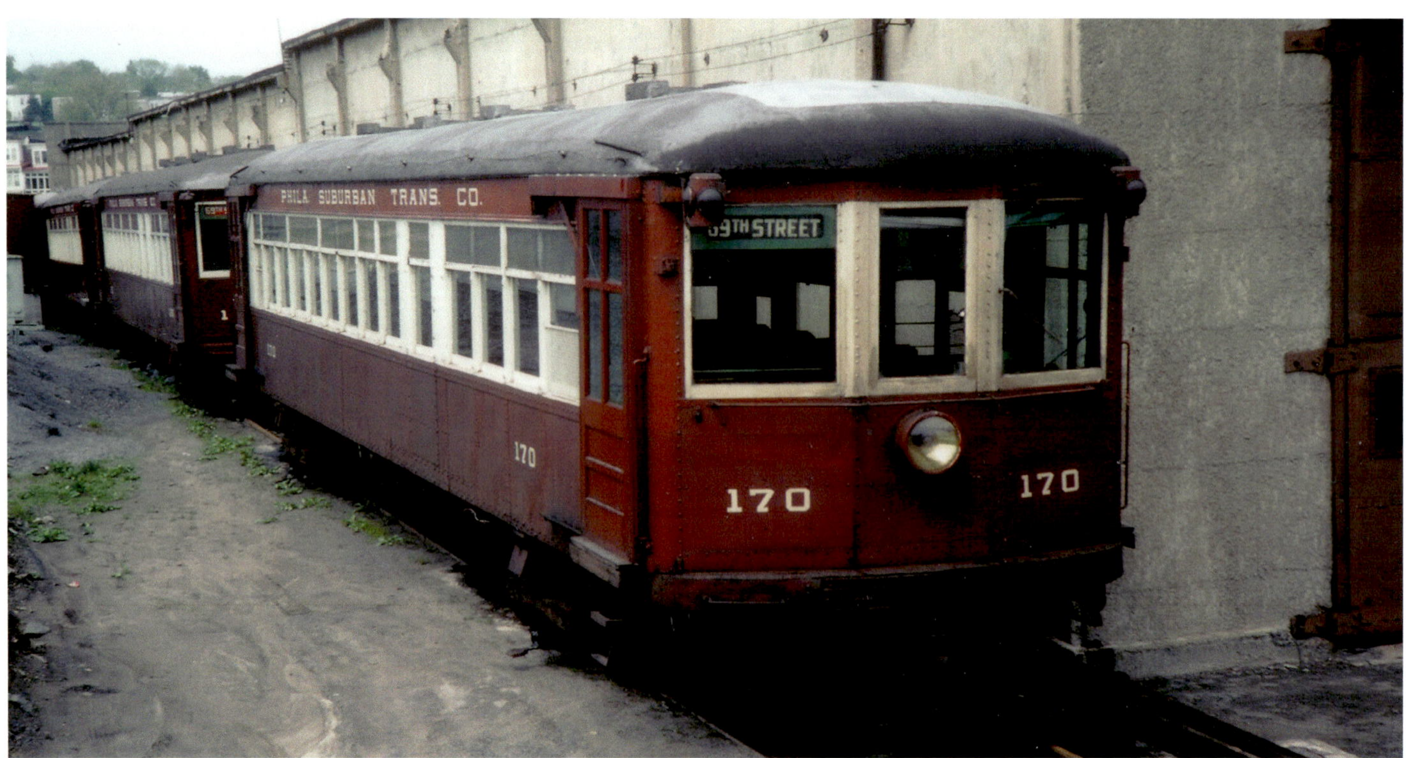

PSTC Strafford car No. 170 is at the 72nd Street shops of the Norristown Line (formerly Philadelphia & Western Railway that became part of PSTC on December 31, 1953) on April 27, 1968. This was one of four cars Nos. 66-70 built by J. G. Brill Company in 1929 powered by four Westinghouse type 535B1 motors. Cars Nos. 66-68 were rebuilt and renumbered 166-168 in 1931. Car No. 69 became car No. 160 in 1935, and car No. 70 became car No. 170 which was scrapped after a collision with *Liberty Liner Independence Hall* on January 17, 1969.

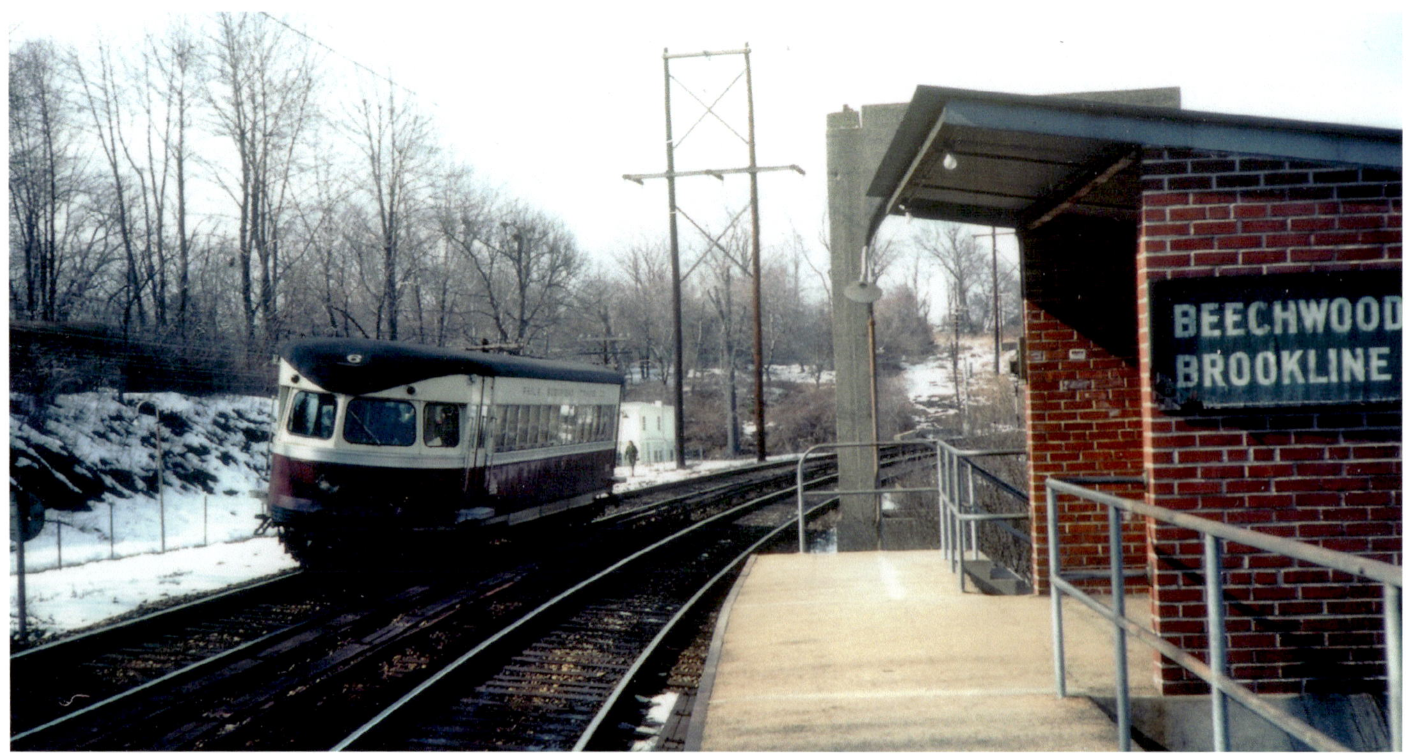

On February 27, 1969, PSTC "Bullet" car No. 206 is near the Beechwood Brookline station on the former Philadelphia & Western Railway Norristown Line. This was one of ten cars numbered 200-209 built by J. G. Brill Company in 1931 and powered by four General Electric type 706A motors. The station is located at Edgewood and Strathmore Roads on south side of the tracks and Beechwood & Karakung Drives on north side of the tracks in Haverford Township.

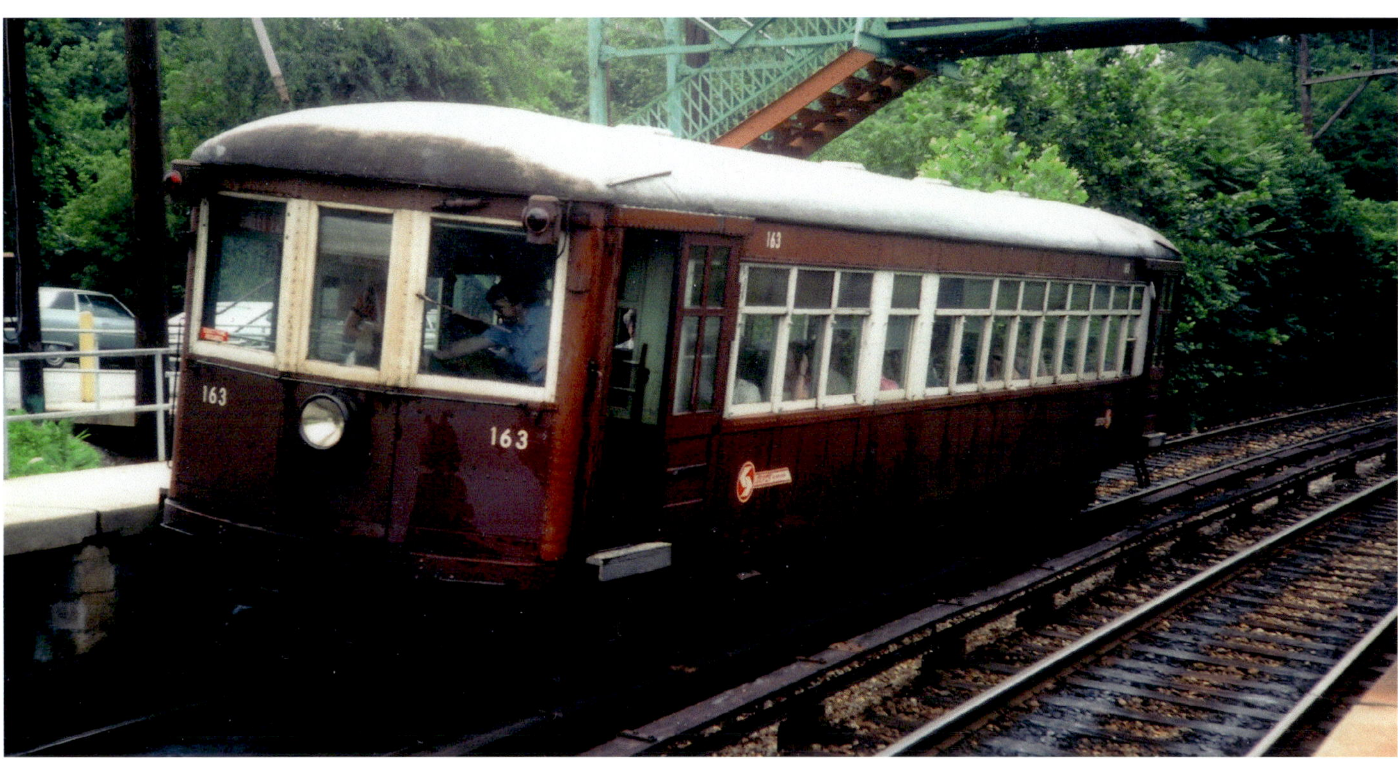

SEPTA "Strafford" car No. 163 is at Radnor station on July 23, 1976. This was one of five cars Nos. 61-65 built by J. G. Brill Company powered by four Westinghouse type 535B1 motors in 1927. Cars Nos. 61-64 were rebuilt to Nos. 161-164 in 1931. Car No. 65 was rebuilt to No. 169 in 1935 and was destroyed in a fire in 1960. Radnor Station is located off King of Prussia Road in Radnor Township near the SEPTA Paoli/Thorndale Regional Rail Line.

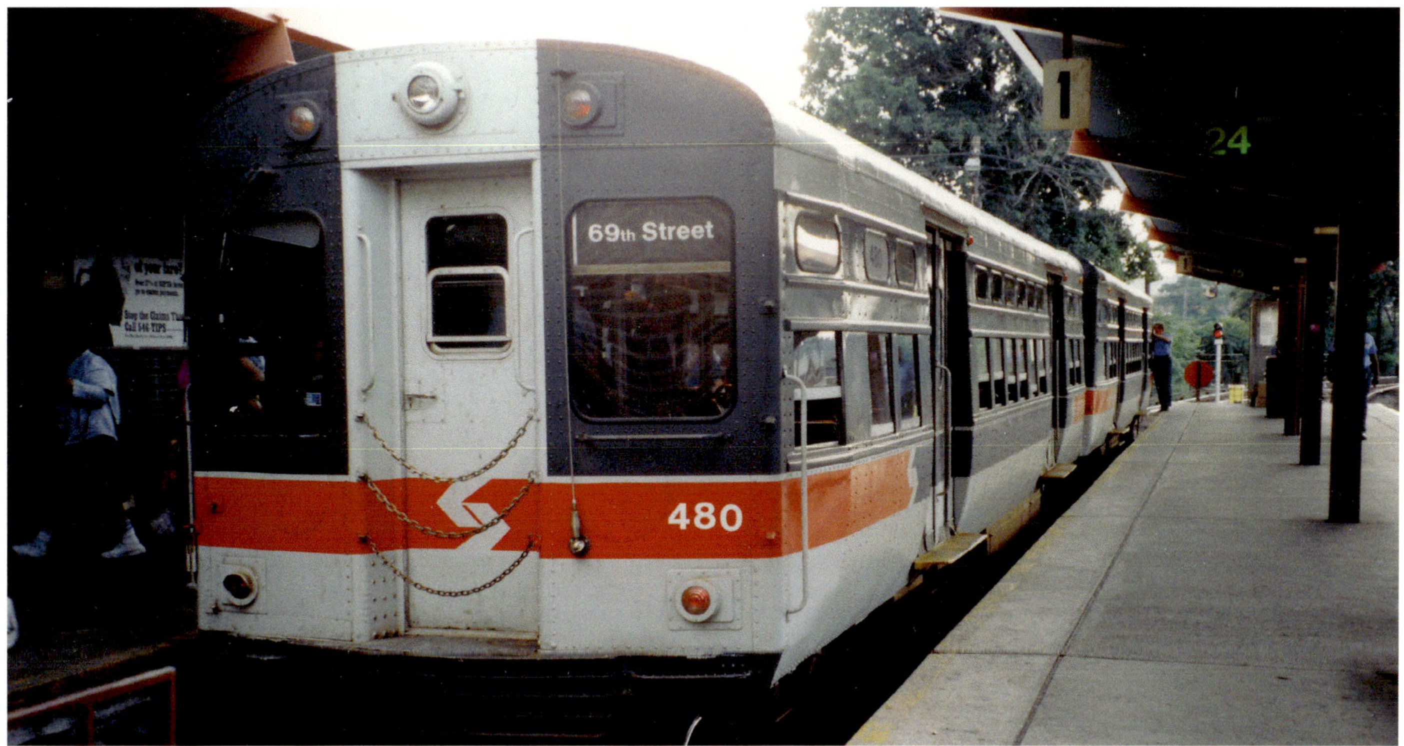

On August 31, 1980, SEPTA car No. 480 acquired from the Chicago Transit Authority is at the 69th Street Terminal on the Norristown Line awaiting departure time. When the Bullet and Strafford cars were no longer able to operate, former CTA 6000 series cars were brought in from Chicago along with five Market Frankford Line type M3 cars (with a sixth one for spare parts) to keep the line in operation.

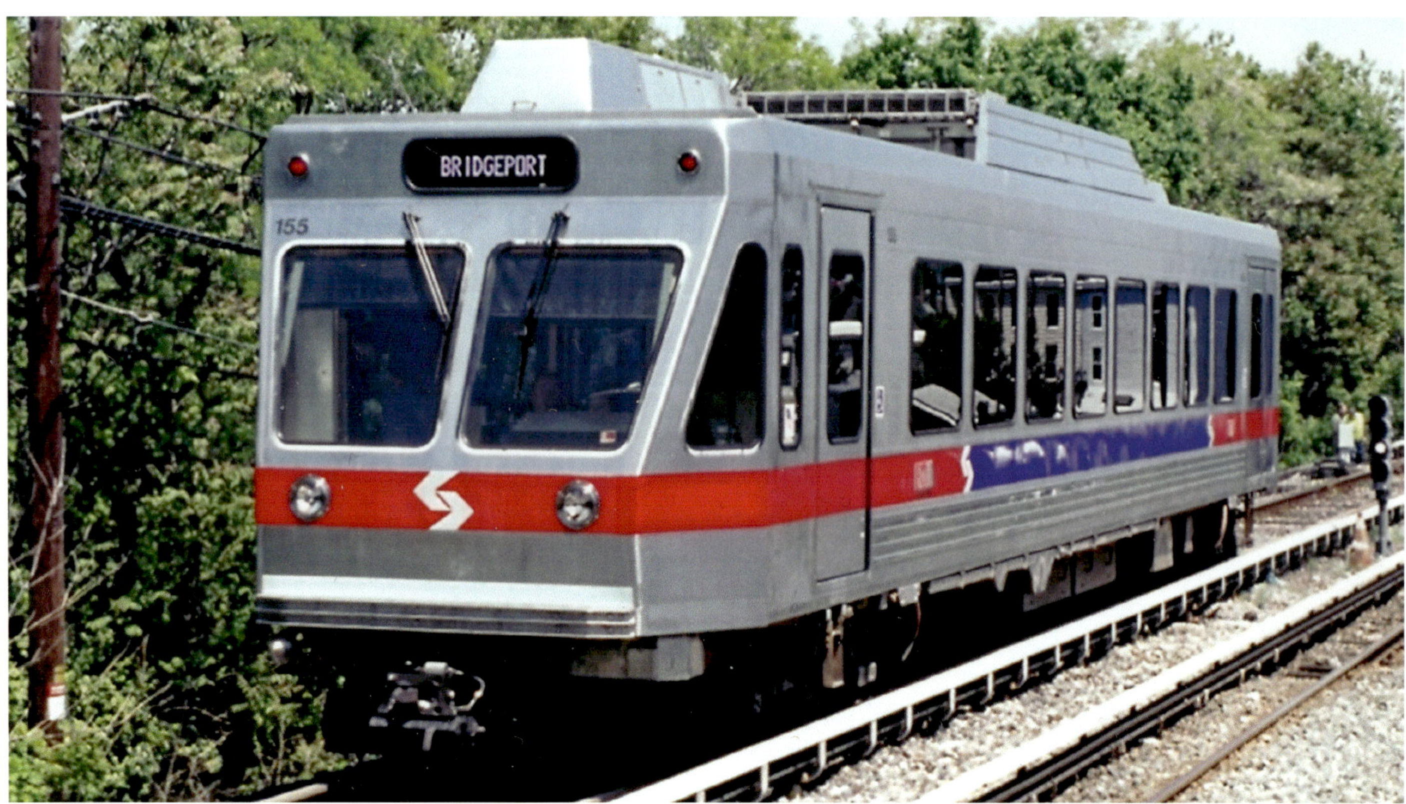

Type N-5 car No. 155, built by Asea Brown Boveri, is at the Bridgeport station of the Norristown Line on May 20, 2007. The station is located near 5th & Merion Streets in the Montgomery County borough of Bridgeport.

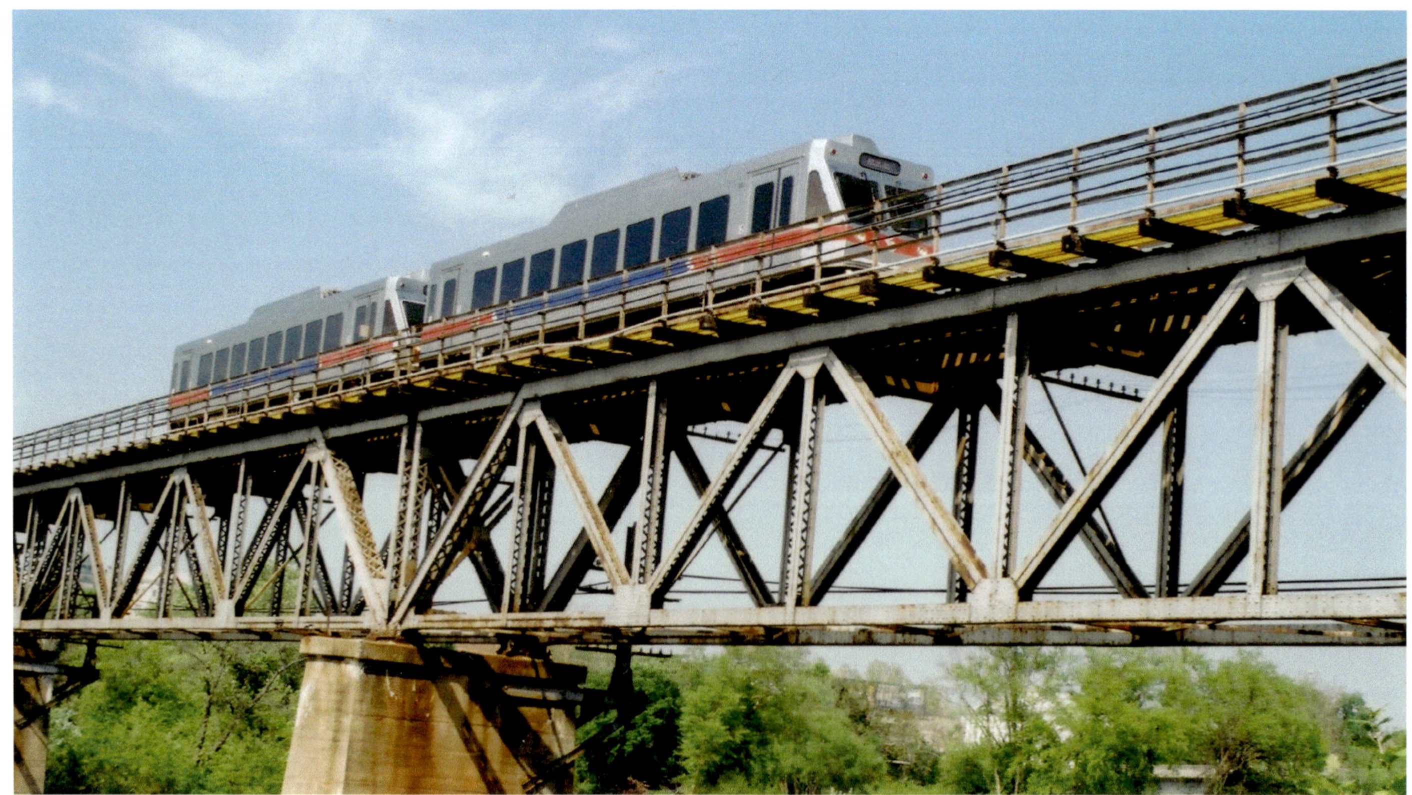

A two car train of type N-5 cars is crossing the Schuylkill River over the single track 3,800 foot long Bridgeport-Norristown Viaduct on May 15, 2013; that over the river section of the viaduct consists of Warren trusses carried on concrete piers. The Philadelphia & Western Railway built this structure with service beginning from 69th Street Terminal via this viaduct to Norristown on August 26, 1912.

Chapter 3

Pittsburgh Trolleys

On January 1, 1902 all Pittsburgh trolley companies were merged into Pittsburgh Railways Company (PRC). As late as 1950, PRC had 542 miles of track and operated 1,187 cars of which 666 were PCC cars on its 5 foot 2.5 inches wide gauge system. PRC converted Route 29 (Thornburg) to bus operation on November 16, 1952. On August 29, 1953, PRC PCC car No. 1711 made the last trip over the twenty-nine mile interurban line to Washington, Pennsylvania. PRC fleet of 666 PCC cars declined to 655 as a result of a May 18, 1955 fire at the Homewood Carbarn. Trolley Car Routes 1 (Spring Garden) and 5 (Spring Hill) were abandoned on October 6, 1957. The June 21, 1959 closure of the 1,120 foot long Point Bridge over the Monongahela River resulted in the end of West End trolley car service for 6 Pittsburgh Railways Company (PRC) Routes 25 (Island Avenue), 26 (West Park), 27 (Carnegie), 28 (Heidelberg), 30 (Crafton–Ingram), and 31/34 (Elliott–Ingram). PRC Trolley Car Routes 18 (Woods Run) and 19 (Western Avenue) were converted to bus operation on November 12, 1961. Because of the expense of renewing track on West Liberty Avenue, PRC combined Route 38 (Mt. Lebanon) and Route 42 (Dormont) into Route 42/38 (Mt. Lebanon via Dormont and Beechview) on May 26, 1963. As a result of a devastating tornado that hit the borough of Glassport in Allegheny County on August 3, 1963, Route 98 (Glassport) was abandoned when it took six hours to get the only car on the line PCC car No. 1412 out of the area. Effective August 6, 1963, PRC turned over the operation of the line to Noble J. Dick Bus Lines.

Western Pennsylvania's last intercity trolley car line closed when PRC converted Route 56 (McKeesport via 2nd Avenue) from Pittsburgh to McKeesport to bus operation on September 1, 1963. The Port Authority of Allegheny County known as Port Authority Transit (PAT) took over Pittsburgh Railways and thirty independent bus companies on March 1, 1964. On September 5, 1965, PAT Trolley Car Routes 8 (Perrysville), 10 (West View), 15 (Belleview), 65 (Munhall–Lincoln Place), and 77/54 (North Side–Oakland) were converted to bus operation plus Route 13 (Emsworth), which shared track with Route 15 from Balph Avenue to downtown Pittsburgh, was combined with Route 6 (Brighton Road) making it 6/13 (Brighton–Emsworth) allowing that trackage on California Avenue parallel to Brighton Road to be abandoned. Because of the deteriorated condition of the Ben Avon and Avalon trolley bridges, on December 31, 1965 trolley car service was discontinued between Emsworth Loop and Avalon Loop, and the route became 6/14 (Brighton–Avalon). In the late evening of April 31, 1966, Route 21 (Fineview) made its last run, and in the early morning of May 1, 1966 Route 6/14 made its last run as a trolley car line. This ended all trolley car service on Pittsburgh's North Side (north of the Allegheny River). Route 85 (Bedford) was converted to bus operation on June 26, 1966.

On September 4, 1966, South Hills Trolley Car Routes 39 (Brookline) and 40 (Mt. Washington) were replaced by buses and East End Route 87 (Ardmore) was cut back from Wilmerding to Wilkinsburg without any bus replacement. Also East End trolley car routes began operating only Monday through Friday, which included 64 (Wilkinsburg–East Pittsburgh), 67 (Swissvale–Rankin–Braddock), 71 (Negley–Highland Park), 73 (Highland Park), 75 (East Liberty–Wilkinsburg), 76 (Hamilton), 82 (Lincoln), the remaining portion of 87 (Ardmore), and 88 (Frankstown) with full bus operation on these East End lines on January 28, 1967. During the early morning hours of March 31, 1968, Trolley Car Route 48 (Arlington) was converted to bus operation by an extension of Bus Route 54A (Arlington Heights), and rush hour Trolley Car Route 47 (Carrick via Tunnel) was replaced by Trolley Car Route 53 that was rerouted into the Tunnel. Trolley Car Routes 44 (Knoxville), 49 (Beltzhoover), and 53 (Carrick) made their last runs on the evening of November 13, 1971 and early morning of November 14, 1971. The track and overhead wire were retained on Warrington and Arlington Avenues (formerly used by Routes 44, 49, and 53) as a tunnel bypass and was served by a new Route 49 (Arlington-Warrington to South Hills Junction). Modern light rail vehicles were placed in service on April 15, 1984, and the 1.1 mile downtown subway opened on July 3, 1985.

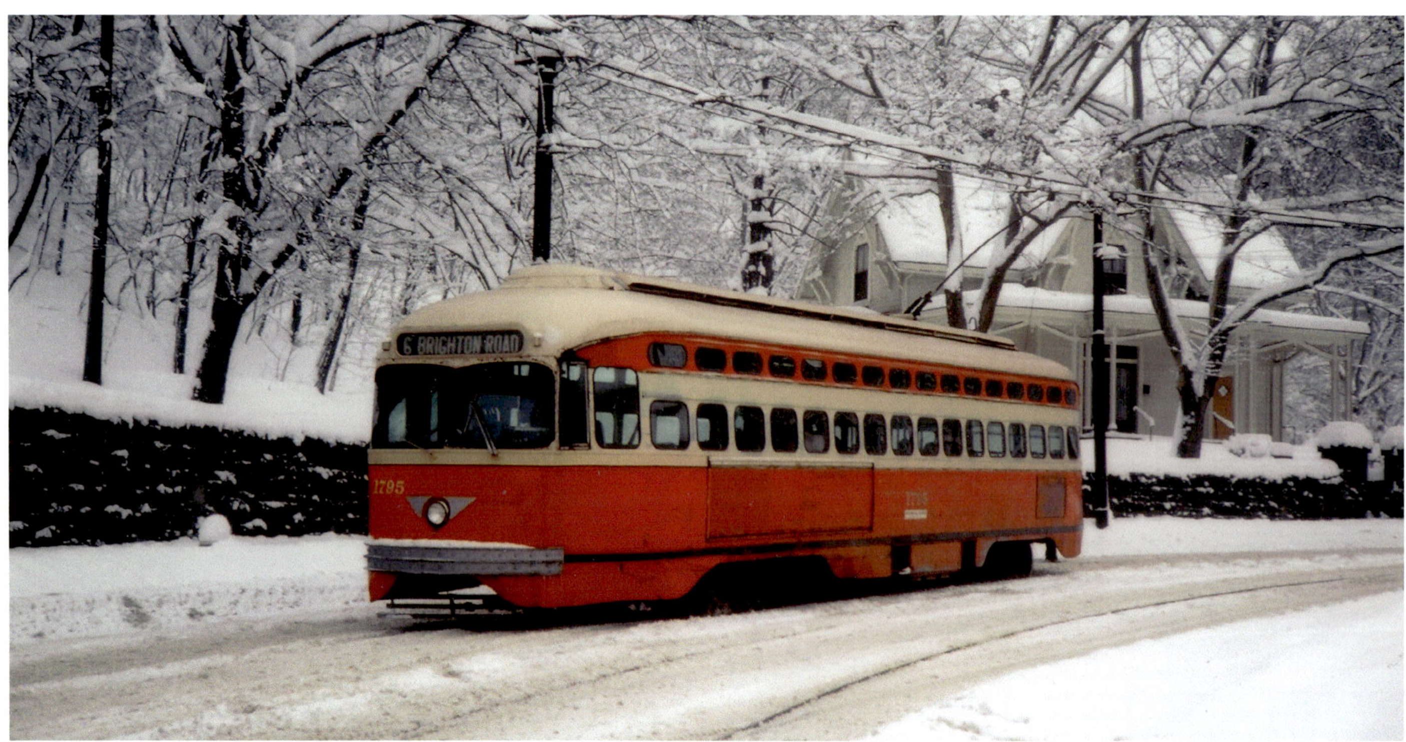

Port Authority Transit (PAT) Route 6 (Brighton Road) PCC car No. 1795 is on Brighton Road amid a cold snowy January 23, 1966. This was one of a hundred cars numbered 1700-1799 built by St. Louis Car Company and delivered between December 1948 and July 1949. These cars featured standee windows, a top roof ventilator, and sealed windows. Route 6 was an all street running mostly on double track line that connected the North Side with downtown Pittsburgh.

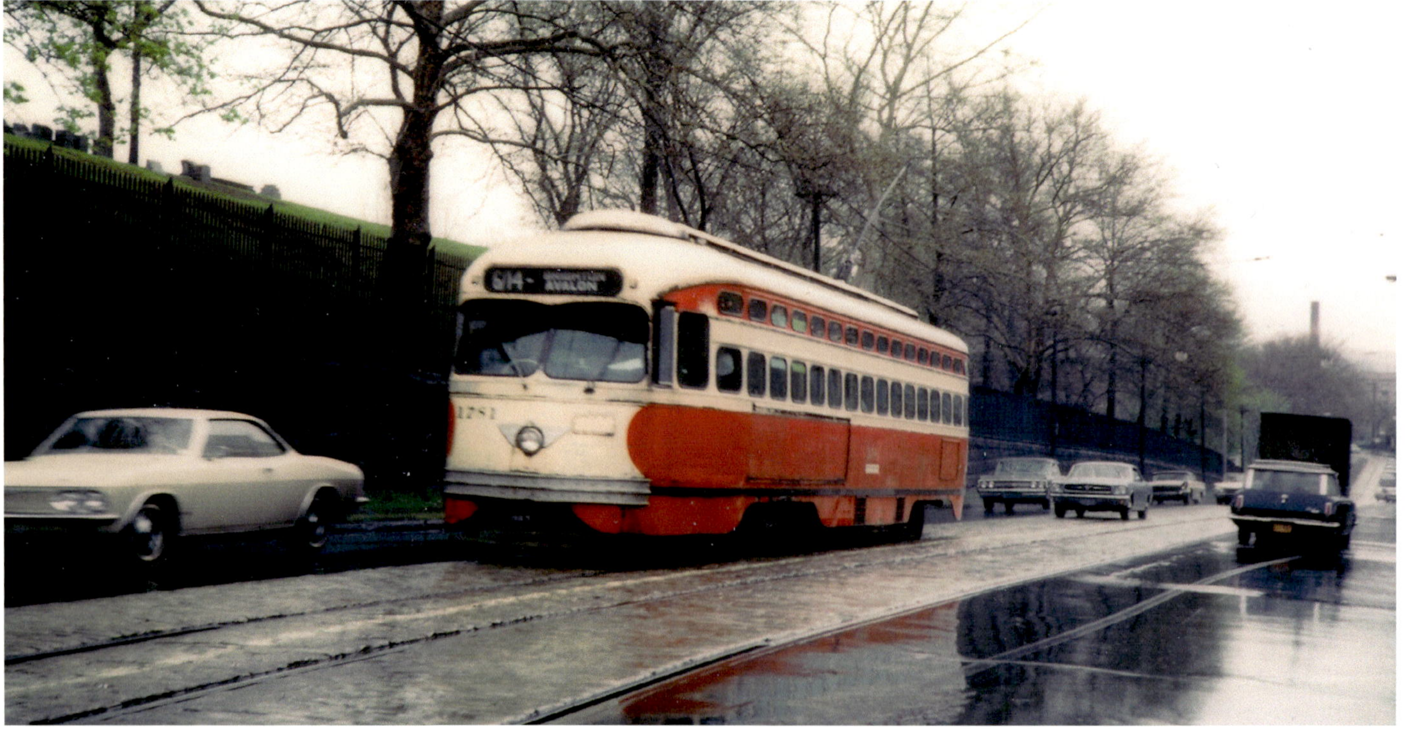

On a rainy April 30, 1966, PAT Route 6/14 PCC car No. 1781 is on Brighton Road. PAT Route 6/13 (Brighton Emsworth) PCC car No. 1795 was the last car to Emsworth Loop leaving downtown Pittsburgh at 12:27 a.m. on December 31, 1965 ending all trolley car service beyond Avalon Loop to Emsworth Loop. The route was now 6/14 (Brighton-Avalon) which ended trolley car service when the last car left 6th and Penn Avenue at 12:27 a.m. on May 1, 1966.

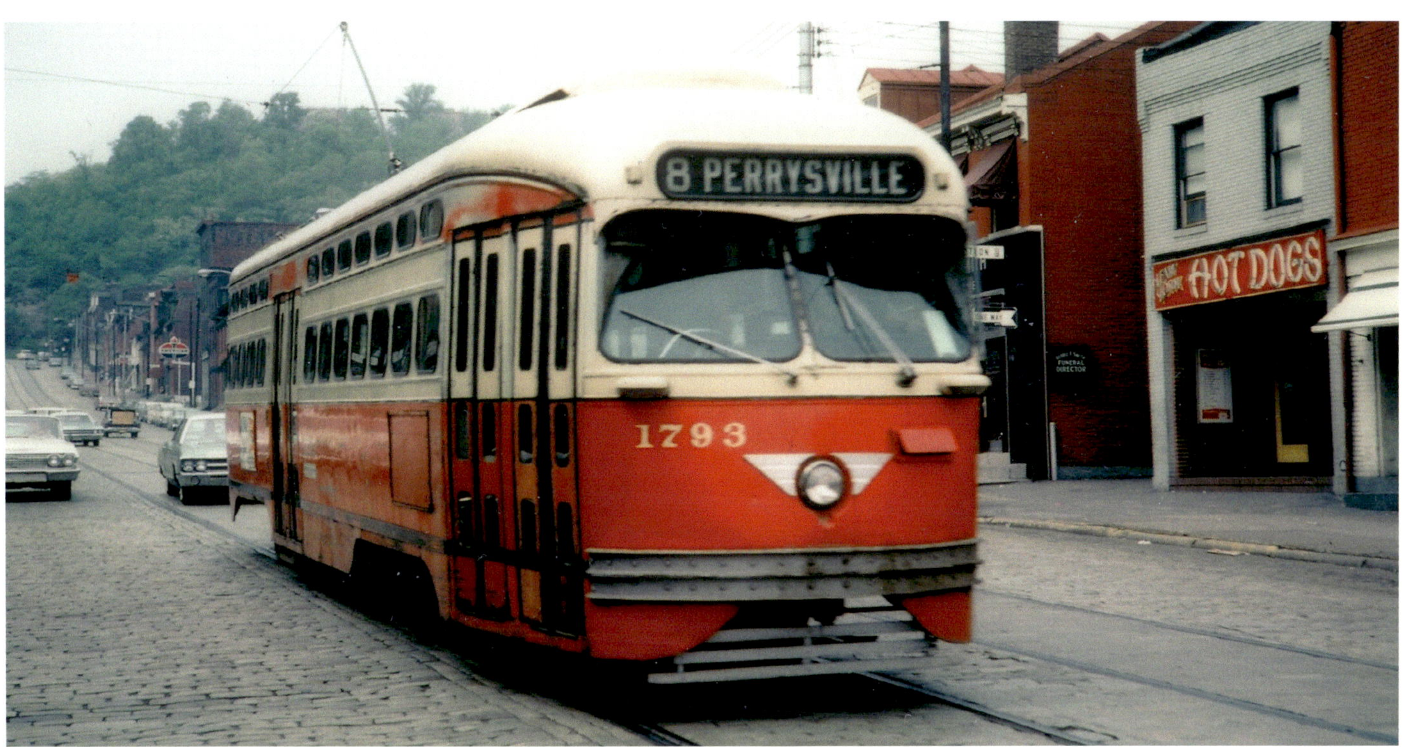

PAT Route 8 Perrysville PCC car No. 1793 is at Federal Street and North Avenue on May 23, 1965. On September 5, 1965 at 5:05 a.m., PCC car No. 1683 made the last trip on Route 8 and arrived at Keating Car House at 5:28 a.m., making it the last trolley car to use Keating Car House. Route 8, the busiest trolley car line on Pittsburgh's North Side, connecting Keating carhouse via winding Perrysville Avenue with downtown Pittsburgh, was now a bus line.

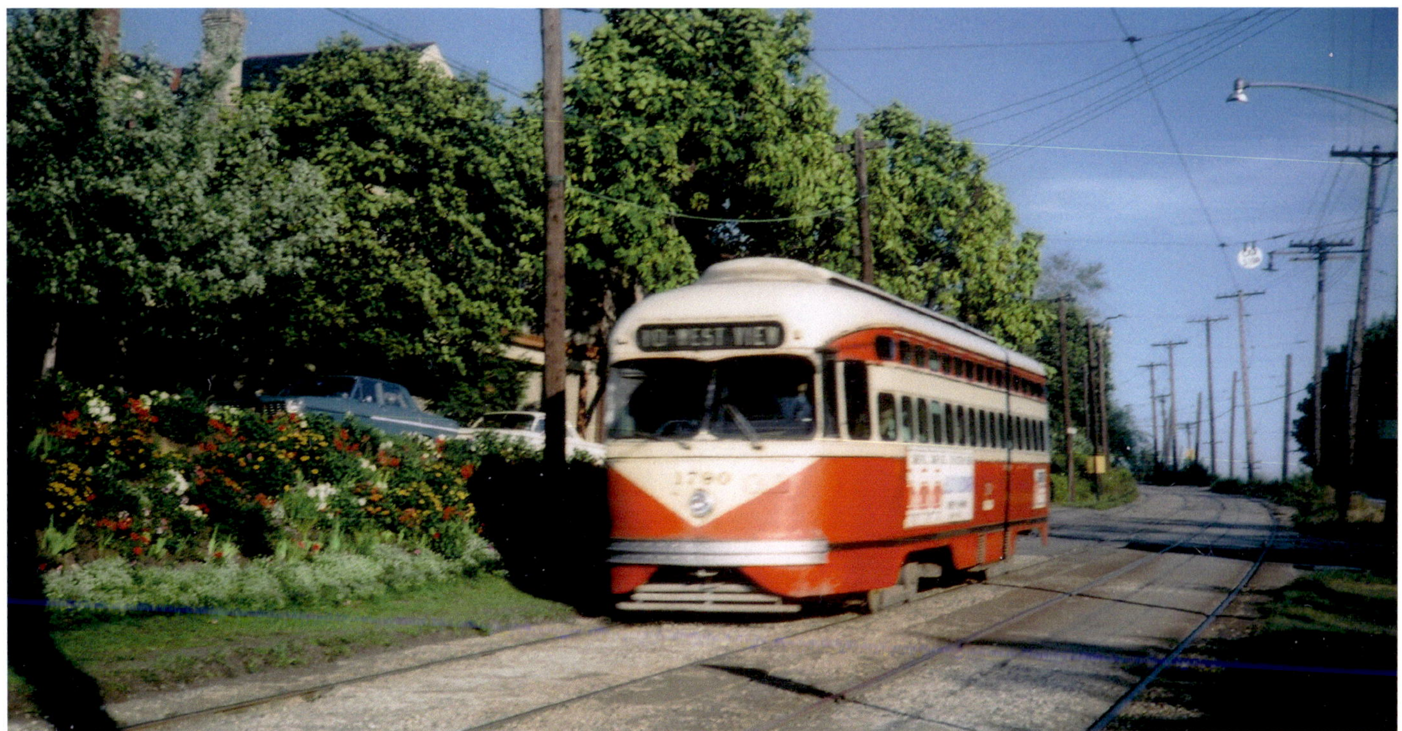

On August 29, 1965, PAT Route 10 (West View) PCC car No. 1790 is parallel to highway Route 19 north of Keating carhouse. On September 5, 1965, this car made the last trolley car trip on Route 10 leaving downtown at 12:52 a.m. and arrived at West View at 1:24 a.m. and buses took over. Route 10, connecting downtown Pittsburgh with the West View Amusement Park, did not have a loop at the end of the line but had three crossovers where cars could lay over or pass each other. Trolleys continued as Route 15 to downtown Pittsburgh. Hence, Routes 10 and 15 were one circular route.

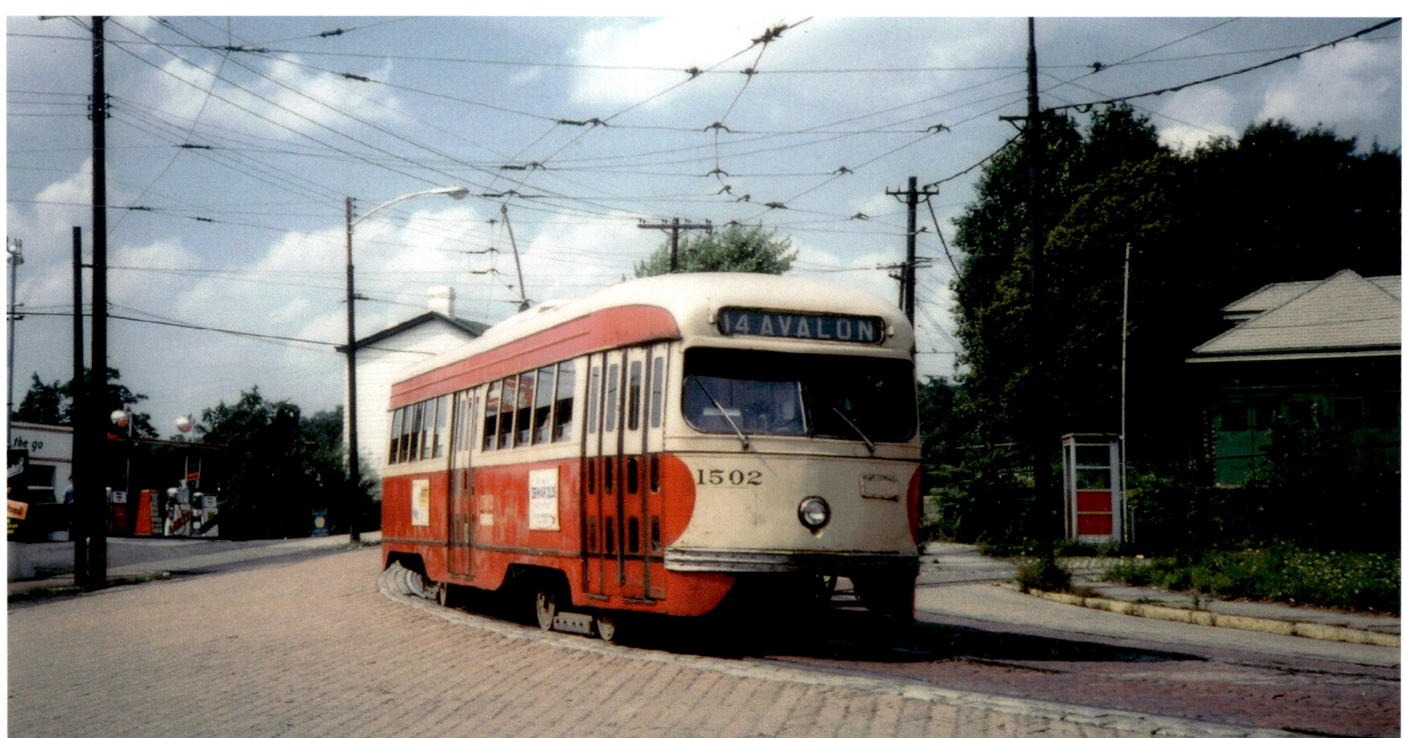

On August 23, 1964, PAT Route 14 (Avalon), a cutback of Route 13 (Emsworth), PCC car No. 1502 is on Lincoln Avenue near the Avalon Loop. This was one of sixty-five cars numbered 1500-1564 (weighing 35,880 pounds and seating 56) built by St. Louis Car Company and delivered between December 1944 and March 1945. None of these cars have survived.

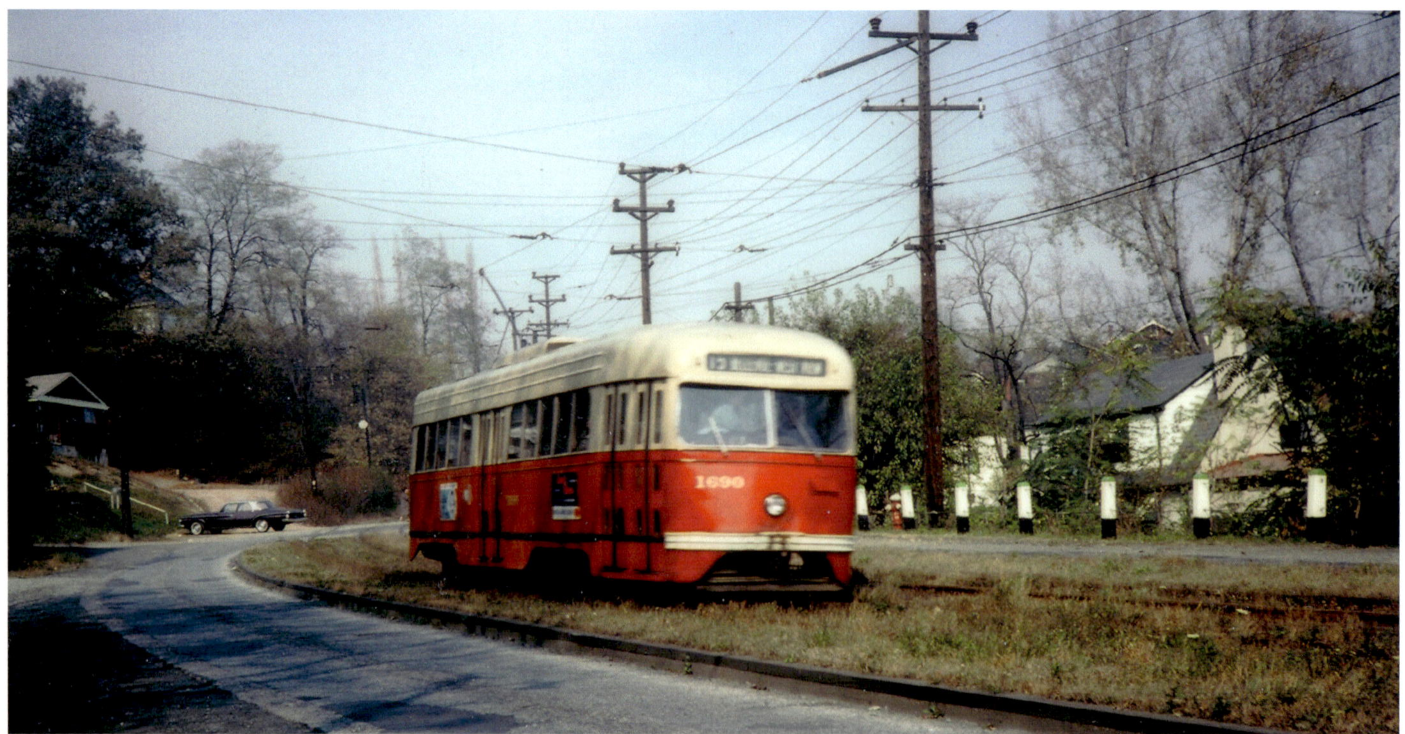

PRC Route 15 (Bellevue) PCC car No. 1690 is at Cornell Avenue in the borough of West View just north of downtown Pittsburgh on October 19, 1963. This was one of a hundred cars numbered 1600-1699 (weighing 36,264 pounds and seating fifty-six) built by St. Louis Car Company and delivered between September 1945 and January 1946. The last Route 15 trolley car was PCC car No. 1777 that left downtown Pittsburgh on September 5, 1965 at 12:07 a.m. and arrived at West View at 12:40 a.m. At the end of the line, there was no loop; the sign was changed for the trip back to Pittsburgh. Route 15 was now a bus line.

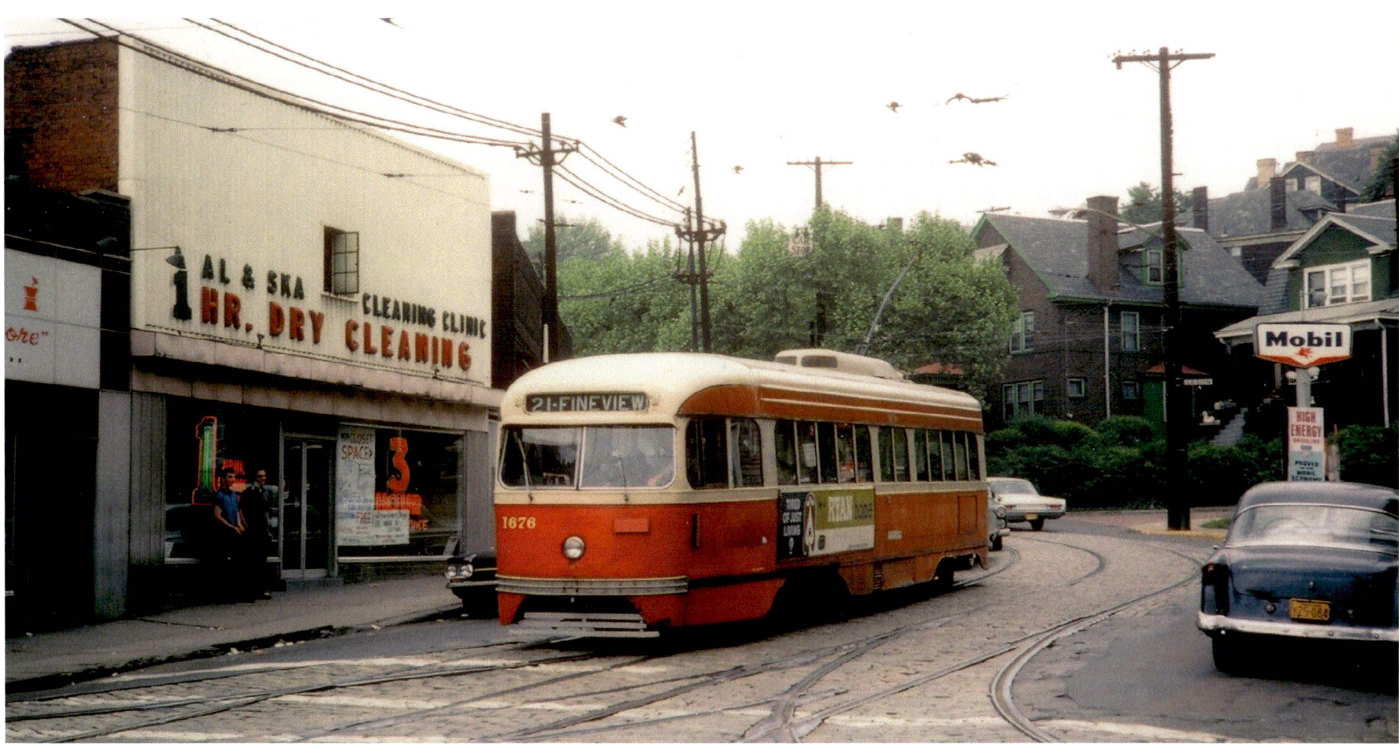

PAT Route 21 PCC car No. 1676 is on Perrysville Avenue at North Charles Street on May 23, 1965. On April 31, 1966, PCC car No. 1678 made the last regular Route 21 run leaving downtown Pittsburgh at 11:26 p.m. and returned to 6th Street and Penn Avenue forty minutes later. Route 21 was a spectacular one directional loop that climbed from downtown Pittsburgh at elevation 730 feet above sea level to a high point at 1185 feet above sea level encountering some of the steepest straight adhesion rail grades in the world.

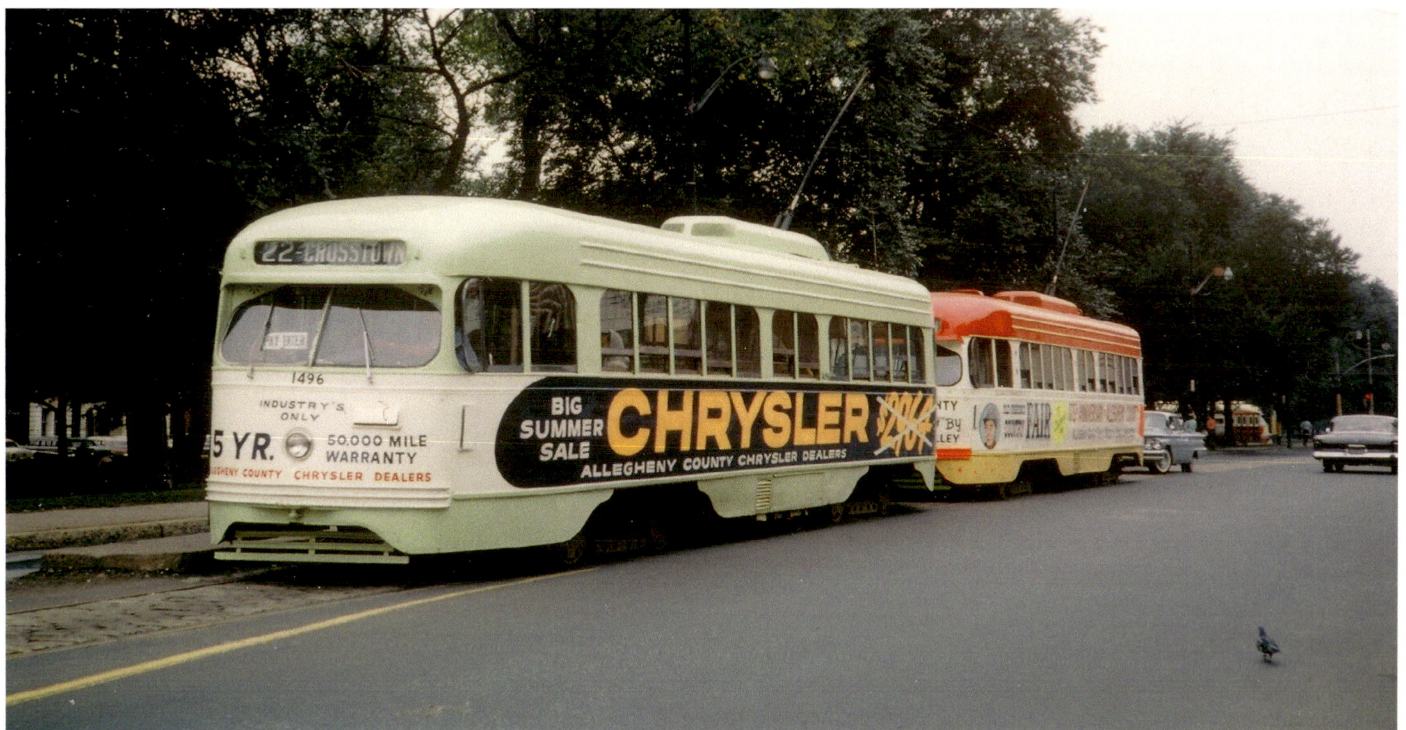

On August 3, 1963, PRC Route 22 PCC cars Nos. 1496 and 1559 are at North Avenue and Sandusky Street awaiting departure time. This was a short line connecting the downtown and North Side Pittsburgh business districts.

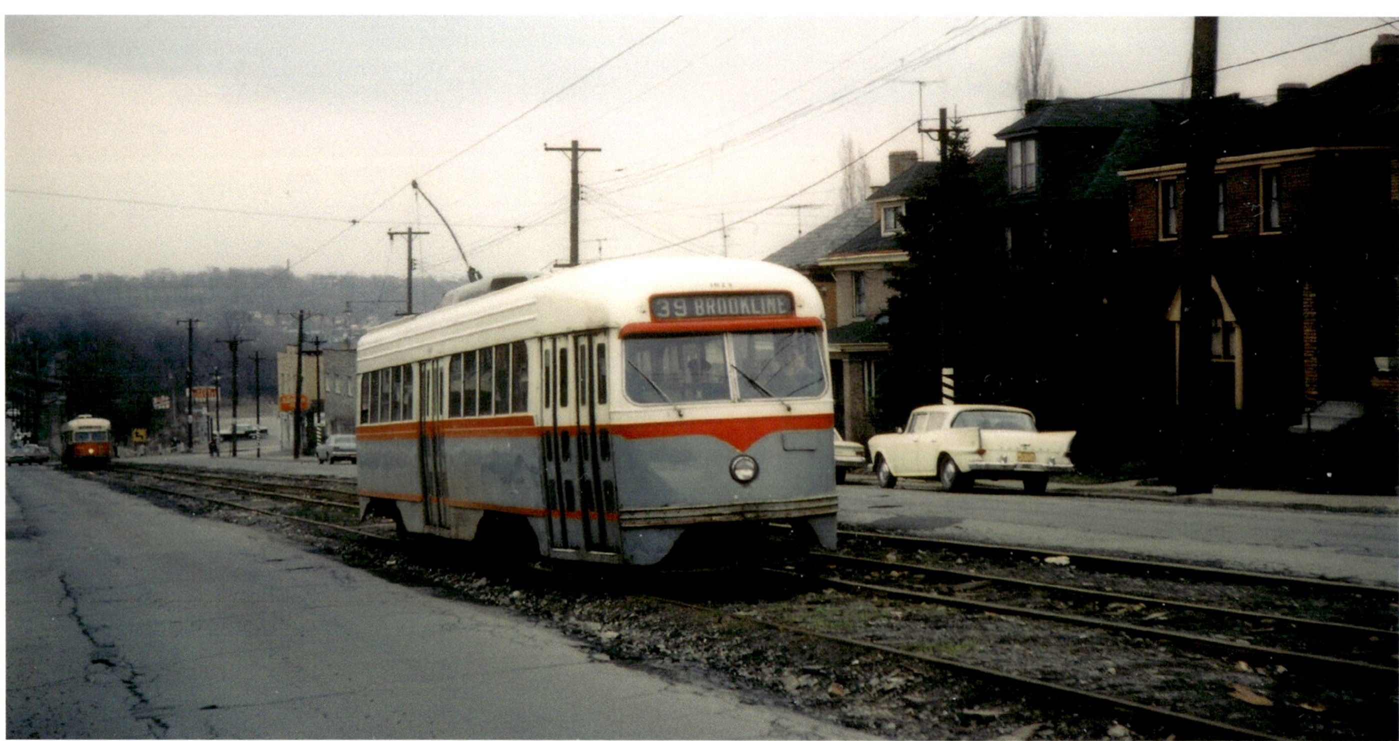

The center-of-the-road private way of Brookline Boulevard eliminates congestion problems on this portion of PAT Route 39 (Brookline) for PCC car No. 1623 on March 20, 1966. Route 39 was converted to bus operation on September 4, 1966. In downtown Pittsburgh, the line crossed the Monongahela River on the Smithfield Street Bridge, used the Mt. Washington Tunnel to South Hills Junction, crossed the Palm Garden Trestle, operated on West Liberty Avenue, and entered the private right of way in the center of Brookline Boulevard to its loop.

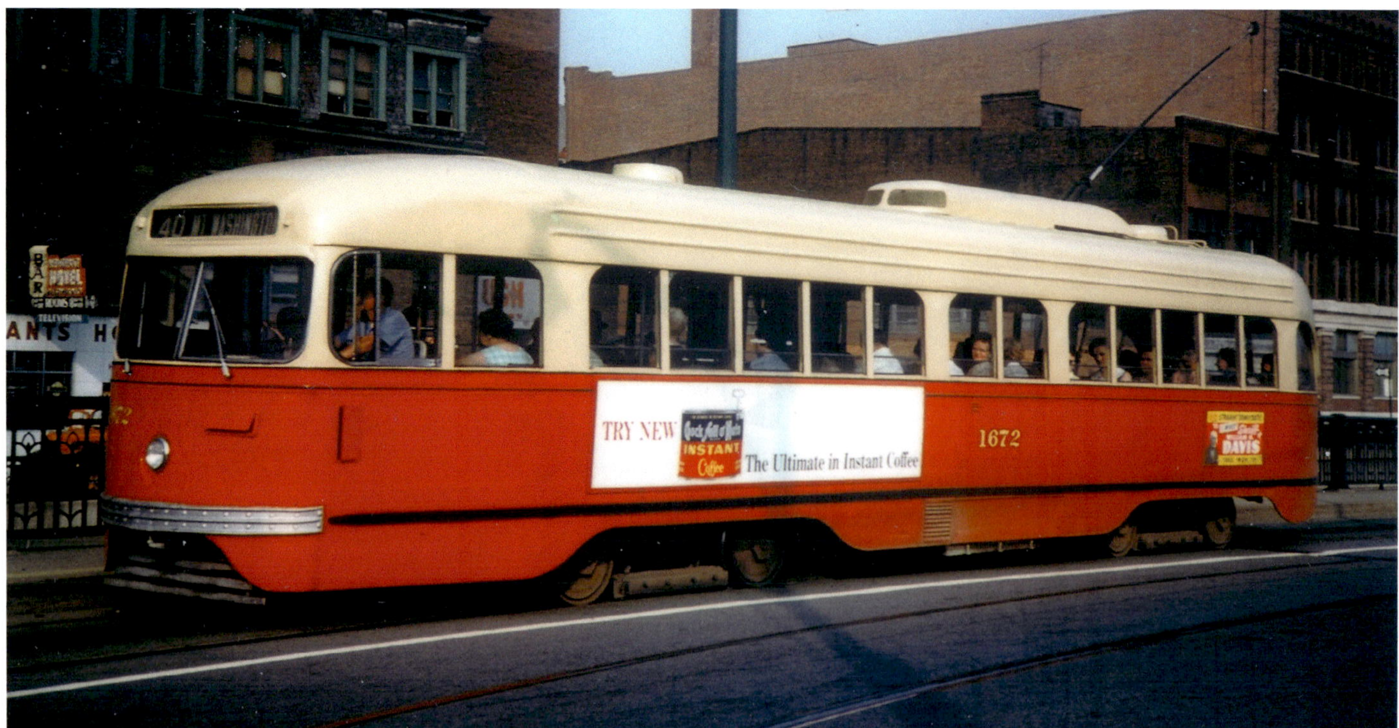

PRC Route 40 (Mt. Washington) PCC car No. 1672 is on Fort Pitt Boulevard near Smithfield Street on September 11, 1961. This repainted car had a new simplified paint scheme with red below the window sills, all above in cream, a minimum of black trim, wings around the headlight removed, and front car number in white. Route 40 was converted to bus operation on September 4, 1966. It used the Smithfield Street Bridge from downtown Pittsburgh to South Hills Junction, and then began climbing entering Grandview Avenue providing a view of the city passing the Monongahela and Duquesne Inclines to its terminal.

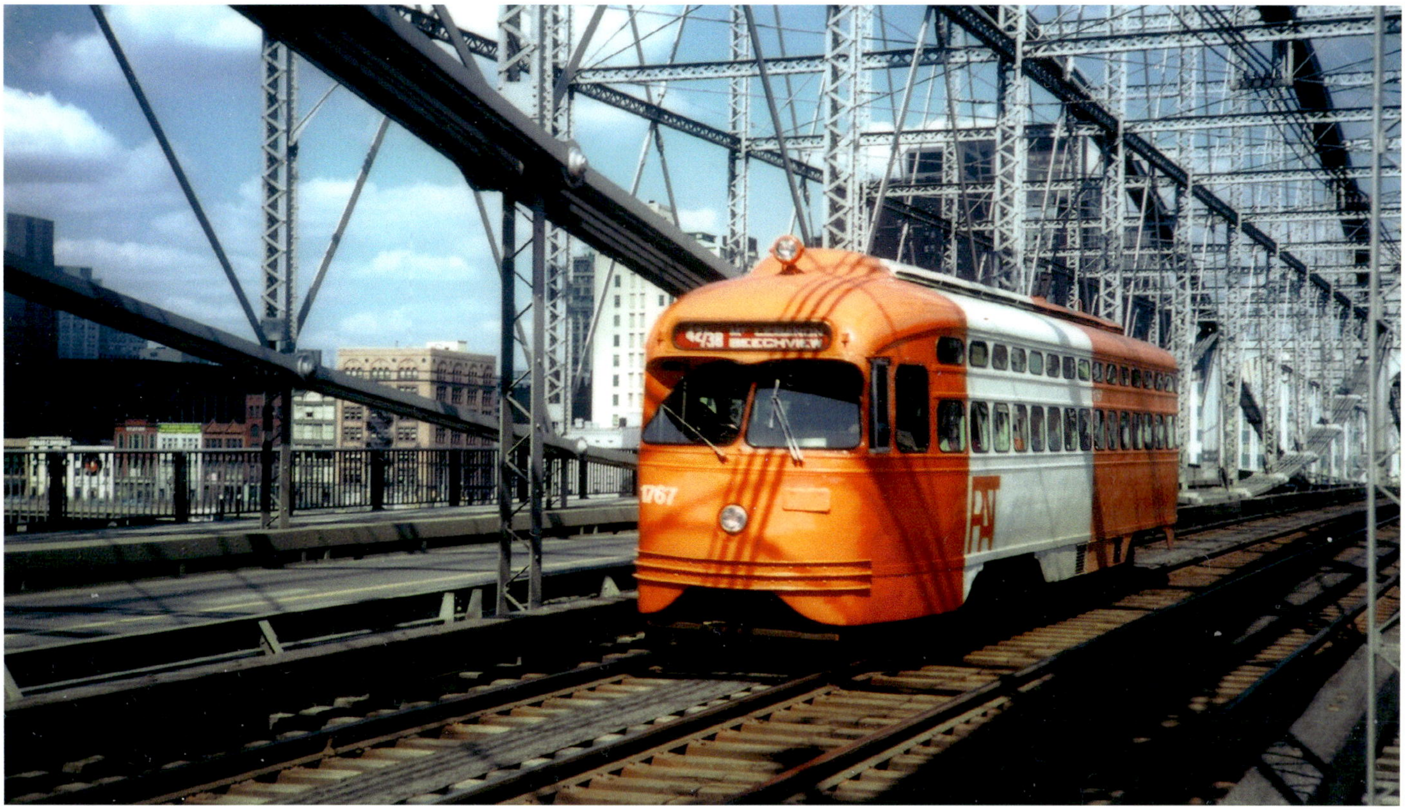

On October 1, 1972, southbound PAT Route 42/38 PCC car No. 1767 is crossing over the Monongahela River on the Smithfield Street Bridge.

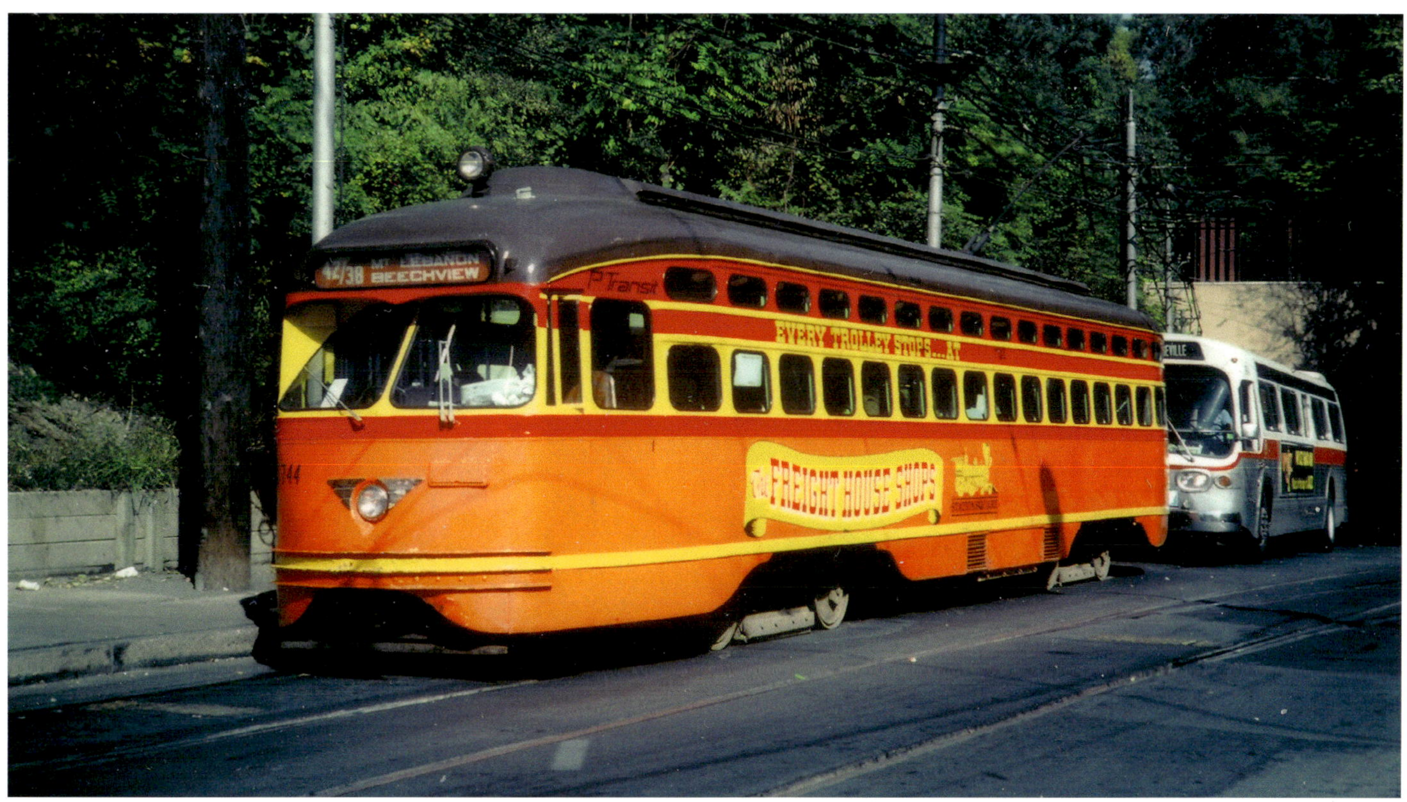

Advertising the Freight House Shops, PAT Route 42/38 PCC car No. 1744 is at South Hills Junction on October 11, 1980. A number of South Hills trolley lines used the double track 3,500 foot long Mount Washington Trolley Tunnel that opened on December 1, 1904 to South Hills Junction where they diverged into four directions at the Junction. Adjacent to the junction was the Tunnel Carbarn and maintenance shops.

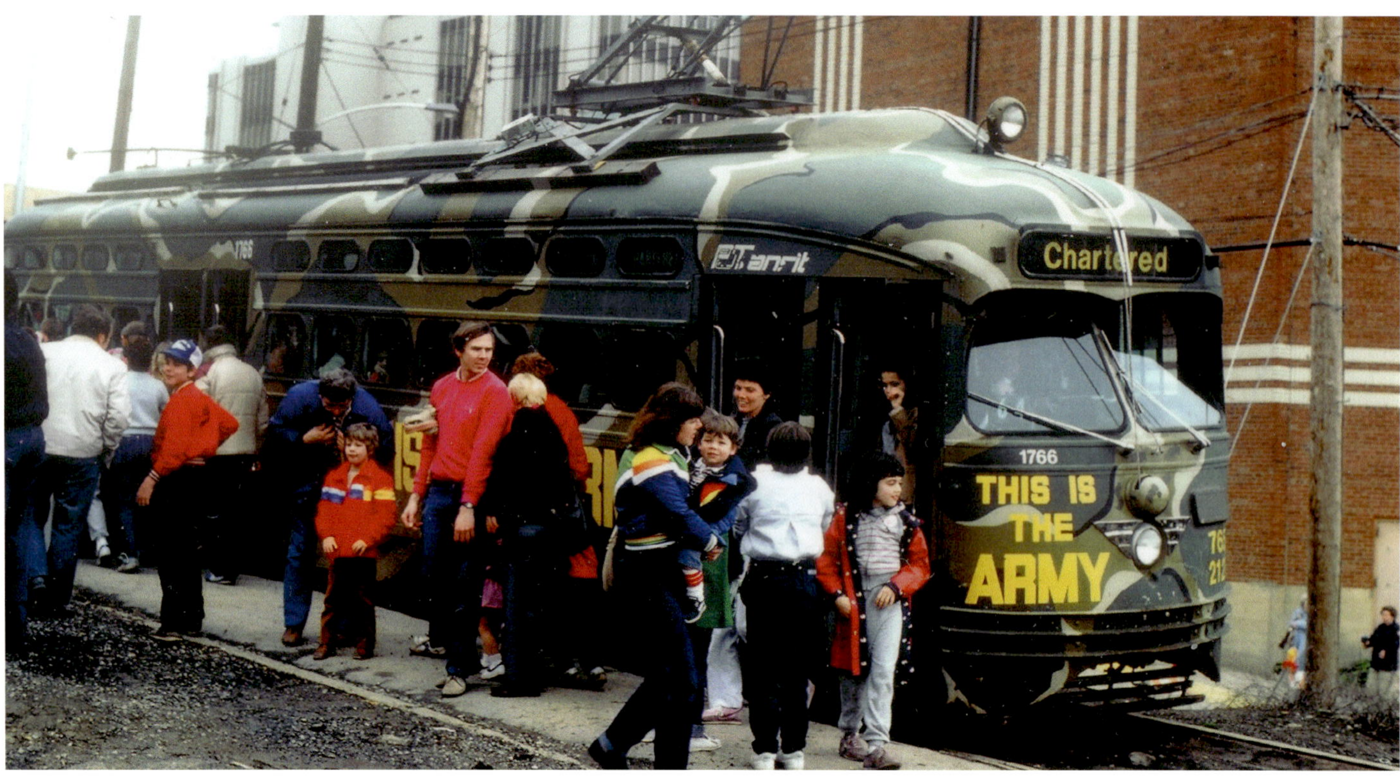

Crowds were riding the last day of trolley car operation on Washington Road in Mount Lebanon as PAT Route 42/38 PCC car No. 1766 is jammed with riders on April 14, 1984.

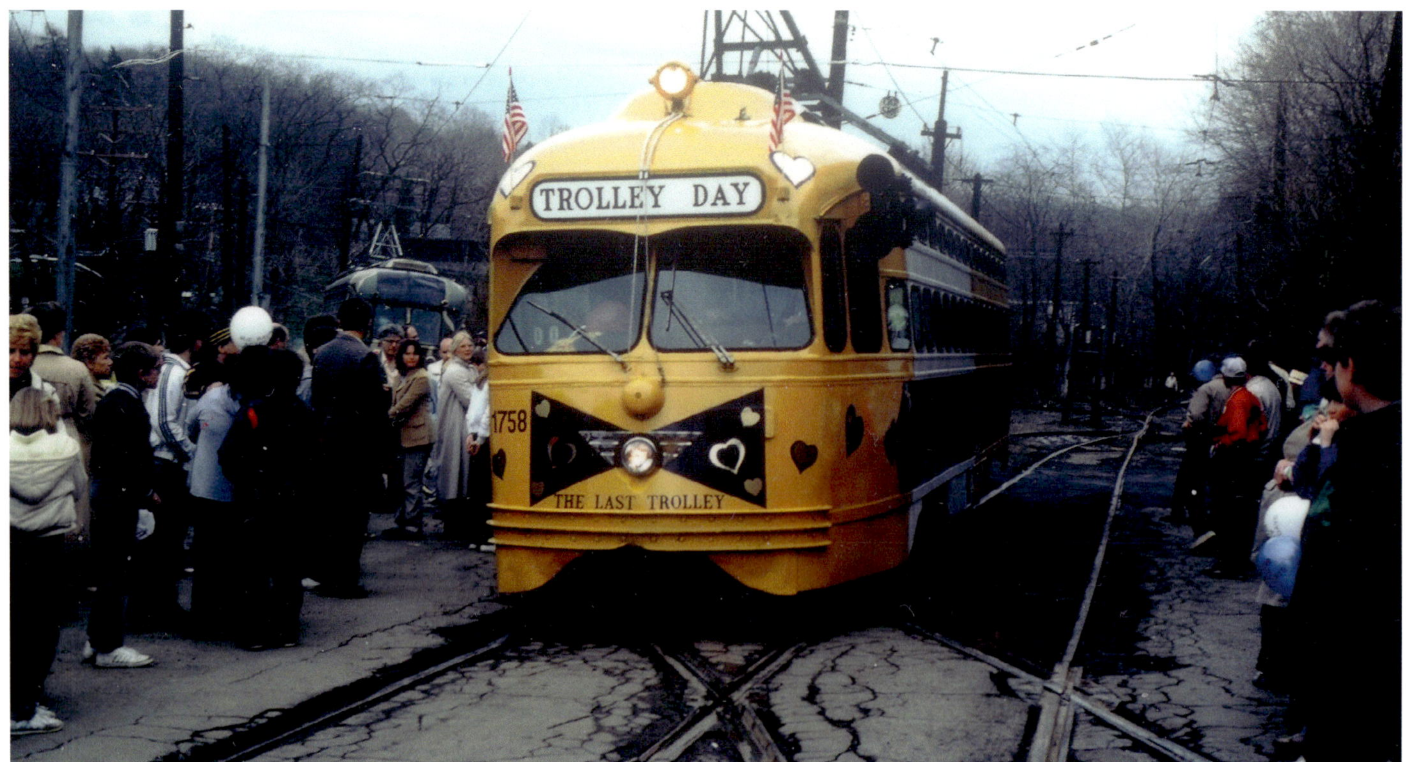

PAT Route 42/38 PCC car No. 1758 is at the Clearview Loop on April 14, 1984, the last day of operation on Washington Road. The line was shut down for the construction of the 3,000 foot long Mt. Lebanon Tunnel that connects the Dormont Junction and Mt. Lebanon stations beneath Washington Road & West Liberty Avenue from Shady Drive to McFarland Road. Using the rock surrounding the hole as the support system, the tunnel was constructed by lining the tunnel cavity with several thin layers of concrete that was blown on under air pressure.

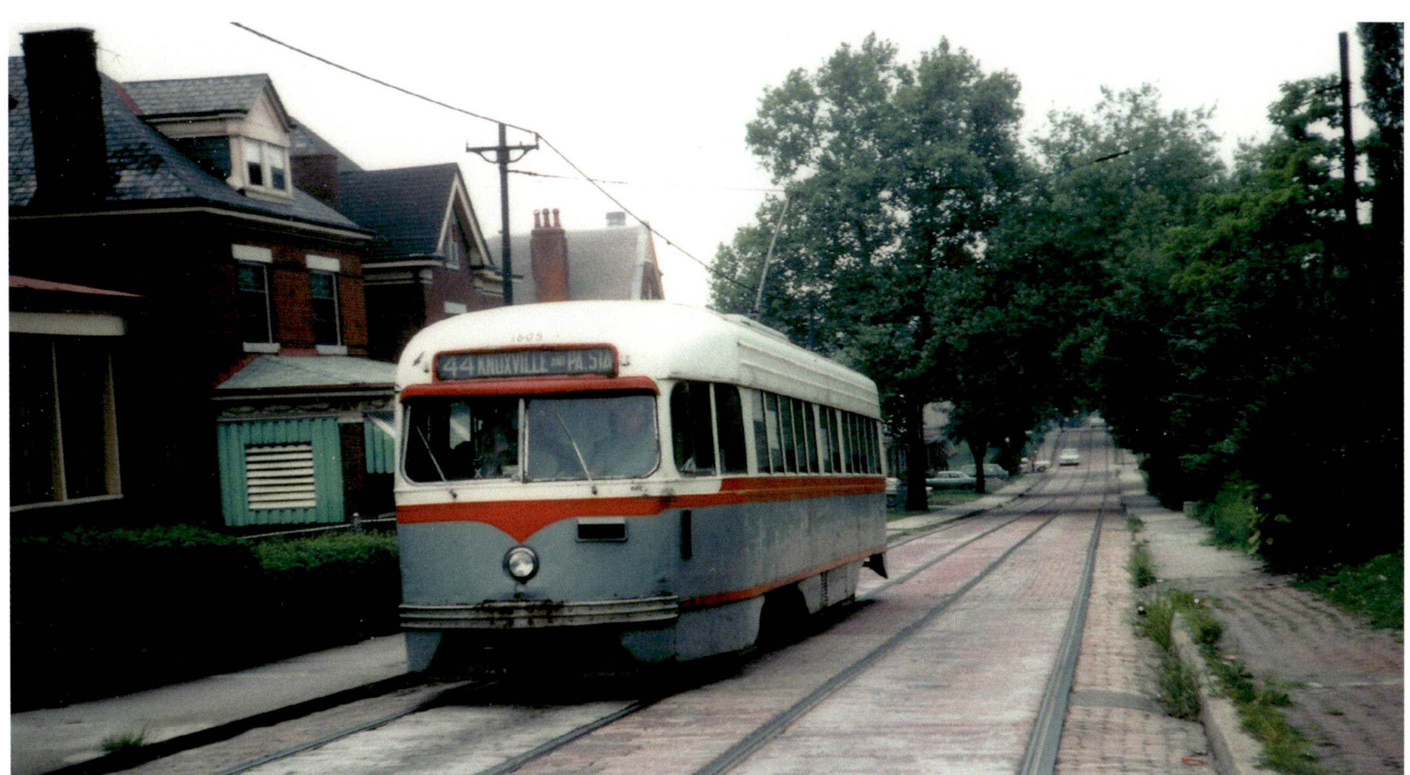

On August 10, 1968, PAT Route 44 PCC car No. 1605 is at Charles Street and Amanda Avenue in the Knoxville neighborhood of south Pittsburgh. This line was converted to bus operation on November 14, 1971. This line's downtown loop served both the Pennsylvania Railroad and Pittsburgh & Lake Erie Railroad stations. At its outer end, it featured two tracks on narrow Charles Street with true curb loading.

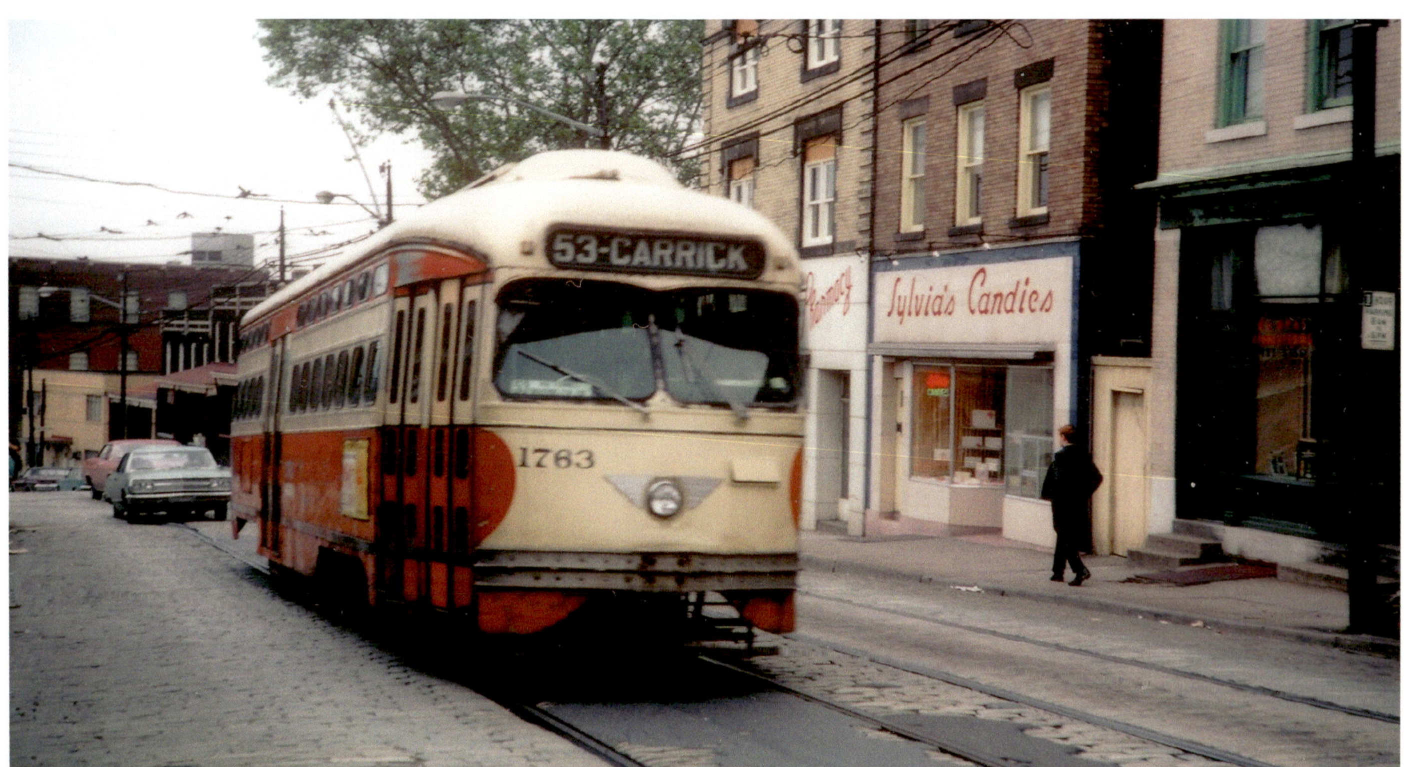

PAT Route 53 PCC car No. 1763 is on Warrington Avenue near Beltzhoover Avenue in the Allentown neighborhood of Pittsburgh on May 26, 1968. On March 31, 1968, rush hour Route 47 Carrick via tunnel was discontinued, and Route 53 which used South 18th Street and Carson Street was rerouted to use Route 47 trackage through the Mount Washington Tunnel. Route 53 was converted to bus operation on November 14, 1971.

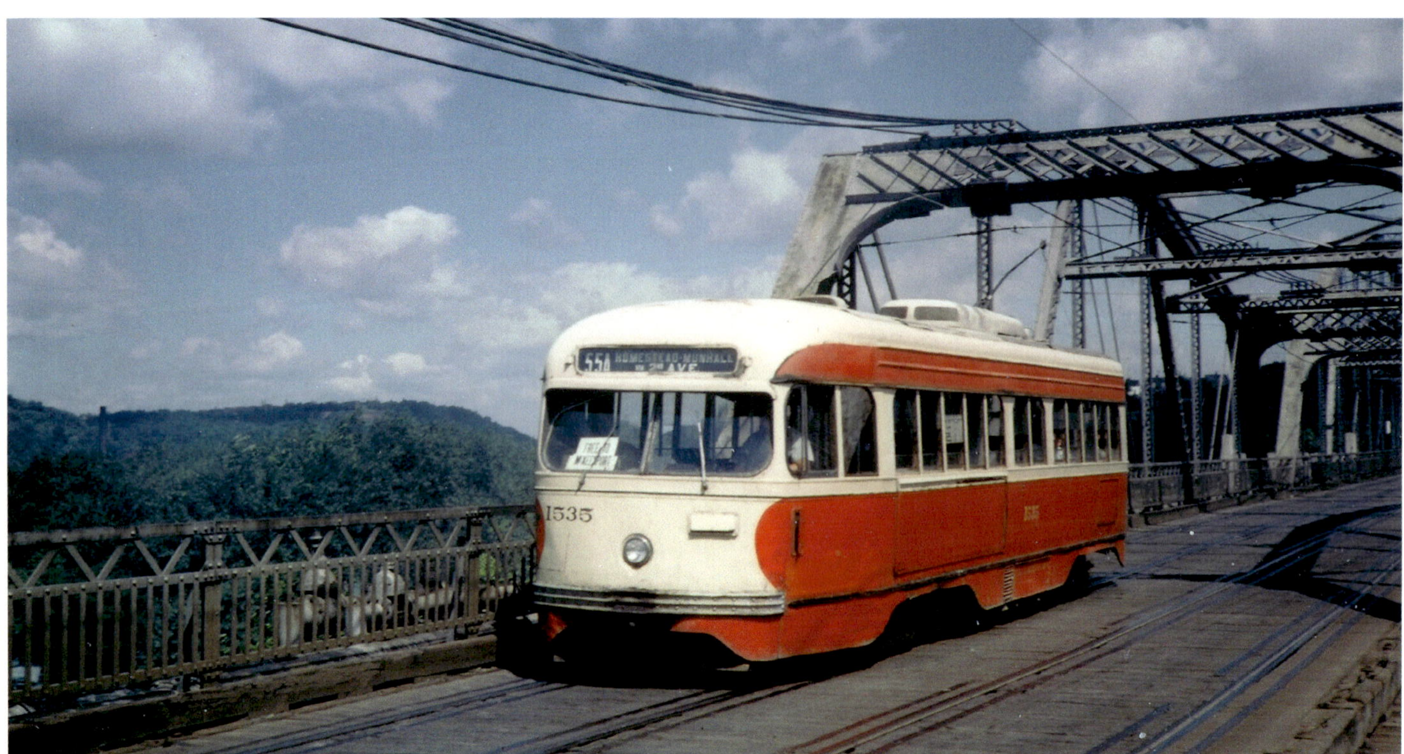

The vintage Glenwood Bridge provides a nice photo stop for a rail excursion on PRC Route 55A using PCC car No. 1535 on August 4, 1963. This trackage was also used by Route 56 (McKeesport) until it became Bus Route 56C on September 1, 1963. Route 55 (East Pittsburgh) and Route 58 (Greenfield) were converted to bus operation on July 5, 1964 plus Trolley Car Route 65 (Munhall-Lincoln Place) was extended over Route 55 trackage from Munhall Loop to East Pittsburgh from 5 a.m. to 8 p.m. Monday thru Friday.

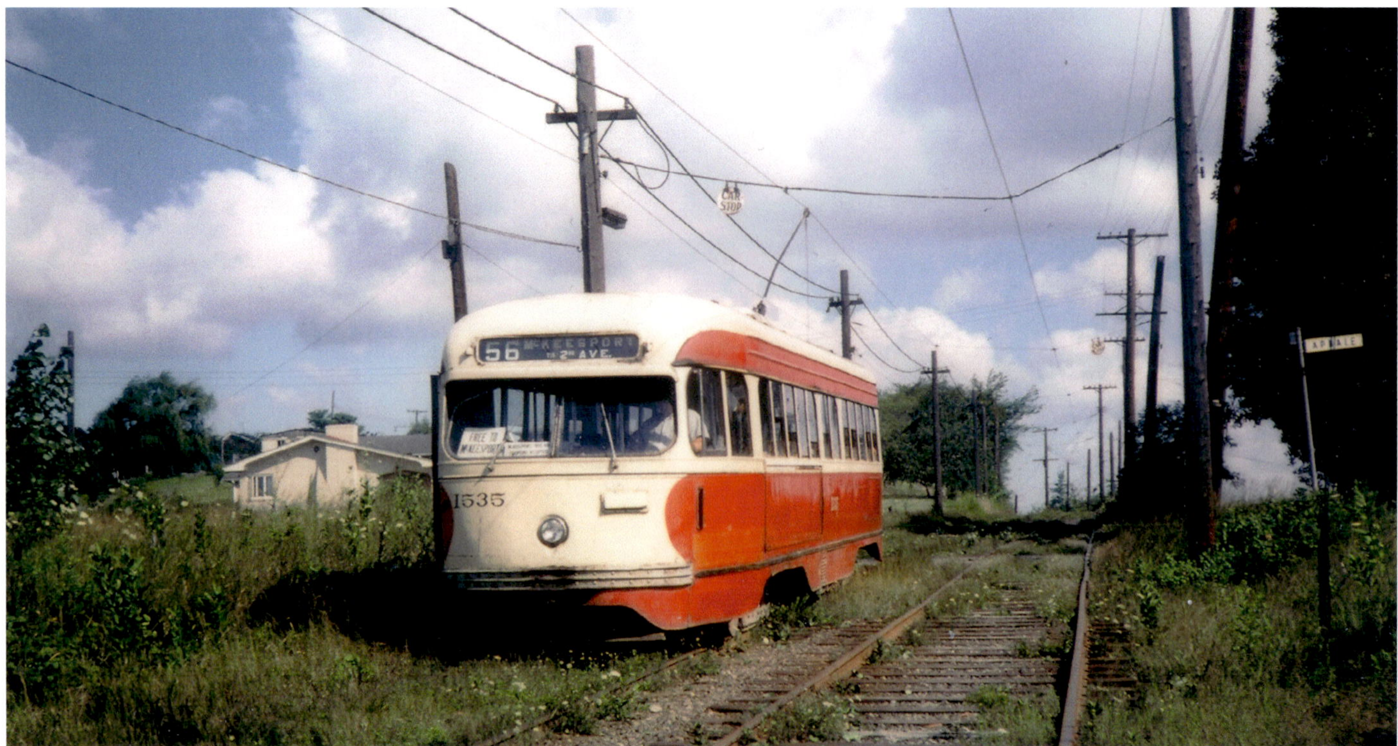

On August 4, 1963, PCC car No. 1535 has taken rail enthusiasts to a private right of way section of Route 56 (McKeesport via 2nd Avenue) at Apdale Street for another photo stop before proceeding to McKeesport. This double tracked line connected Pittsburgh with McKeesport featuring private right of way through wooded valleys and hills. With plans to replace the Glenwood Bridge, Route 56 was converted to bus operation on September 1, 1963.

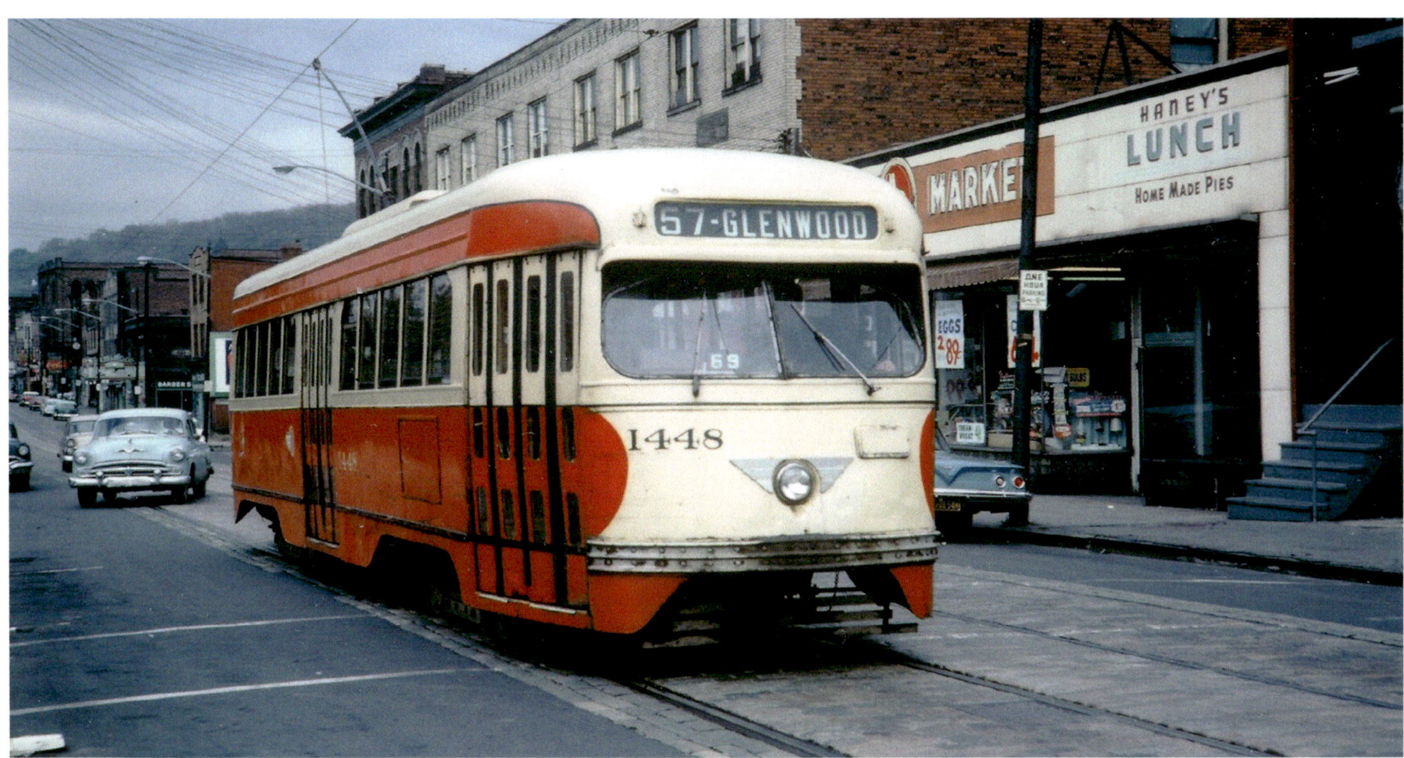

PRC rush hour Route 57 PCC car No. 1448 is on 2nd Avenue on October 21, 1962. This line was replaced by Bus Route 56D on July 5, 1964. Car No. 1448 was one of a hundred cars numbered 1400-1499 (weighing 36,080 pounds and seating fifty-six) built by St. Louis Car Company and delivered between February 1942 and May 1942. A similar Pittsburgh PCC car No. 1440 was acquired by the Seashore Trolley Museum in 1968.

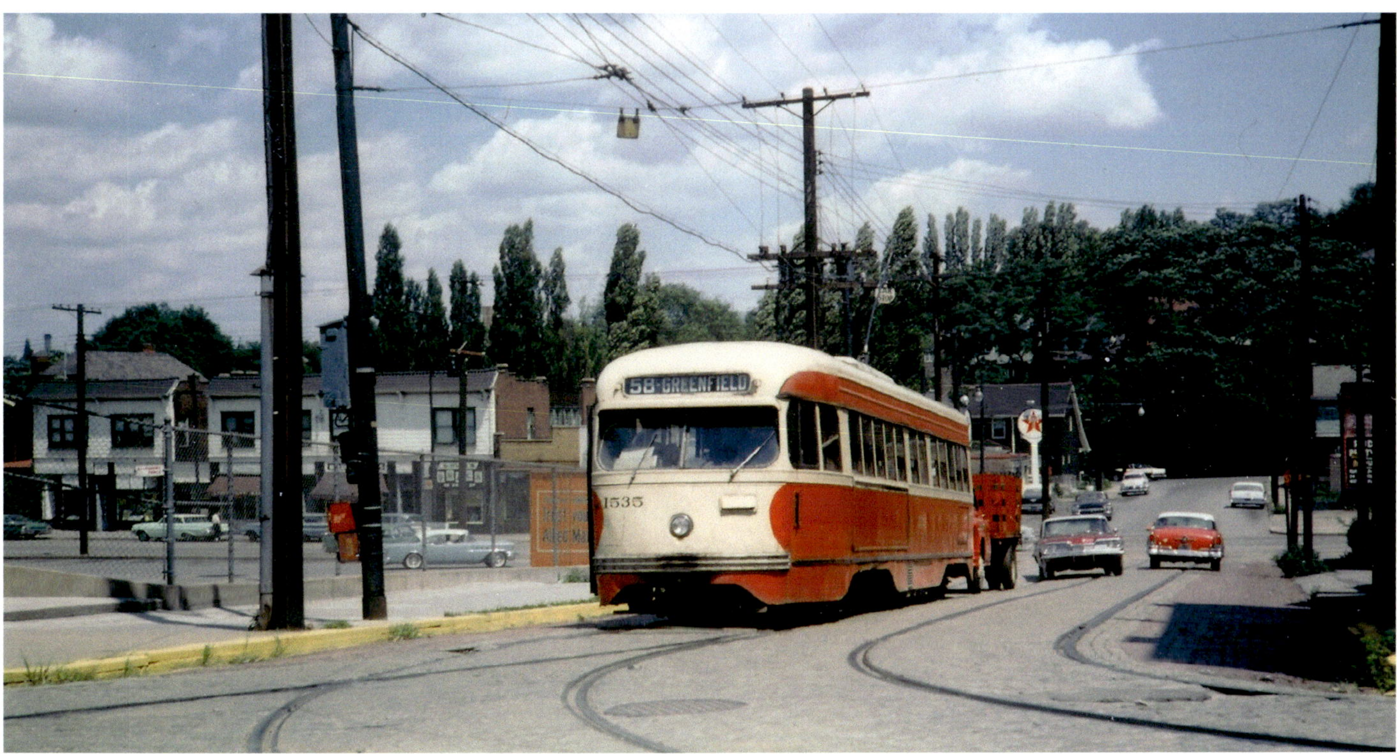

On August 4, 1963, a rail excursion is at Greenfield Avenue and Loretta Street on PRC Route 58 using PCC car No. 1535. Route 58 Greenfield was replaced by Bus Route 56E on July 5, 1964. This line entered downtown Pittsburgh along 2nd Avenue which was also used by Routes 53, 55, and 56.

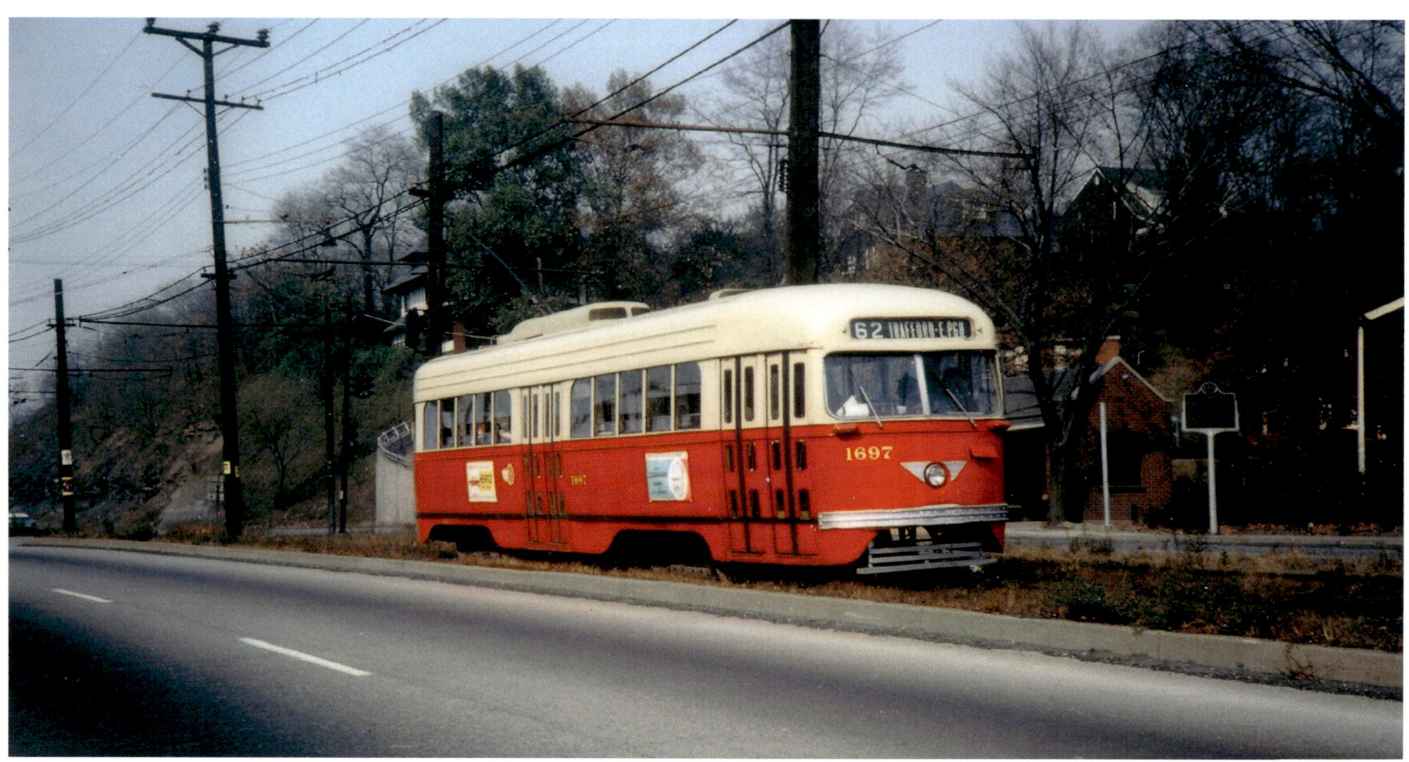

The center-of-the-road private right of way of Ardmore Boulevard provides the setting for PRC newly repainted PCC car No. 1697 with a Route 62 Trafford–E. Pittsburgh destination sign for the benefit of photographers on this October 20, 1963 rail excursion. Route 62 was abandoned on May 2, 1962.

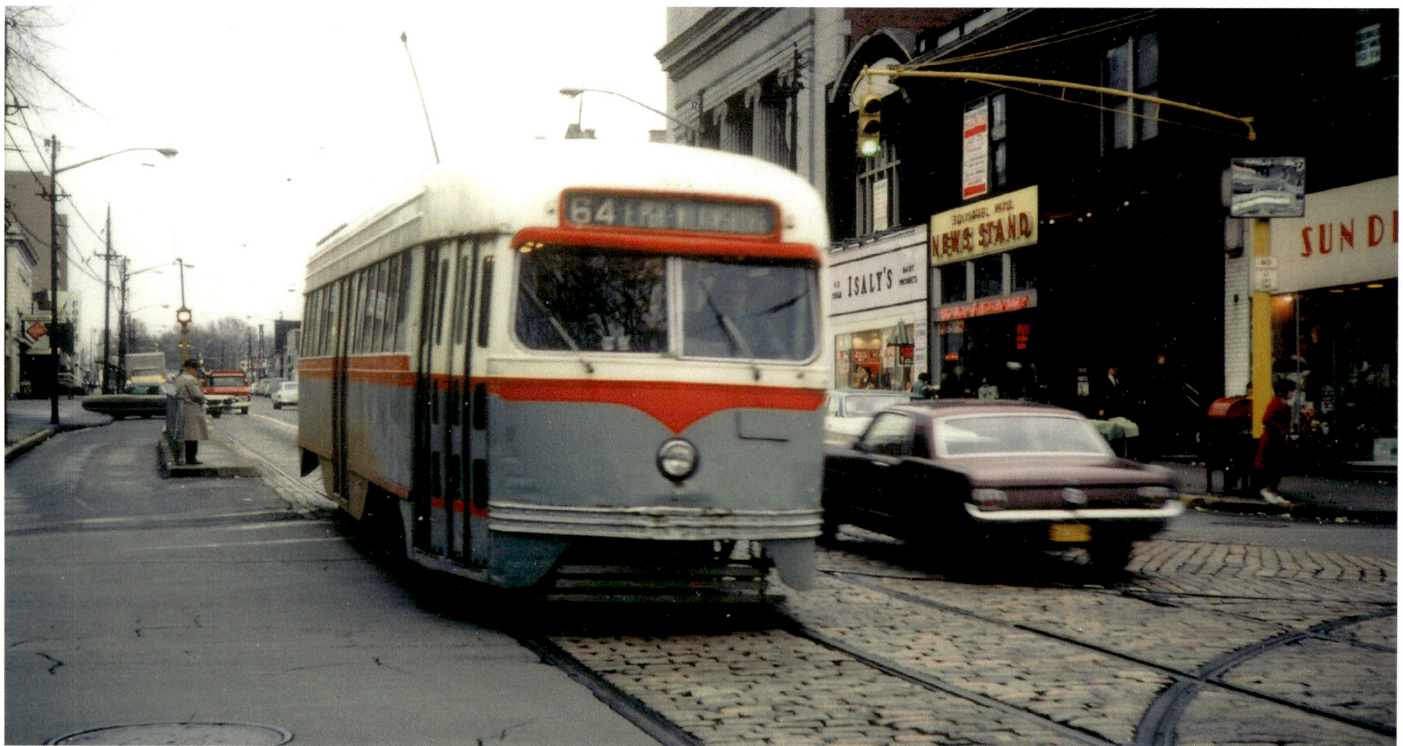

On November 8, 1966, PAT Route 64 (Wilkinsburg–East Pittsburgh) PCC car No. 1605 is on Forbes Avenue at Murray Avenue. Beginning September 4, 1966 this line operated trolley cars Monday through Friday with buses on weekends. This line, the fastest trolley route from Wilkinsburg to downtown Pittsburgh, was converted to full bus operation on January 28, 1967.

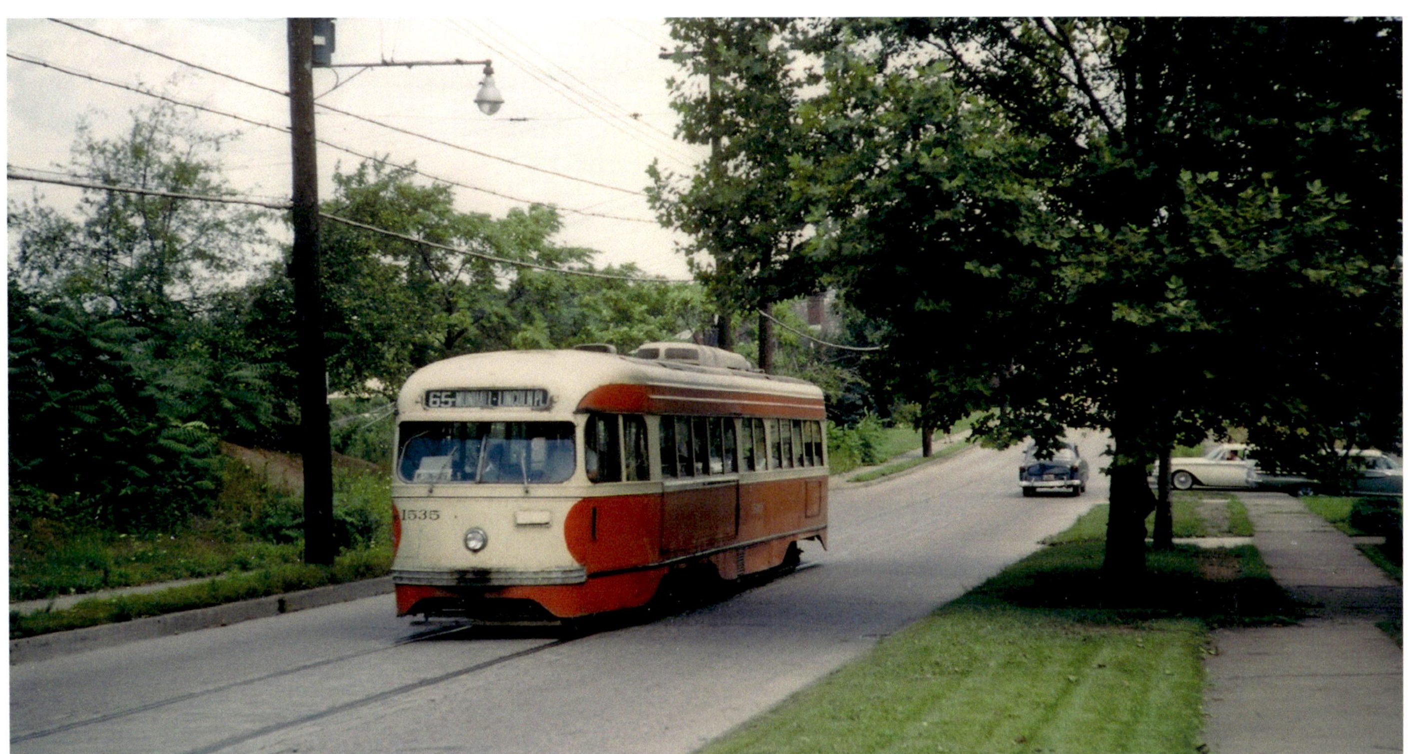

On August 4, 1963, PRC Route 65 PCC car No. 1535 is on Main Street at Brierly Lane. The line started at Munhall Loop with double track along 8th Avenue passing the Homestead steel mills, turned up Amity and entered single track with passing sidings to its terminus at Muldowney Loop. On September 5, 1965, PCC car No. 1673 made the last trolley car trip on Route 65 leaving Muldowney Loop in Lincoln Place at 12:33 a.m. and arriving at Craft Avenue Car House at 1:26 a.m.

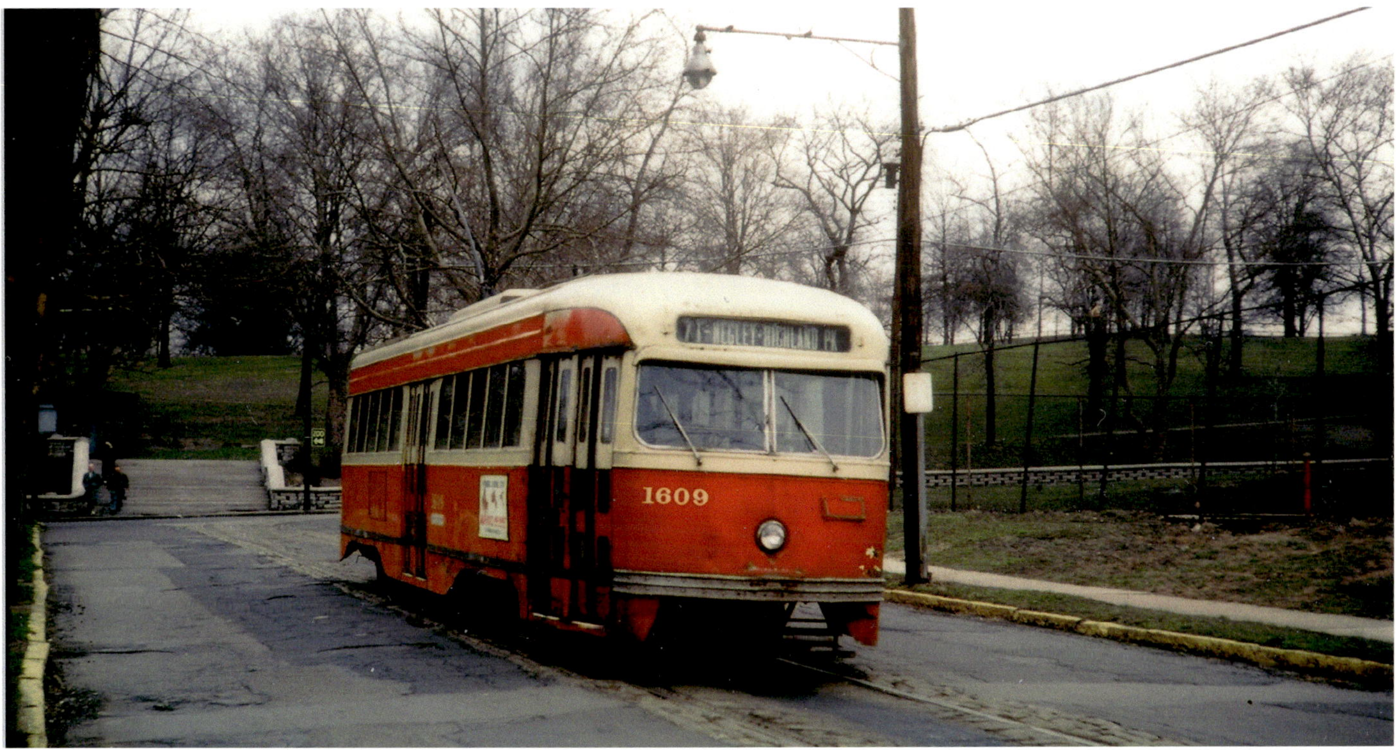

PAT Route 71 (Negley–Highland Park) PCC car No. 1609 is at Bunker Hill Street and North St. Clair Street in the Highland Park neighborhood of Pittsburgh on March 19, 1966. This line connected high density East End residential and business areas with downtown Pittsburgh. Beginning September 4, 1966, the line operated trolley cars Monday through Friday with buses on weekends. This line was converted to full bus operation on January 28, 1967.

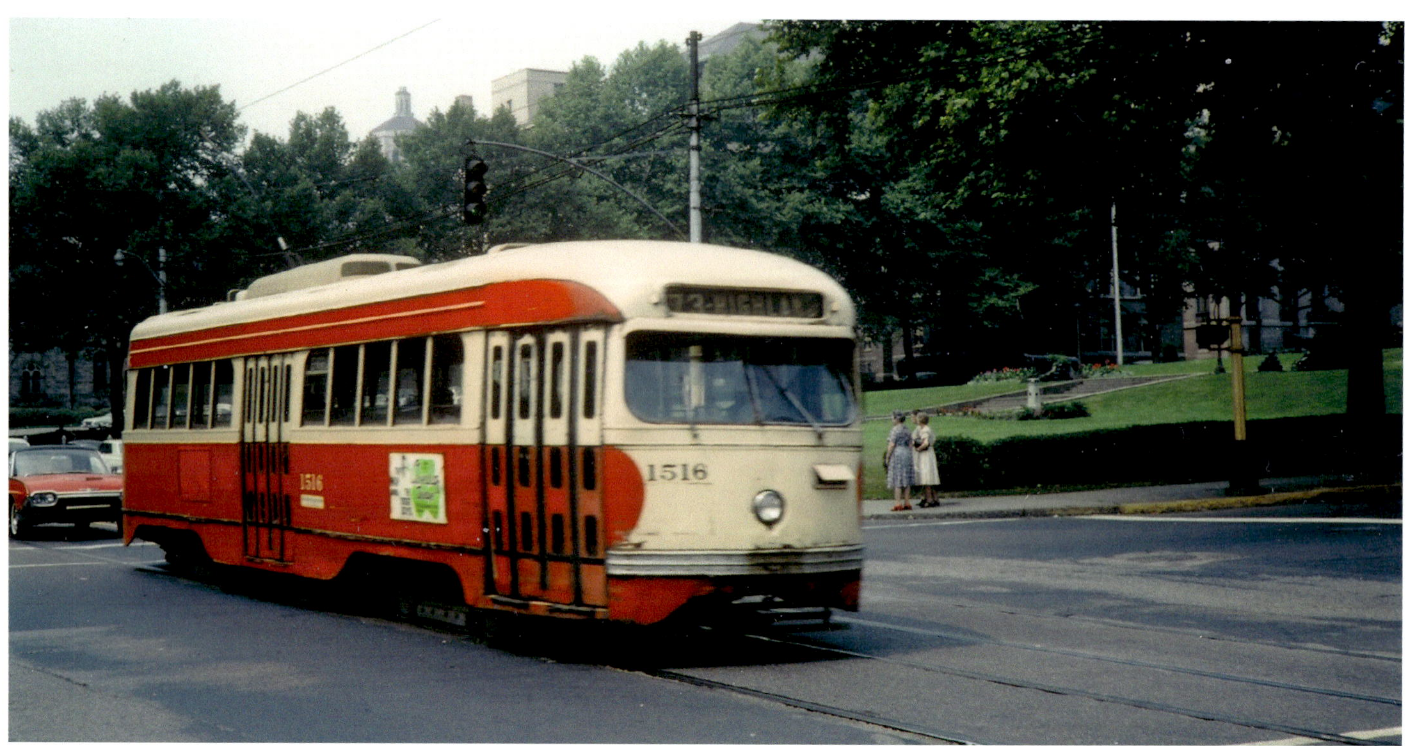

On July 24, 1964, PAT Route 73 (Highland Park) PCC car No. 1516 is on Fifth Avenue at Bigelow Boulevard in the Central Oakland neighborhood of Pittsburgh. Beginning September 4, 1966 this line operated trolley cars Monday through Friday with buses on weekends. This line was converted to full bus operation on January 28, 1967.

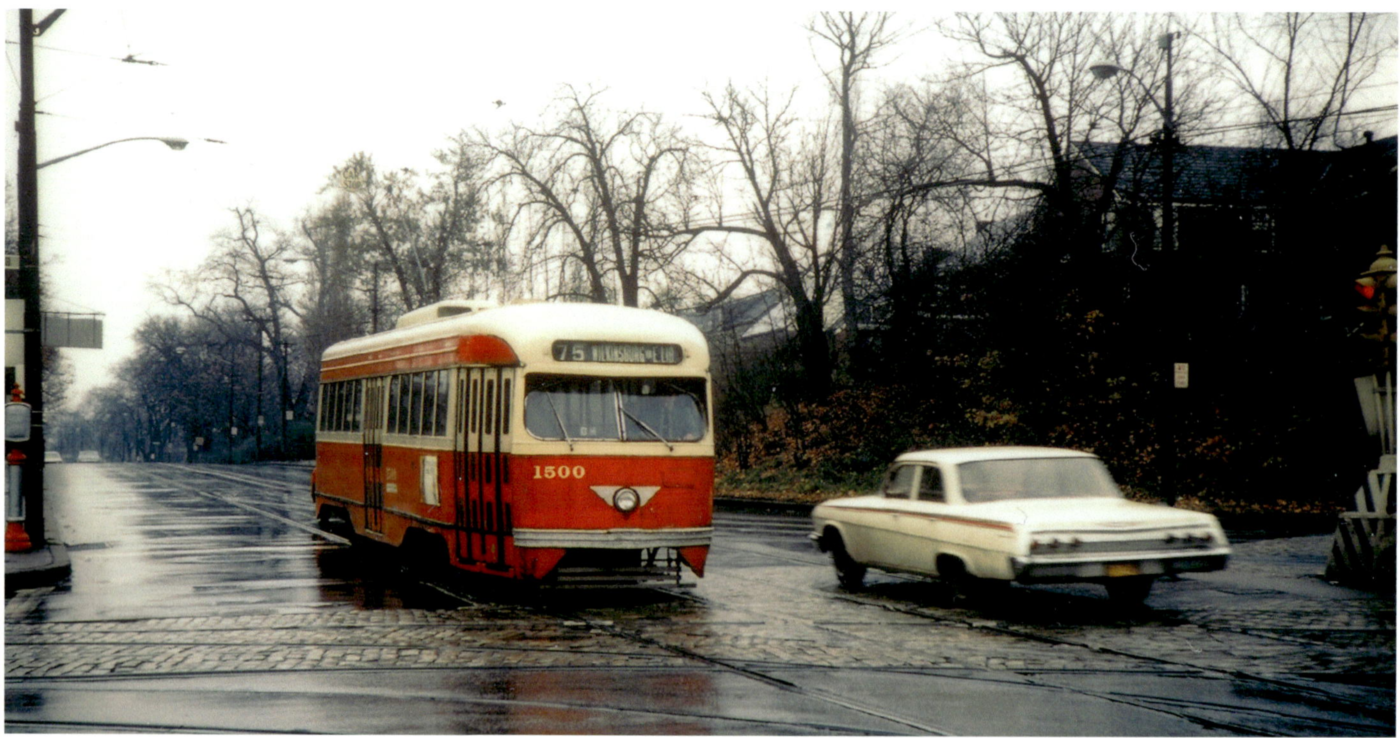

On a rainy November 8, 1966, PAT Route 75 (East Liberty–Wilkinsburg) PCC car No. 1500 is on Penn Avenue at 5th Avenue crossing Route 76 trolley car line. Beginning September 4, 1966, this line operated trolley cars Monday through Friday with buses on weekends. This line was converted to full bus operation on January 28, 1967.

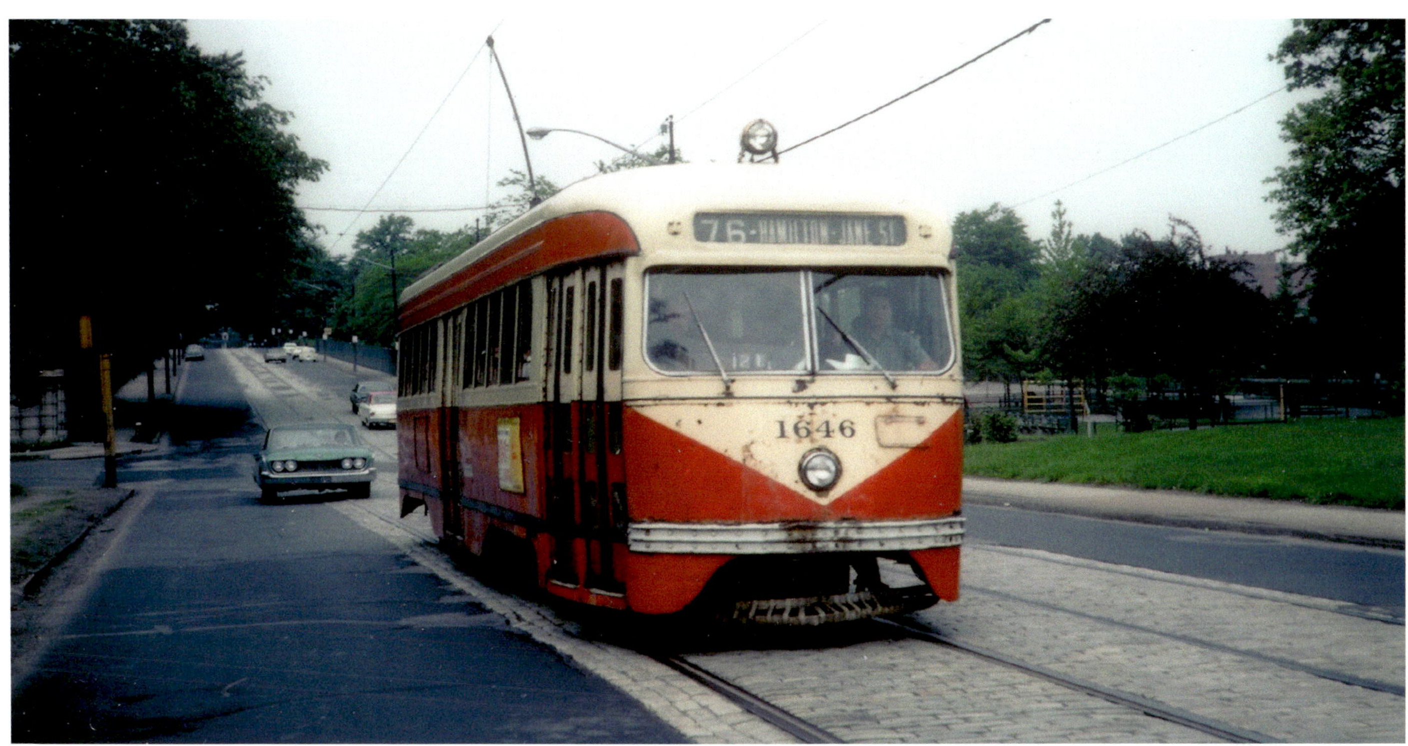

PAT Route 76 (Hamilton) PCC car No. 1646 is on 5th Avenue south of Penn Avenue on May 26, 1968. This car had a "V" shaped area in the center in cream and the remainder in red, car number centered above the headlight in black, and the headlight wings were removed. Beginning September 4, 1966, Route 76 operated trolley cars Monday through Friday with buses on weekends. The line was converted to full bus operation on January 28, 1967.

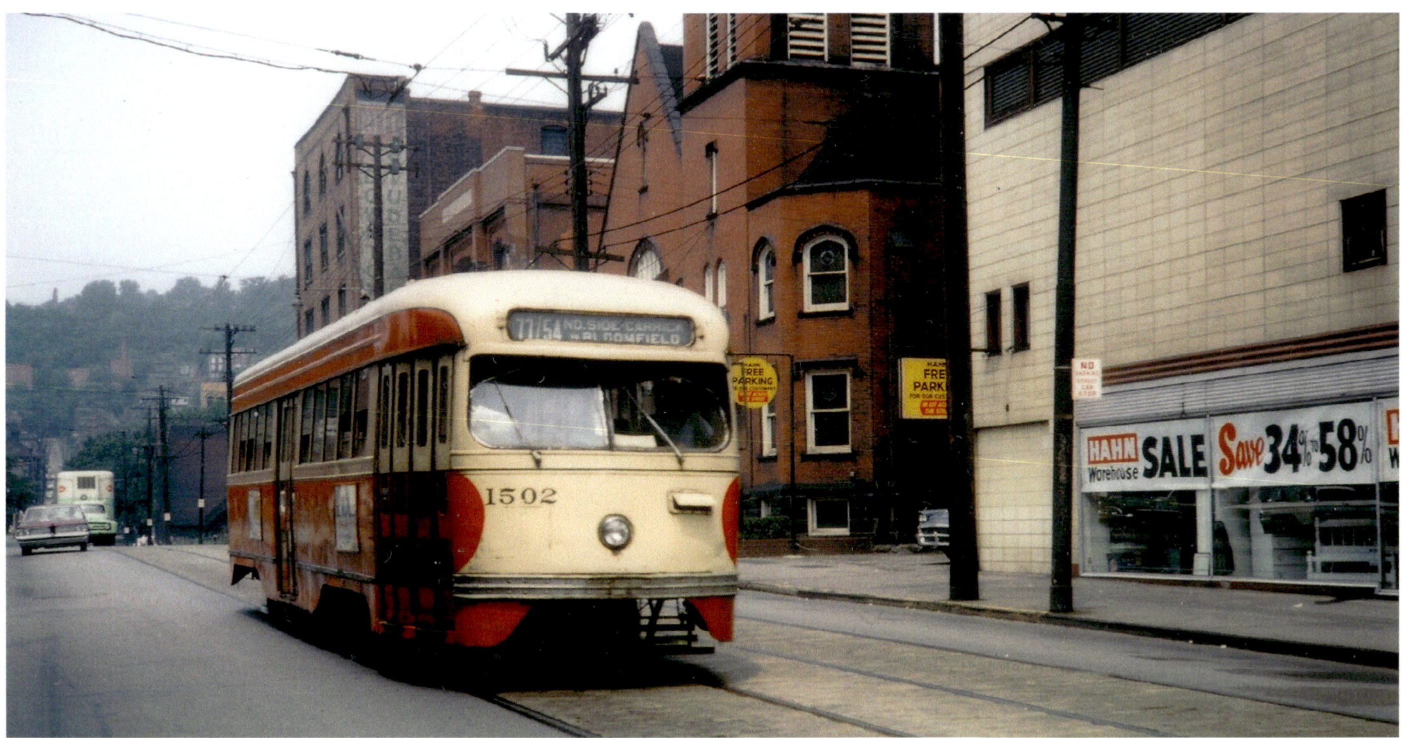

On July 23, 1964, PAT Route 77/54 (North Side–Carrick via Bloomfield) PCC car No. 1502 is at Sandusky Street and E. Ohio Street on the North Side. This line started on the North Side at Robinson and Sandusky Streets and traveled over double track in city streets using the 16th Street Bridge over the Allegheny River and the 22nd Street Bridge over the Monongahela River to reach Brentwood Loop on the South Side. The last trolley car trip on Route 77/54 was made by PCC car No. 1438 which left Robinson and Sandusky on the North Side at 2:00 a.m. on September 5, 1965, Route 77/54 was now a bus line.

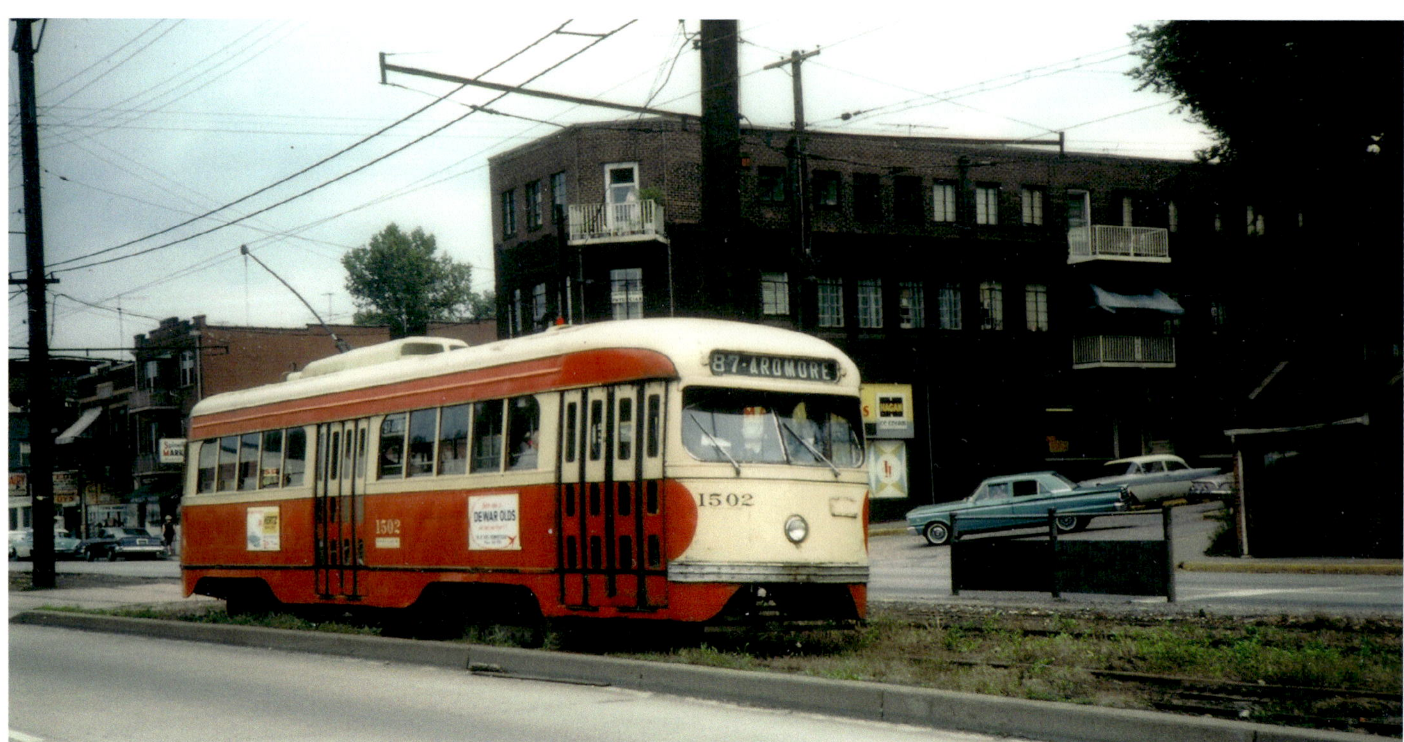

PAT Route 87 PCC car No. 1502 is on the center-of-the-road private right of way, Ardmore Boulevard at Summer Avenue, on August 23, 1964 in the borough of Forest Hills in the eastern suburbs of Pittsburgh. The outer end of this line was cutback from Wilmerding to Wilkinsburg on September 4, 1966, and the line now only operated trolley cars Monday through Friday with buses on weekends. This line was converted to full bus operation on January 28, 1967.

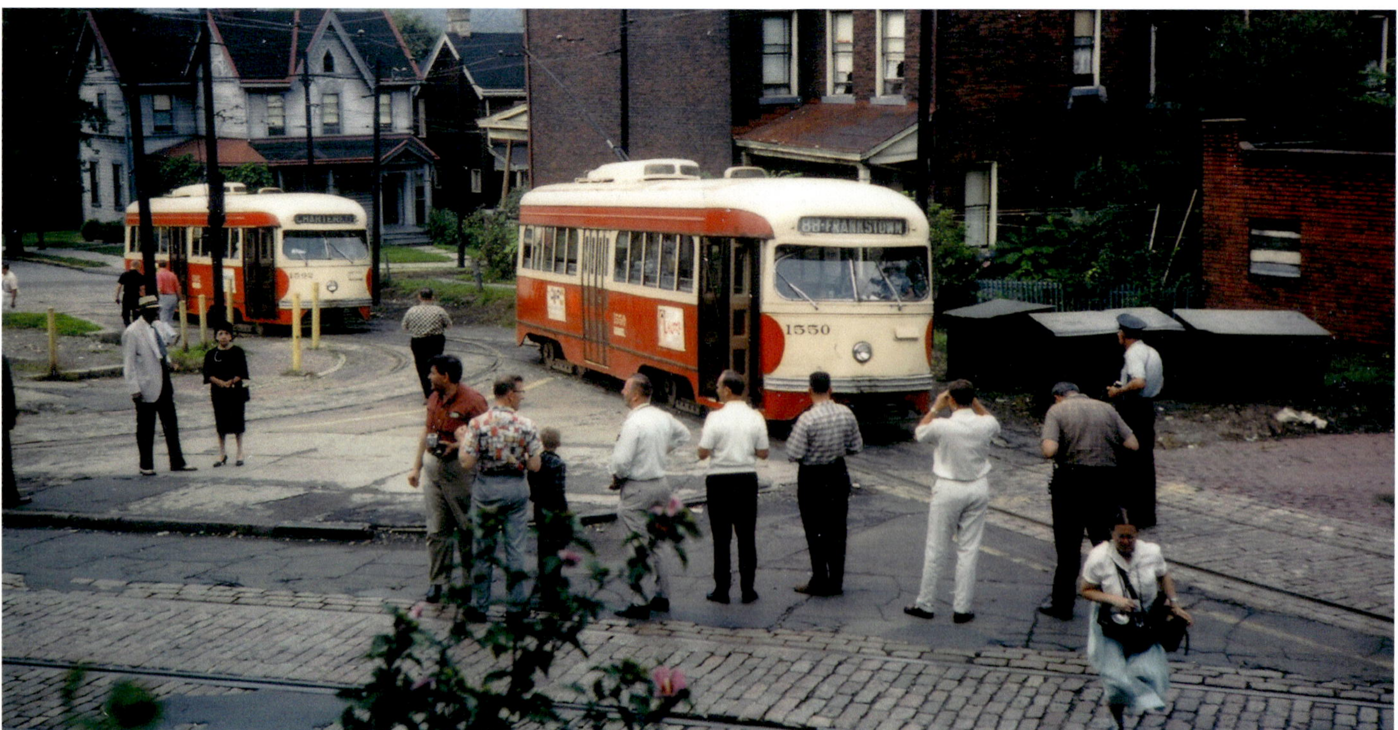

On August 23, 1964, PAT Route 88 PCC car No. 1550 with PCC car No. 1502 behind it on a rail excursion charter trip are at the Tioga Loop. This loop was a full circle formed by Tioga Street behind car No. 1502 and Oakwood Street in the lower portion of the picture, and it provided a convenient photo stop for the group of rail enthusiasts. Effective September 4, 1966, the line operated trolley cars Monday through Friday with buses on weekends. This line was converted to full bus operation on January 28, 1967.

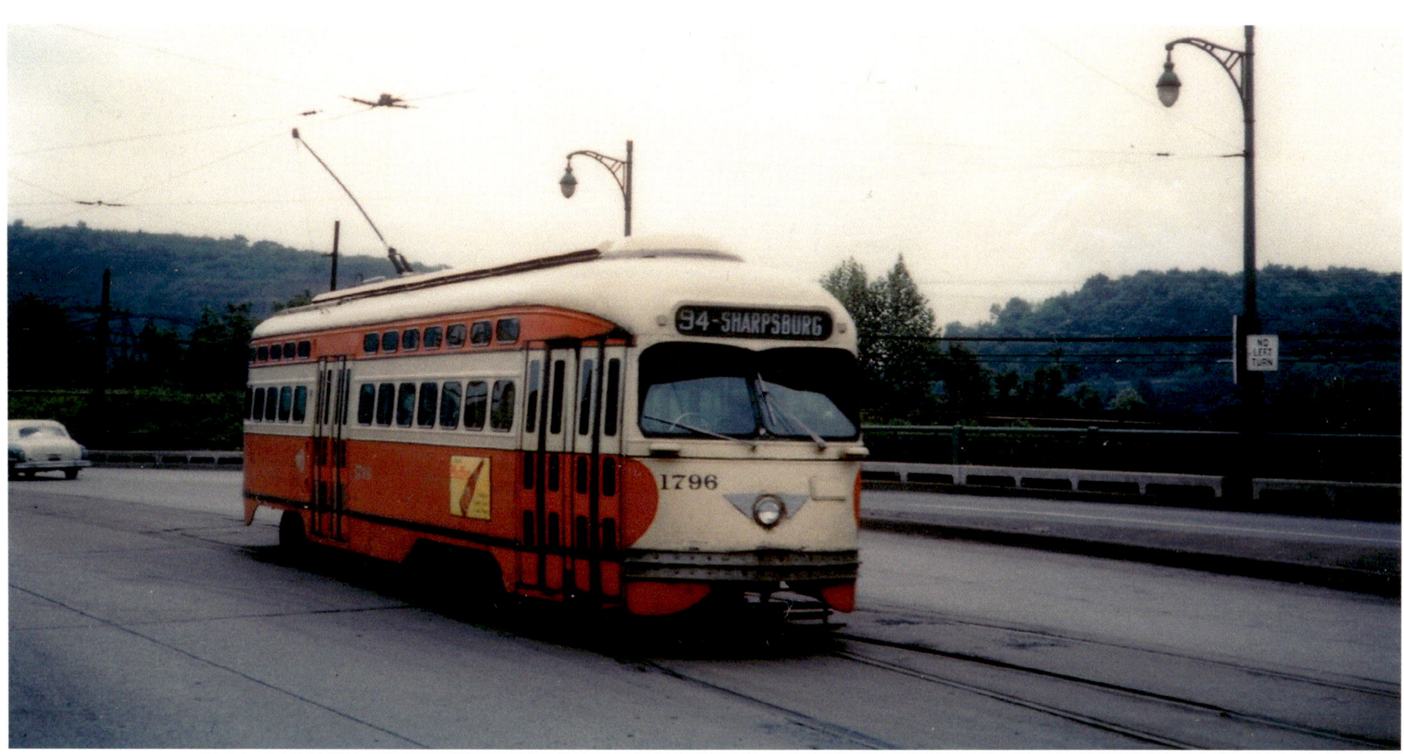

Highland Park Bridge is the location of PRC Route 94 PCC car No. 1796 on May 29, 1960. On November 12, 1960, trolley car service was discontinued on Routes 94 (Aspinwall), 95 (Butler Street), and 96 (E. Liberty–E. 62nd Street).

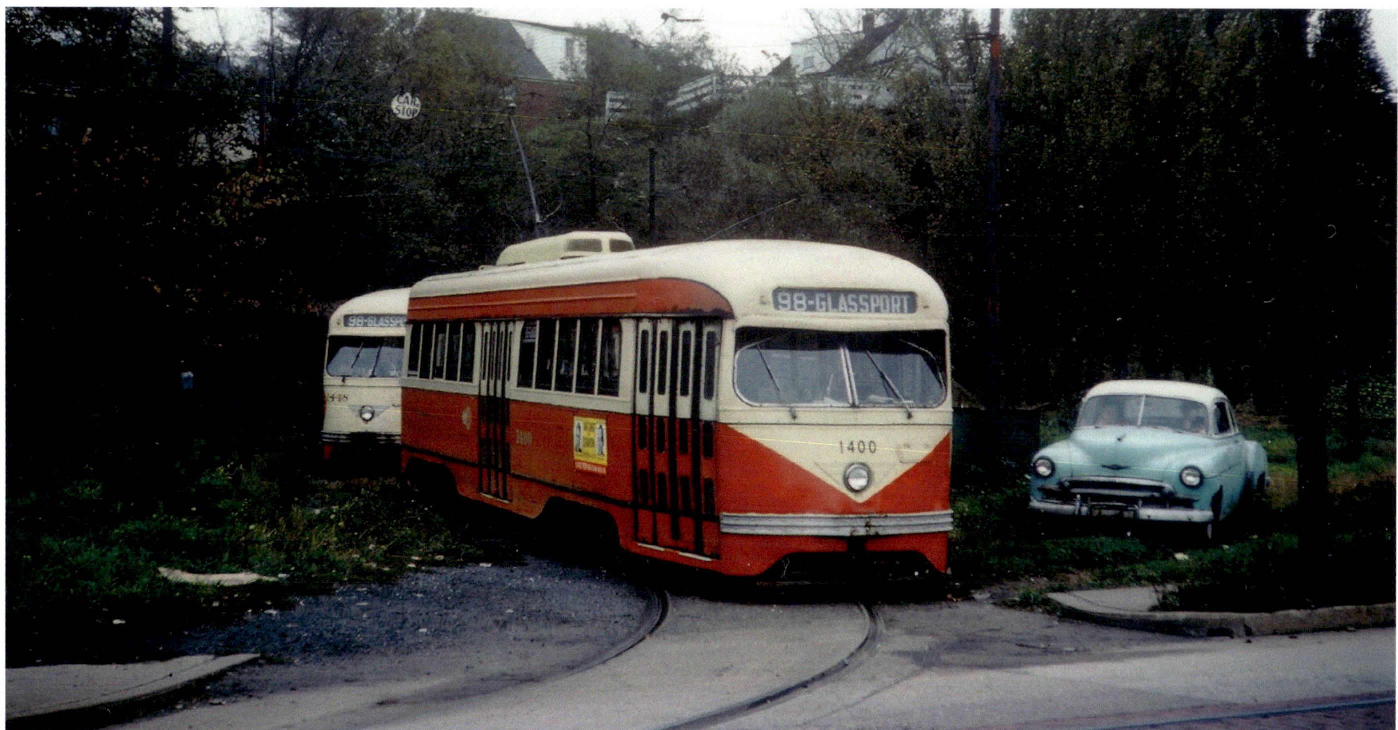

PRC Route 98 PCC cars Nos. 1400 and 1448 are at the Glassport Loop on October 21, 1962. The borough of Glassport located along the east side of the Monongahela River has suffered a severe economic decline like many communities in the "Mon Valley" with a population decline from 8,748 in 1940 to 4,483 as of the 2010 census. On August 3, 1963, a tornado struck Glassport with high winds damaging the overhead wire of Route 98 ending trolley car service, and the eighty foot tower of the United States Glass Company collapsed, shutting down the furnaces. The liquid glass cooled leaving a 250 ton block of glass too costly to rebuild.

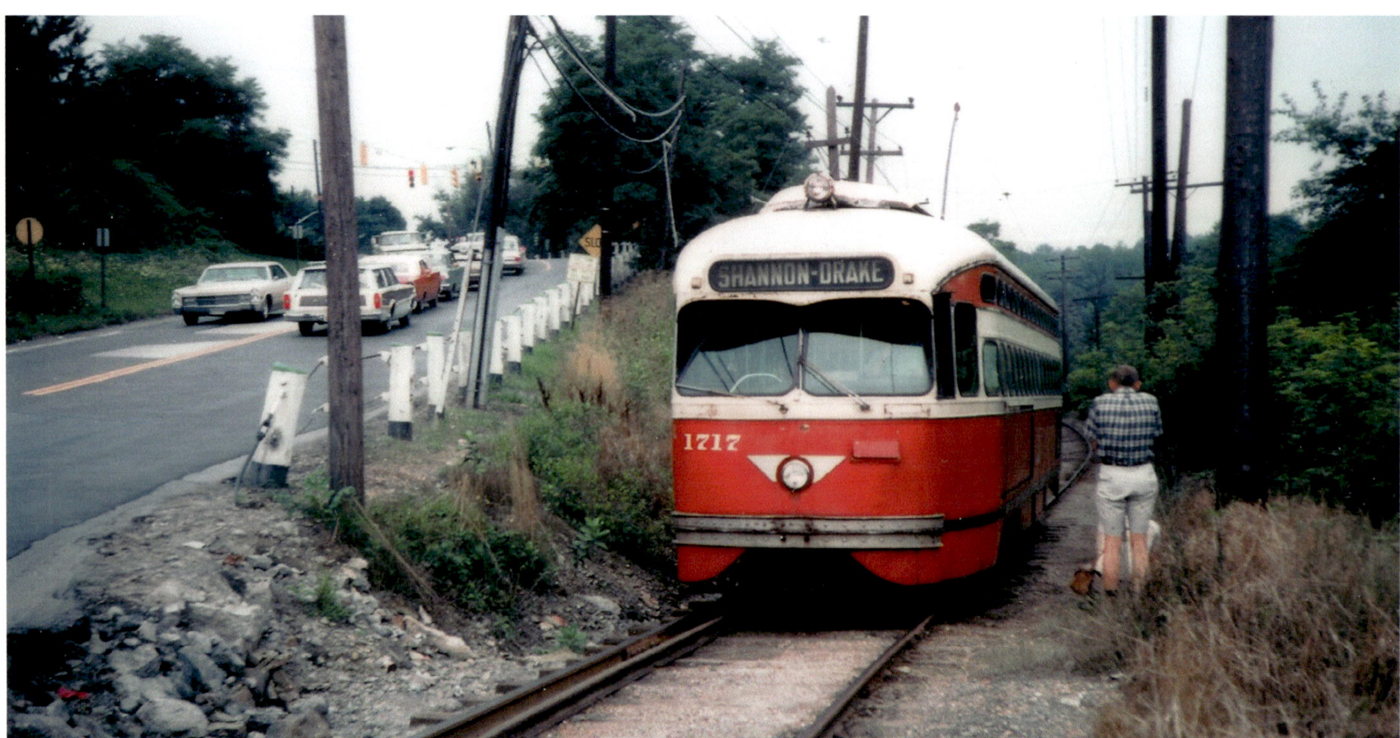

On August 10, 1968, PAT silver winged PCC car No. 1717 is at the Fort Couch Road crossing on the Shannon Drake Line in the Municipality of Bethel Park south of Pittsburgh. The Drake Line was originally built in 1909 as part of the line from Pittsburgh to Washington, Pennsylvania. In August 29, 1953 it was cut back to the Allegheny County Line at Drake and became Route 36 (Shannon–Drake). In 1984 the Drake Line from Castle Shannon to Dorchester was upgraded with double track and a short spur was built from Dorchester to South Hills Village. The outer portion of the Drake Line from Dorchester to Drake remained in service.

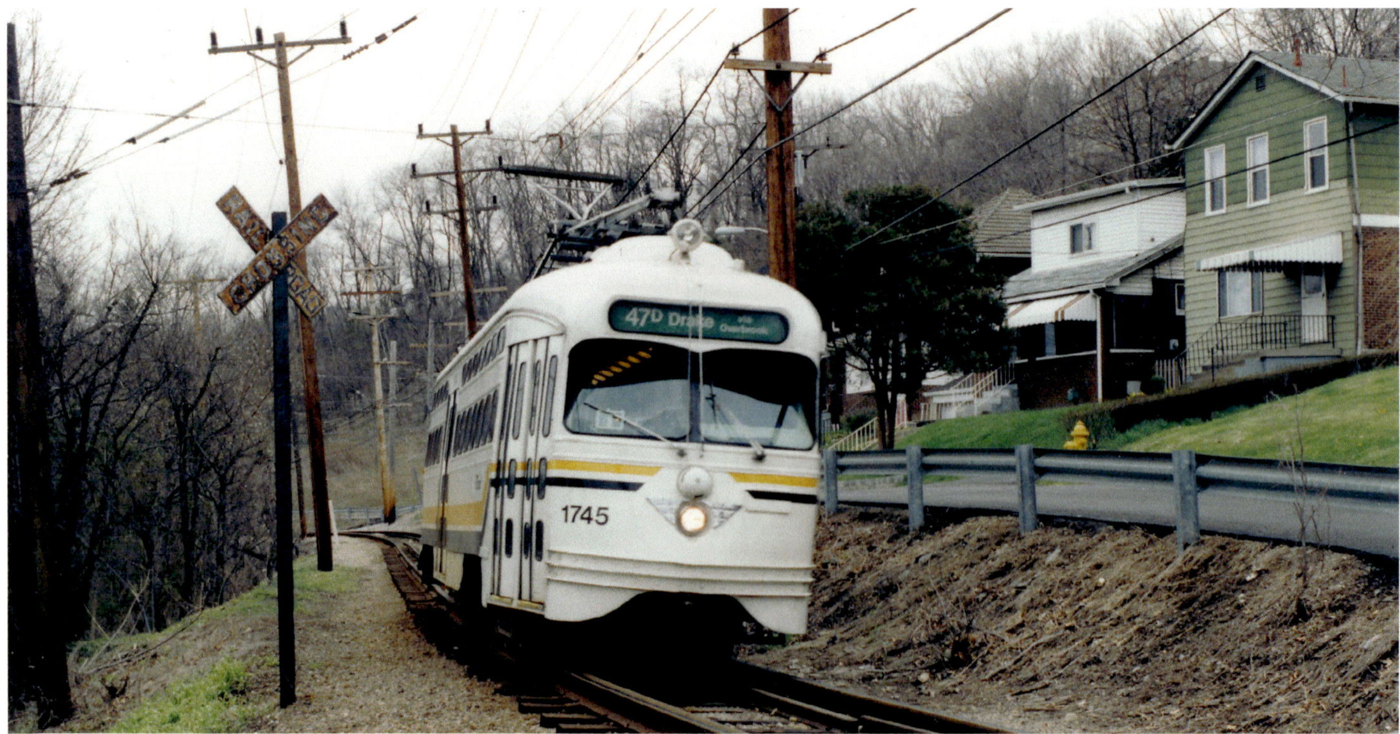

PAT Route 47D (Drake via Overbrook) car No. 1745 is ready to cross Smith Road in the borough of Castle Shannon south of Pittsburgh on April 14, 1990. After 1993, Route 47D operated as a shuttle between Castle Shannon and Drake. Passengers transferred between 47D and either 42L or 42S at Castle Shannon or Washington Junction to travel to or from downtown Pittsburgh. Trolley car service on Route 47D was discontinued on September 4, 1999.

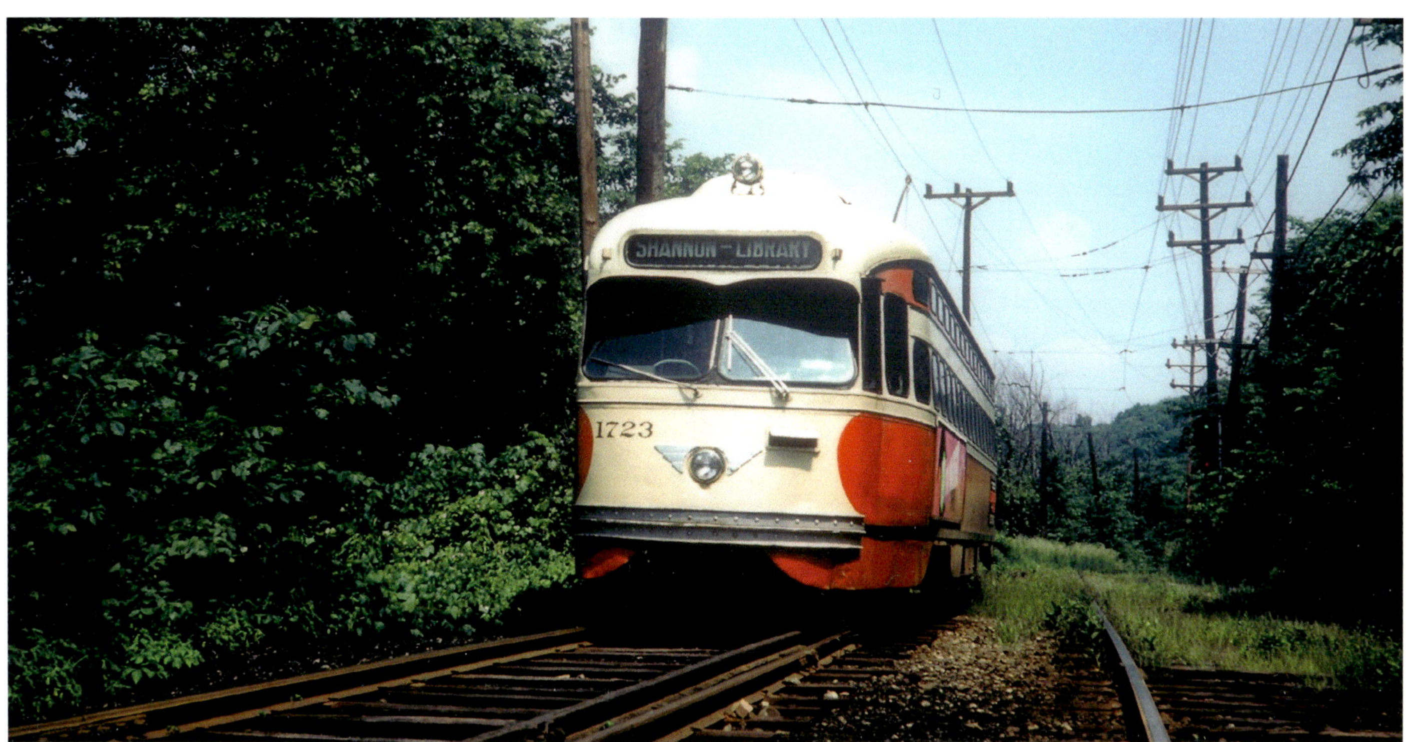

On June 11, 1961, PCC car No. 1723, in the familiar PRC paint scheme, is approaching the Hillcrest station stop in this wooded area on the Library Line. This line opened to Roscoe on June 10, 1910 and was cut back to Library on June 28, 1953. The line to Washington, Pennsylvania, was also cut back on August 29, 1953 to Drake, and a new loop was built at Drake.

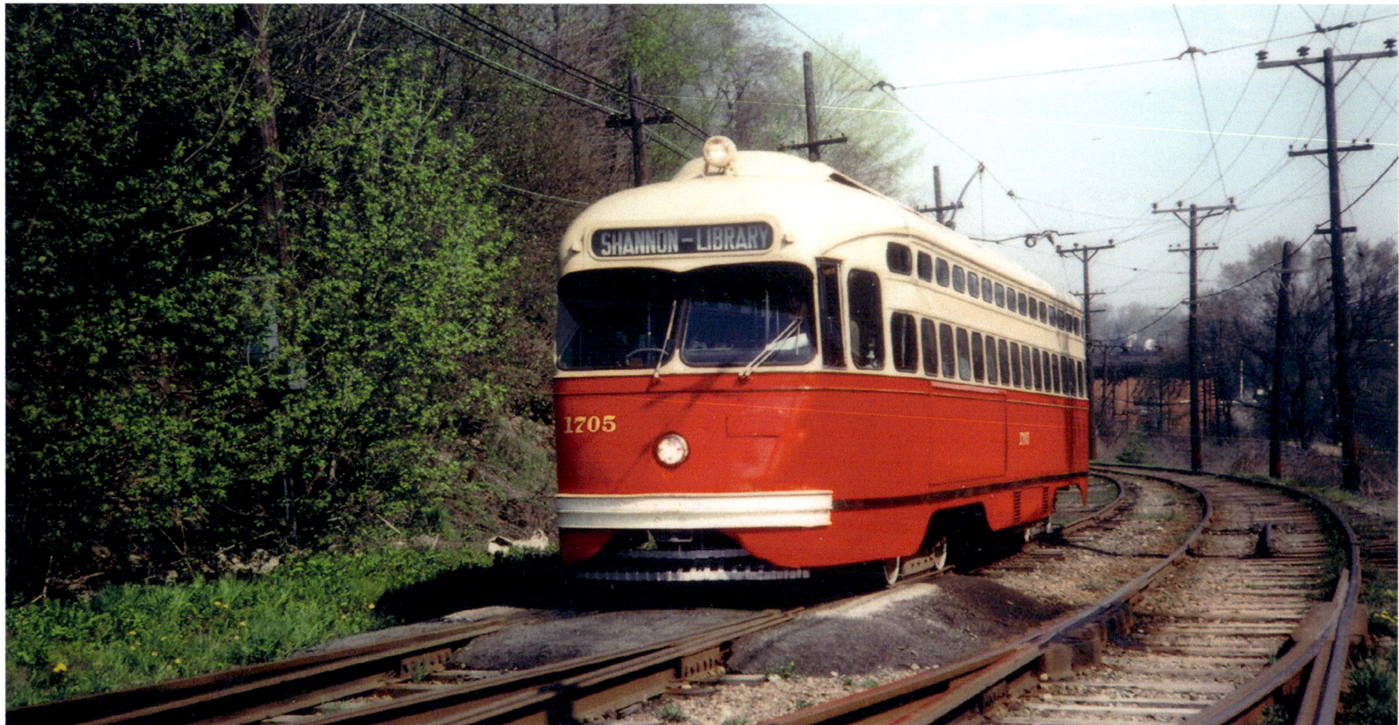

PRC smartly repainted PCC car No. 1705 is at Washington Junction where the Drake Line splits off to the left, and the car signed "Shannon Library" will go straight on April 21, 1963.

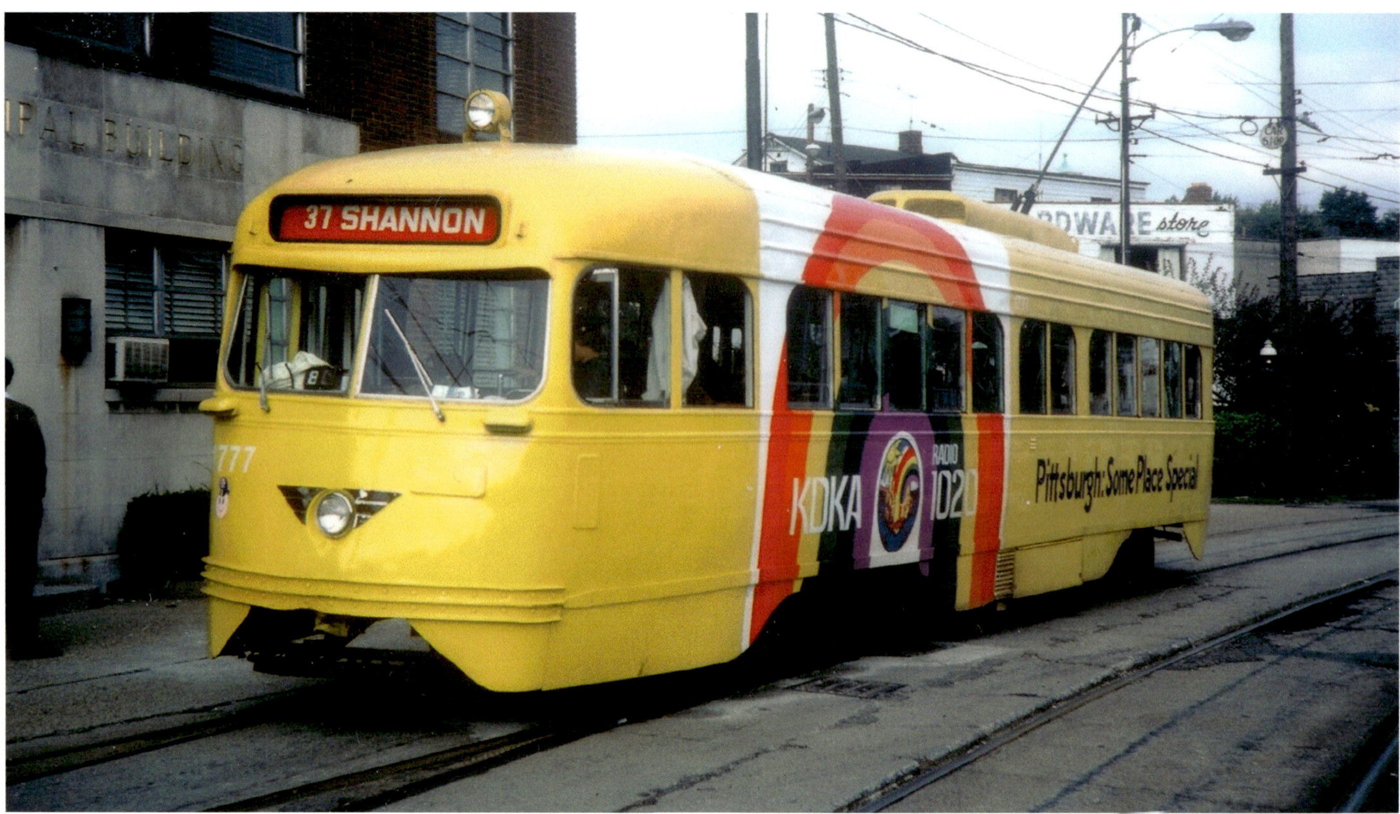

Featuring a colorful radio station advertisement, PAT Route 37 PCC car No. 1777 is at Castle Shannon on September 22, 1974. This car was rehabilitated from car No. 1615.

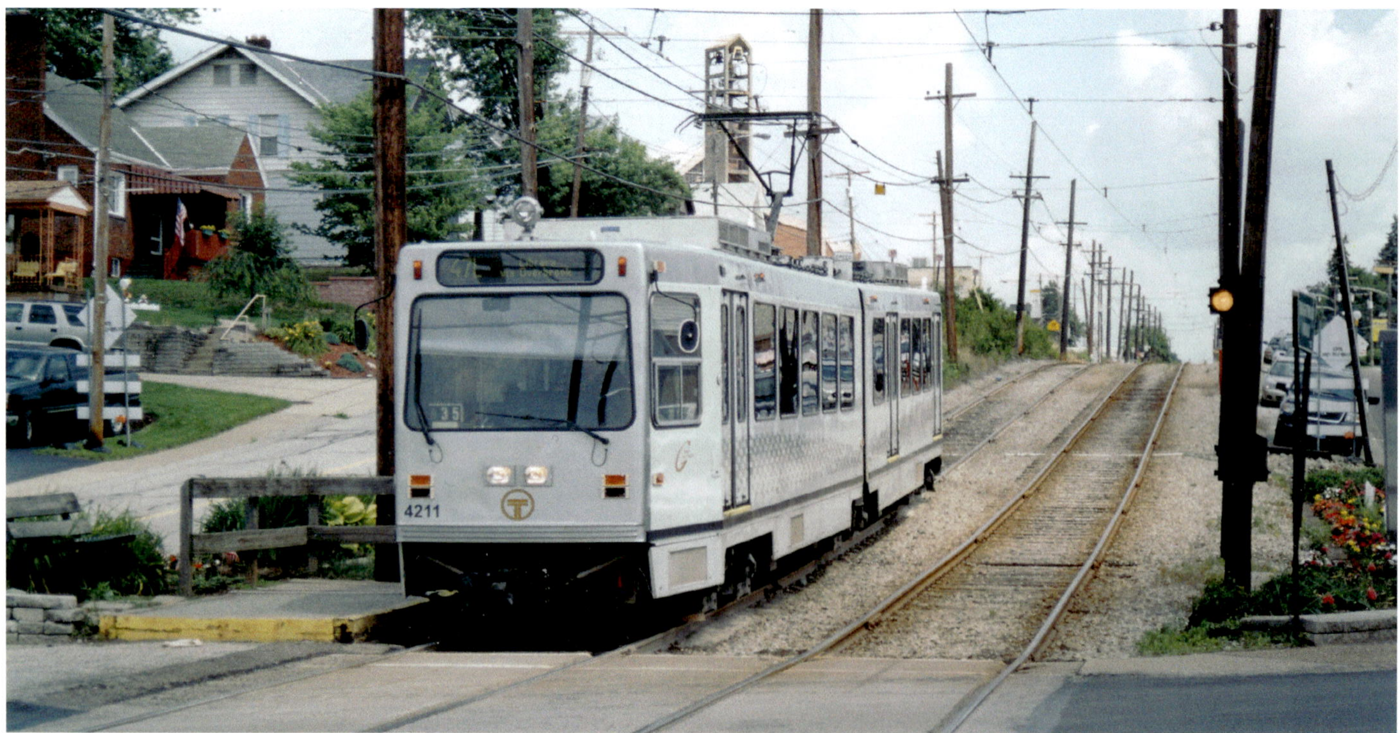

On June 30, 2006, PAT Route 47L (Library) light rail vehicle car No. 4211 is at South Park Road in Bethel Park. This was one of fifty-five model SD-400 cars numbered 4101-4155 built by Siemens Transportation Systems during 1985-1987. They were rebuilt by Construcciones y Auxiliar de Ferrocarriles (CAF) during 2005-2006 and renumbered 4201-4255. The line from South Hills Junction via Overbrook to Castle Shannon that was used by Library cars was rebuilt and opened on June 2, 2004.

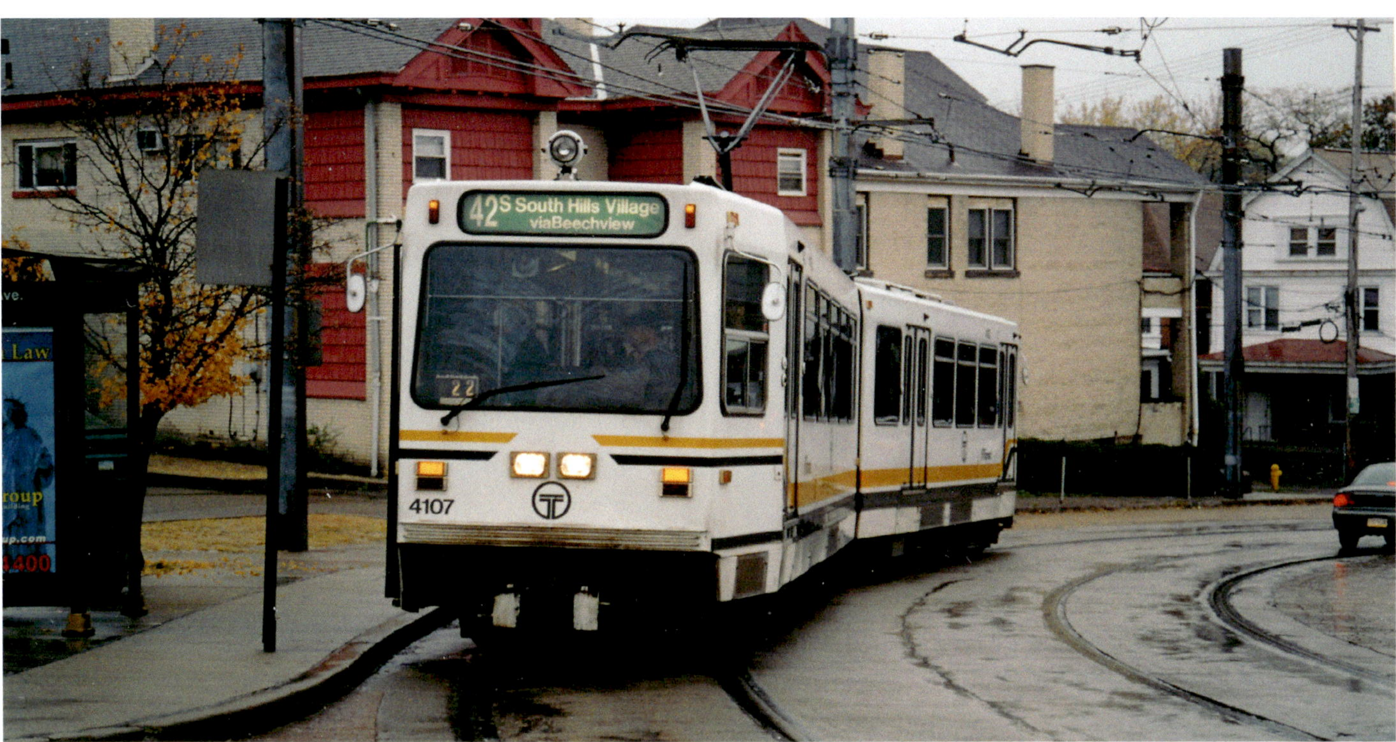

A rainy November 8, 2005 finds PAT Route 42S light rail vehicle car No. 4107 rounding the curve on Broadway Avenue at Coast Avenue in the Beechview neighborhood in the southwestern part of Pittsburgh on June 30, 2006. The first modern light rail cars began operation from South Hills Village to Castle Shannon on April 15, 1984 with the 1.1 mile downtown subway added to the system on July 3, 1985. The modern suburban "Beechview" Line (from Castle Shannon to South Hills Junction via Mt. Lebanon and Beechview) opened on May 22, 1987 completing PAT's 10.5 mile Stage I Light Rail Transit project.

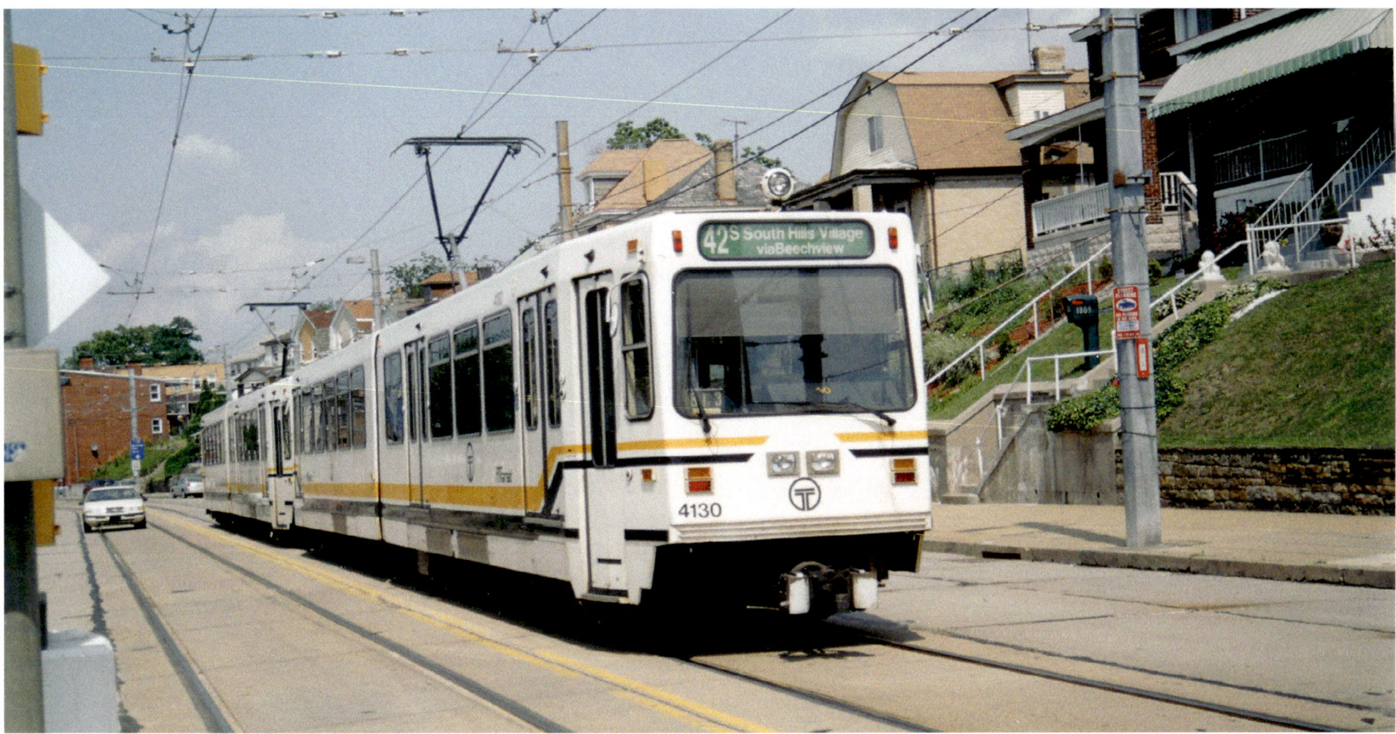

PAT Route 42S light rail vehicle car No. 4130 is on Broadway Avenue at Belasco Avenue in the Beechview neighborhood of Pittsburgh on June 30, 2006. This neighborhood has benefitted by its proximity to downtown Pittsburgh and its convenient access by trolley car now also known as light rail transit.

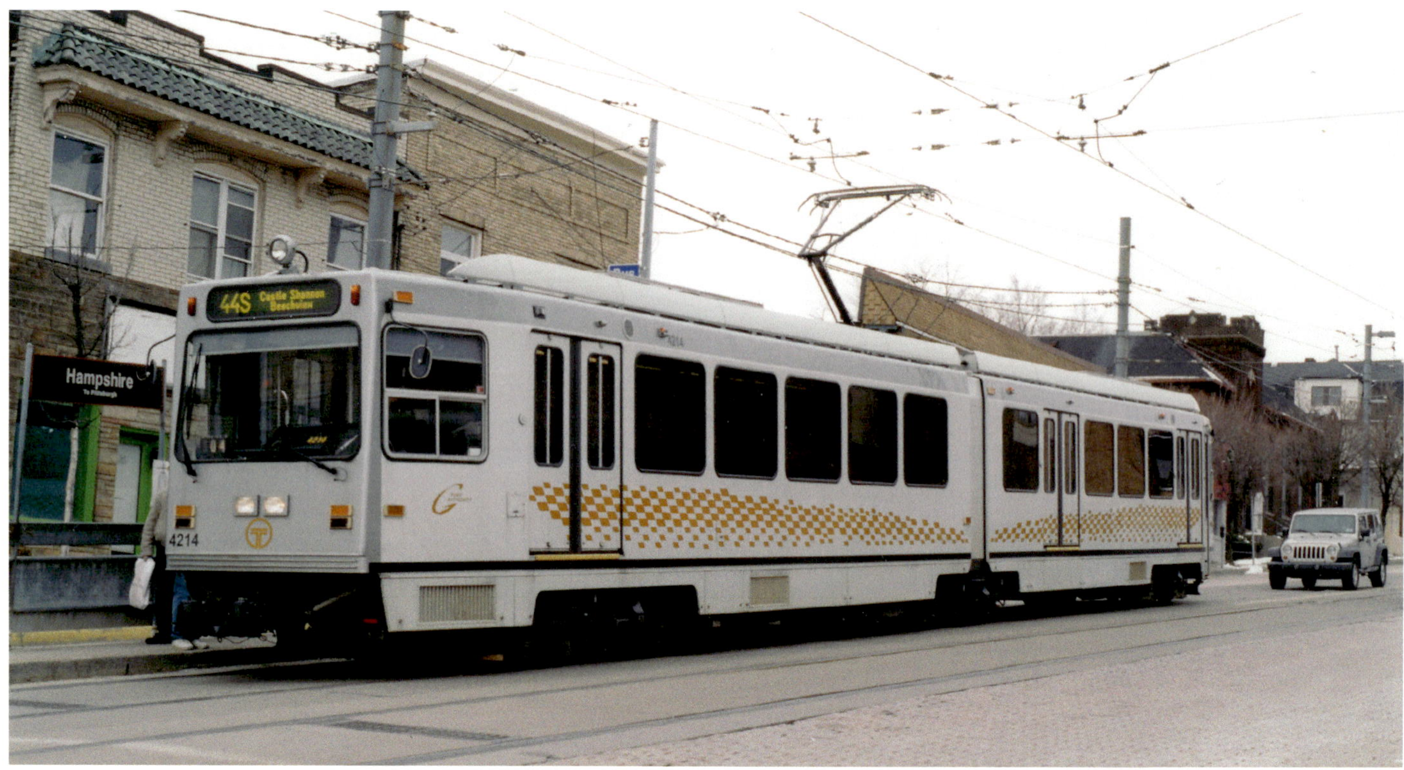

On March 19, 2007, PAT Route 44S light rail vehicle car No. 4214 on Broadway Avenue at Hampshire Avenue was running between Castle Shannon and Beechview as a shuttle service because the closure of the Palm Garden Bridge cut off the Beechview Line from downtown Pittsburgh. The 44S was discontinued when the Palm Garden Bridge re-opened on September 2, 2007.

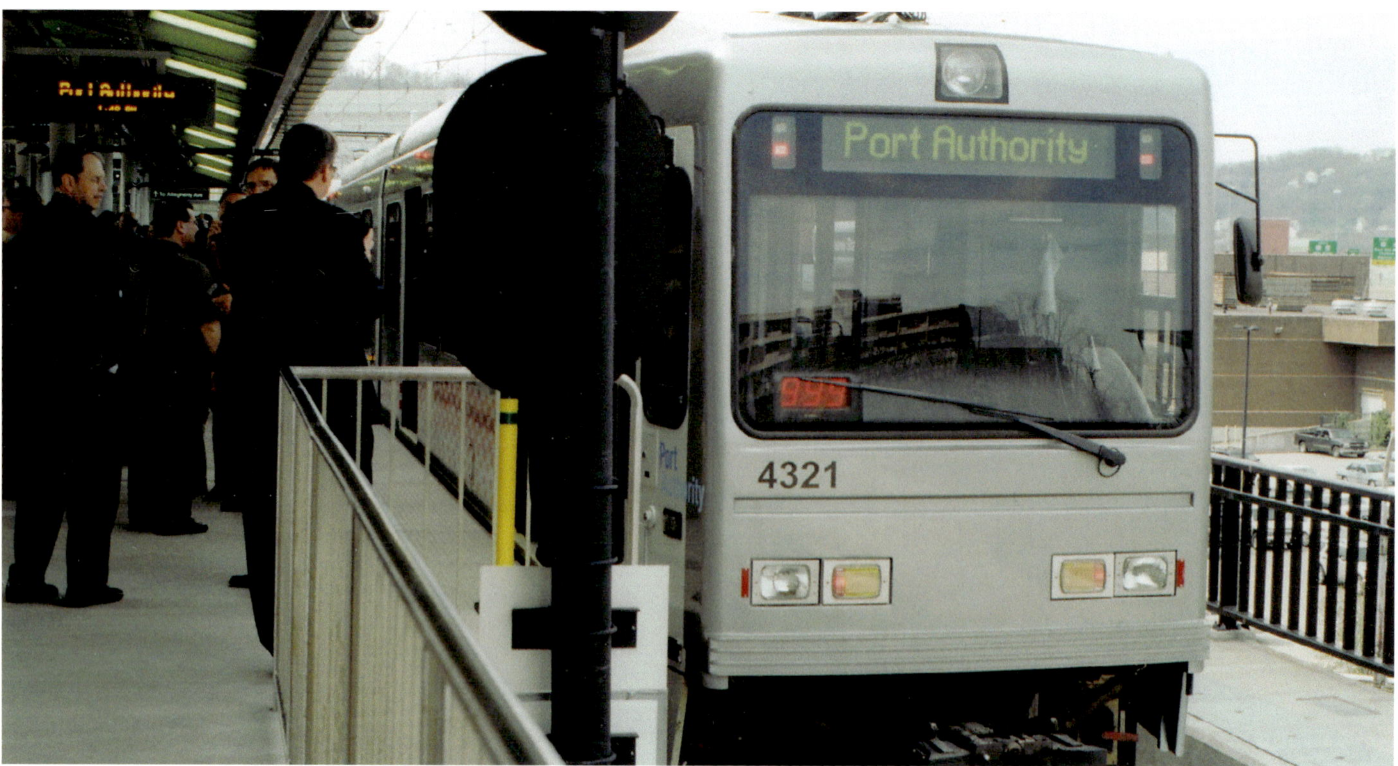

On the March 23, 2012 opening day of the North Side Connector, PAT light rail vehicle car No. 4321 is at the Allegheny Station. This car was one of twenty-eight numbered 4301-4328 built by CAF during 2003-2004. The Port Authority began construction of the North Side Connector in October 2006, with the first bore completed on July 10, 2008 and the second tunnel under the Allegheny River completed in 2009. Service began on March 25, 2012 with a final cost of $523.4 million.

Chapter 4

Harmony and Mars Routes

There were two interurban trolley lines between Pittsburgh and Butler. On March 9, 1905, several Pittsburgh entrepreneurs organized the Pittsburgh, Harmony, Butler & New Castle Railway Company to build a line from Pittsburgh to Butler and New Castle, and it became known as the Harmony Route. Russell H. Boggs was elected president of the company and was part owner along with Henry Buhl of the Boggs and Buhl department store in Pittsburgh. After the store opened, Boggs, using a horse-drawn wagon, became a traveling salesman from Pittsburgh stopping in Evans City, Prospect, Portersville, and at various farms along the way for the three-day round trip back to the store. During the trip he delivered products and took orders for the next trip. He also purchased everything from eggs to homemade items which he sold at the store or to others along the trip. His years of friendly contact made it possible for him to acquire the right of way needed for the new trolley line. Each property owner was given a dollar, and the promise of a station with the owner's name on it as well as on the route map. Construction began in 1905 starting from Pittsburgh. Local labor by pick and shovel did the excavation and some cuts were made with a horse-drawn scoop. Where needed large rocks were dynamited.

After track was laid, a small rail car was used for installing the poles and to string the overhead electric wire. With improved lighting in the summer of 1907, crews worked around the clock. The line was completed to Butler and New Castle in May 1908. A test run was made from the Harmony Carbarn to Ellwood City on July 2, 1908. Hundreds of people greeted the official opening of the line when the first car arrived in Ellwood City on July 23, 1908. Four months later, the line was completed to Pittsburgh. It was now possible to travel from Fairchance in southwestern Pennsylvania via Pittsburgh and New Castle in Pennsylvania; Youngstown, Akron, Cleveland, Sandusky, and Lima in Ohio; Fort Wayne, Peru, South Bend and Gary in Indiana; Chicago and Waukegan in Illinois; and Milwaukee to Elkhart Lake, Wisconsin by trolley car. The Harmony Route used Pittsburgh Railways track and then proceeded on its own track through Ross, Ingomar, Warrendale, to Evans City where one branch headed northeast via Connoquenessing, Meridian, and Lyndora to Butler. The other branch went northwest via Harmony, Zelienople and Ellwood City to New Castle. In January 1915, trolley car service began from Ellwood City to Beaver Falls.

Trolley car service began in Butler on August 20, 1900 and the trolley company opened Alameda Park, an amusement park served by the trolley system in 1903. On April 24, 1907, the Pittsburgh & Butler Street Railway Company opened a direct line between Pittsburgh and Butler which became known as the Mars Route. Leaving Main Street in downtown Butler, the Mars Route headed south through McCandless, Mars, Gibsonia to Etna where it used Pittsburgh Railway trackage to downtown Pittsburgh. In 1914, the Butler Railways Company, operating trolley car service in and around Butler, became the city division of the Pittsburgh & Butler Street Railway Company which failed in 1917 and was reorganized as the Pittsburgh, Mars & Butler Railway Company. In 1918, both companies were acquired by the holding company Pittsburgh, Butler & Harmony Consolidated Railway & Power Company. The holding company was reorganized in 1928 as the Harmony Short Line Railway, Bus and Land Company which established bus service in the region. With a decline in ridership, the Mars Route from Pittsburgh to Butler operated its last trolley car on April 22, 1931. The April 23, 1931 *Butler Eagle* newspaper reported the last run was made by "car No. 103 with G. W. Johnson of Mars, motorman and W. J. Weissert of Renfew conductor in charge." On June 15, 1931 the Beaver Falls–Ellwood City–New Castle portion of the Harmony Route was converted to bus operation. The last trolley car operated on the remaining portion of the Harmony Route on August 15, 1931 Butler Railways Company ended trolley car service on January 30, 1941. Harmony Short Line buses replaced the trolley cars.

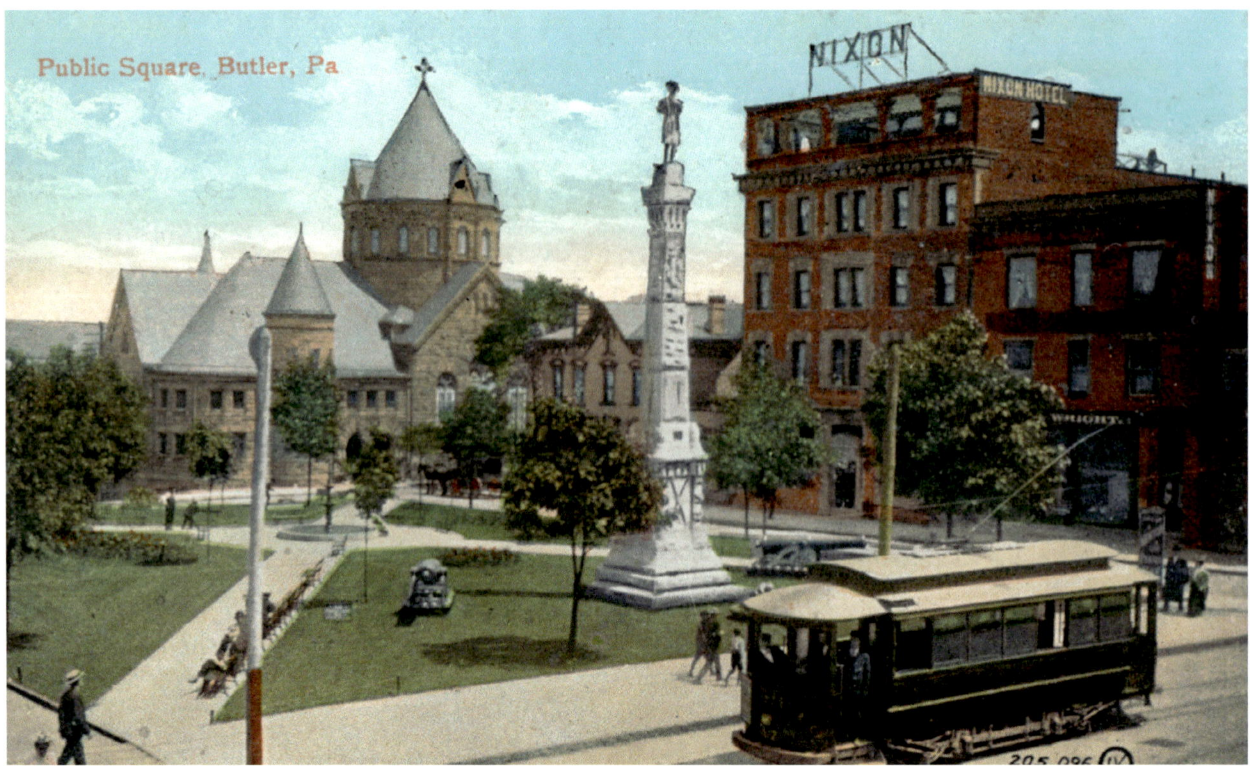

Public Square in downtown Butler is the location of a Butler Passenger Railway Company trolley car in this postcard scene around 1910. Organized in October 1899, construction began in June 1990, and by August 20, 1990 trolley car operation had started. This became the city division of the Pittsburgh & Butler Street Railway Company in 1914.

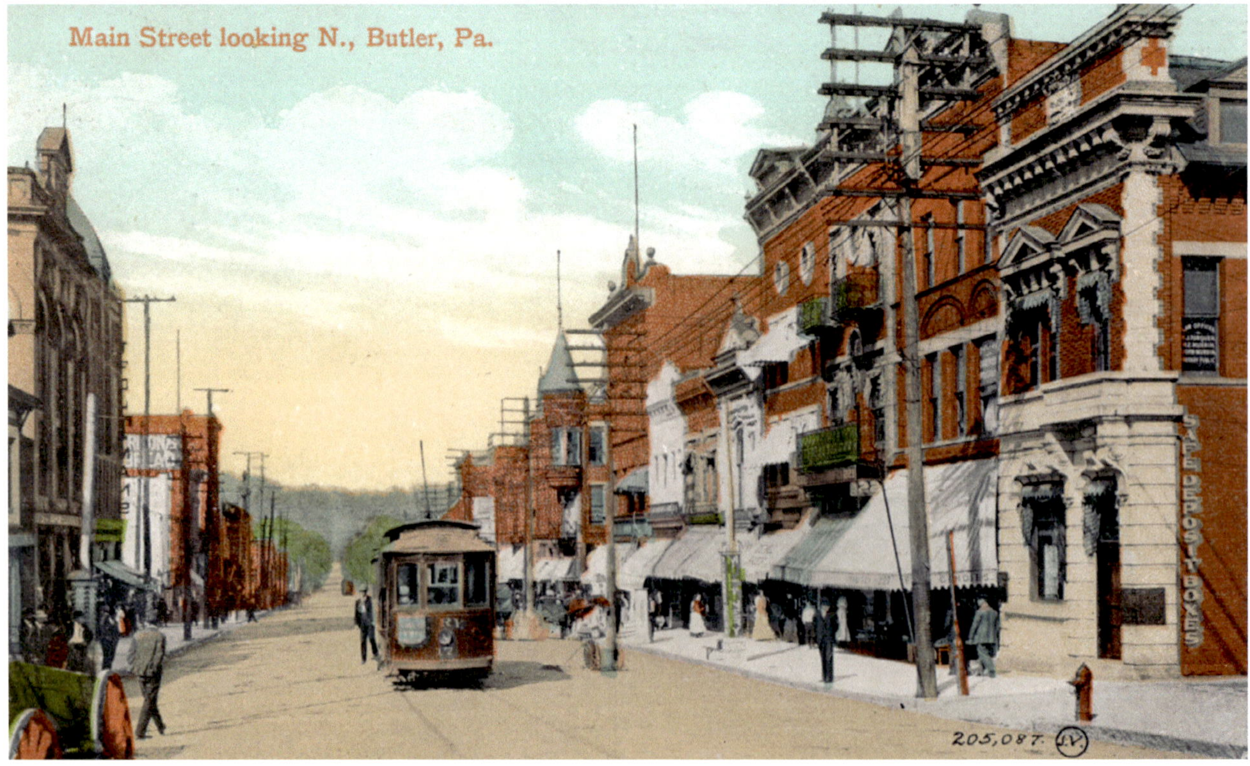

There are no traffic congestion issues for this Butler Railways Company trolley on Main Street in this 1910 postcard scene. The Pittsburgh & Butler Street Railway, which completed a line between Butler and Pittsburgh on April 24, 1907, took over the Butler Passenger Railway Company. Financial problems resulted in reorganization as the Pittsburgh, Mars & Butler Railway Company which was acquired by the Pittsburgh, Harmony, Butler, and New Castle Railway Company in 1918.

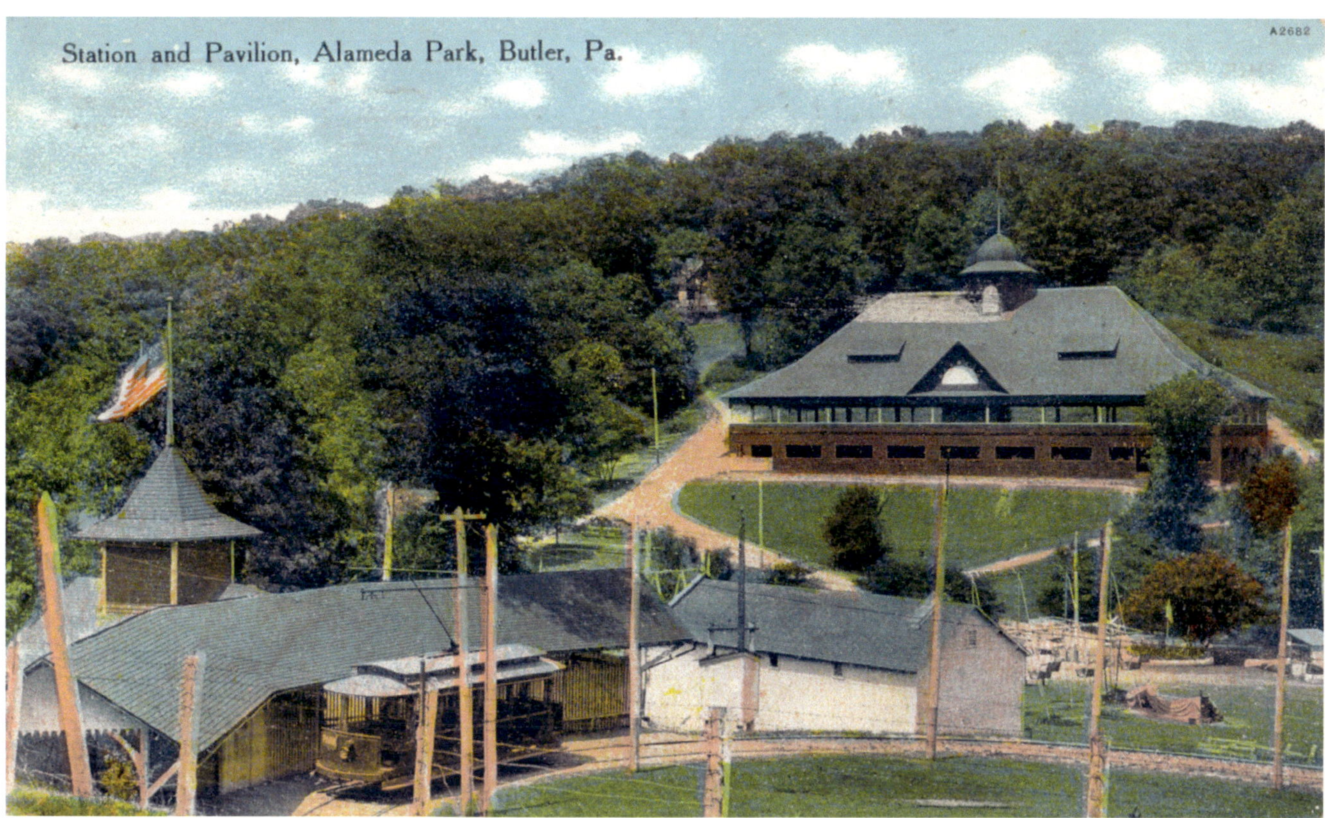

A Butler Railways Company car is at Alameda Park in this postcard postmarked February 23, 1910. The Butler Railways Company purchased sixty acres of land two miles west of Butler and established Alameda Park, which opened in 1903, served by the trolley system.

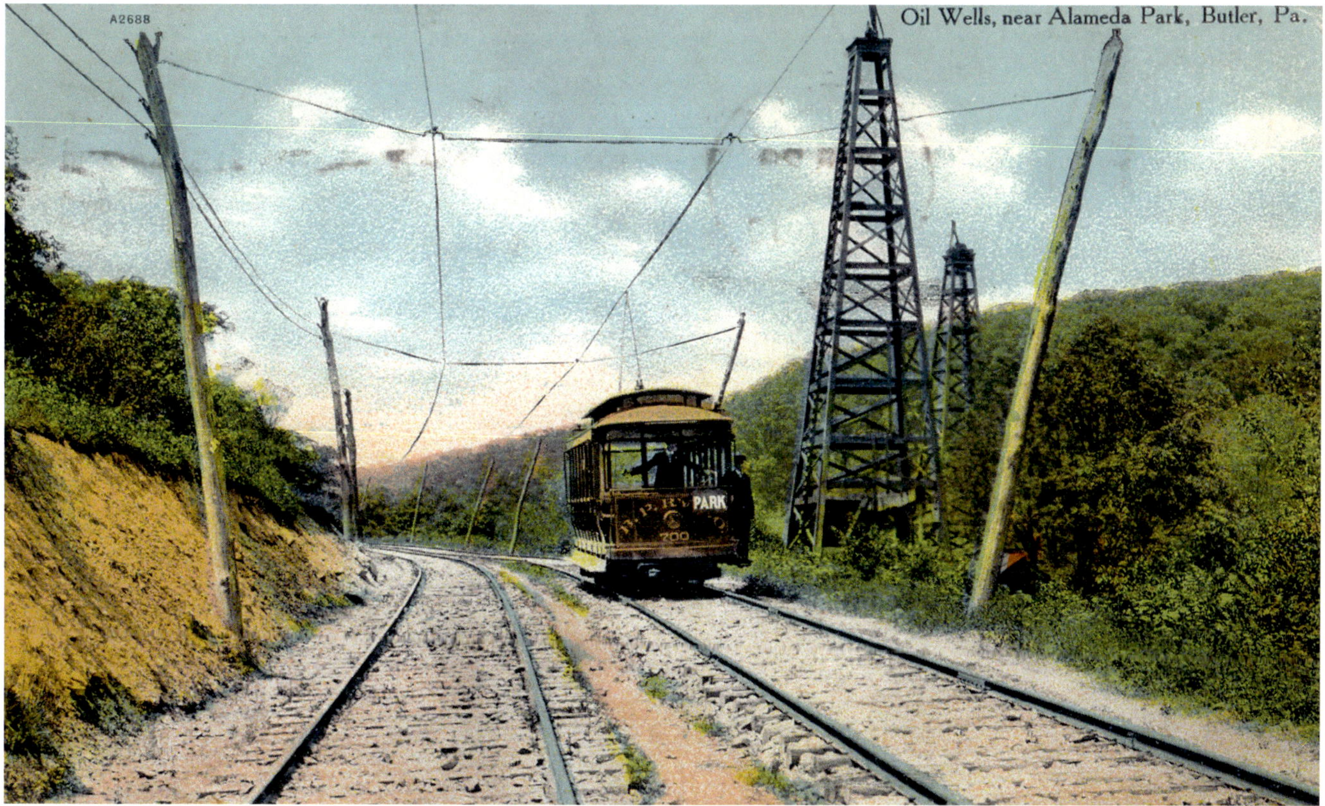

Butler Railways Company car No. 700 passes by oil derricks as it heads for Alameda Park in this postcard postmarked May 29, 1910. According to the *McGraw Electric Railway Directory 1924*, the Butler Railways Company operated twenty-nine cars on 15.34 miles of track.

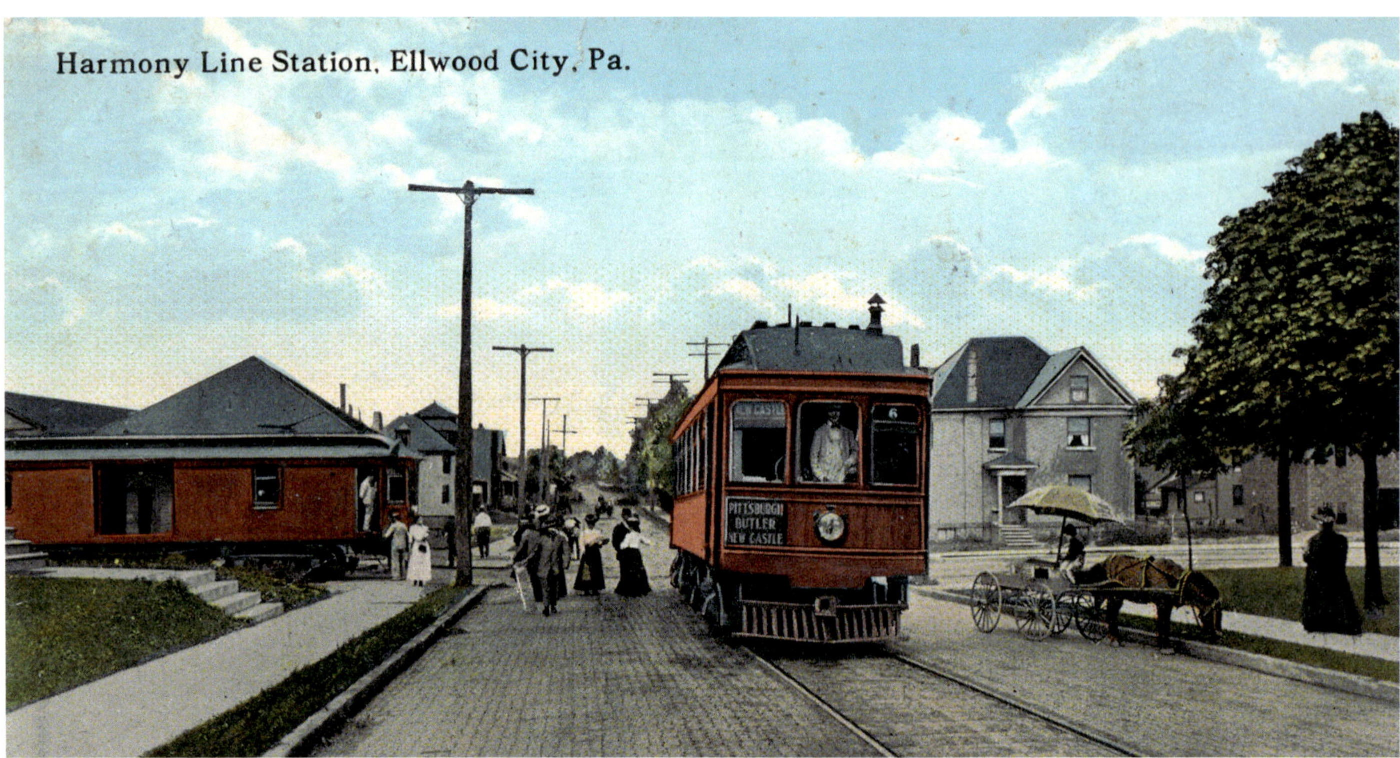

A Pittsburgh, Harmony, Butler, and New Castle Railway commonly called the Harmony Route trolley car is at the station (shown on the left) in the borough of Ellwood City in the southern part of Lawrence County loading passengers in this postcard scene. The fare from Pittsburgh to Evans City was $0.85, Pittsburgh to Ellwood City was $1.30, and Pittsburgh to New Castle was $1.50. Before the coming of the trolley car, travel was not easy over rutted dirt roads that were at times impassable during wet weather.

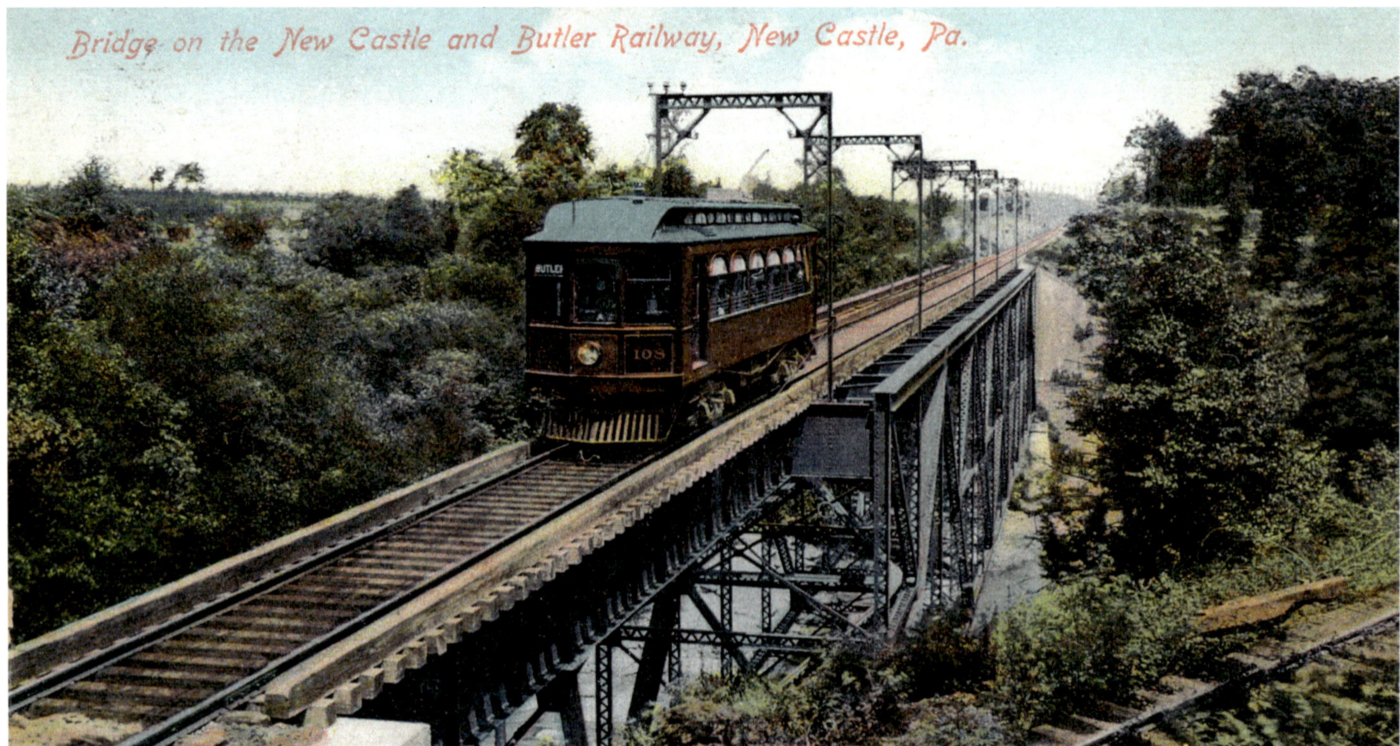

A Harmony Line trolley car is crossing the Knox Bridge over the Connoquenessing River (about a fifty mile long tributary of the Beaver River) in Ellwood City in this postcard scene postmarked July 7, 1909. The line was divided into three divisions: Pittsburgh division from Pittsburgh to Evans City, twenty-three miles; Butler division from Evans City to Butler, twelve miles; and the New Castle division from Evans City to New Castle, twenty-eight miles.

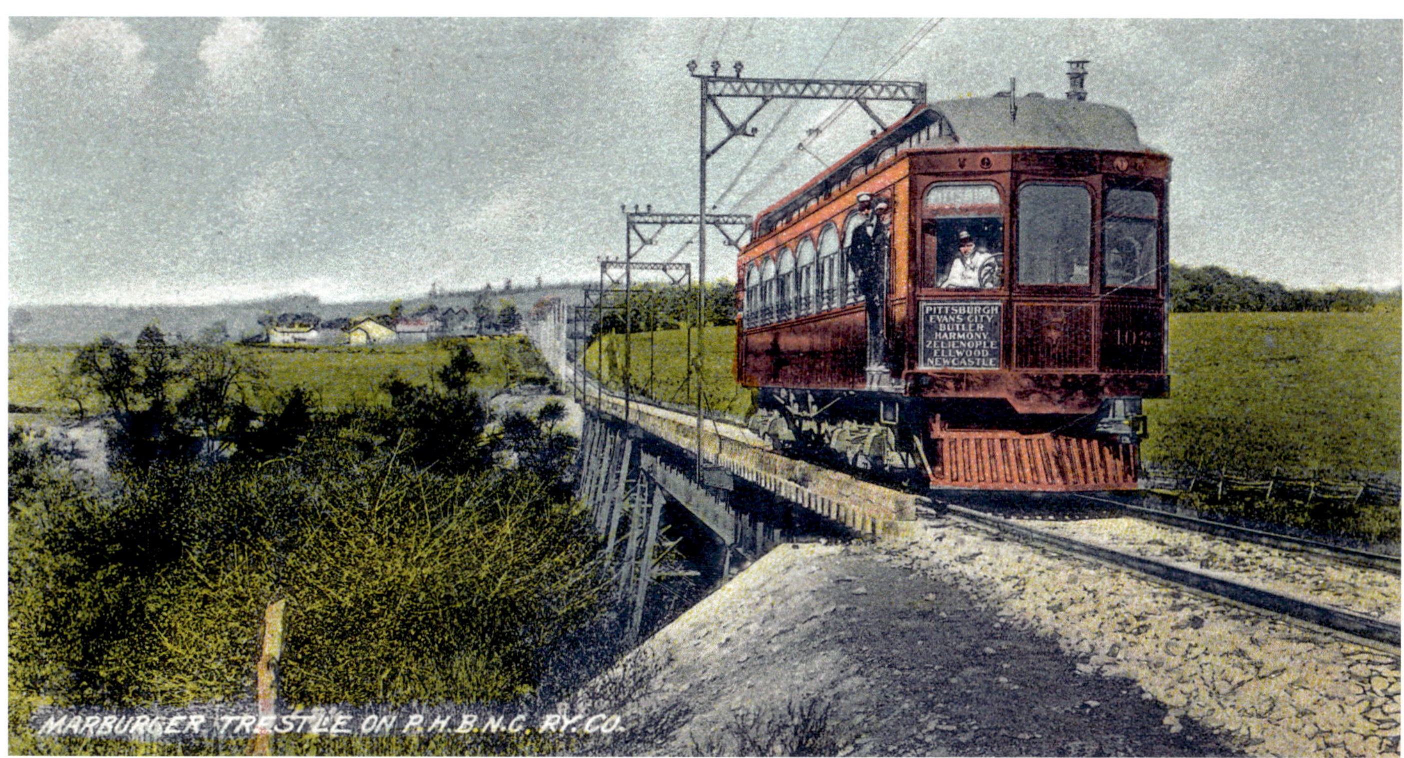

The Marburger Trestle is the site of a photo stop for Harmony Line trolley car No. 102 in this postcard, postmarked March 16, 1911. In addition to passengers, milk and farm produce was shipped from Butler, Beaver, and Lawrence County farm to Pittsburgh by trolley car. Milk cans were picked up at specified locations along the line and placed on special racks in the cars. On the return trip, the empty cars were dropped off to be used again the next day.

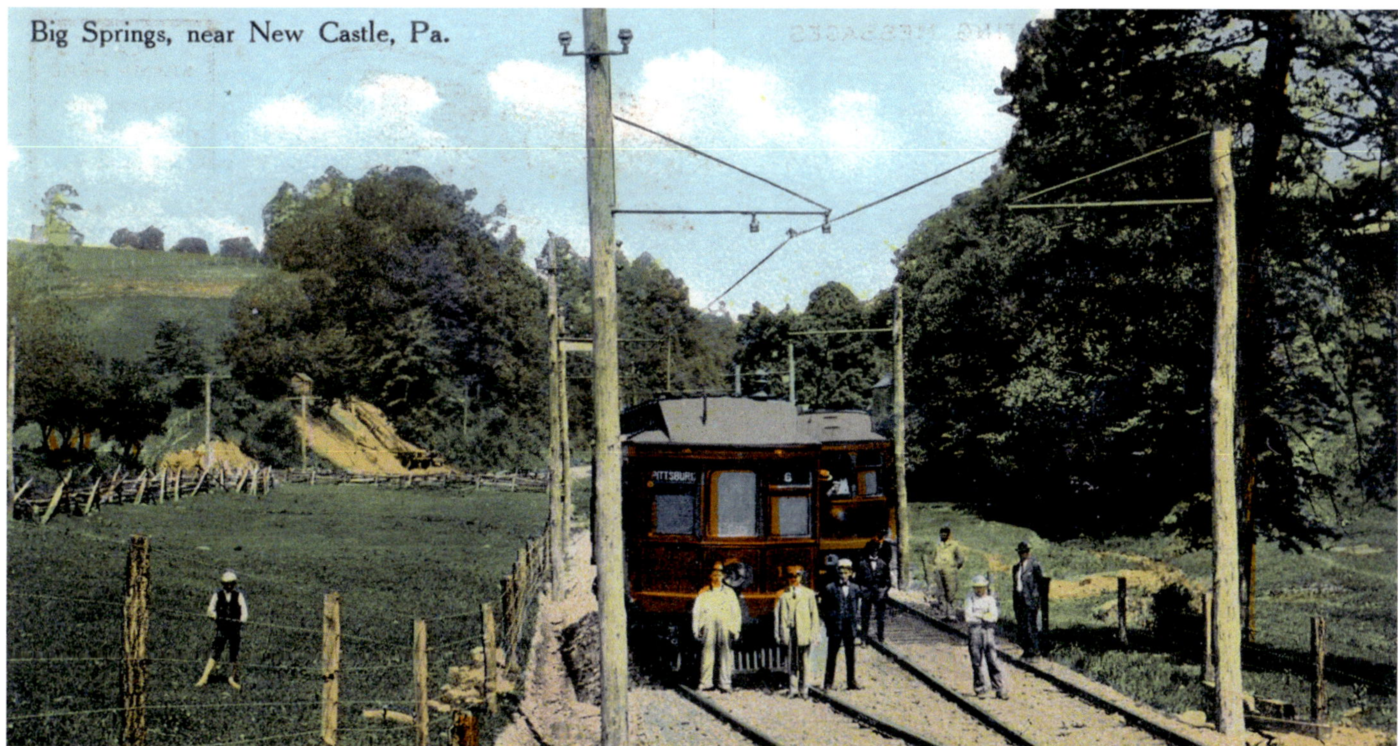

Two Harmony Line trolley cars pose with their crew at Big Springs siding near Marquis Station stop in Shenango Township in this postcard scene around 1911. Factory and office workers commuted by trolley car to their jobs in Pittsburgh, Butler, Ellwood City, and New Castle. Harmony Junction, midway between Pittsburgh and New Castle, was the location of the main power station, carhouse, and executive office.

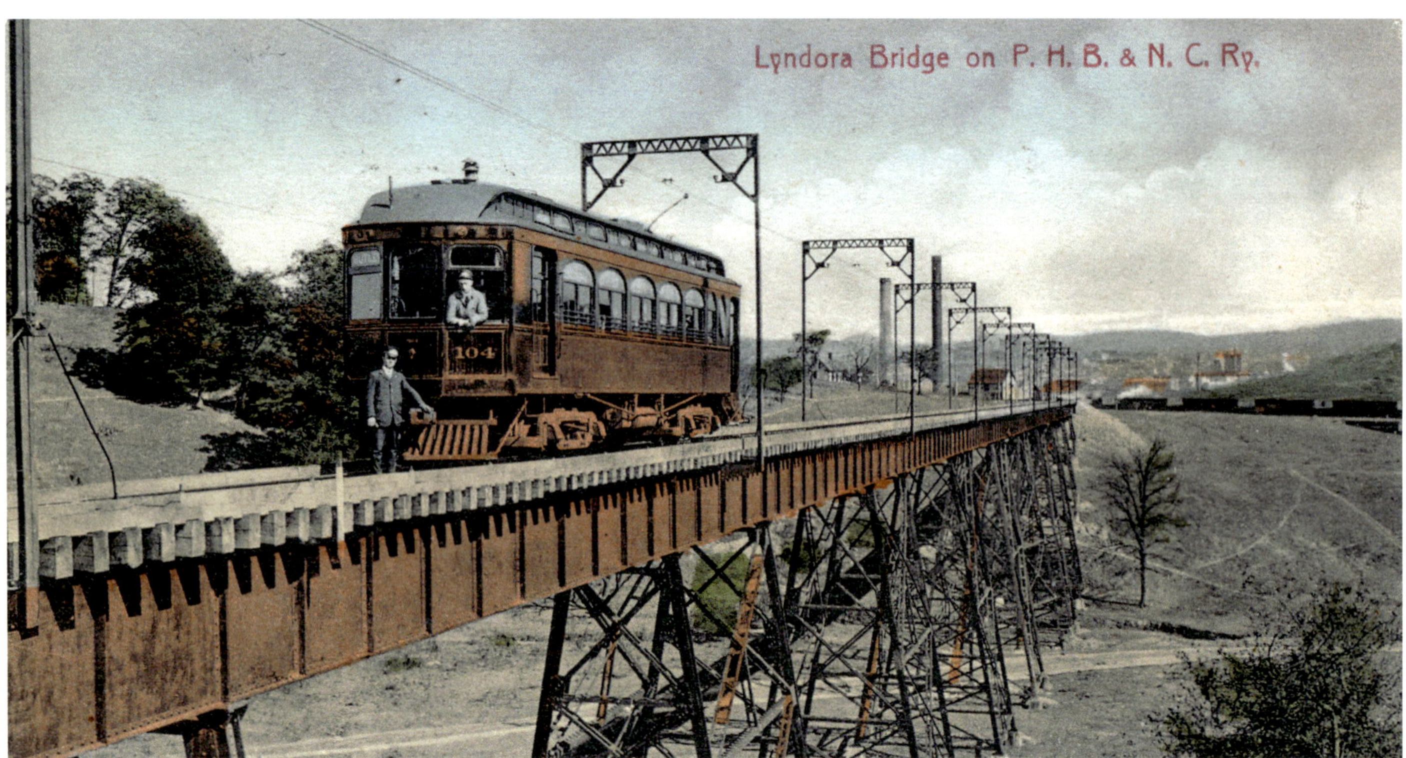

Harmony Line trolley car No. 104 poses on the Lyndora Bridge in this postcard postmarked August 9, 1911. On Sunday families rode the trolley to attend church services. People rode the trolleys to go shopping, to amusement parks for picnics and outings, and to visit friends and relatives. Special party cars could even be rented. One trolley car was outfitted at the company's shop at Harmony Junction to show motion pictures projected on a screen at one end of the car.

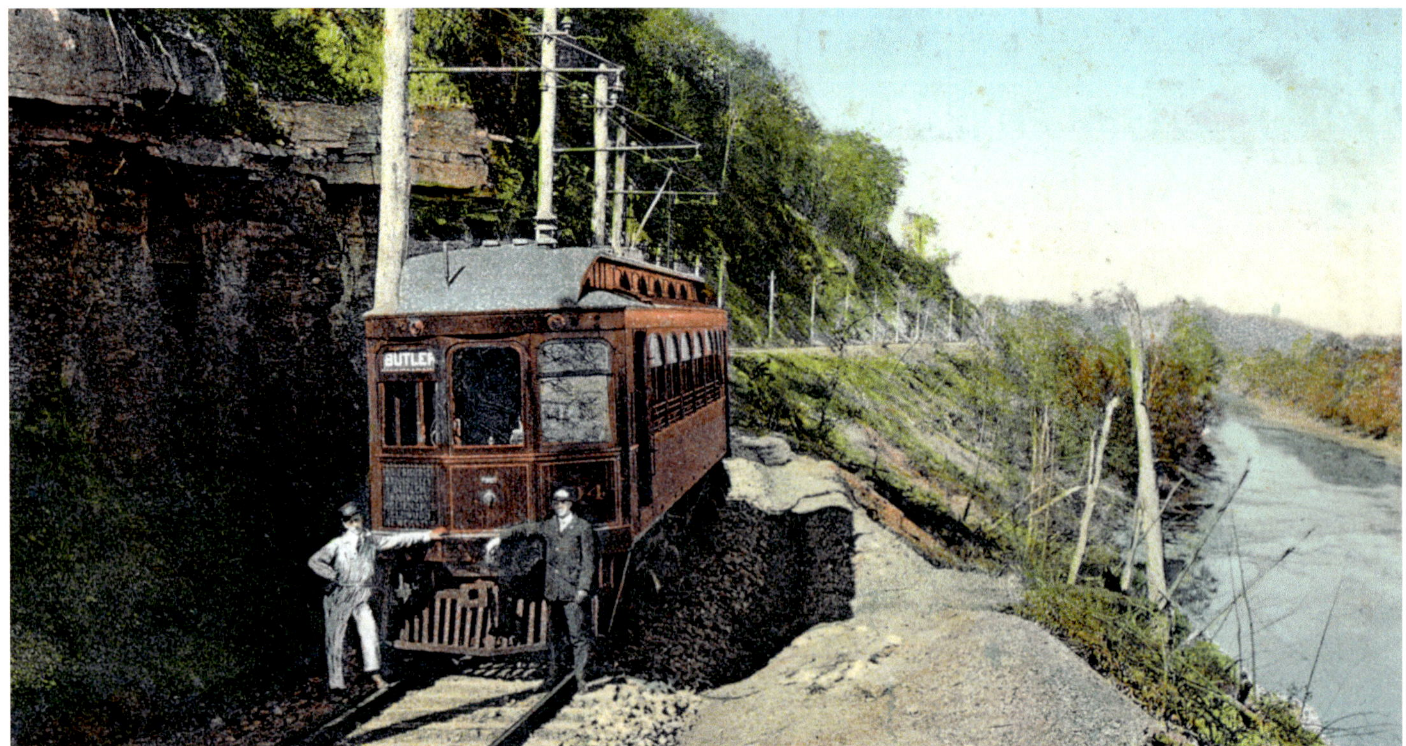

In this 1911 postcard scene, Harmony Line trolley car No. 104 is having a photo stop with two crew members at Pine Hill near the borough of Zelienople in Butler County. According to the *Electric Railway Journal Volume 43, 1914*, page 1034, the first freight train was operated in May 1910. The system grew, employing, "thirty-three persons and operates six motor or freight cars, eight box cars, three gondola cars, one flat car, and forty dump cars." From 1908 to 1931, the Harmony Route served the region with dependable, frequent, and low cost public transportation.

Chapter 5

Johnstown Trolleys

The May 31, 1889 flood wiped out the Johnstown Passenger Railway Company horse car system. Tom L. Johnson of the Johnson Steel Works purchased the company, and it was rebuilt as an electric trolley car system. The cabarn and company office were built at Central Avenue in Moxham, and the first trip was made on July 28, 1891. After the new carbarn was destroyed by fire on March 11, 1893, a new carbarn was built further south on Central Avenue at Bond Street. The Johnstown Passenger Railway Company was merged into the Johnstown Traction Company (JTC) on February 13, 1910. The line to Southmont opened in 1911, and track was extended into Morrellville with an extension into Oakhurst in 1911.

A subsidiary, the Traction Bus Company, on November 22, 1922, began bus service from the Dale trolley loop to Scalp Level. In November 1931, JTC went into receivership, and was reorganized under the same name on December 3, 1932. All of the trolley lines were closed by the March 17, 1936 flood. The Windber Line was not rebuilt after the flood. However, the section from Ferndale to Benscreek continued to have trolley car service. With the bus system growing, the bus operation was merged into the parent company on January 1, 1937 to achieve closer control. During 1938 bus service was initiated using the Johnstown Incline to Westmont. The Dale Line was converted to bus operation on August 2, 1940 due to a street reconstruction project.

A dividend was paid in 1942, 1943, and 1944. Ridership increased during World War II from 19,130,285 in 1942 to 24,722,124 in 1947, and then declined to 4,443,777 in 1962. In March 1945, JTC ordered seventeen new PCC cars and fourteen new buses. On January 25, 1947, car No. 401 was first of the new PCC cars to arrive in Johnstown. A trainer from Pittsburgh Railways Company instructed the operators on the new PCC cars. In a month, they were in service on the Morrellville, Roxbury, Ferndale, Franklin, and Coopersdale lines. On November 20, 1951, the Horner Street Line was the first line converted to trackless trolley operation. In 1953 the Oakhurst shuttle was converted to bus operation and

was extended to serve a new residential development. PCC car No. 406 was hit by a train on the Franklin Line and was scrapped in 1953 leaving sixteen PCC cars in service. After a rockslide, the Southmont Line was converted to bus operation on October 9, 1954.

During 1956 the Franklin Line was temporarily cut back while a new bridge was erected. New rail was installed on the bridge, and trolley car service was restored. In 1957 the Benscreek Shuttle Line that operated during rush hours between Ferndale and Benscreek was converted to bus operation. In preparation for the conversion of the Roxbury–Morrellville Line to trackless trolley operation, overhead wire work was started in 1957. During June 1957, JTC purchased ten second-hand trackless trolleys from Wilmington, Delaware, and eleven second-hand trackless trolleys from Covington, Kentucky. These vehicles were refurbished and repainted in the company's shops. Buses took over the Ferndale and Coopersdale Lines on November 25, 1959. The Ferndale Line crossed the Baltimore & Ohio Railroad tracks, and the railroad wanted the crossing repaired or removed. It was removed by JTC, and the trolley cars were replaced by buses. Trolley car service remained on the Roxbury–Morrellville Line and during rush hours to Franklin using the Ferndale Line to reach the Moxham Carbarn. In addition to the sixteen PCC cars, in 1960 there were ten of the twenty cars Nos. 350-369 built in 1926 by St. Louis Car Company on the property along with "Birney Safety" car No. 311 (built in 1922 by Wason Manufacturing Company) purchased second hand from the Bangor Railway & Electric Company in 1941.

All trolley car service ended on June 11, 1960 with temporary operation by buses, because the city had initiated a new system of one way streets. Trackless trolley service began on September 26, 1960. The Conemaugh Line was converted from bus to trackless trolley operation in July 1965. Trackless trolley operation in Johnstown ended on November 11, 1967. With ridership declining, JTC could no longer operate the system. The Cambria County Transit Authority, formed on December 1, 1976, began providing bus service.

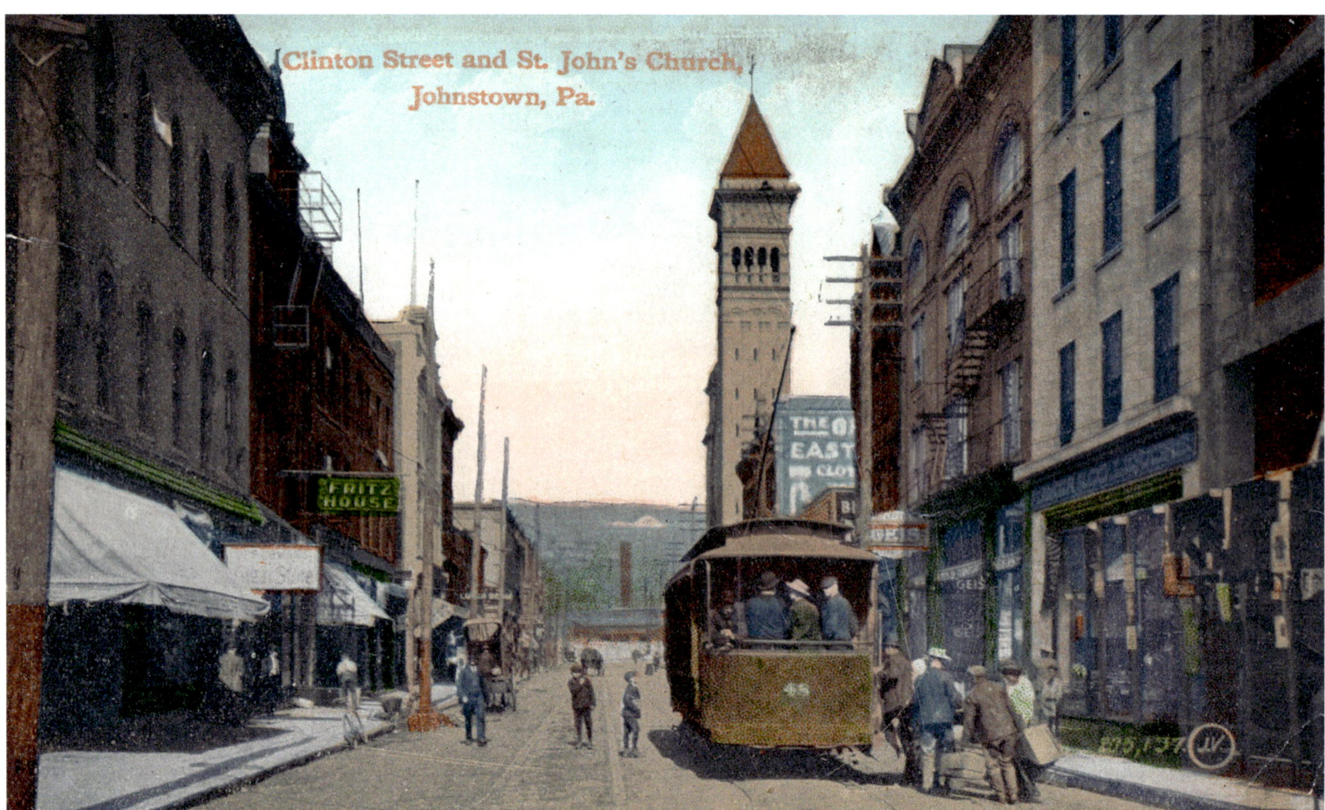

Johnstown Traction Company trolley car No. 48 is on Clinton Street around 1910. This was one of sixteen single truck, deck roof, open type trolley cars numbered 34 to 49 built by St. Louis Car Company in 1899 and were retired in the mid-1920s. Ahead is the 180 foot Italianate style 180 foot high tower of St. John Gualbert Church located at 117 Clinton Street in downtown Johnstown that was completed in 1895.

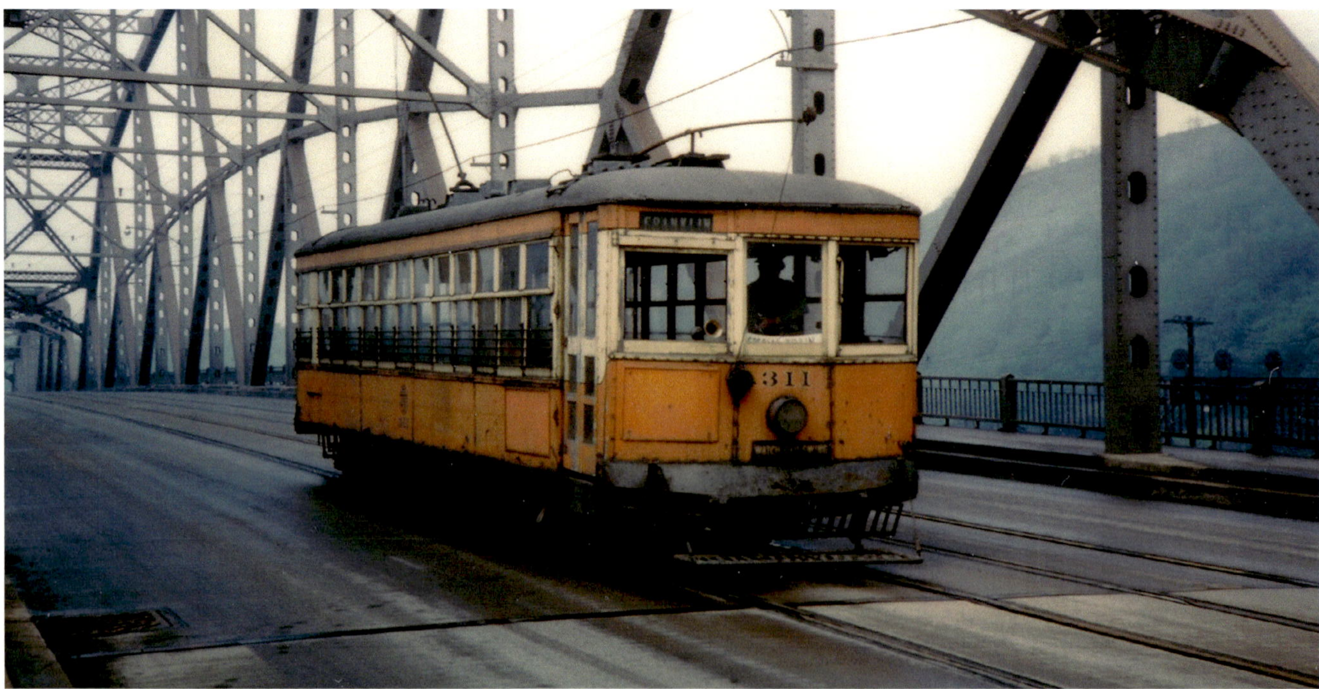

On May 30, 1960 JTC trolley car No. 311 is on the Maple Avenue Bridge on the Franklin Line. This double truck Birney car was built by Wason Manufacturing Company of Springfield, Massachusetts, in 1920 as No. 14 for the Bangor Railway & Electric Company of Bangor, Maine, and was acquired by JTC in 1941. The car was designed for one person operation having safety equipment that brought the car to a stop if the operator became disabled. It operated until trolley car service ended in 1960. This car has been preserved at the Rockhill Trolley Museum where it was the first trolley to operate on any museum line in Pennsylvania.

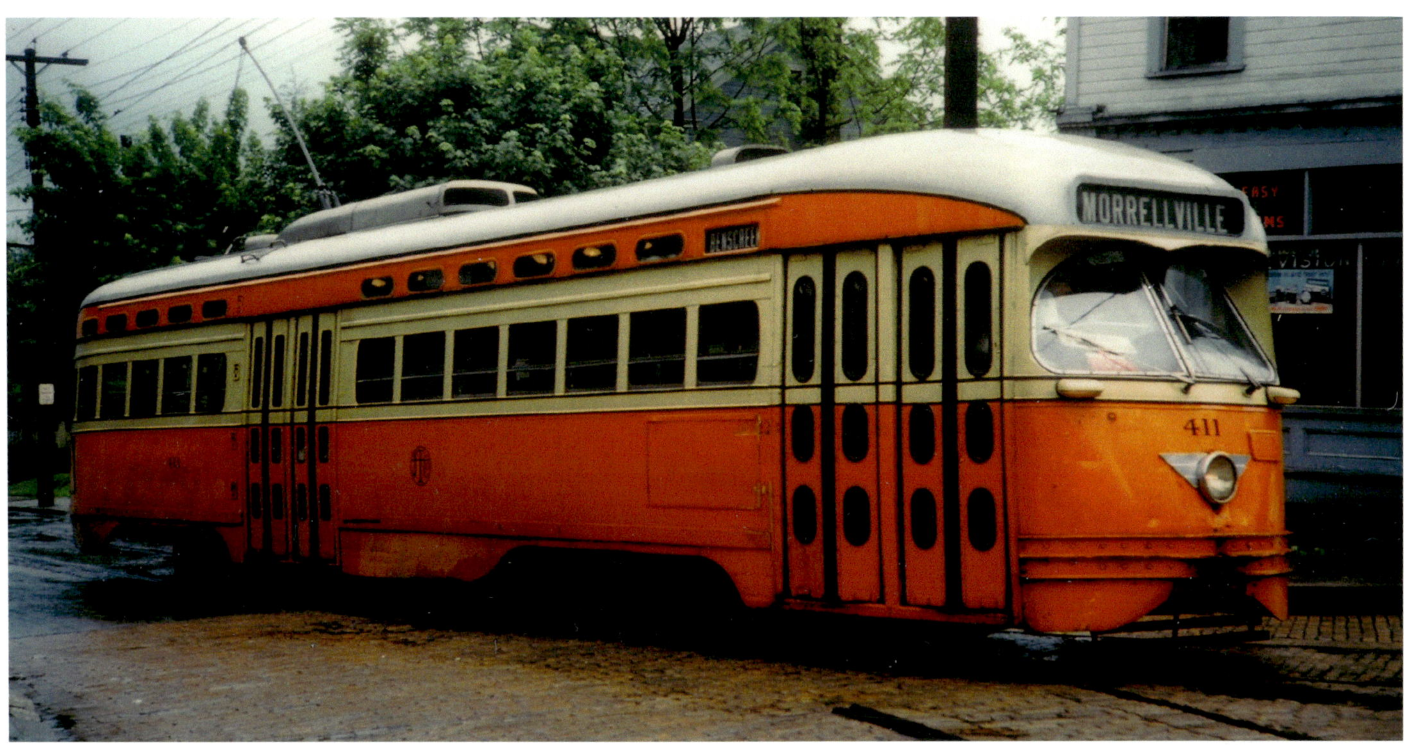

On May 30, 1960, Johnstown Traction Company PCC car No. 411 is on Chandler Avenue ready to turn onto Strayer Street. This was one of seventeen PCC cars numbered 401 to 417 built by St. Louis Car Company in 1947. Car No. 406 was scrapped after an accident with a train on May 18, 1953. The disconnected track in the bottom right hand side of the picture was for the abandoned Oakhurst Shuttle, which had been replaced by buses in 1953.

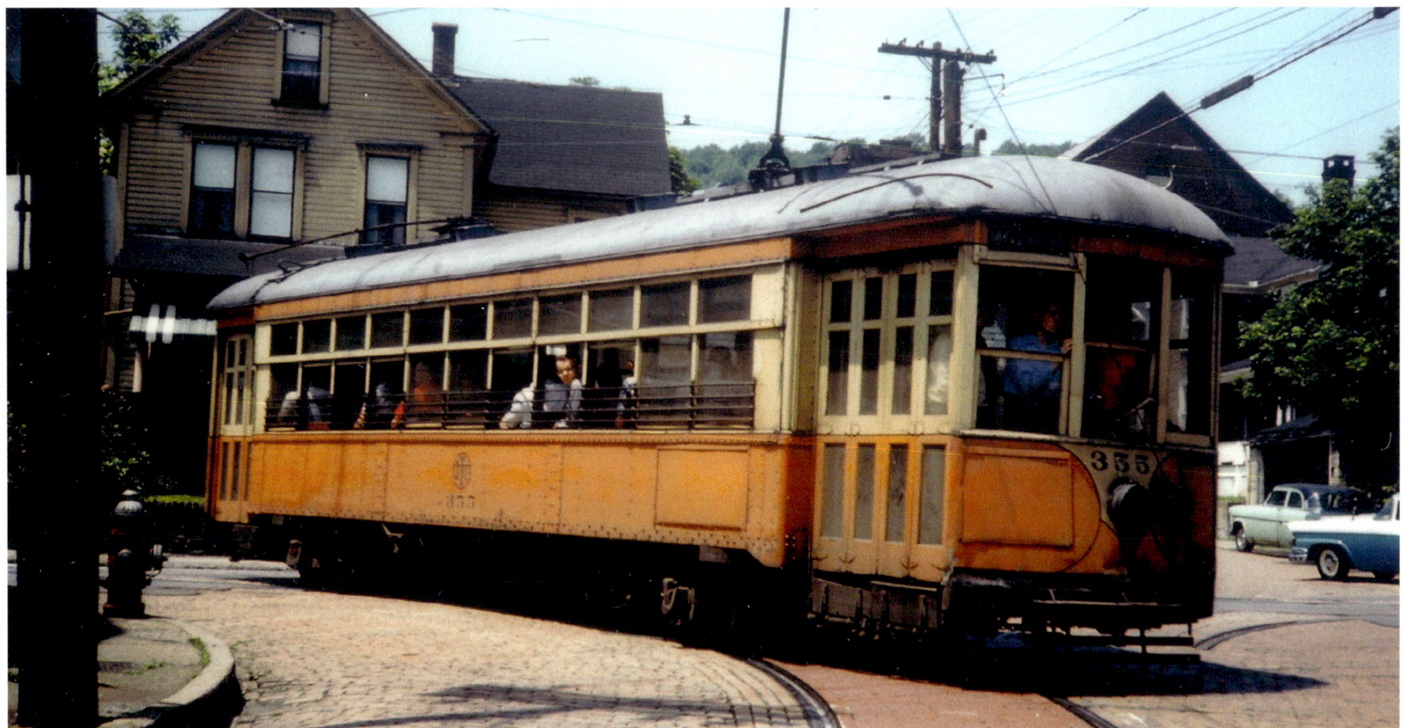

Car No. 355 is turning from Chandler Avenue onto Strayer Street on June 11, 1960, the last day of trolley car operation in Johnstown. This was one of fifteen double truck, single end, arch roof cars built by St. Louis Car Company in 1926. Cars numbered 355 to 358 were later converted to double end operation. After trolley car service ended in Johnstown, the car left for a museum in New Hampshire that never developed and was acquired by the Rockhill Trolley Museum in 1970. The car running gear has been extensively rebuilt plus all major areas received new materials including steel siding, air piping, flooring and electrical wiring.

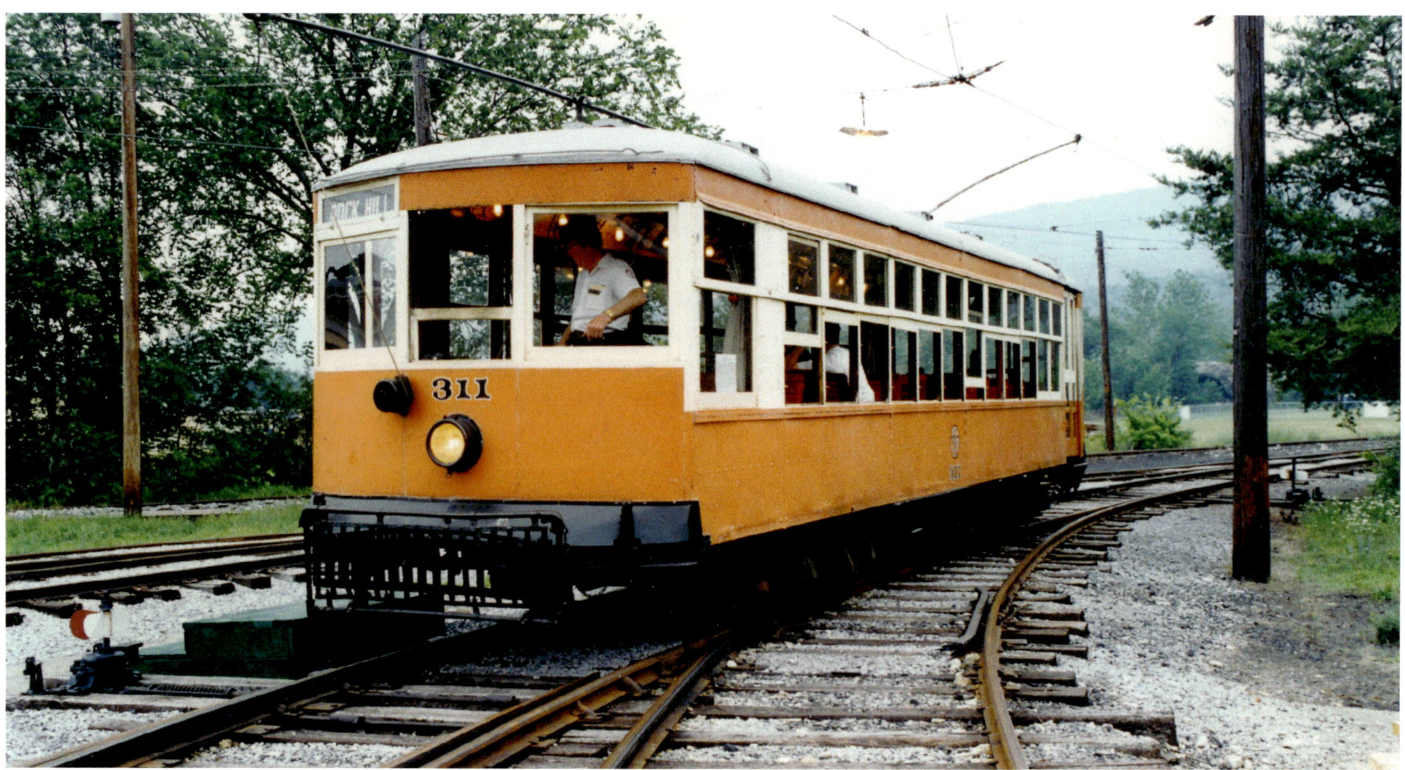

Former Johnstown Traction Company trolley car No. 311 is at the Rockhill Trolley Museum in this June 22, 1996 view. This car operated in Bangor, Maine from 1920 to 1941 and operated in Johnstown serving the system well until the end of service on Jun 11, 1960. The car was a favorite for many rail enthusiasts to charter in Johnstown.

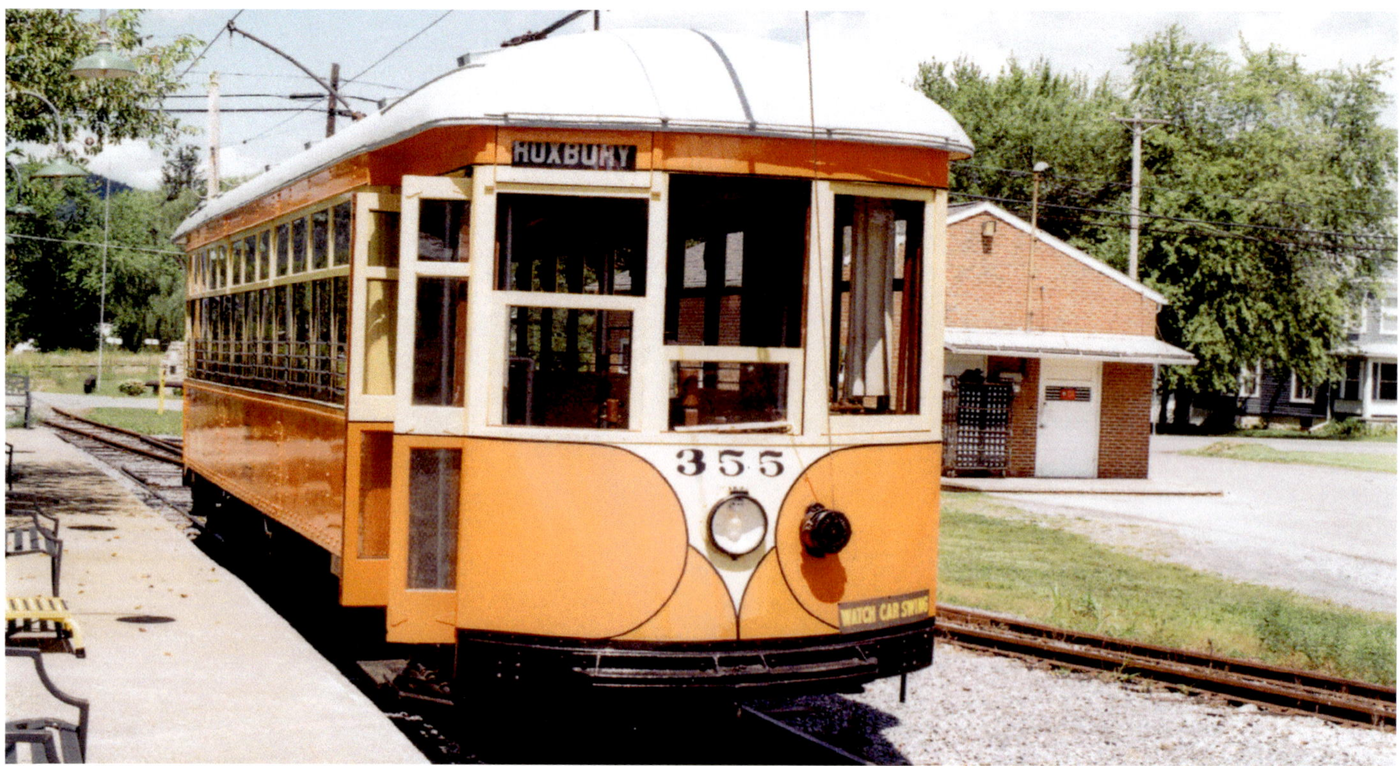

On a bright summer August 17, 2014, former Johnstown Traction Company trolley car No. 355 is ready to receive passengers for the next trip. This car originally had controls only at one end and was later equipped with controls at both ends. It has a safety brake system that allowed for one man operation. If the motorman became disabled while the car was running, the safety brake system automatically stopped the car. Instead of a conductor, passengers paid when boarding or leaving the car.

Chapter 6

Altoona Trolleys

The City Passenger Railway Company, incorporated on March 10, 1882, began construction of a horse car line in Altoona which opened on July 4, 1882 with eighteen horse cars, thirty-three horses, and eight mules. The 3.5 mile loop operated over 8th Avenue, 17th Street, 11th Avenue, and 11th Street. On the north side of Chestnut Avenue east of 1st Street, the carbarn was located and was connected to the line by trackage on Chestnut Avenue. A decision was made to electrify the line and on July 4, 1891 the first electric trolley car operated around the loop. The City & Park Railway Company opened a 7.5 mile line into Altoona from the southeast that was completed by the end of 1892. On June 1, 1892, the Tyrone Electric Railway was incorporated. The Altoona & Logan Valley Electric Railway (ALV) received its charter on December 12, 1892 and gained control of the City Passenger Railway Company and the City & Park Railway Company on April 17, 1893. In 1894 trolley lines were completed to Bellwood and via Lakemont Park to Hollidaysburg. The Tyrone Electric Railway Company began construction in 1900 and on July 4, 1902 opened their line to Bellwood where passengers could board an ALV car to Altoona and Lakemont Park. On August 3, 1903, the Tyrone Electric Railway Company was merged into the ALV.

With construction of a route along Sixth Avenue to 58th Street in the Eldorado neighborhood in 1908, the Altoona trolley system had 54.28 miles of track. The trolley system had an influence on the development of the city of Altoona and suburban residential areas. In November 1923 the Logan Valley Bus Company, a subsidiary of the trolley company, was operating seven buses on trolley feeder lines. The fare for a trolley car was seven cents while the fare for the bus was ten cents. During this period, employees of the Pennsylvania Railroad were the company's major customers. Hundreds of employees arriving for work used public transit. Railroad workers completing their shift would use public transit to get home. The company went into bankruptcy and was sold at foreclosure on December 8, 1933 for $800,000. It reorganized on January 3, 1934. Under new management, the 18th Street and 3rd Street Lines were discontinued in 1934. Following severe flood damage, the Tyrone Line was cut back to East Altoona, and the isolated Tyrone local line was discontinued on March 31, 1938. The East Juniata Line was discontinued on April 14, 1938. With the abandonment of the Fairview Line on April 15, 1940, 36.9 miles of track remained.

During World War II, a shortage of rubber and gasoline limited the use of automobiles and heavy demands on the Pennsylvania Railroad resulted in increased ridership, and no trolley routes were abandoned. However, after the war ridership declined, and the conversion to bus operation resumed. Buses took over the 2nd Avenue Line on August 1, 1948 followed by the East Altoona Shuttle and 8th Avenue Lines on September 4, 1949, and the 3rd Avenue Line on September 11, 1949 with 25.71 miles of track remaining. In 1946 more than 15 million passengers were carried, and in 1947 figures were slightly higher. By late 1950, buses were used after 6 p.m. daily and provided all service on weekends except for rail excursions. Trolley car operation was reduced to tripper runs. The last regular service trolley car operation ended on June 2, 1954. Charter trips continued on the El Dorado, Hollidaysburg, and Juniata Lines until Saturday August 7, 1954 when five trolley cars, carrying about 500 passengers decorated with banners proclaiming the end of sixty-three years of trolley car operation in Altoona, made the final trip. In December 1956 the ALV announced that it had filed with the Public Utilities Commission to terminate bus service and cease operation on March 31, 1957 due to ongoing operating losses. On May 27, 1958, the city of Altoona and Logan Township voted to create the Transportation & Motor Buses for Public Use Authority, generally known as the Altoona & Logan Valley Bus Authority, which took over bus operation on November 1, 1959. In 1977 the authority adopted the name AMTRAN for Altoona Metro Transit.

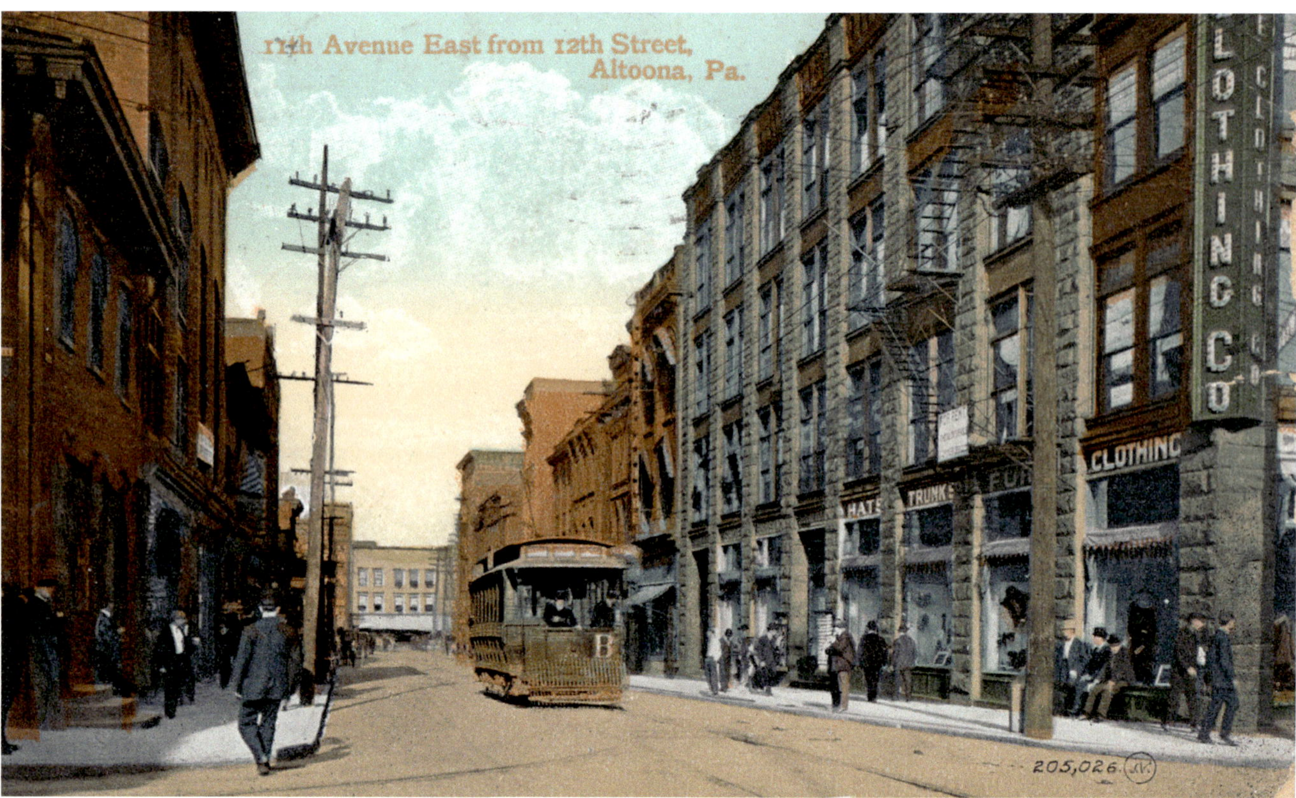

In this postcard postmarked December 31, 1909, an Altoona & Logan Valley Electric Railway Company trolley car is on 11th Avenue east from 12th Street in downtown Altoona.

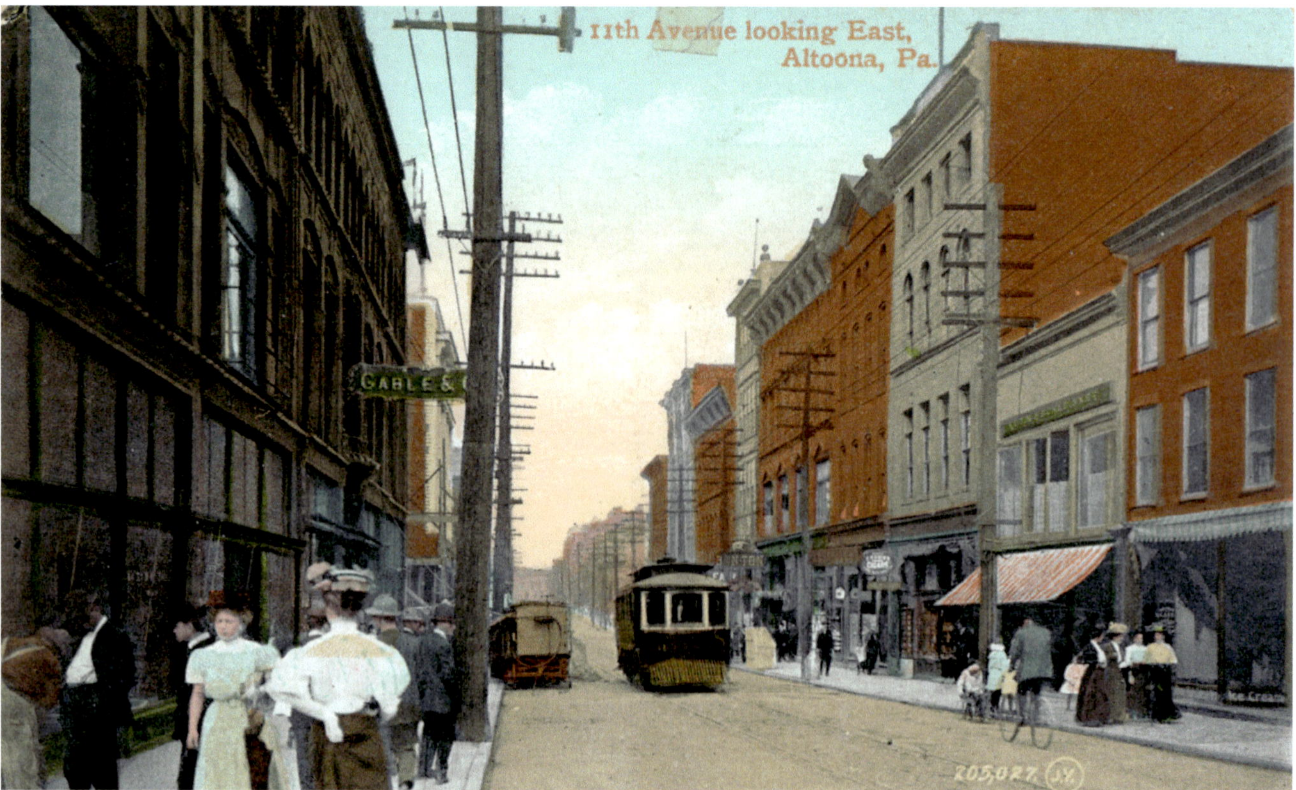

An Altoona & Logan Valley Electric Railway Company trolley car is on 11th Avenue in this downtown Altoona 1910 postcard scene looking east. According to the *McGraw Electric Railway List August 1918*, the company had 54.28 miles of track and operated 105 trolley cars and fourteen trailer cars.

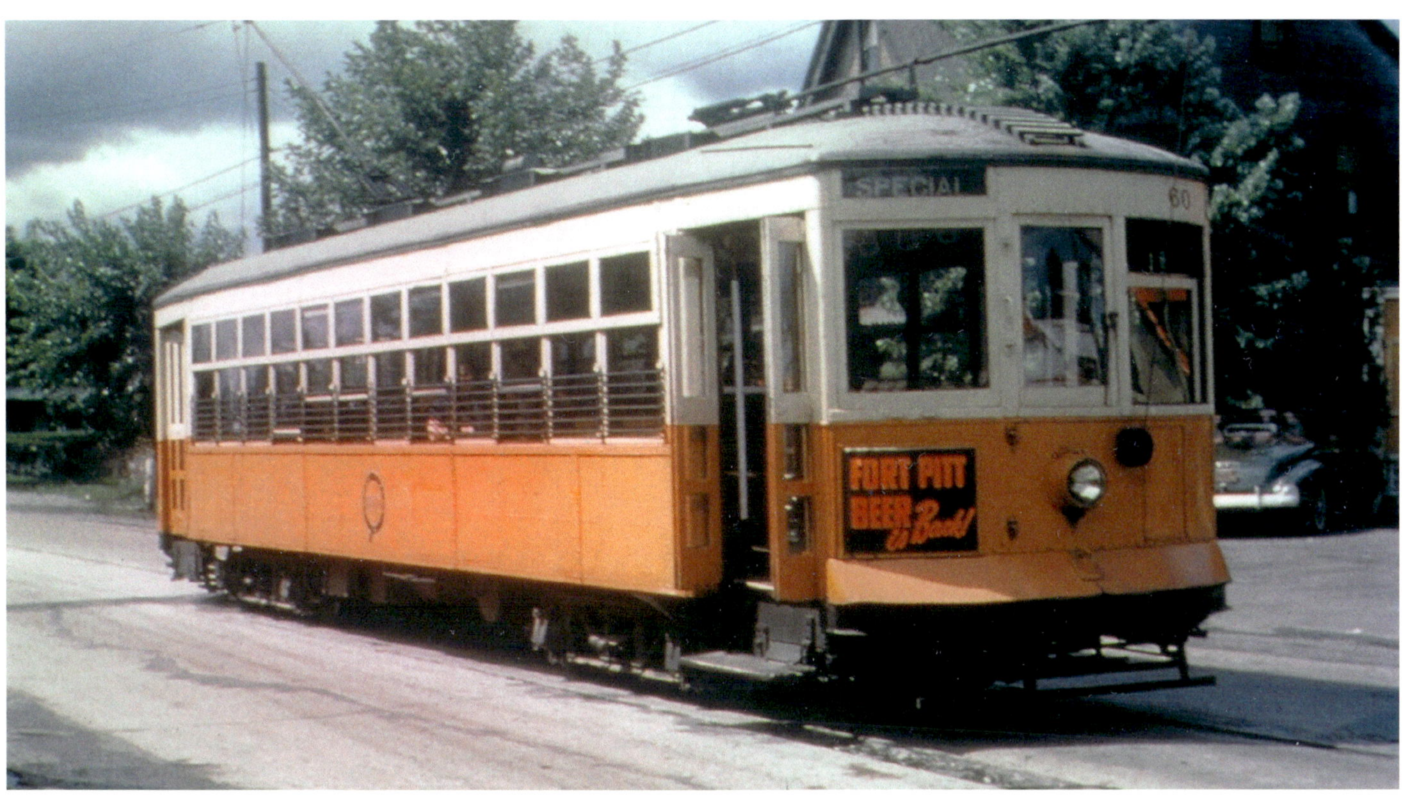

Altoona & Logan Valley Electric Railway Company trolley car No. 60 is at 6th Avenue and 58th Street on August 8, 1953. This was one of thirteen double truck, double end, arch roof trolley cars numbered 50 to 62 built by Osgood Bradley Car Company in 1925 and were retired in 1954. (C. R. Scholes collection.)

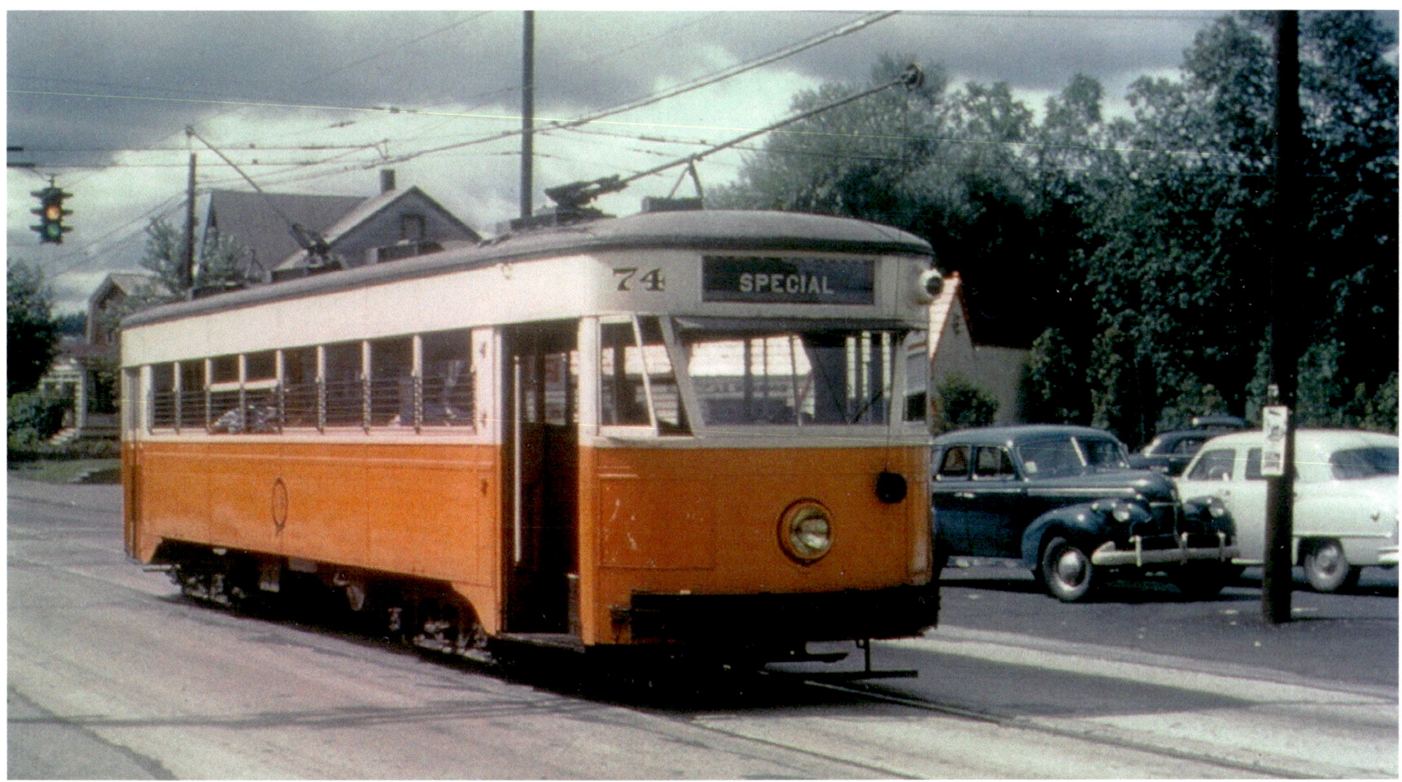

With "Special" on the destination sign, Altoona & Logan Valley Electric Railway Company trolley car No. 74 is on 6th Avenue and 58th Street on August 8, 1953. This was one of five double truck, double end, arch roof cars numbered 70 to 74 that were built by Osgood Bradley Car Company in 1929 and were retired in 1954. (C. R. Scholes collection.)

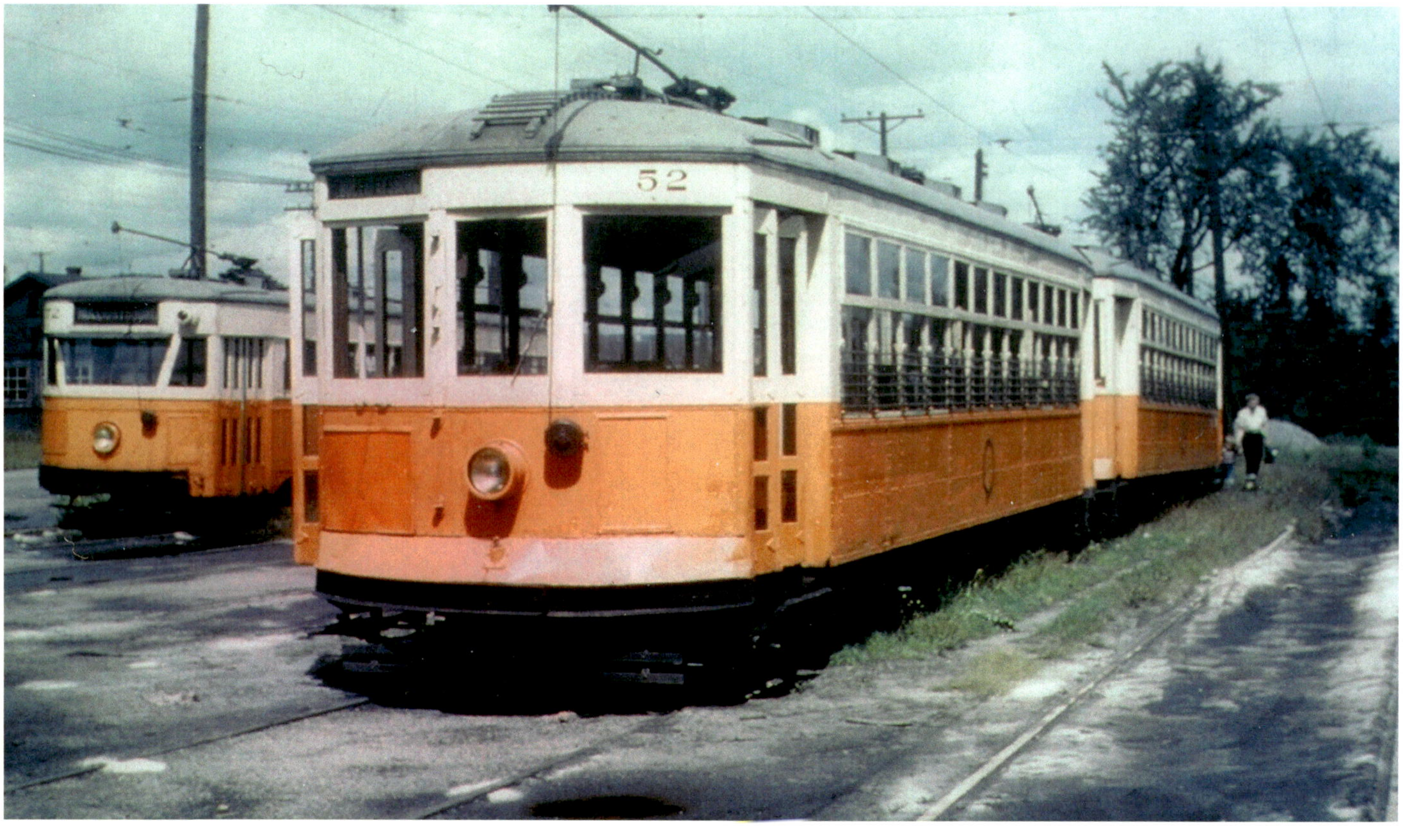

The 5th Avenue Carbarn is the location of Altoona & Logan Valley Electric Railway Company car No. 52 on August 8, 1953, and car No. 72 is on the left side of the photograph.

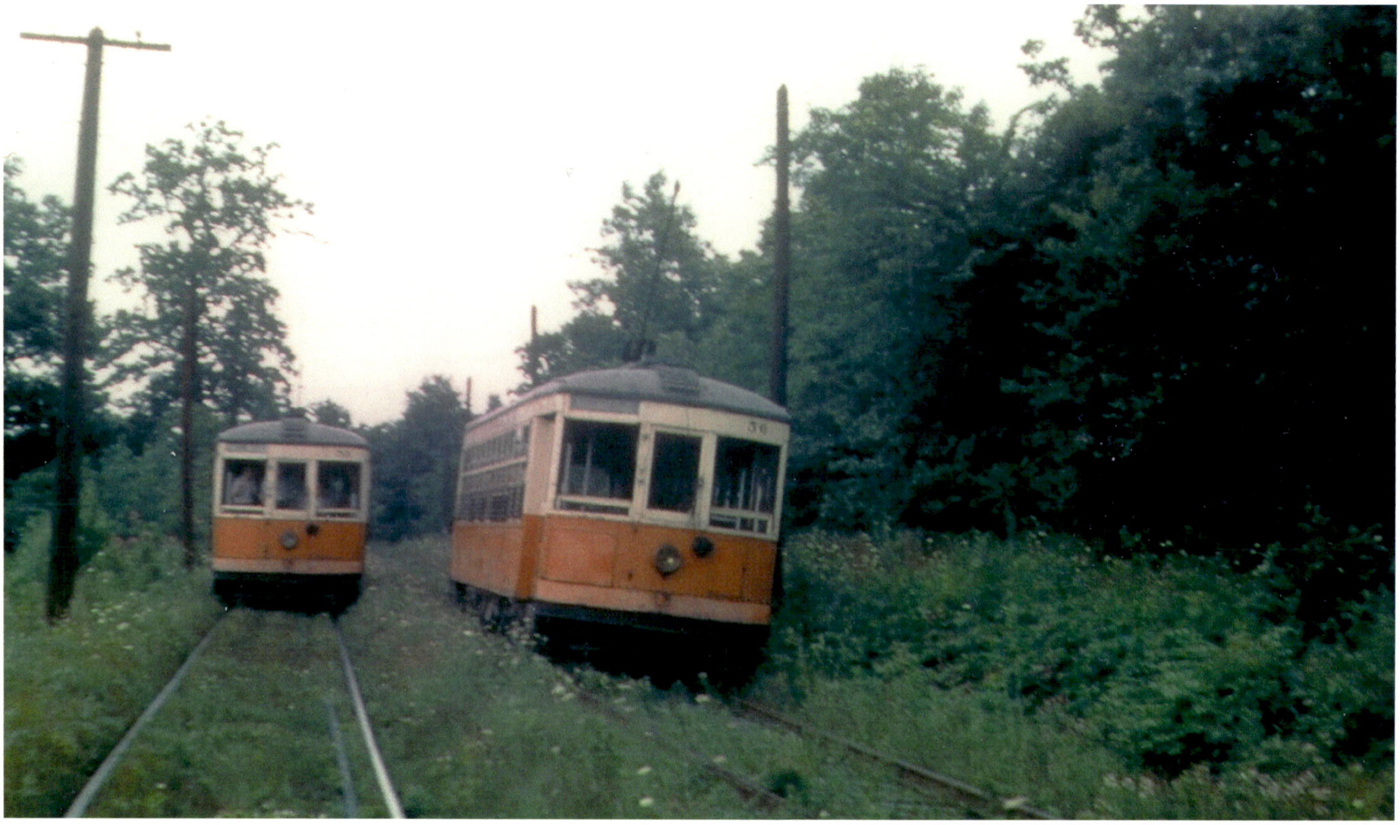

On August 8, 1953, Altoona & Logan Valley Electric Railway Company car No. 53 is passing car No. 56 on the Hollidaysburg Line.

Chapter 7

Reading Trolleys

On December 1, 1888, the Reading & St. Lawrence Railroad began electric trolley car service in Reading. Under reorganization, a number of Reading trolley car lines were leased by the United Traction Company on January 1, 1896 which by 1898 operated eighty-five trolley cars and forty-eight miles of track. A holding company, United Power & Transportation Company, created in 1899, eventually controlled and managed seventy-five companies including systems in Reading, Lebanon, Norristown, and Philadelphia. By 1904 there was trolley service from Reading northeast to Allentown, east to Boyertown, southeast to Birdsboro, southwest to Adamstown, and westward to Womelsdorf. On May 21, 1908, it was possible to ride on trolley cars from Philadelphia through Reading to Womelsdorf. Effective January 12, 1910, the Reading Transit Company was chartered to lease the trolley lines and was succeeded in 1913 by the Reading Transit & Light Company. In 1924 the name of the operating company was changed back to Reading Transit Company. The Reading Transit Bus Company, an affiliate, opened a bus line on September 12, 1926 to the Reading Fairgrounds that operated during the Reading Fair.

Buses replaced trolley cars on the Boyertown–Pottsville Line on August 22, 1927 and on the Allentown–Reading Line on October 5, 1930. Emerging from receivership, it became the Reading Street Railway Company on December 27, 1930. Trolley car service on Route 7 (P&R Depot) and Route 8 (Mineral Spring–2nd & Penn) ended in 1931. Trolley car service to Boyertown ended on July 21, 1932. The Adamstown Line was cut back to Mohnton on January 29, 1933. Ridership increased during World War II from 10,149,362 in 1939 to 23,085,492 in 1943 due to a shortage of gasoline and an increased work force because of defense work. After the war, ridership declined to 17,000,000 by 1947. Conversion of trolley car routes to bus operation temporarily halted during the war resumed in 1946. Following the conversion of the Albright Loop Line on May 17, 1947, only the Shillington–Mohnton Trolley Car Line remained because of a 999 year lease that called for a $50,000 forfeiture if trolley car service was stopped or if there was substitution of another type of vehicle. After considerable litigation, the penalty was voided, and trolley car service ended on January 7, 1952 with car No. 807 making the final trip.

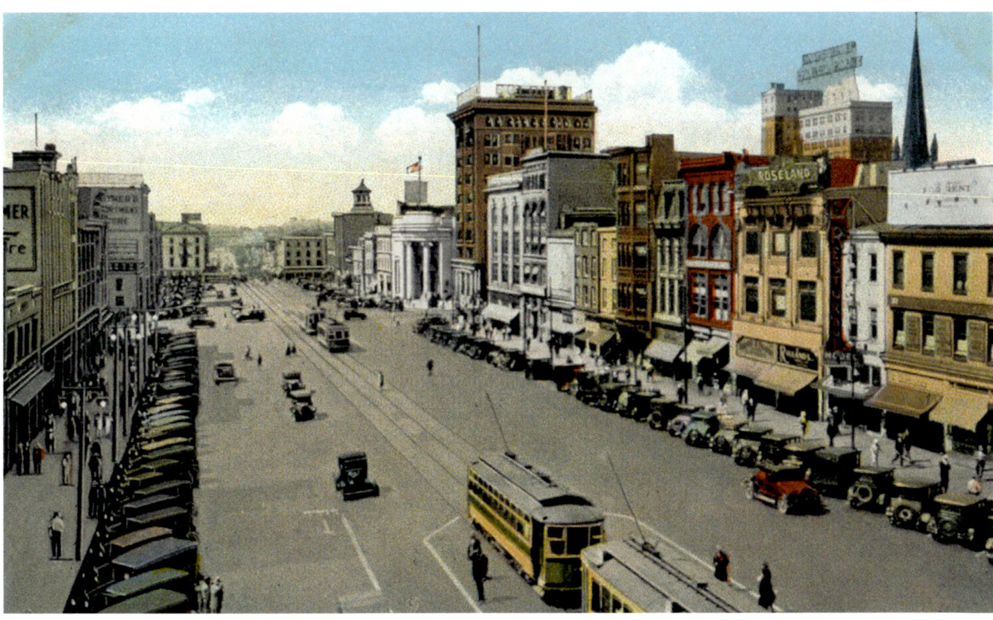

Four Reading Transit & Light Company trolley cars are in this June 2, 1929 postcard scene at Penn Square in Reading.

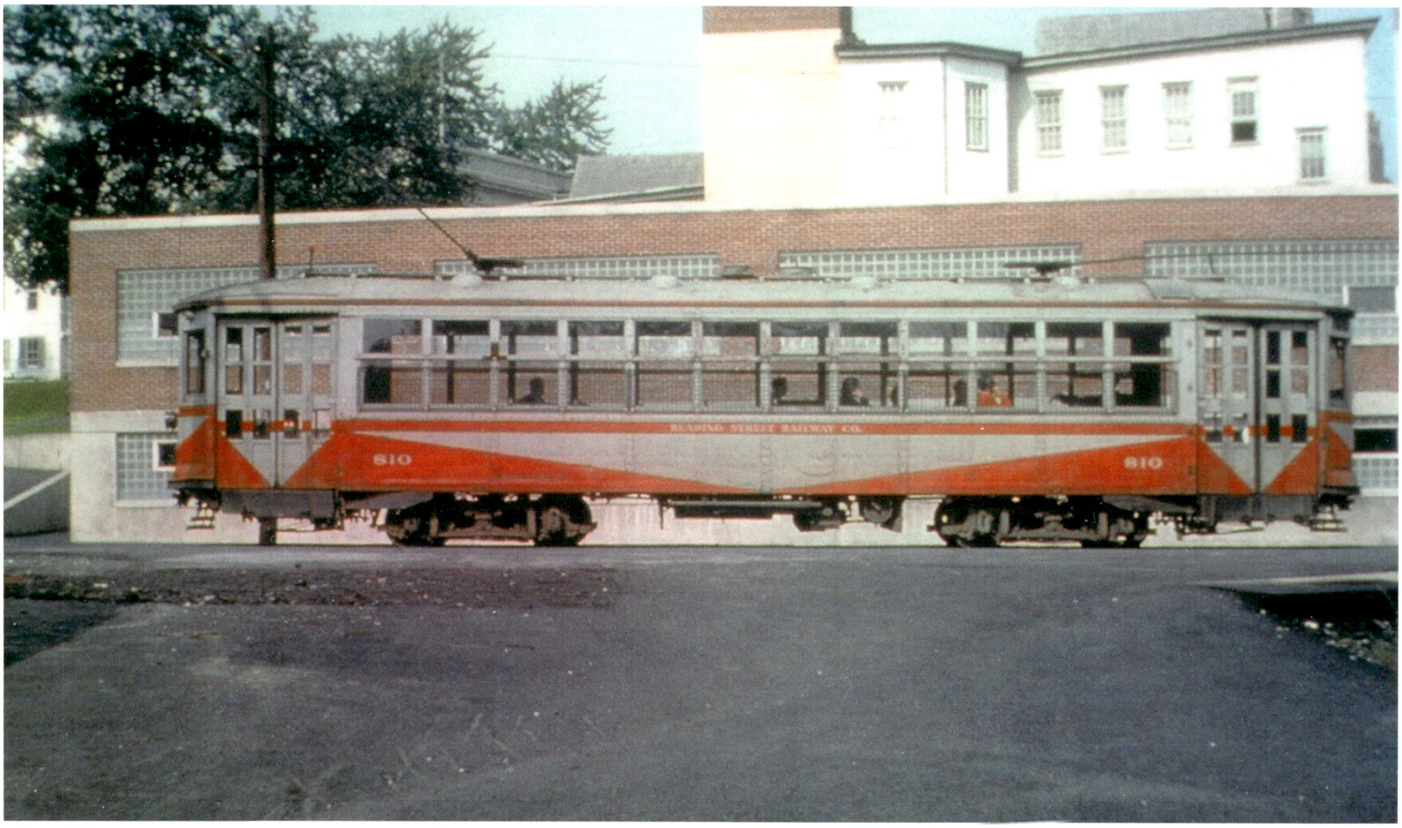

Reading Street Railway Company trolley car No. 810 is at the Mohnton terminal in 1951. This double truck car was built by the J. G. Brill Company in 1926 and was retired in 1952. (C. R. Scholes collection.)

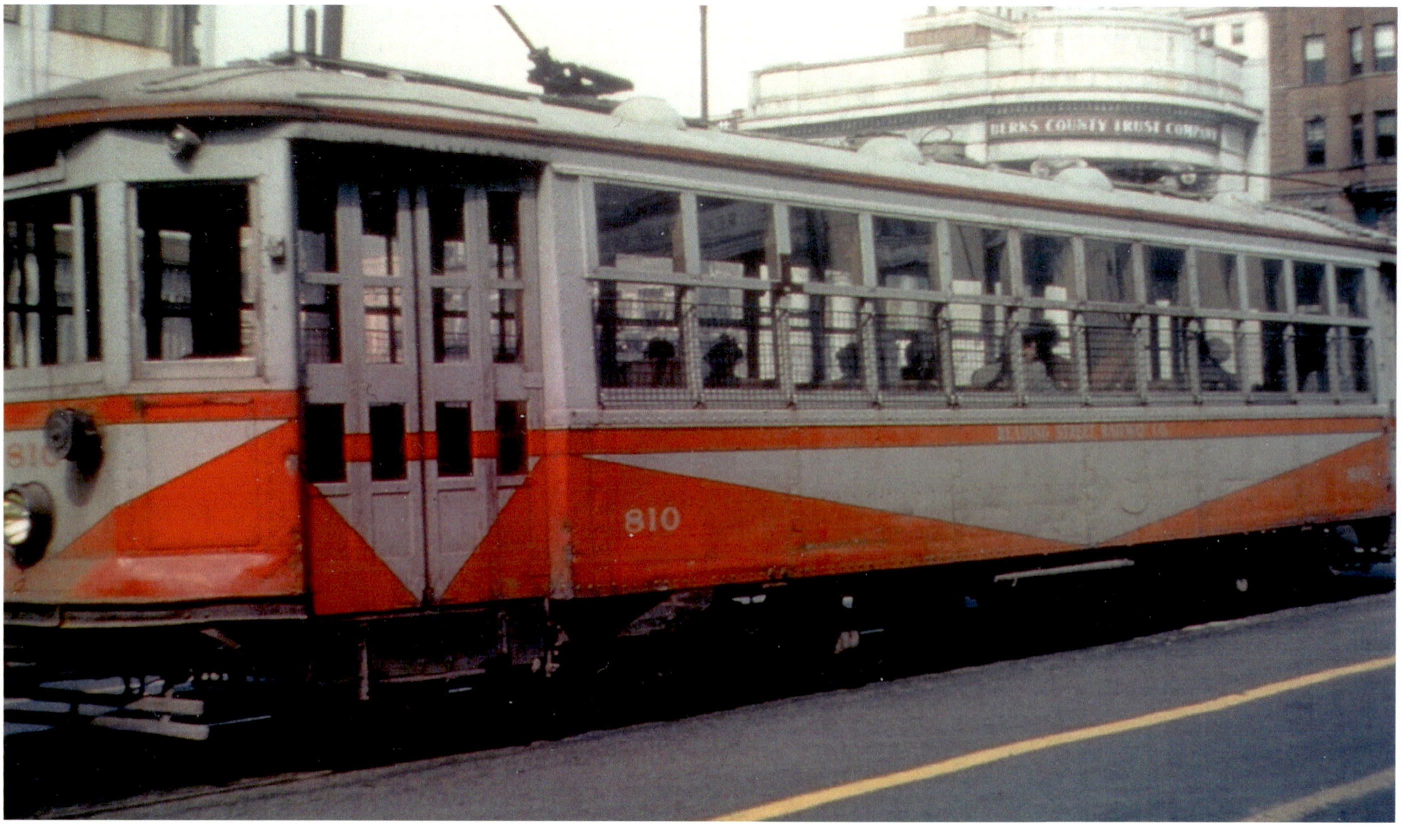

In 1951, Reading Street Railway trolley car No. 810 is on 5th Street at Penn Square. (C. R. Scholes collection.)

Chapter 8

Lehigh Valley Transit

Numerous trolley companies were merged into the Lehigh Valley Transit Company (LVT) on July 20, 1905. The transit company expanded with new routes and additional trolley cars to service a growing Allentown. On October 25, 1911 the wide gauge line of the Montgomery Traction Company between Lansdale and Norristown was acquired to achieve a more direct route to Philadelphia which opened on December 12, 1912. The Allentown to Philadelphia Liberty Bell Line was an overhead trolley wire single track operation with frequent passing sidings that made good time in open country but slow going through towns where it made frequent stops. In Norristown, its third-rail-equipped cars operated on the high-speed Philadelphia & Western Railway (P & W) to the 69th Street Terminal, which was the western terminus of the Market Frankford Subway Elevated serving center city Philadelphia. Much of the LVT's Liberty Bell Route was paralleled by the Reading Railroad's Bethlehem Branch. In Lansdale, the two stations faced each other. The Reading Railroad operated passenger service to Reading Terminal in center city Philadelphia. However, the LVT was less expensive and made many more village, local, and roadside stops.

Between 1920 and 1923, the company refurbished most of its trolley car fleet. The LVT leased the Easton Transit Company on March 1, 1922, making it the Easton Division. During the Depression, buses replaced a number of rural trolley car routes. As the LTV started to recover by 1937, the company rehabilitated many of the cars it had stored. Between 1936 and 1940, the company purchased twenty-two second-hand light weight double truck city/suburban type trolley cars. In addition, twenty-three interurban type cars were purchased second hand, of which four were assigned to the Easton Division, plus thirteen limited and six local cars for the Philadelphia Division. The thirteen limited cars were purchased from the Cincinnati & Lake Erie Railroad Company in 1938-1939 and extensively rehabilitated becoming the 1000 series. Car No. 1004 was destroyed by fire on December 20, 1940 and was replaced by Indiana Railroad Company car No. 55 which was acquired in February 1941, extensively rehabilitated, and renumbered 1030.

During World War II, the LVT with its rehabilitated fleet and additional cars that had been purchased was able to handle the increased traffic. The additional miles put on the cars plus the difficulty in getting supplies had a serious impact on the rolling stock and track. Following the end of World War II, ridership and revenues declined. On August 15, 1949 the Allentown–Bethlehem–Easton trolley car service ended followed on September 26, 1949 cutting back the Allentown to 69th Street Terminal Liberty Bell Line to Norristown requiring passengers to change to the P & W at Norristown to reach the 69th Street Terminal. In April 1950, the Cincinnati, Newport & Covington Railway Company purchased National Power and Light Company's common stock holdings in LVT and began the conversion of the remaining trolley car lines to bus operation. Norristown–Allentown trolley service ended on September 6, 1951 with car No. 1006 leaving Allentown at 11:05 p.m. making the final southbound trip from Allentown to Norristown and arriving back in Allentown at 2:41 a.m. on September 7, 1951. Allentown trolley routes were converted to bus operation as follows: Allentown–Greenawalds on June 1, 1952; Allentown–South Bethlehem–Hellertown on October 26, 1952; Allentown–Catasauqua–Northampton via 2nd Street on May 10, 1953; and Allentown–Fullerton via 7th and Washington Streets on June 7, 1953. Trolley car service ended when decorated car No. 912 made the last run on June 8, 1953 from Broad and Linden Streets in Bethlehem to the Fairview Carbarn in Allentown. LVT completed its conversion to bus operation. The Lehigh and Northampton Transportation Authority (LANTA) was created by the counties of Lehigh and Northampton in March 1972 to operate transit service in the two counties as LVT could no long afford to operate the system.

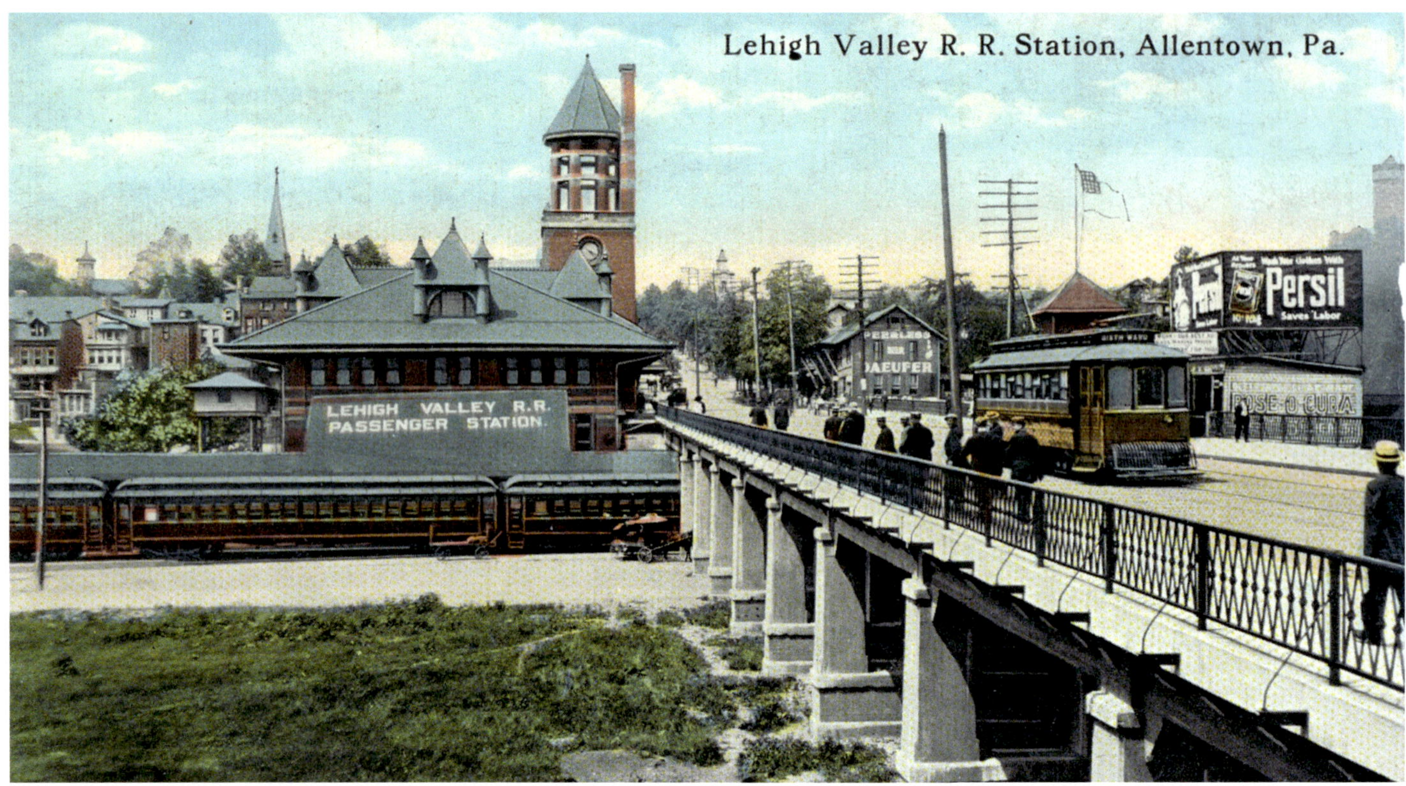

A Lehigh Valley Transit Company (LVT) trolley car is providing convenient service to the Lehigh Valley Railroad Station (built in 1899) that was located at the Hamilton Street Bridge over Jordan Creek in Allentown in this 1915 postcard scene. Passenger train service to this station ended in 1961, and the station was torn down in 1972.

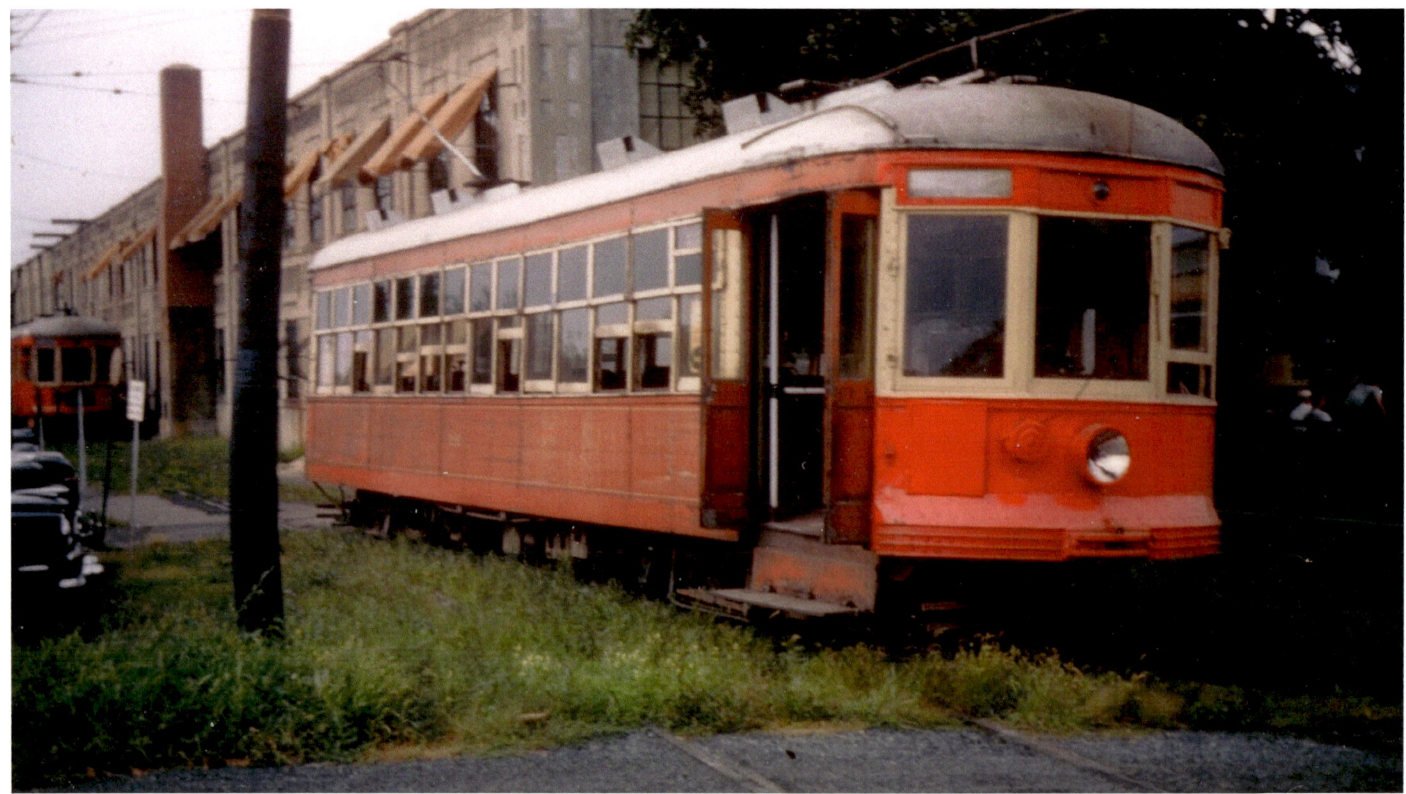

On August 28, 1949, LVT car No. 923 is at the Fairview Carbarn. This was one of twenty-four cars numbered 900 to 923 built by the J. G. Brill Company in 1918. By June 12, 1953, all of these cars had been scrapped. (C. R. Scholes collection.)

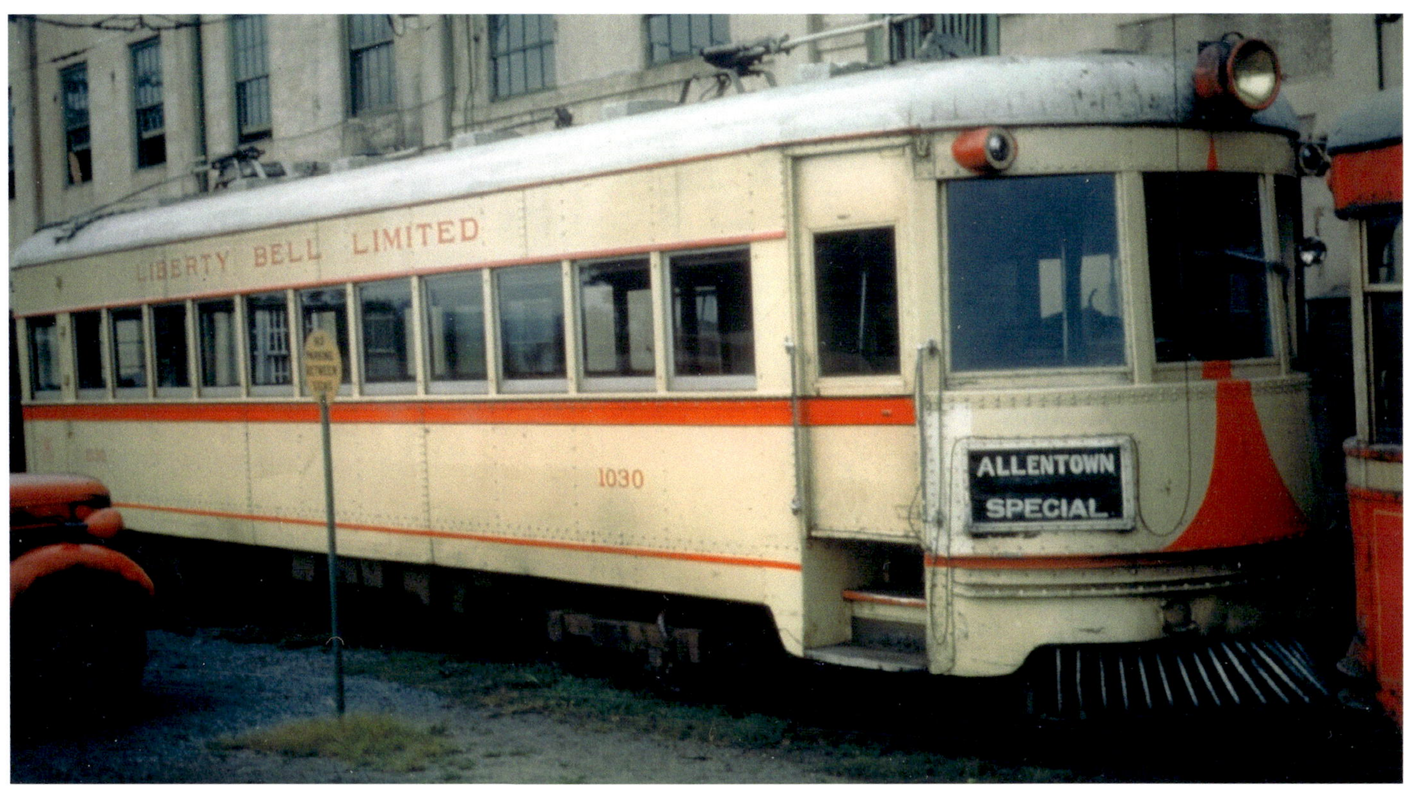

LVT car No. 1030 is at the Fairview Carbarn on August 28, 1949. The car was built by the American Car & Foundry Company of Jeffersonville, Indiana as car No. 55 for the Indiana Railroad Company of Indianapolis, Indiana. It was purchased by LVT in January 1941. After rebuilding, the car entered revenue service on October 3, 1941. This car was sold to the Seashore Trolley Museum at Kennebunkport, Maine in 1952. (C. R. Scholes collection.)

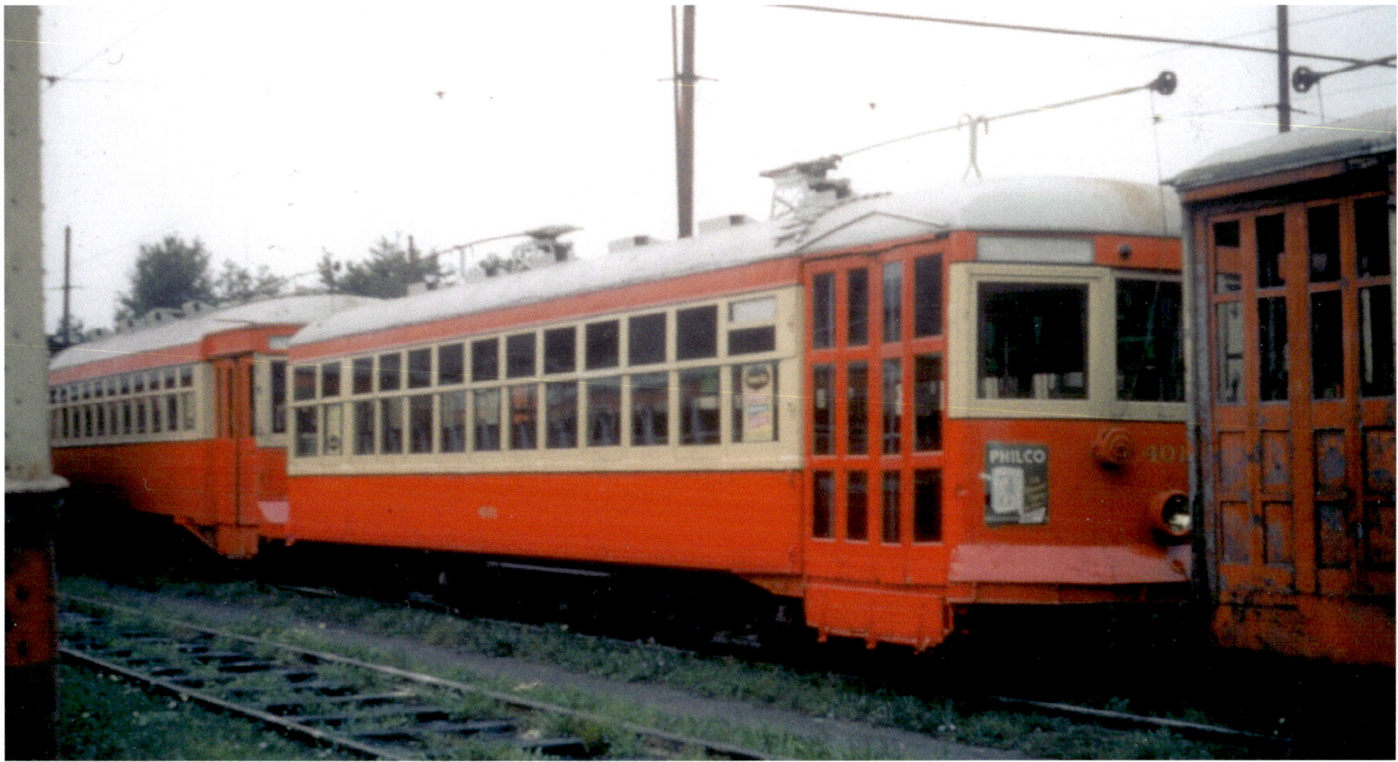

On August 28, 1949, LVT car No. 401 is in the lineup of cars at the Fairview Carbarn. This car (built by the St. Louis Car Company in 1926) was acquired from Wisconsin Public Service Corporation in 1938, and was scrapped on August 11, 1952. (C. R. Scholes collection.)

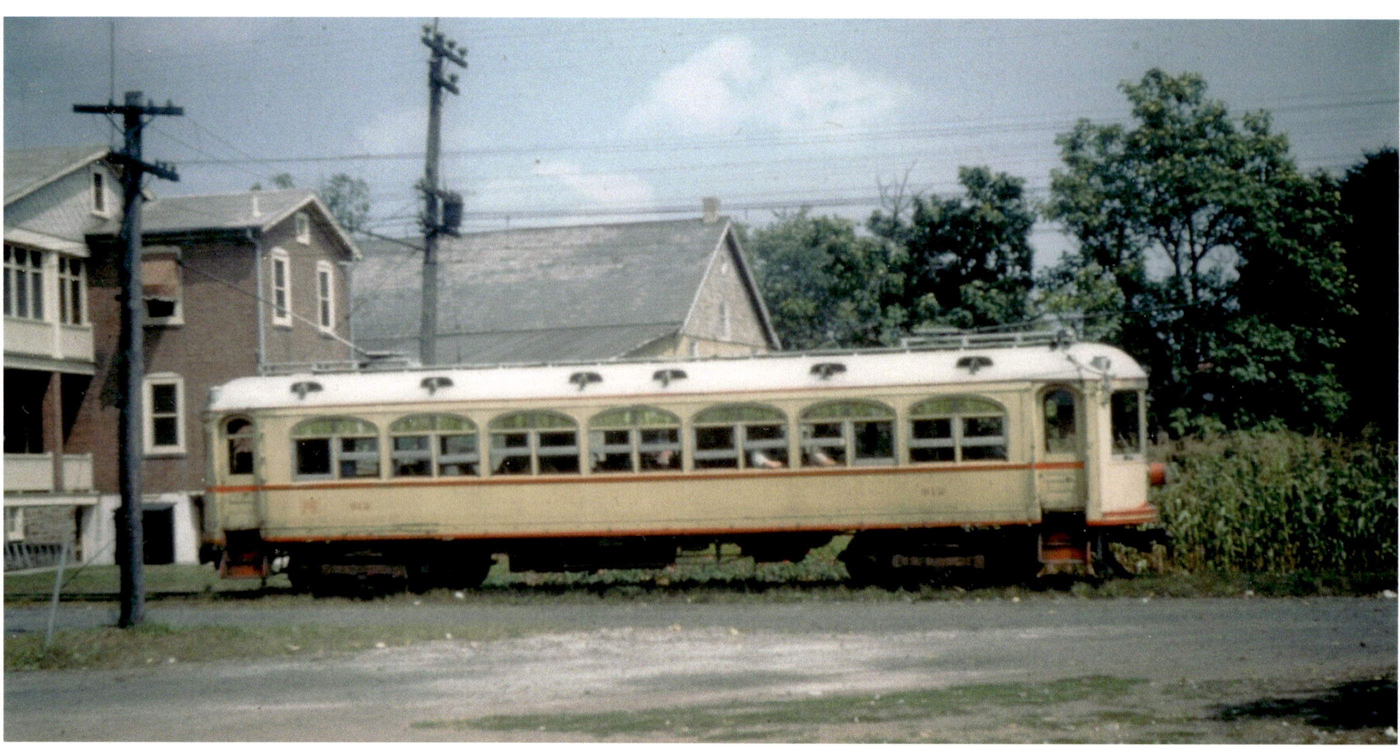

LVT car No. 812 is at the Hatfield Station on August 28, 1949. This car was originally private interurban car Co. 999 which had been built at the LVT's 14th Street shop and was converted into passenger car No. 812. It was assigned to the Fairview Carbarn and entered revenue service on July 4, 1921. During 1932 the car was modified for one man operation. In 1936 its windows were enlarged at one end and a rear passenger entrance was added. The car was scrapped on November 4, 1951. (C. R. Scholes collection.)

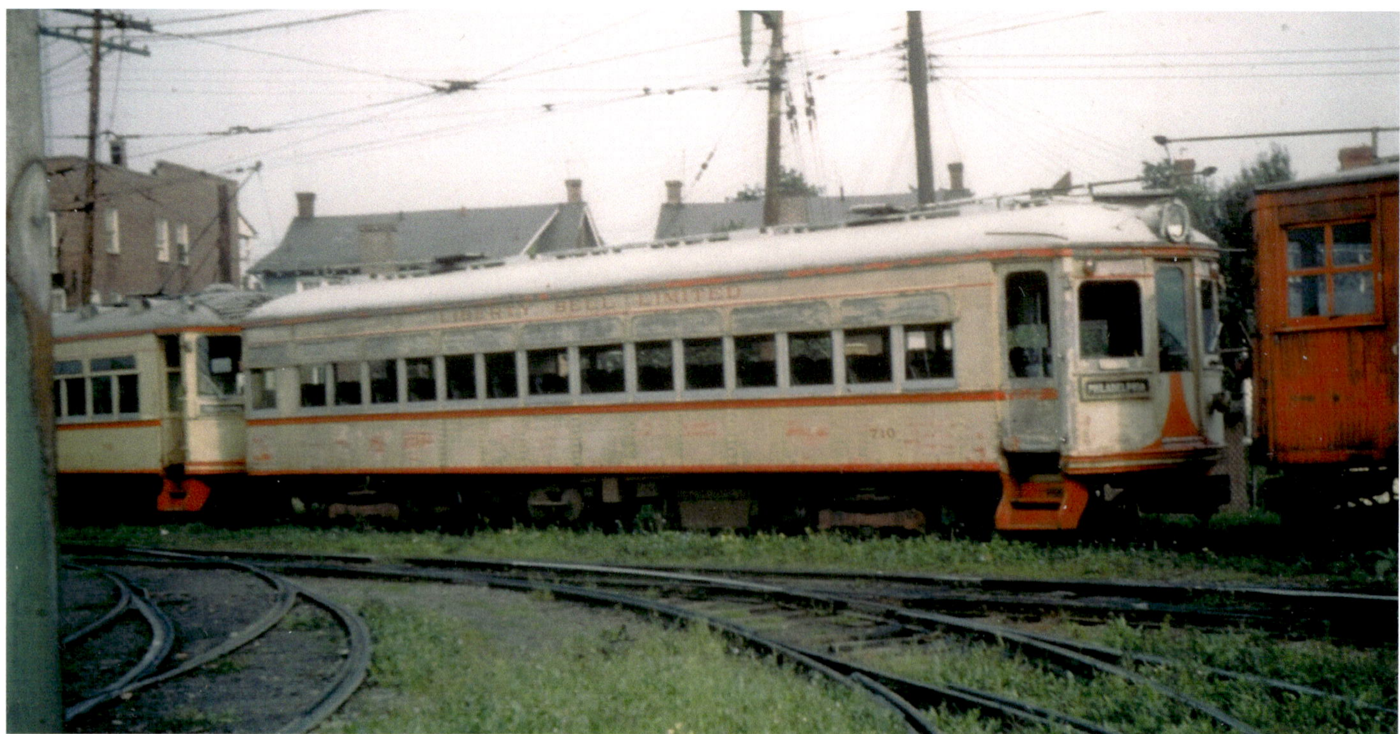

On August 28, 1949, Lehigh Valley Transit Company car No. 710 is at the Fairview Carbarn. This was one of twelve cars numbered 700 to 711 that were delivered in August 1916 from the Southern Car Company of High Point, North Carolina. The Souderton Carbarn received eleven of these cars, and one was assigned to the Fairview Carbarn as a spare and for emergency service. Car 710 went out of service on July 24, 1922 because a fire damaged the reverser. It was rebuilt as a chair car and was back in service as a chair car in 1923. In September 1931, it was rebuilt as a deluxe limited. The car was scrapped on November 14, 1951. (C. R. Scholes collection.)

Chapter 9

Sampling of Trolley Lines

The West Penn Railways at its peak operated 339.5 miles of track comprised of sixty-two trolley car companies. Among the early companies was the Connellsville Suburban Street Railway which was chartered on September 15, 1896. Although the McKeesport–Duquesne Line was abandoned in 1932, much of the system remained intact until 1950. The Irwin–Greensburg Line was abandoned on July 12, 1952 followed by the Latrobe–Hecla Line on August 2, 1952. On August 9, 1952, the remaining two lines, Connellsville–South Connellsville and Greensburg–Connellsville–Uniontown Lines, of the West Penn Railways were abandoned.

Inventor Charles J. Van Depoele supervised the installation and operated the first test trip for the Scranton Suburban Electric Railway Company (SSERC) on November 29, 1886. Van Depoele had earlier supervised the electrification of the Capital City Street Railway at Montgomery, Alabama, which began operation on April 15, 1886. The SSERC extended northward to Carbondale and Forest City, and southward to Moosic and Pittston. The Scranton Railway Company (SRC), formed on December 18, 1896, consolidated about twenty different trolley companies. For the year ending June 30, 1917, SRC operated 183 cars on 102 miles of track. After the Scranton Bus Company was incorporated in 1924, conversion to bus operation began and continued until World War II. It reorganized as the Scranton Transit Company on July 27, 1934. After World War II, conversion to bus operation resumed and the last trolley line, Green Ridge Suburban, was replaced by buses on December 18, 1954.

The East Harrisburg Passenger Railway made its first trial run with electric trolley cars on July 4, 1888. A number of trolley companies were merged into the Harrisburg Traction Company on June 18, 1895. The cost of expansion to outlying areas resulted in a reorganization into the Harrisburg Railways Company on November 29, 1912. Ridership peaked in 1923 with 34,560,000 passengers. With a decline in ridership, conversion to bus operation began in 1933, and trolley service ended when the Harrisburg to Middletown Line closed on July 16, 1939.

The York Street Railway Company formally opened its first electric trolley line on August 19, 1892 from the Square to Highland Park. By 1901 the York County Traction Company consolidated a number of trolley systems and on November 15, 1907 was reorganized into the York Railways Company. At the end of 1921, the company operated sixty-eight cars on 85.4 miles of track. Ridership peaked in 1923 with 10,950,000 passengers carried. Ridership declined, and the Broad Street Line made its last run on December 1, 1931 followed by the Dover Line on May 1, 1932. February 4, 1939 was the last day of trolley car operation in York.

The Fairmount Park Transportation Company opened the first part of the trolley car line in Fairmount Park in Philadelphia on November 10, 1896, and it was completed on June 13, 1897. It went into receivership, was sold on December 13, 1917, and was reorganized as the Fairmount Park Transit Company. Declining ridership and the fact that it was busy for only a brief period each year resulted in its last trolley operating on September 9, 1946.

The Wilkes-Barre & Suburban Street Railway operated the first electric trolley car in Wilkes-Barre in March 1888. On January 1, 1910, the Wilkes-Barre Railway Company leased all the equipment and lines of the various companies. The North Pennsylvania Trolley Line was abandoned on December 23, 1929, and elimination of trolley car lines began with a halt during World War II; however, resumed after the war with the heaviest lines converted to trackless trolley operation. Trolley car service ended on October 14, 1950 when the Nanticoke and Hanover Lines made their last runs.

The Beaver Valley Traction Company operated its first electric trolley car on December 5, 1891 from New Brighton to Beaver. According to the *McGraw Electric Railway Directory 1924*, the Beaver Valley Traction Company operated thirty-two trolley cars on 32.86 miles of track. On August 10, 1937, the last trolley car left the Junction Carbarn for Morado at 4:45 p.m., and Beaver County was now served by buses.

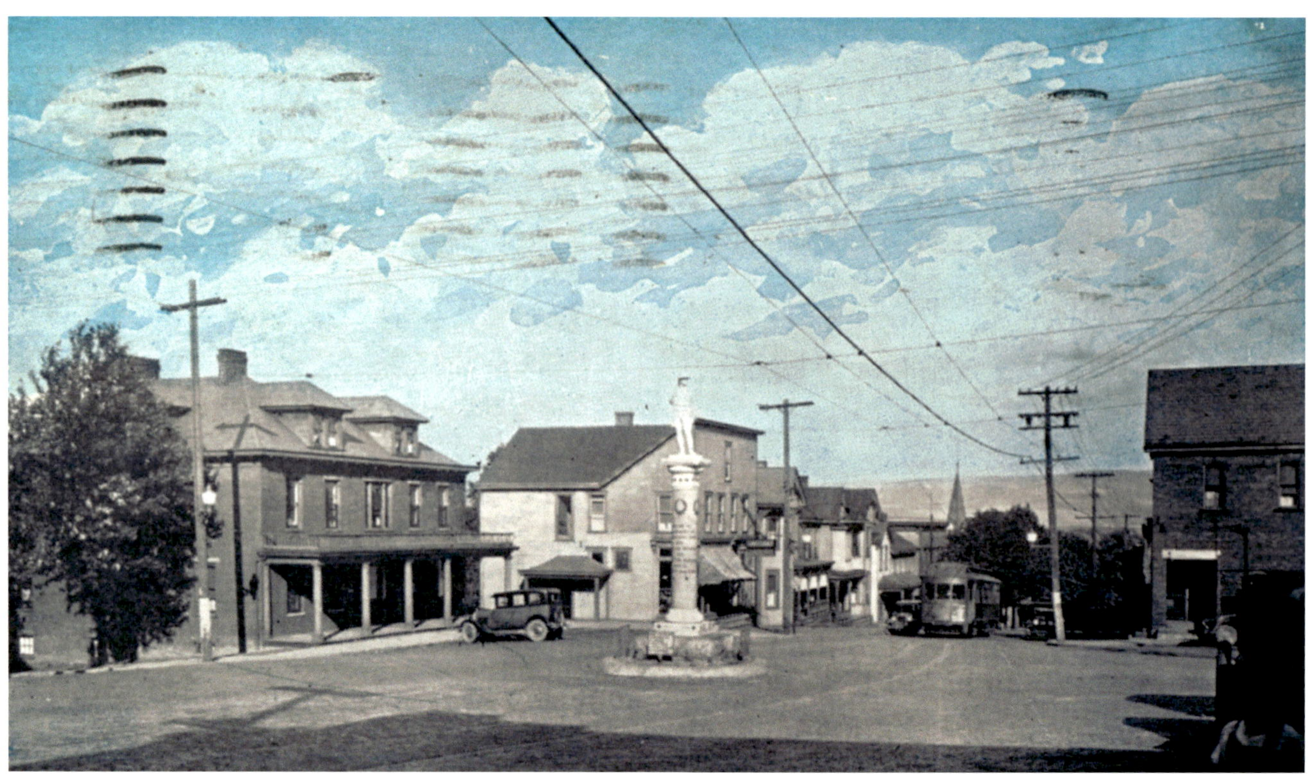

The Diamond and Soldiers Monument are shown with a West Penn Railways Company trolley car in Mt. Pleasant in this postcard view around 1920. The main line of the system was the 30.6 mile line from Greensburg via Hecla, Mount Pleasant, Scottdale, and Connellsville to Uniontown. Service was every thirty minutes and a one way trip took two hours and twenty-five minutes. There also was service from Mt. Pleasant to Tarr every thirty minutes.

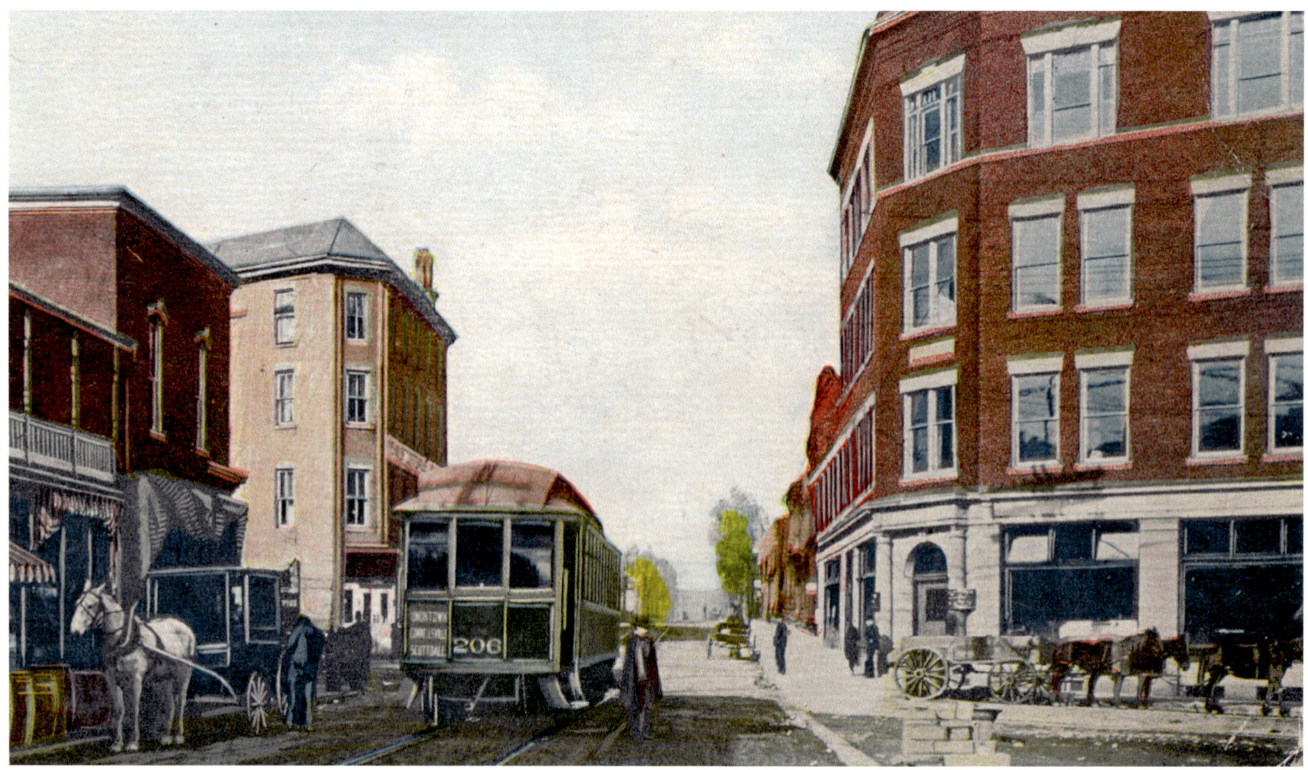

Broadway Street in Scottdale is the scene for this West Penn Railway Company trolley in this 1910 postcard scene. Scottsdale was an important junction point with service north via Mt. Pleasant to Greensburg or north to Greensburg via Hunker. South from Scottsdale the line went to Connellsville and Uniontown with connection to Fairchance.

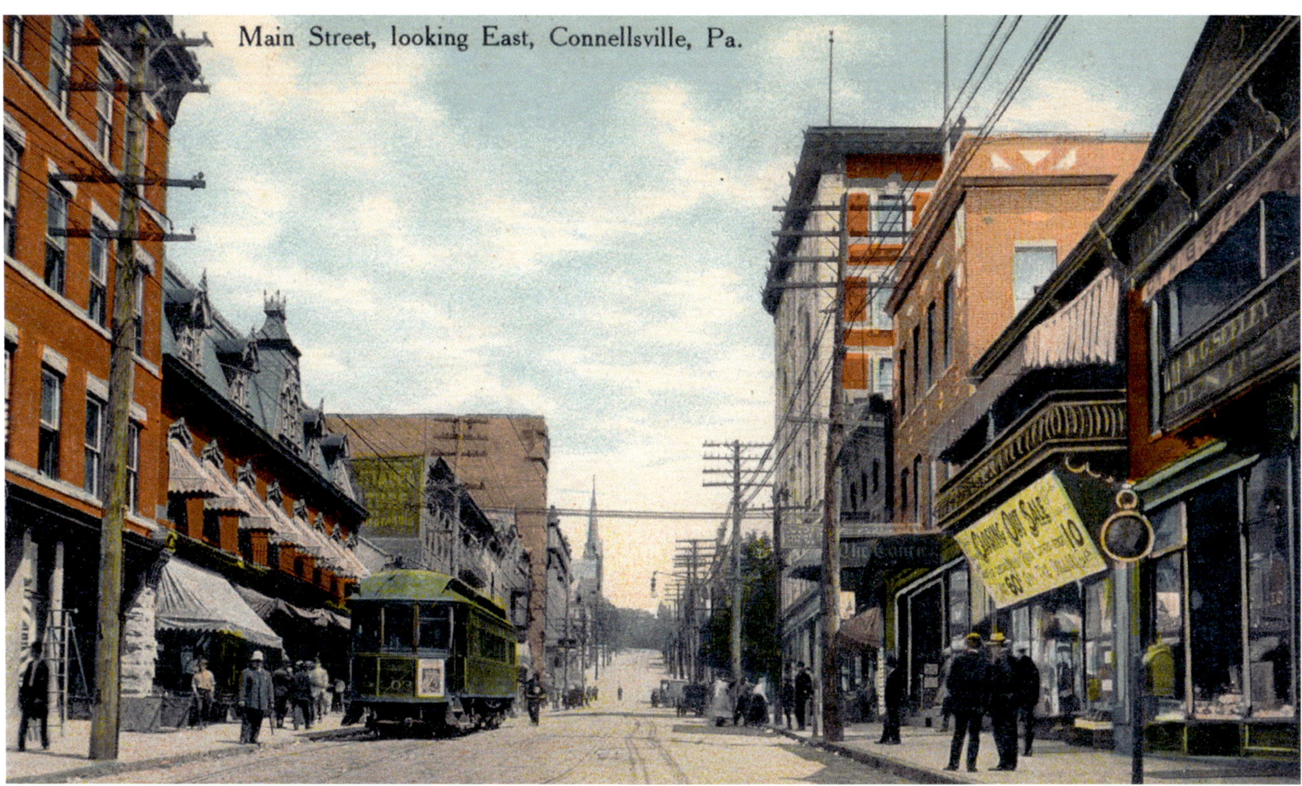

Main Street looking east finds a West Penn Railway Company trolley car coming through traffic free Main Street in this 1910 postcard scene. The trolley system in the 1930s and 1940s was busy bringing residents from outlying areas into nearby towns for work, shopping and entertainment.

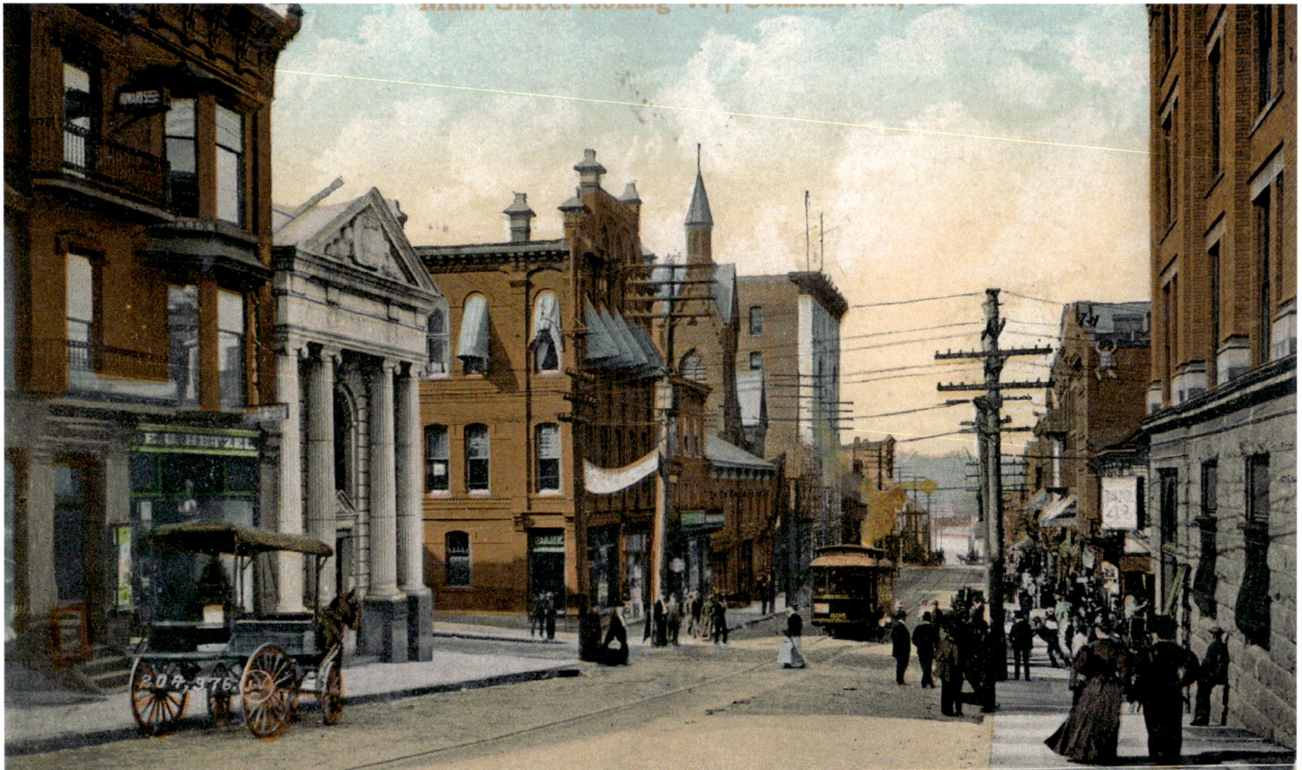

In this postcard postmarked September 21, 1908, a West Penn Railways Company trolley car is moving along Main Street in Connellsville where pedestrians outnumber the horse-drawn vehicles. The decline in area mining plus the construction of better roads which increased automobile ownership resulted in fewer trolley car riders.

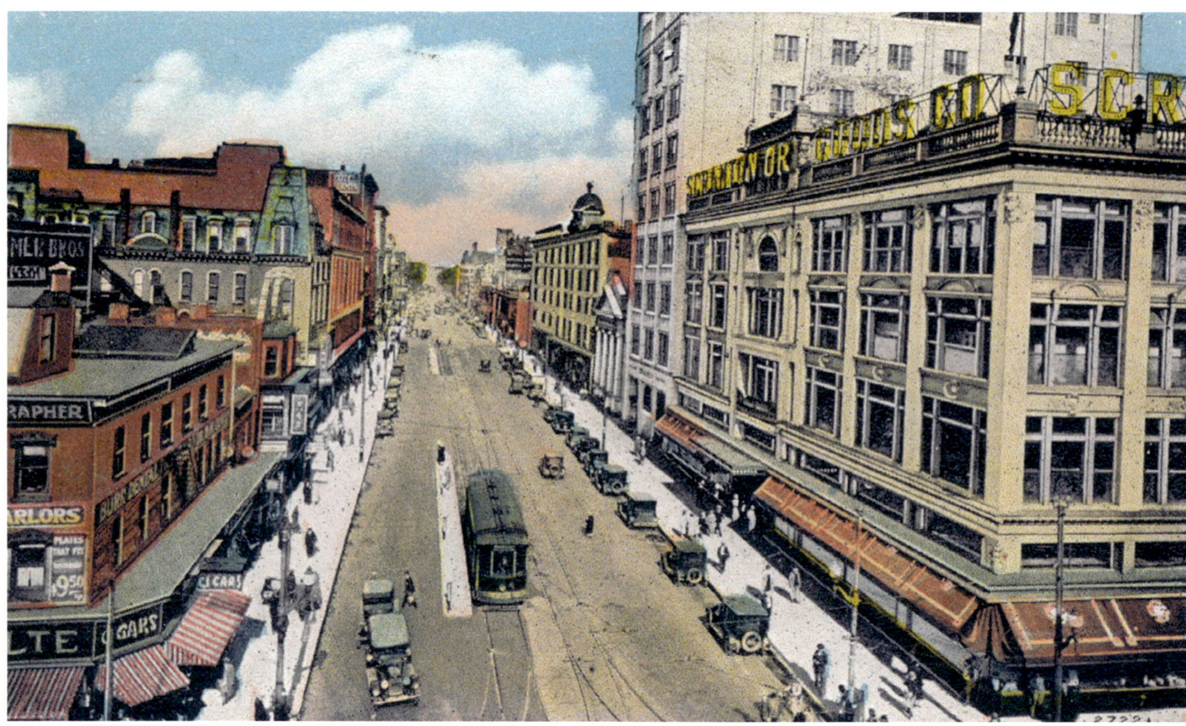

Wyoming Avenue in Scranton is the location of a Scranton Railway Company trolley car in this postcard scene around 1920. The company went into receivership and was reorganized as the Scranton Transit Company on July 27, 1934. Conversion of trolley car to bus operation began in 1935. World War II brought a temporary halt in the abandonment process, but conversion to bus operation resumed in 1947, and was completed when the Green Ridge Suburban Line made its last trolley car run on December 18, 1954.

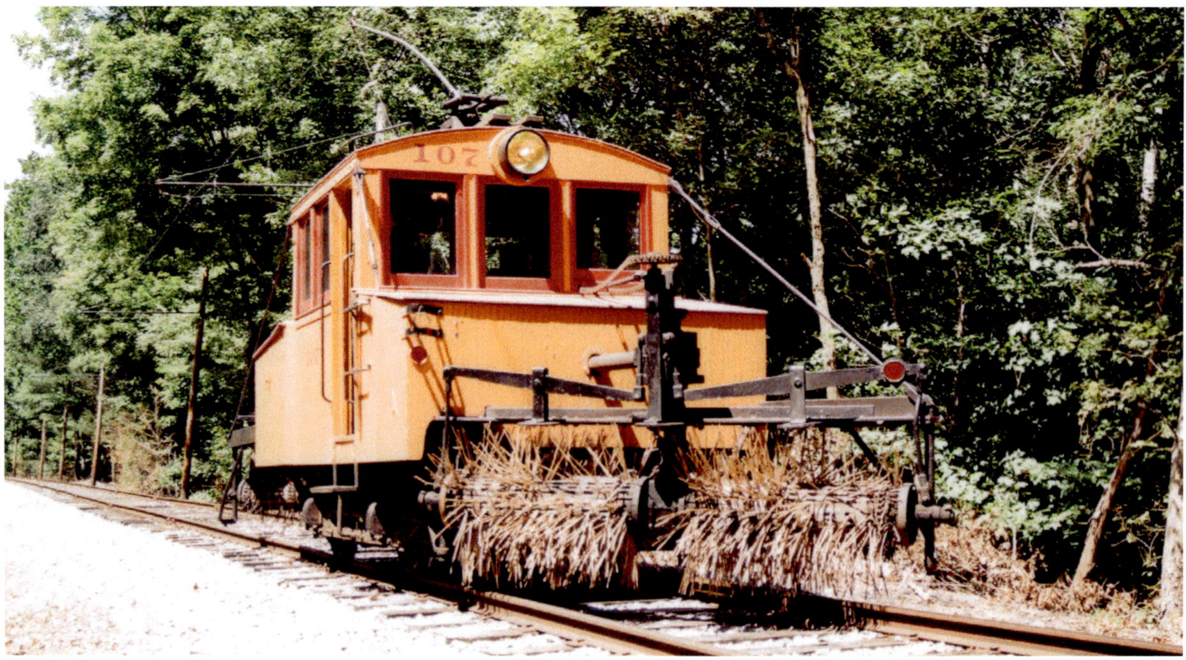

Former Scranton Transit Company single truck, four-wheeled snow sweeper car No. 107 with rotating brooms at each end is on a run at the Rockhill Trolley Museum in this August 17, 2014 scene. It is a "steeple cab" design, with operator controls in the middle of the car, built by the master mechanic of the Chicago and Joliet Electric Railway (CJER) in 1910. After the CJER ended service in 1933, it was acquired by the Scranton Transit Company and used until that system was completely converted to bus operation on December 18, 1954. The snow sweeper was at the Rail City Museum in Sandy Pond, New York, the Magee Transportation Museum in Bloomsburg, Pennsylvania, and was acquired by the Rockhill Trolley Museum in 1973.

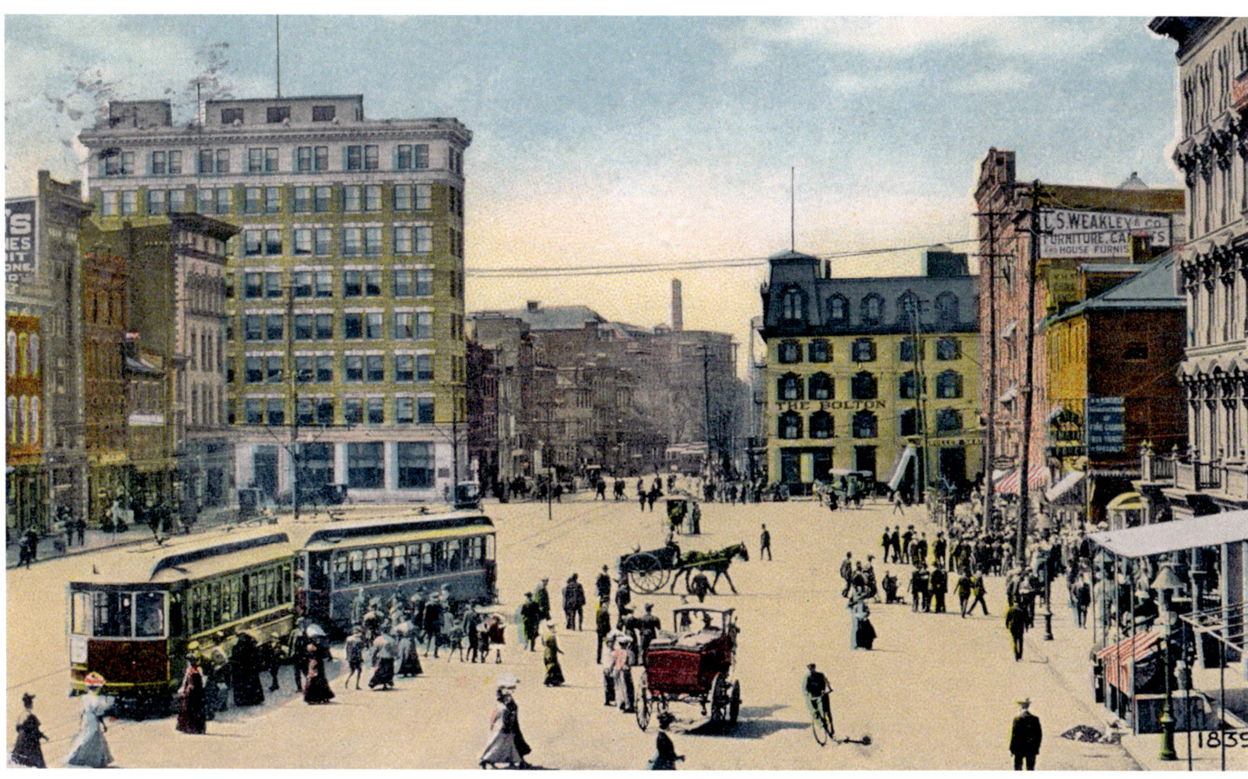

Market Square in Harrisburg is busy with riders at two trolley cars and plenty of pedestrians in this postcard postmarked July 25, 1911. After World War I, Harrisburg Railways faced the expansion of the state capitol grounds and construction of new office buildings which disrupted trolley car routings. Ridership peaked in 1923 with 34,560,000 riders.

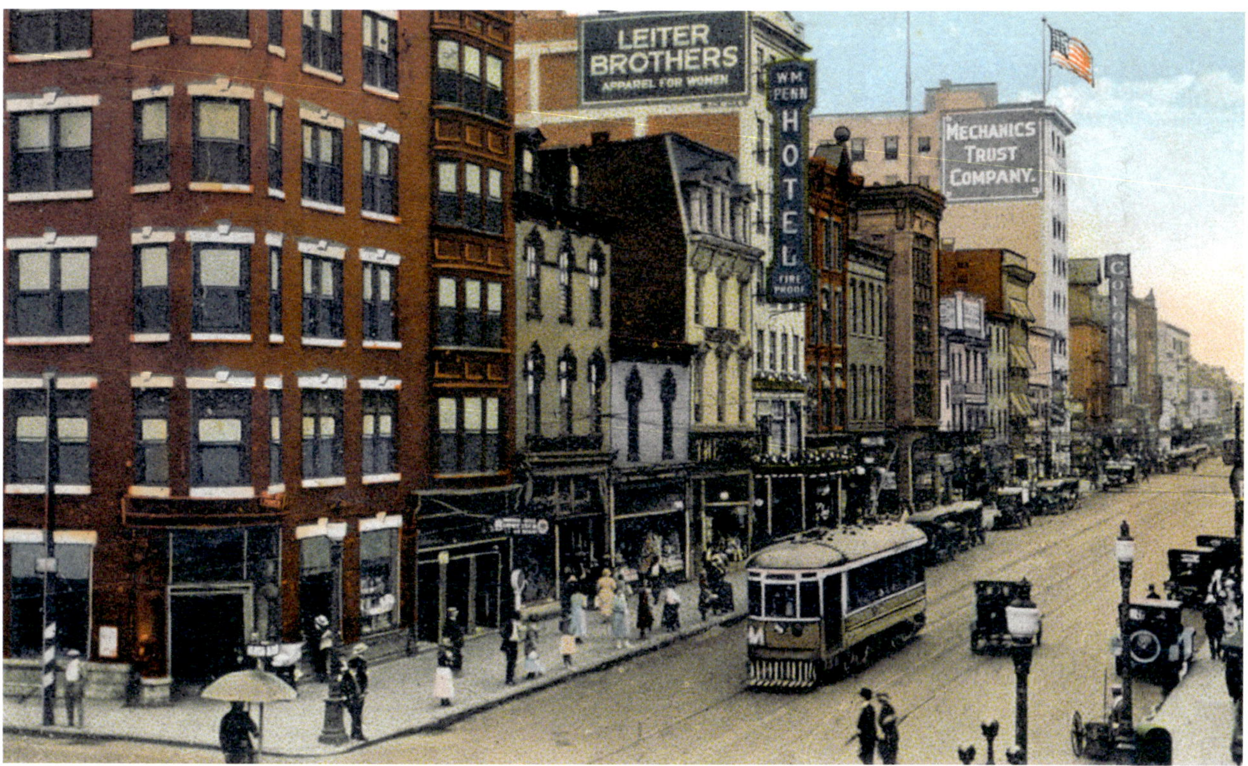

In this postcard postmarked September 4, 1922, a Harrisburg Railways Route M (Steelton–Middletown) trolley car is on Market Street in downtown Harrisburg. The Steelton–Middletown Line was the first electric trolley car line in Harrisburg. On May 17, 1931, Middletown cars were through routed to Hummelstown as Route 7, and Steelton cars went to 23rd and Derry as Route 8. These were the last two trolley lines in Harrisburg, and they made their last run on July 16, 1939.

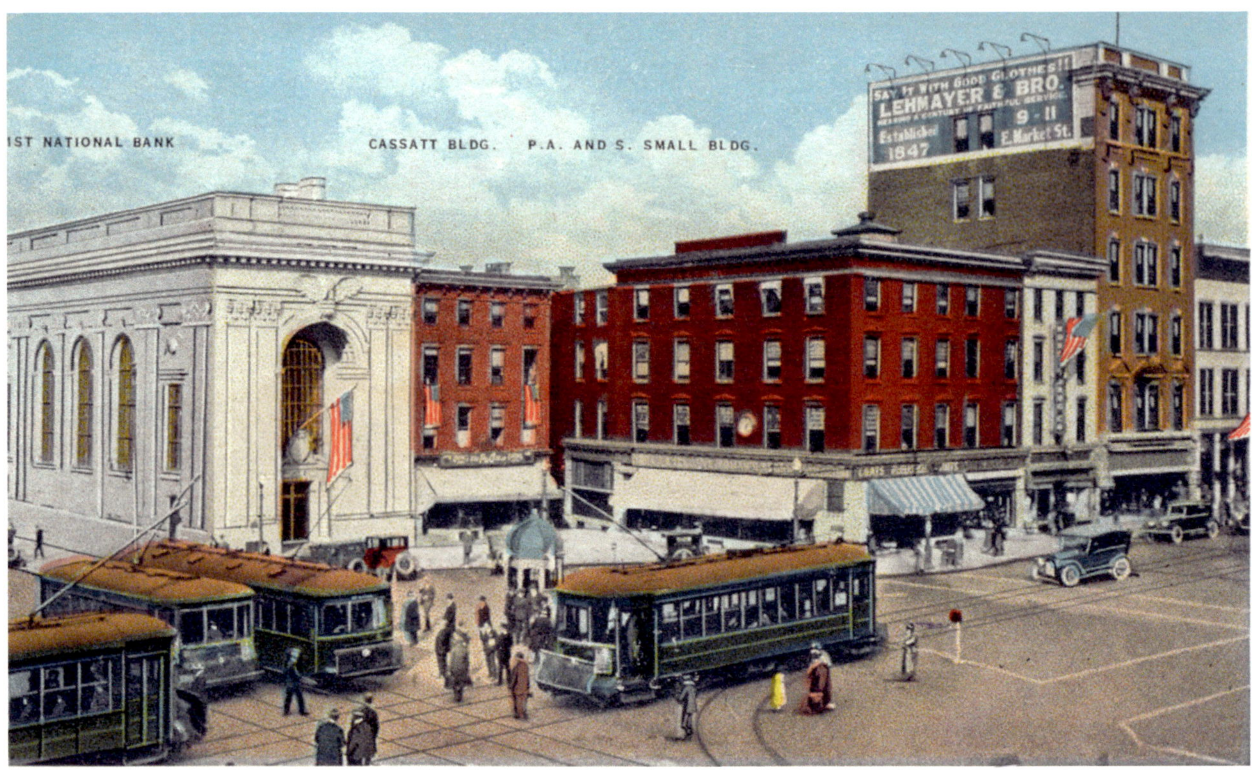

Center Square in York shows four York Railways Company trolley cars in this postcard view around 1920. At the end of 1921, the company operated sixty-eight cars on 85.4 miles of track. Ridership peaked in 1923 with 10,950,000 passengers carried. The last trolley car run in York was made on February 4, 1939.

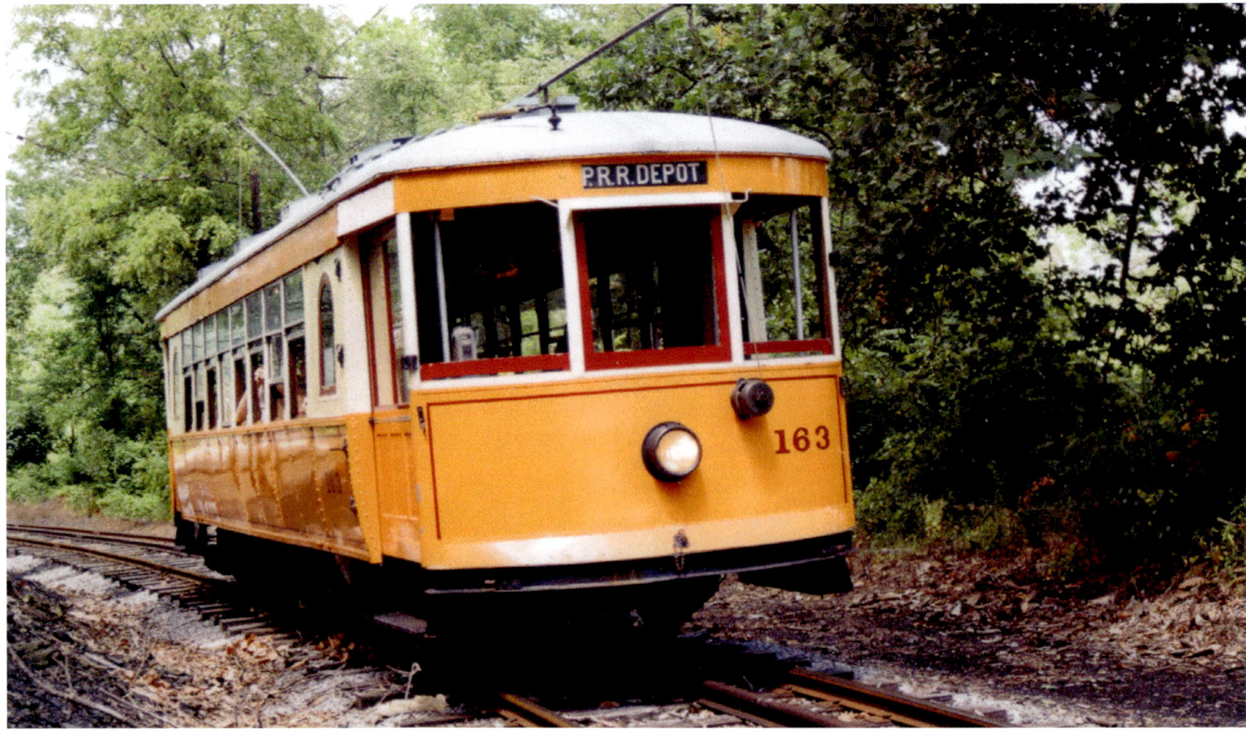

Former York Railways Company trolley car No. 163 is shown at the Rockhill Trolley Museum on August 17, 2014. After York Railways Company ended trolley car operation on February 4, 1939, the car was sold and became a summer home along Conewago Creek. After Hurricane Agnes completely flooded the car in 1972, the owners donated the car to the museum. A worldwide search was conducted to get all the parts needed, and over seventeen years of volunteer labor went into restoring the car to beautiful operating condition. The car was dedicated at the Rockhill Trolley Museum on September 16, 1989.

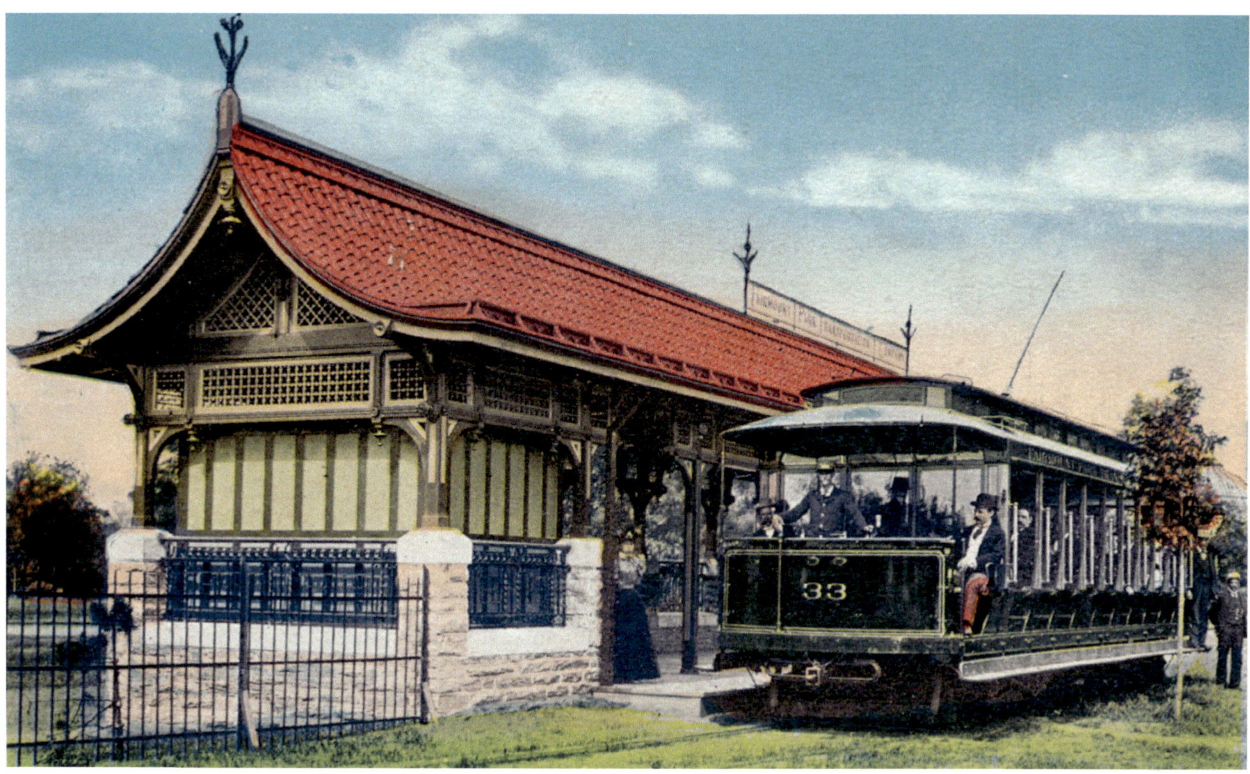

Around 1900, Fairmount Park Transit Company car No. 33 is shown in this postcard view at the ornate Chinese style Dauphine Street terminus of the line instead of 44th and Elm noted on the postcard. In 1896, J. G. Brill Company built thirty trailer cars Nos. 32 to 61. Hence there may have been some later renumbering. The completely grade separated 8.8 mile line, with stone tunnels under roads, had seventy cars because the seasonal business required a large number of cars and operated entirely in Fairmount Park in Philadelphia. Regular service on this line ended on September 9, 1946.

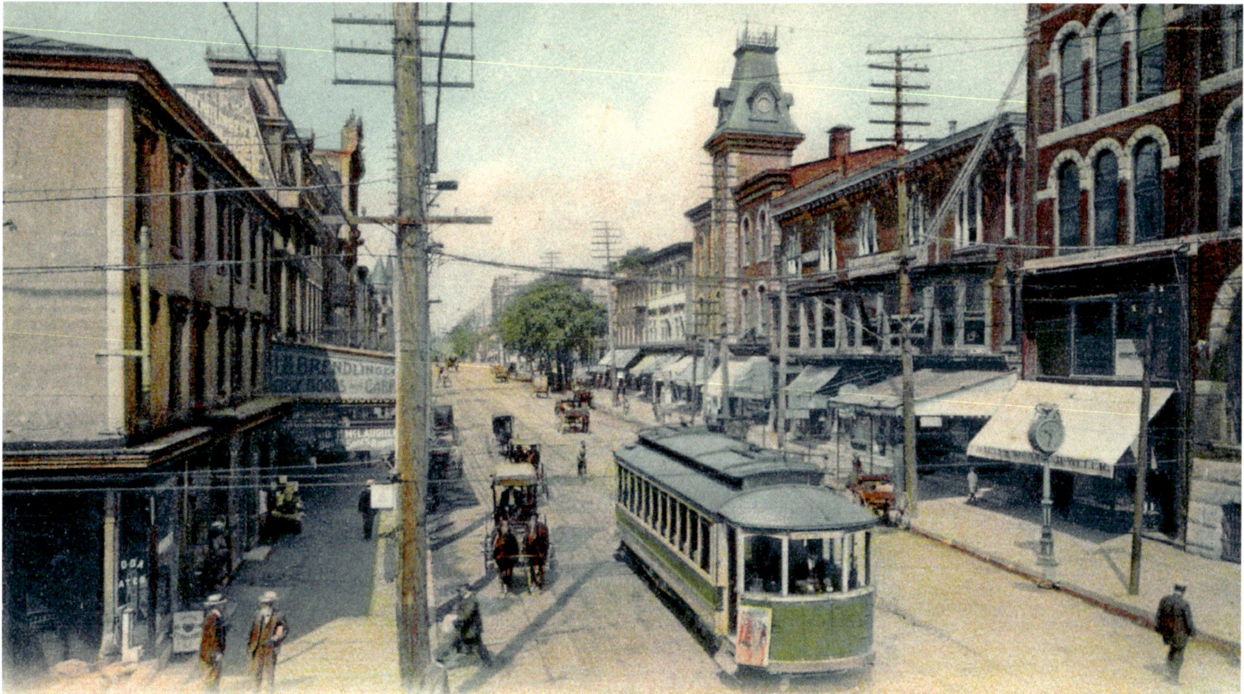

Main Street in Norristown is the location of a Schuylkill Valley Traction Company car in this postcard scene around 1910. The Norristown Passenger Railway Company began electric trolley car service on August 9, 1893 and became part of the Schuylkill Valley Traction Company on January 14, 1895. During the Great Depression, passenger riding declined. On September 9, 1933, all trolley car service ended. Buses of the reorganized Schuylkill Valley Lines replaced the trolley cars on September 10, 1933.

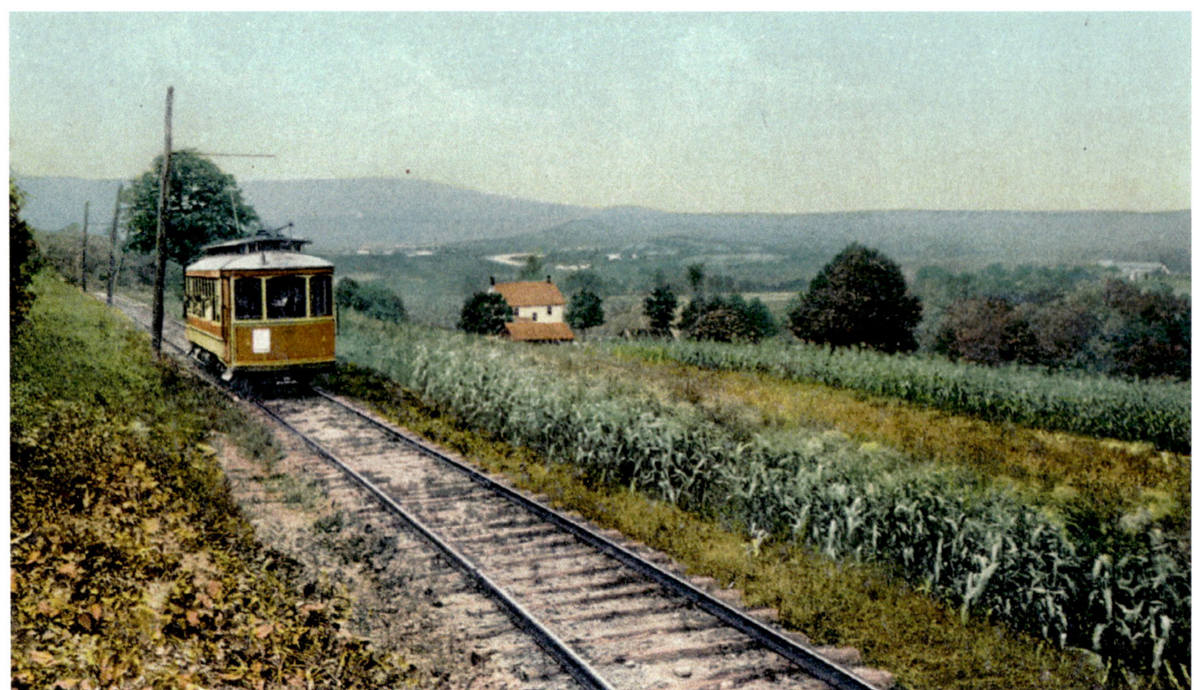

A Stroudsburg, Water Gap & Portland Railway Company (SWGP) trolley car is operating on the thirteen mile Stroudsburg via the Delaware Water Gap to Portland Line in this postcard scene around 1915. The Stroudsburg Passenger Railway Company electrified the line from Stroudsburg to East Stroudsburg on March 11, 1902 and became the Stroudsburg & Water Gap Railroad which merged with the Water Gap & Portland Street Railway Company to form the SWGP on April 1, 1911. In 1917, it emerged from receivership as the Stroudsburg Traction Company. Service was cut back to the Delaware Water Gap on November 30, 1926, and trolley car service ended on September 4, 1928.

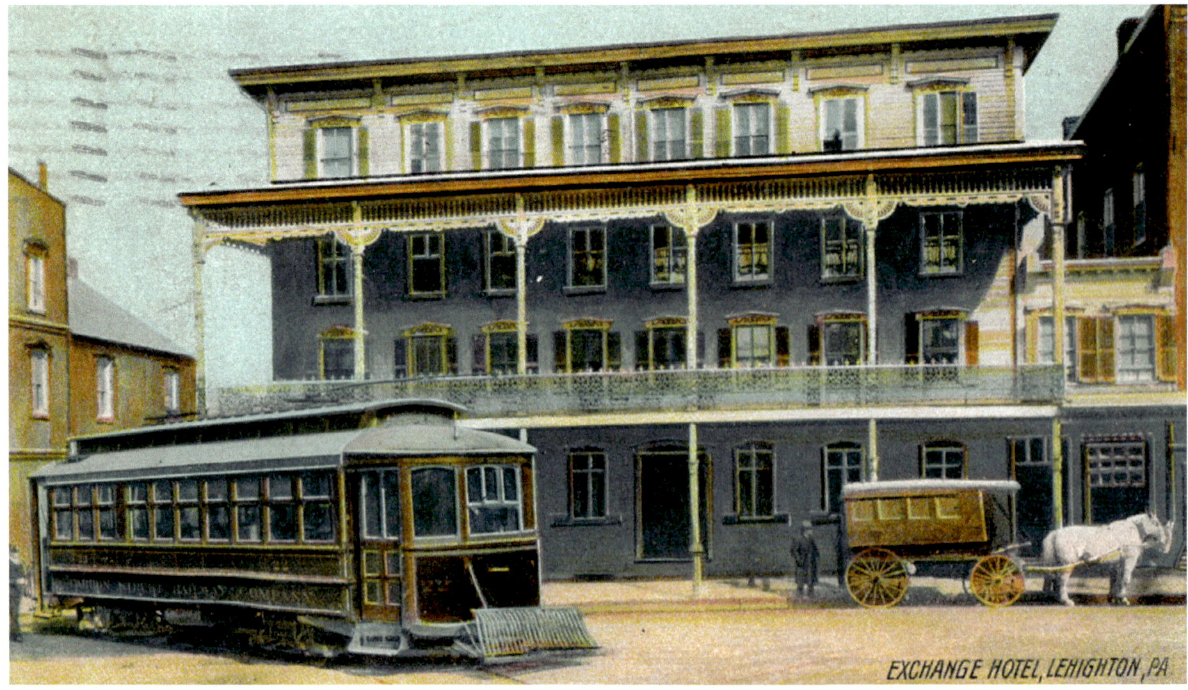

A Carbon Transit Company trolley car is passing by the Exchange Hotel in the borough of Lehighton in Carbon County in this postcard postmarked October 4, 1916. On September 5, 1893, the Carbon County Electric Railway Company began trolley service from Mauch Chunk to Lehighton and in 1898 extended the line from Mauch Chunk to East Mauch Chunk. It became the Carbon Transit Company on July 27, 1908. The line was sold at foreclosure and became the Mauch Chunk & Lehighton Transit Company on March 13, 1919. Unable to meet bond interest payments, the line was reorganized as the Mauch Chunk Transit Company on June 30, 1925. Ridership declined, and trolley service ended on October 28, 1931.

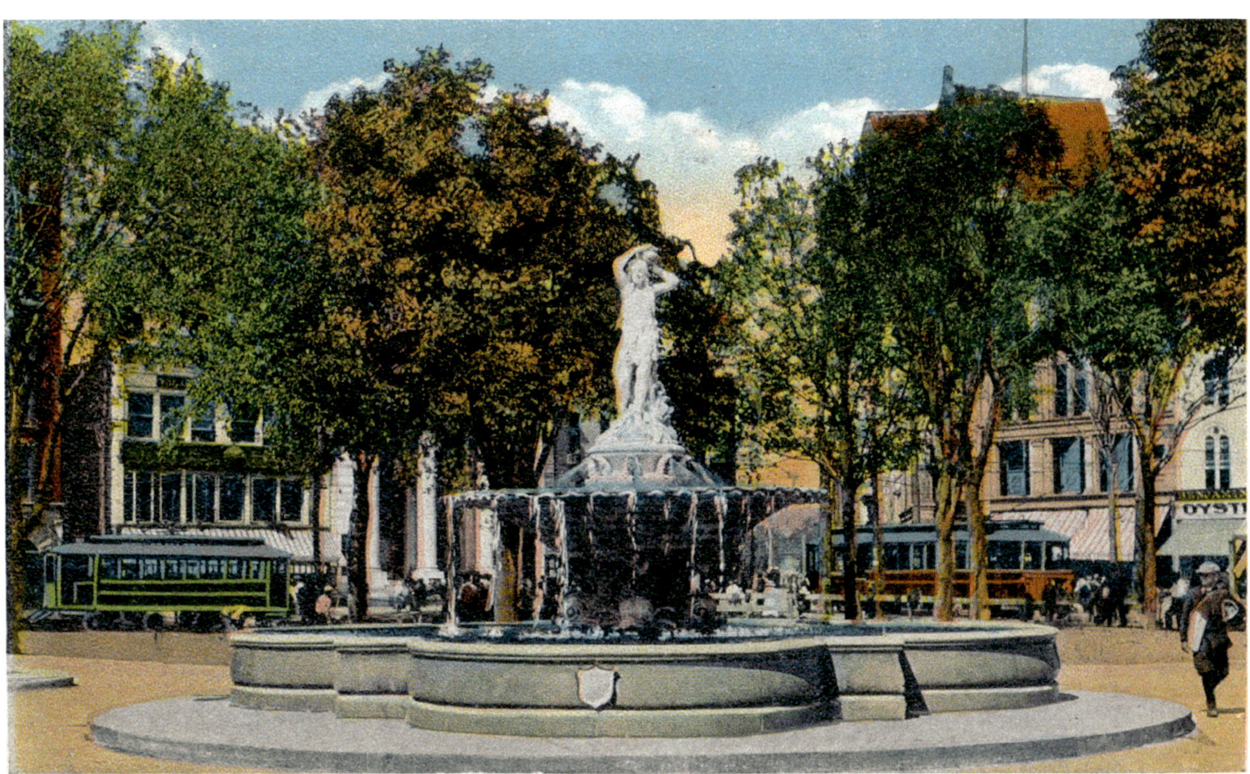

In this postcard postmarked September 1, 1920, a Wilkes-Barre Railway Company trolley car is passing Public Square in the city of Wilkes-Barre. The first trolley car line converted to bus operation was North Pennsylvania Avenue on December 23, 1929. Starting in 1939, the heaviest patronized trolley car routes were converted to trackless trolley. World War II temporarily halted the conversion program which resumed after the war. Trolley car service ended on October 14, 1950, and on October 17, 1958 buses replaced trackless trolleys.

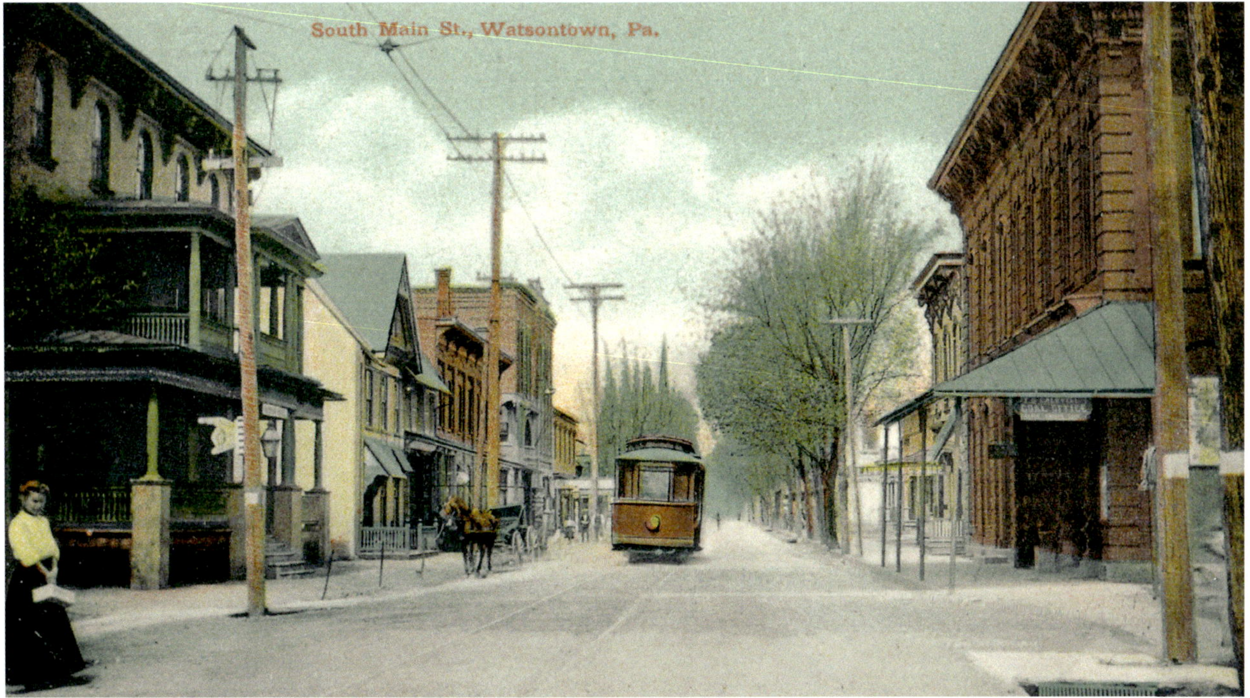

A Lewisburg, Milton & Watsontown Passenger Railway Company trolley car is on South Main Street in the borough of Watsontown in Northumberland County in this postcard postmarked October 6, 1908. The line opened from Lewisburg to Watsontown on April 4, 1898. A dramatic drop in ridership because of increased use of automobiles resulted in the abandonment of trolley car service on July 26, 1928.

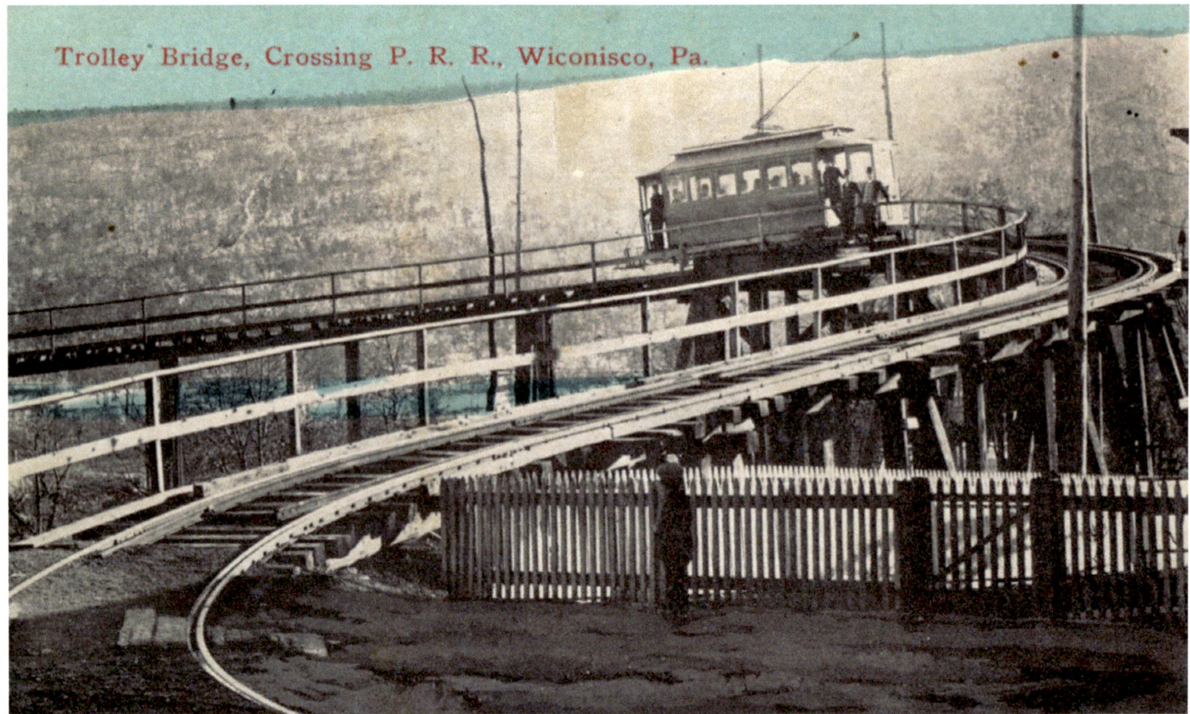

In this 1915 postcard scene, a Lykens Valley Railway Company trolley car is crossing the Pennsylvania Railroad over a horseshoe type trestle. Trolley service began on April 1, 1899 by the Lykens & Williams Valley Street Railway Company. The completed ten mile line had hourly service between Lykens and Reinerton. It reorganized as the Lykens Valley Railway Company on January 1, 1915. The Reinerton–Williamstown section closed in August 1924, and in December 1924 the remainder of the line from Williamstown to Lykens closed.

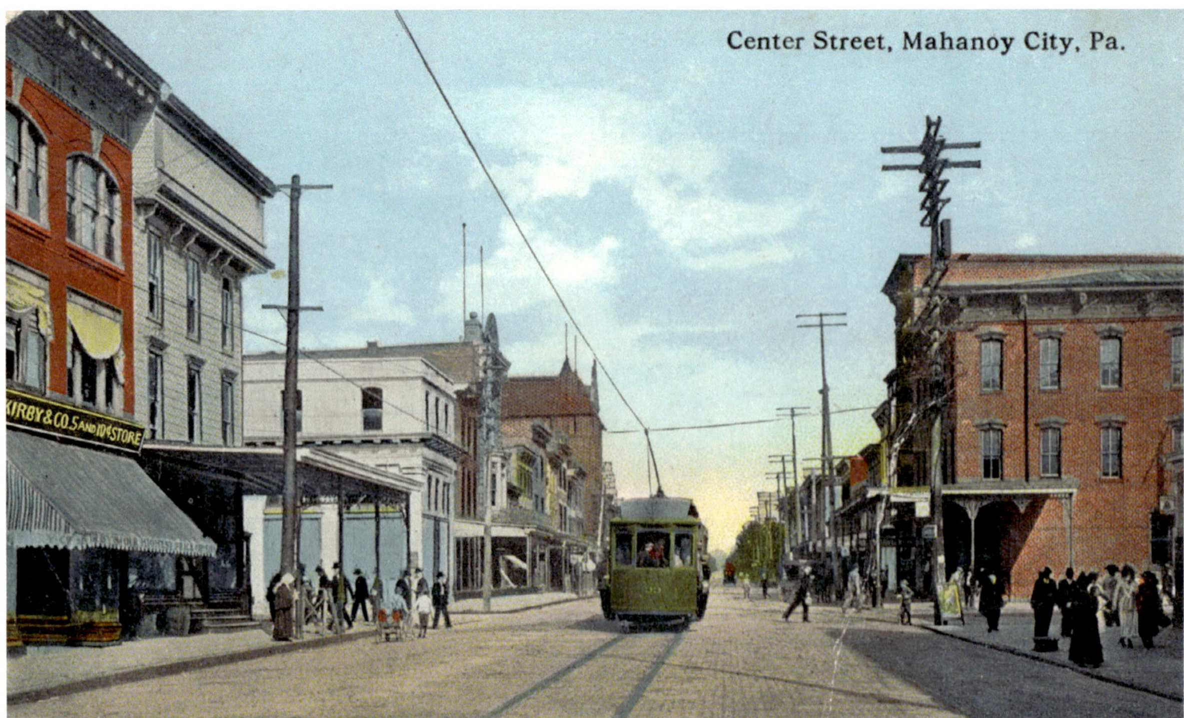

A Schuylkill Railway Company trolley car is on Center Street in Mahanoy City in this postcard postmarked July 19, 1913. The Schuylkill Traction Company was chartered on September 26, 1882, and it became part of the Schuylkill Railway Company on February 20, 1903. The forty mile line (according to the *McGraw Electric Railway List* August 1918) had fifty-four cars and two snow sweepers, connected Mahanoy City with Ashland and Frackville to St. Clair. From its beginning, there were financial difficulties, and trolley car service ended in 1927.

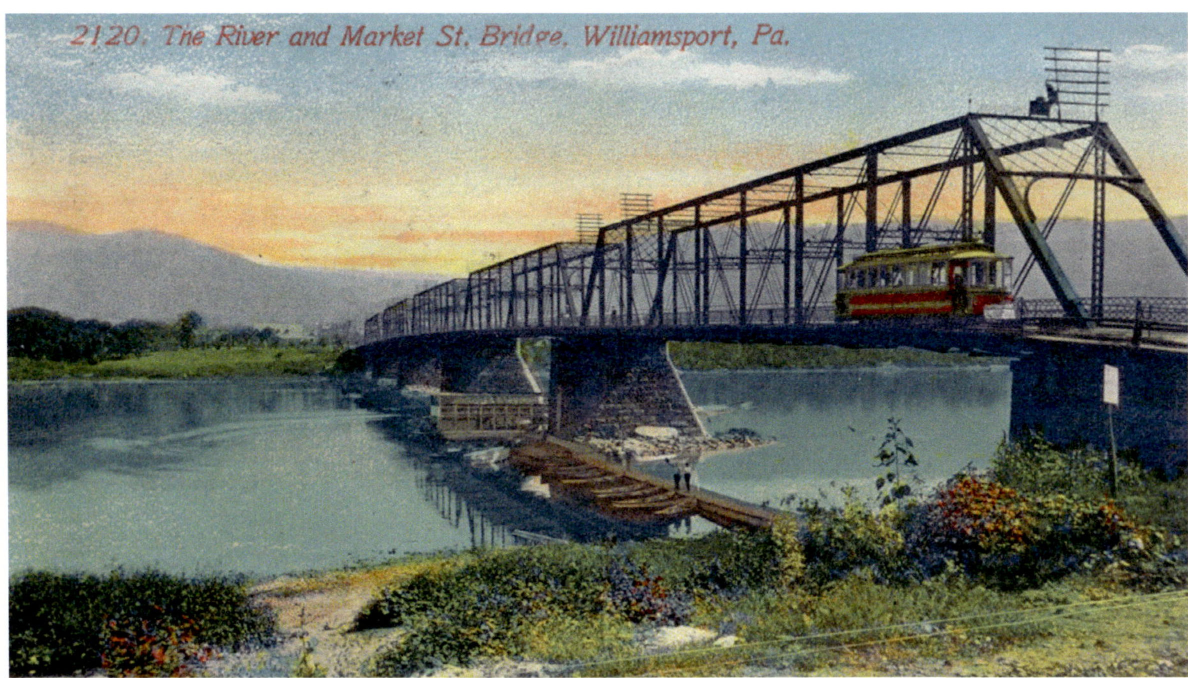

In this postcard postmarked September 22, 1911, a Williamsport Passenger Railway Company trolley car is crossing the Susquehanna River over the Market Street Bridge. Electric trolley car service started in Williamsport on August 5, 1891. Four trolley car companies, consolidated in 1927, formed the Williamsport Railways Company which built a new carbarn at West Third and Park Streets, purchased five new cars, rehabilitated some of the older cars, and rebuilt much of the track. Ridership increased for a brief period but then declined and with the Great Depression was losing money. The decision was made to convert to bus operation. At 1 a.m. on Sunday June 11, 1933, trolley car service ended.

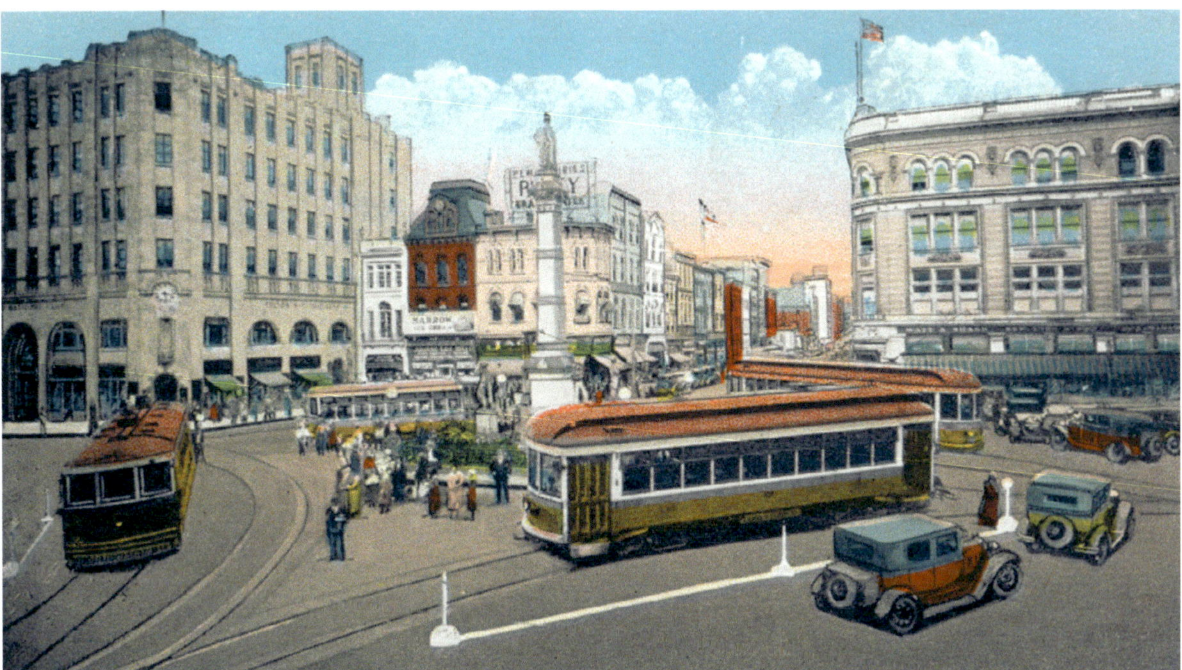

Penn Square in Lancaster is the location of a number of trolley cars in this postcard scene around 1920. In May 1890 the Lancaster City Street Railway Company began electric trolley car service. By July 1, 1891, all of the trolley lines serving Lancaster were converted to electric operation. The trolley lines were consolidated under Conestoga Traction Company on November 15, 1899. On December 24, 1931, the company emerged from receivership as the Conestoga Transportation Company, and trolley lines were converted to bus operation with only three lines remaining by 1942. No lines were converted to bus operation during World War II. After the war, conversion to bus operation resumed. The Rocky Springs line, the last trolley car line, closed on September 21, 1947.

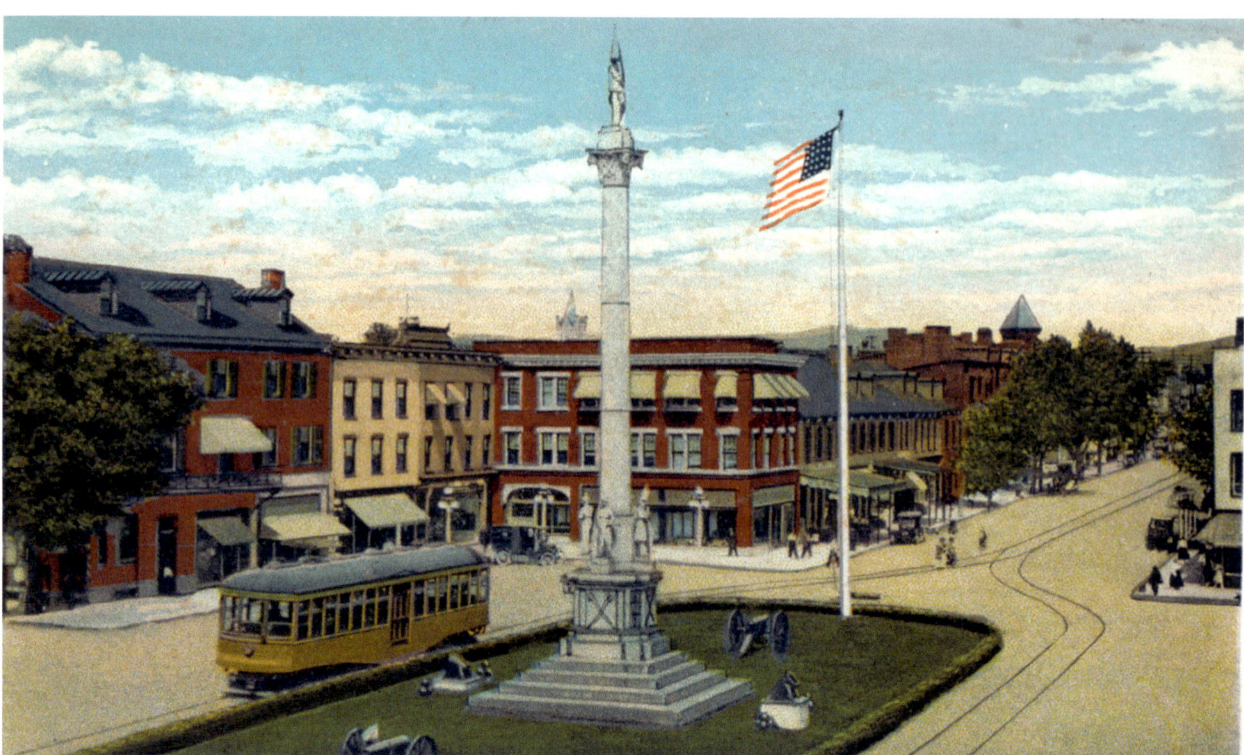

Monument Square in Lewistown is the location of a Lewistown & Reedsville Electric Railway Company trolley car in this postcard scene around 1910. The line opened from the Juniata River to Burnham on March 13, 1900, and service from Lewistown to Reedsville began in the spring of 1901. Later the Juniata River was crossed, and the line reached the Pennsylvania Railroad station at Lewistown Junction. Lewistown to Pennsylvania Railroad Depot service was every twenty minutes. Lewistown to Reedsville service was every thirty minutes.

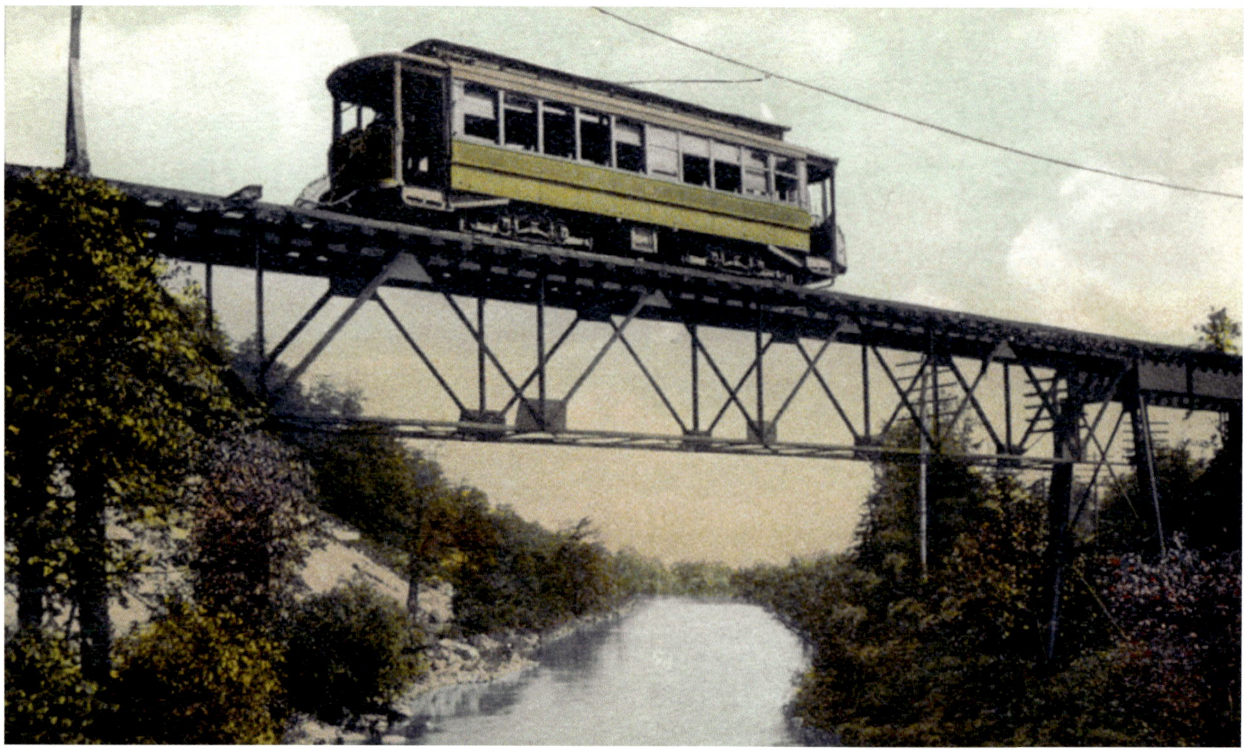

A Lewistown & Reedsville Electric Railway Company trolley car is crossing a trolley bridge at Mann's Narrows. The *McGraw Electric Railway List August 1918* noted the company operated 10.5 miles of track with twenty-one cars. Bus service began in 1923. Reedsville to Yeagertown trolley car service was reduced to one trip daily in 1928. Trolley car service ended on July 1, 1932.

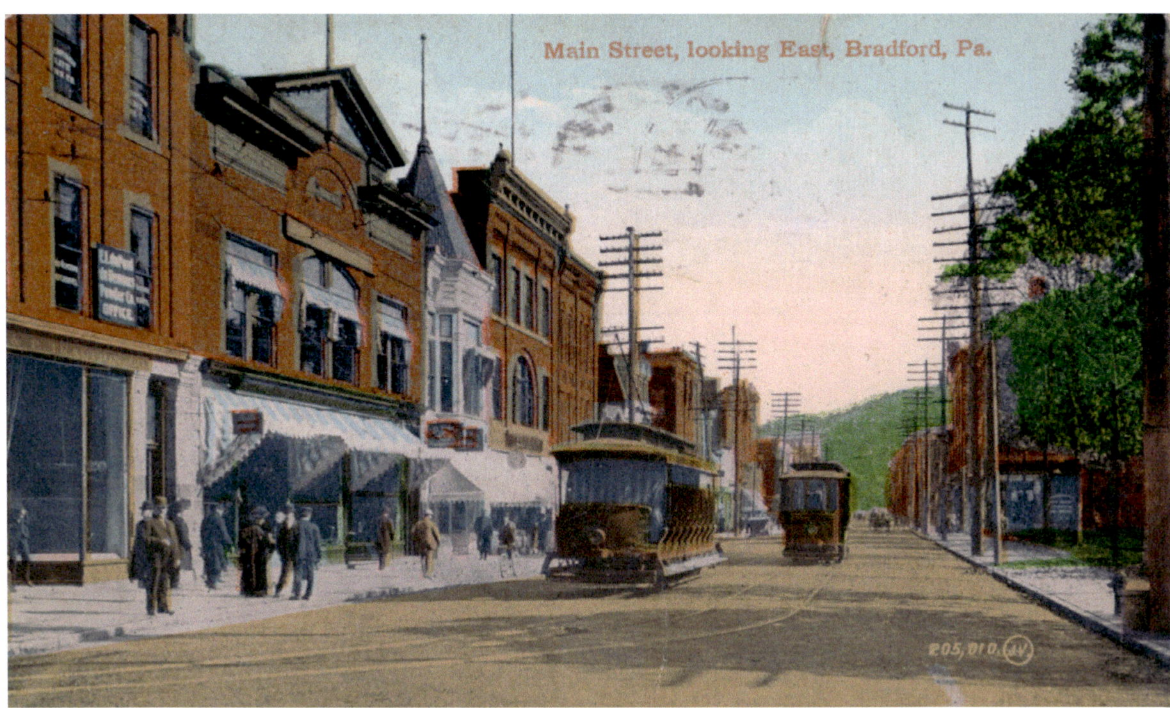

In this postcard postmarked February 23, 1912, two Western New York & Pennsylvania Traction Company (WNYPTC) trolley cars are on Main Street in Bradford. The Bradford Electric Street Railway Company began electric trolley car service in June 1896. On November 14, 1906, the Bradford Street Railway and Olean Street Railway were consolidated into the Western New York & Pennsylvania Traction Company. The *McGraw Electric Railway List August 1918* noted the 99.3 mile line had fifty-five cars. On October 1, 1921, the company reorganized as the Olean, Bradford & Salamanca Railway Company.

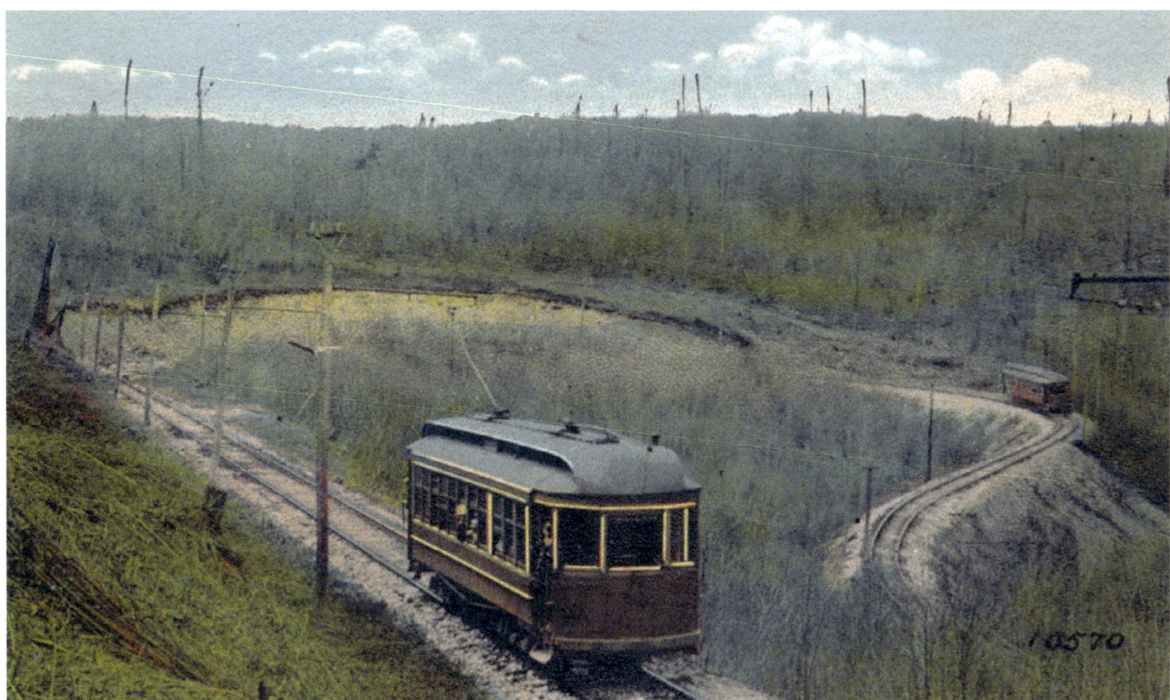

A trolley car is on the horseshoe curve of the WNYPTC between Olean, New York, and Bradford, Pennsylvania, in this postcard scene around 1910. This curve was constructed to reduce the steep grade approaching Rock City. The Olean, Bradford and Salamanca Bus Lines, a subsidiary, converted the Salamanca–Little Valley Line to bus operation on November 14, 1925 because of a land slide in Salamanca. Service ended on the Ceres–Bolivar Line in 1926. On August 31, 1927, the rest of the system was abandoned except for the lines in Bradford which closed on September 30, 1927 and Olean which closed on May 25, 1928.

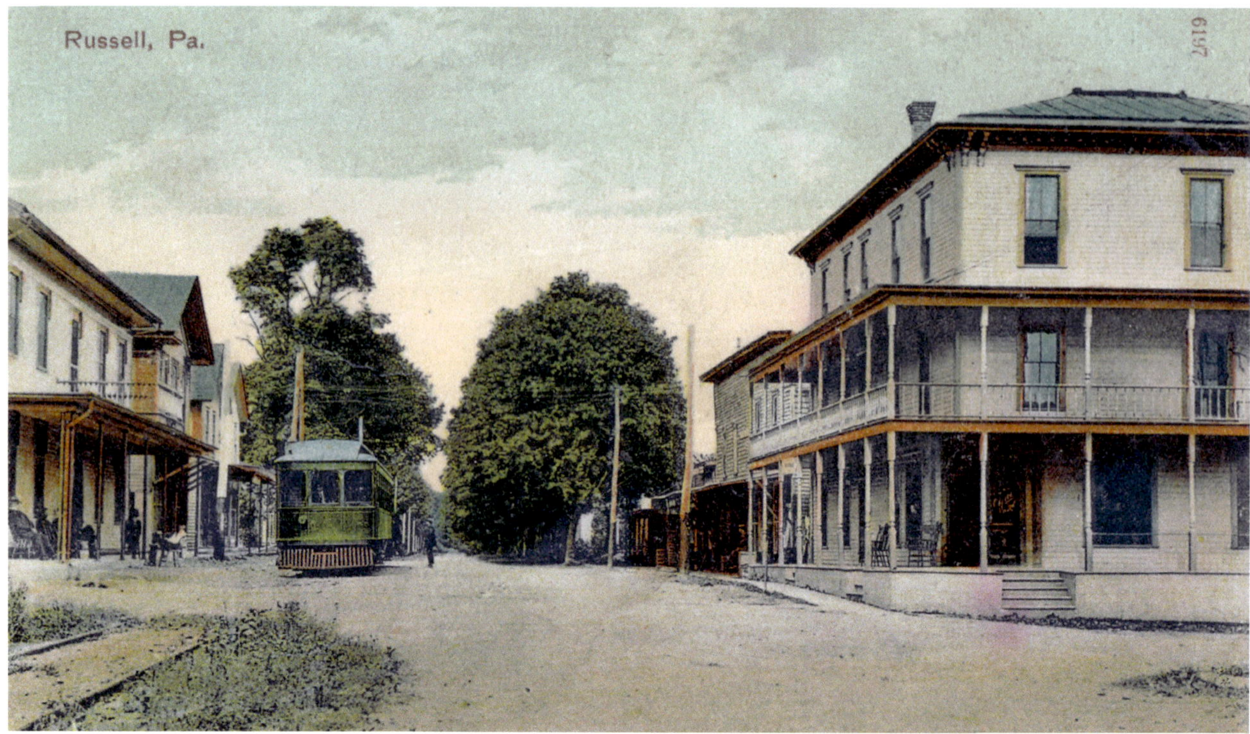

In this postcard postmarked September 18, 1908, a Warren & Jamestown Street Railway car is at Russell, Pennsylvania. This line began service on September 1, 1905 linking Jamestown, New York, with North Warren, Pennsylvania, operating on single phase alternating current. The line was later converted to direct current and operated to downtown Warren, Pennsylvania. On April 10, 1924, the line was sold to the Penn Public Service Corporation. Trolley car service ended on December 2, 1929.

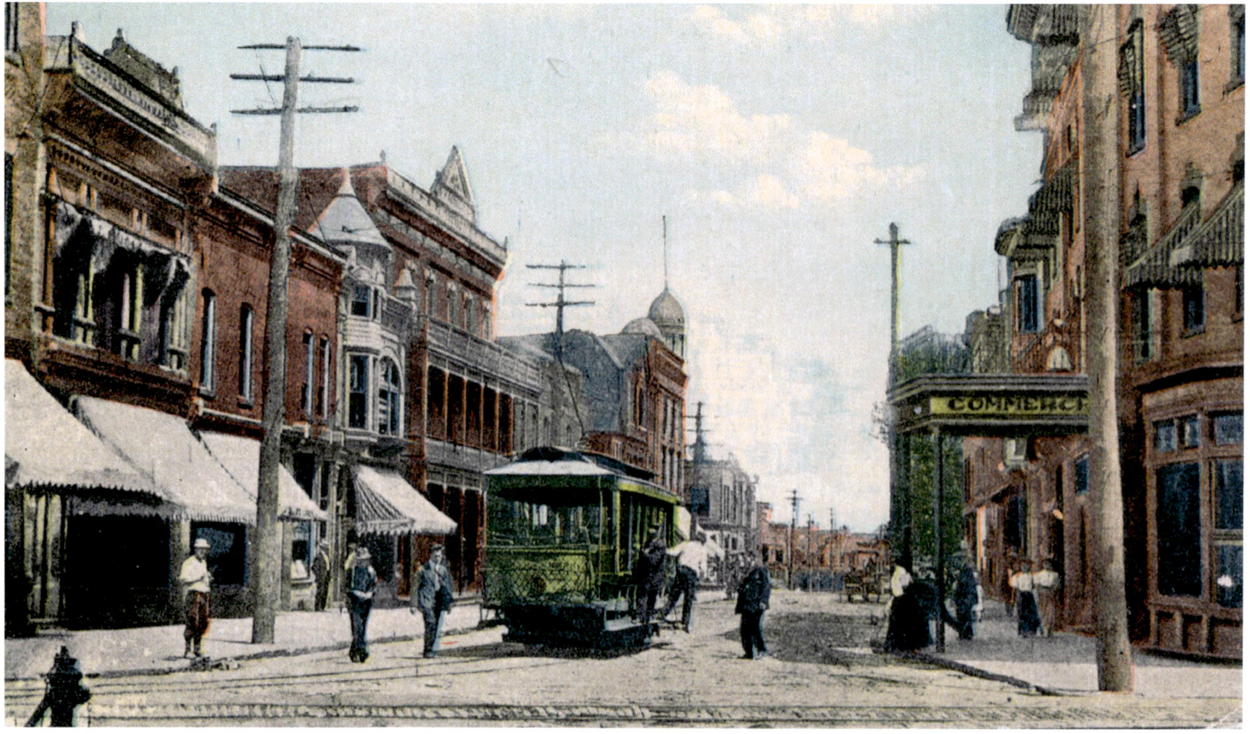

A DuBois Traction Company trolley car is on Brady Street in the city of DuBois (named for lumber businessman John DuBois who was one of the city's founders and inventor of the log slide and a technique for erecting bridge piers under water). The DuBois Traction Passenger Railway began electric trolley car service on October 17, 1891 and reorganized as the DuBois Traction Company on September 2, 1897. When state highway construction would have forced an expensive relocation of much of the company's trackage, the company abandoned all trolley car service on December 25, 1926.

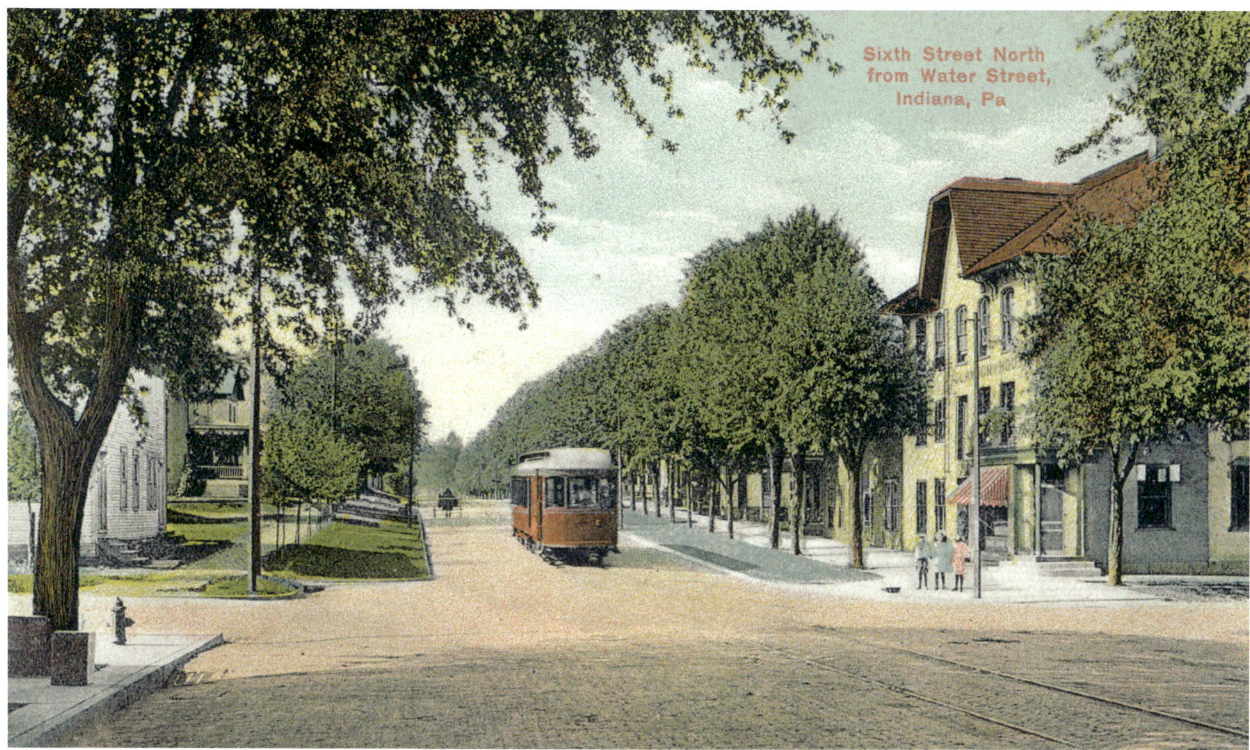

In this postcard postmarked November 9, 1910, an Indiana County Street Railway Company trolley car is on Sixth Street north from Water Street in the borough of Indiana (county seat of Indiana County). Several companies were merged into the Indiana County Street Railway Company on August 6, 1907. The line to Ernest opened in 1907 and to Blairsville in 1909.

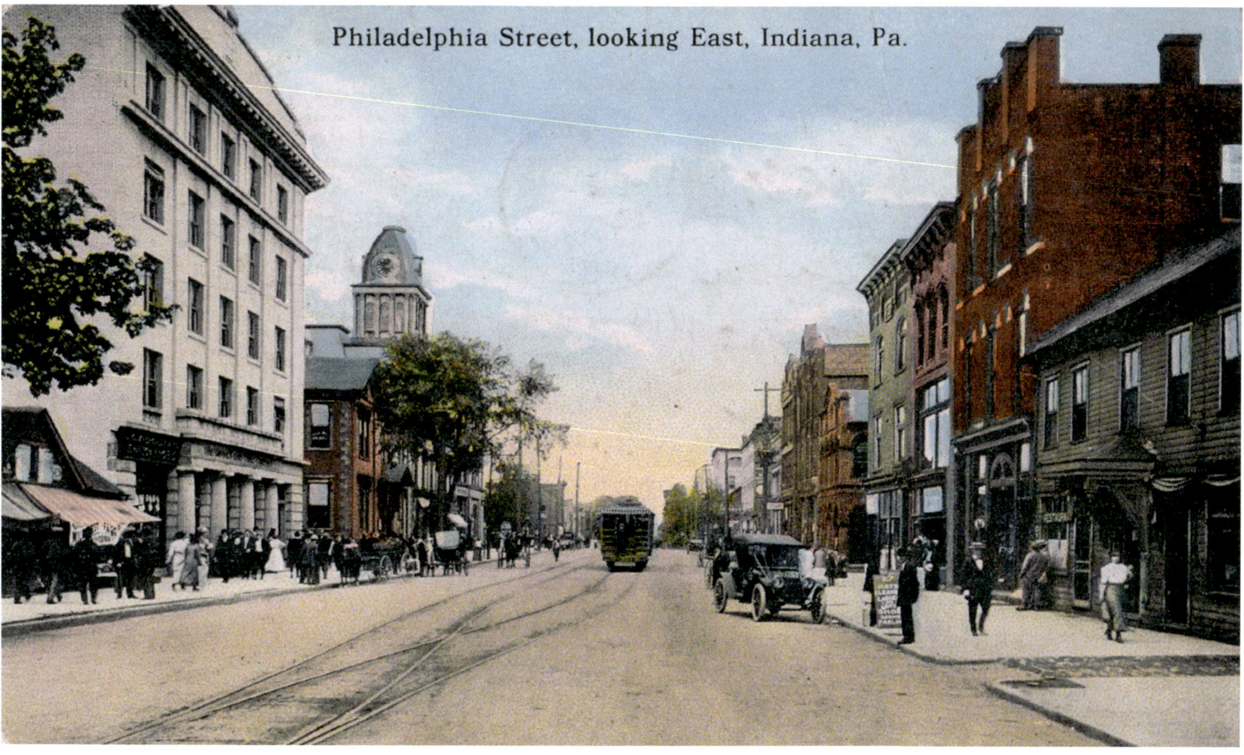

Philadelphia Street looking east in Indiana is the setting for an Indiana County Street Railway Company trolley car in this postcard postmarked December 8, 1913. The company operated an eighteen mile line from Indiana to Blairsville with service every fifty minutes, a six mile line to Creekside with service every seventy minutes, and a twelve mile line to Clymer with service every hour. From a peak ridership of 3,216,031 in 1923, ridership declined to 346,480 in 1932 because of tough economic times for the coal industry. The last trolley car operated on July 1, 1933.

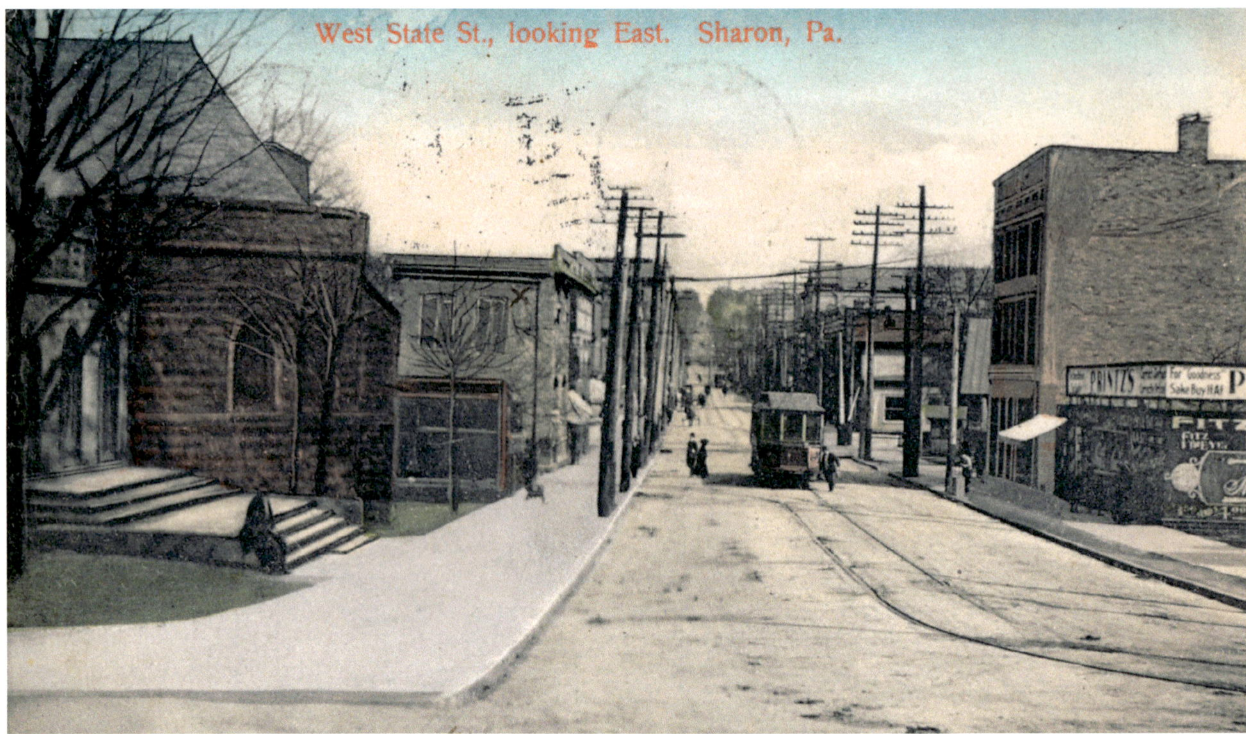

In this postcard postmarked July 19, 1909, a trolley car is on West State Street in the city of Sharon in Mercer County. Sharon had local service plus suburban trolley service from Sharon to Sharpsville every thirty minutes, Sharon to Wheatland every thirty minutes, and hourly interurban service from Sharon to New Castle. Interurban service from Youngstown to Sharon opened on 1901 with hourly service. On October 20, 1920, Sharon area trolley lines came under the control of the Shenango Valley Traction Company.

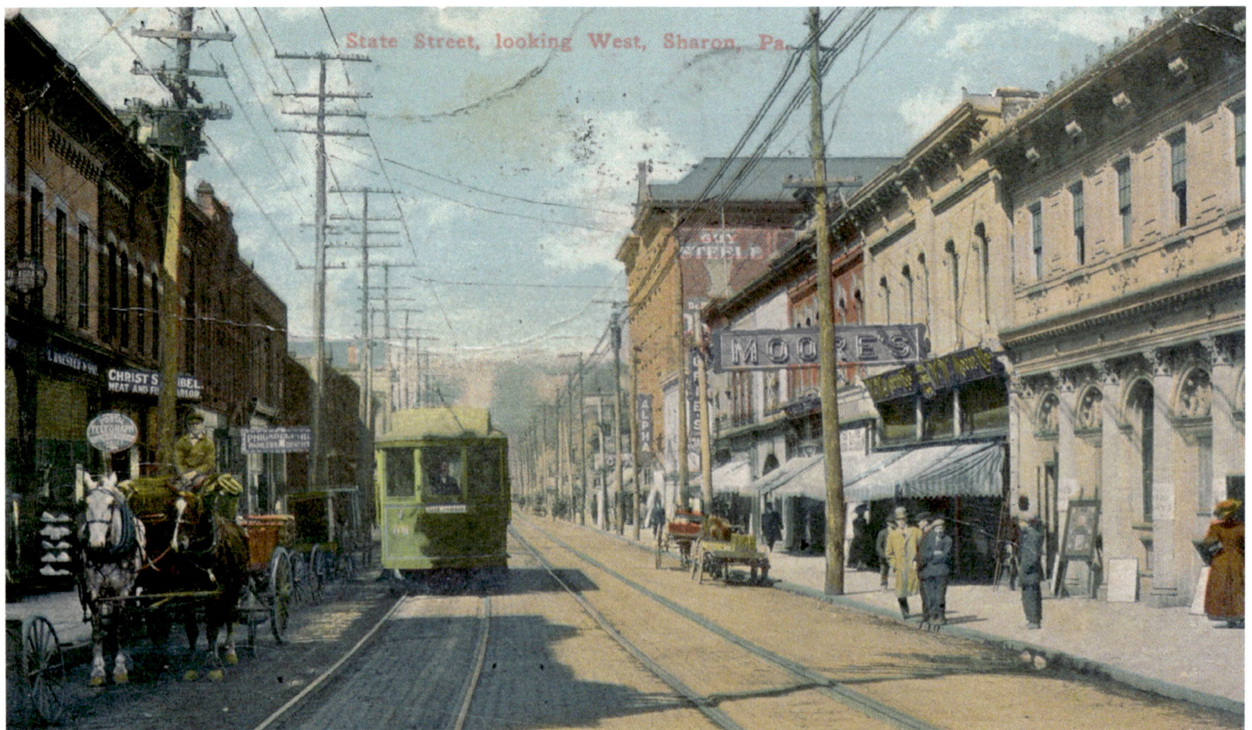

State Street in downtown Sharon shows a trolley car ready to pass a horse-drawn wagon in this postcard postmarked October 31, 1911. According to the *McGraw Electric Railway Directory 1924*, the Shenango Valley Traction Company operated 17.53 miles of track with twenty-five cars. Sharon to Youngstown interurban service closed in 1939. Local trolley service in Sharon ended on October 5, 1939.

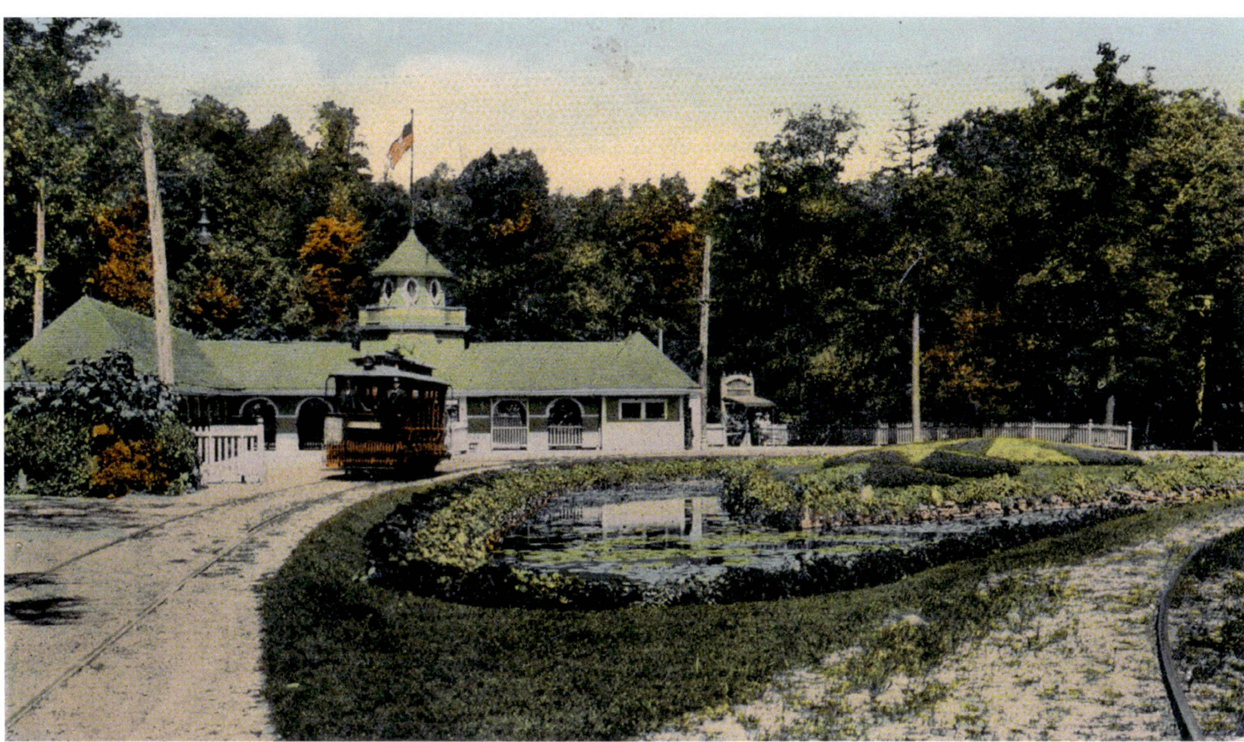

A New Castle Electric Street Railway Company (NCESR) trolley car is at the entrance to Cascade Park in New Castle in this postcard, postmarked October 10, 1913. NCESR opened Cascade Park on May 29, 1897 and over the years added an outdoor theatre, a fifteen acre lake, a zoo, a carousel, concession stands, an outdoor dance pavilion, and a small rollercoaster. While Cascade Park has seen change and challenging times, since the late 1980s several groups have been working to restore its natural beauty, and it is in active use in 2015.

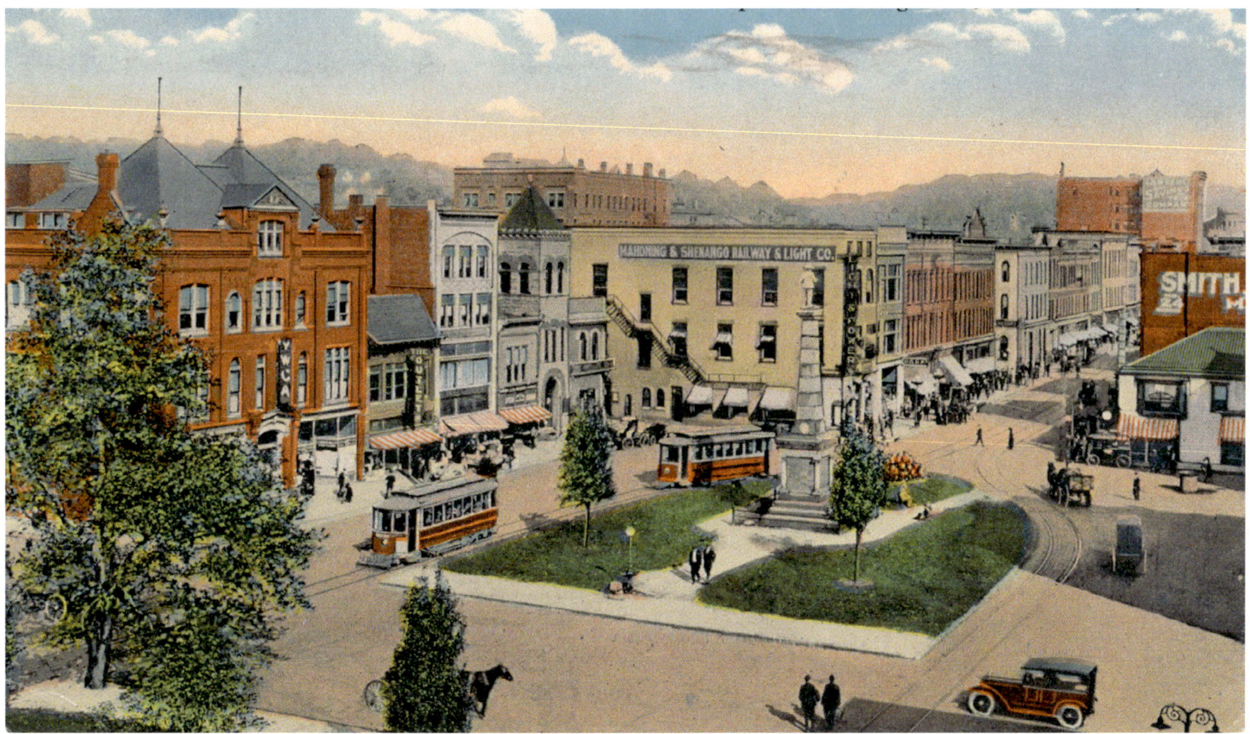

In this postcard, postmarked July 21, 1919, two New Castle Electric Street Railway Company trolley cars are passing around Public Square in New Castle. New Castle had hourly trolley service to Youngstown, hourly service to Hubbard, and service every thirty minutes to Mahonington. Trolley service from New Castle to Hubbard ended in 1925, New Castle to Youngstown ended in 1933, and local service in New Castle ended in December 11, 1941.

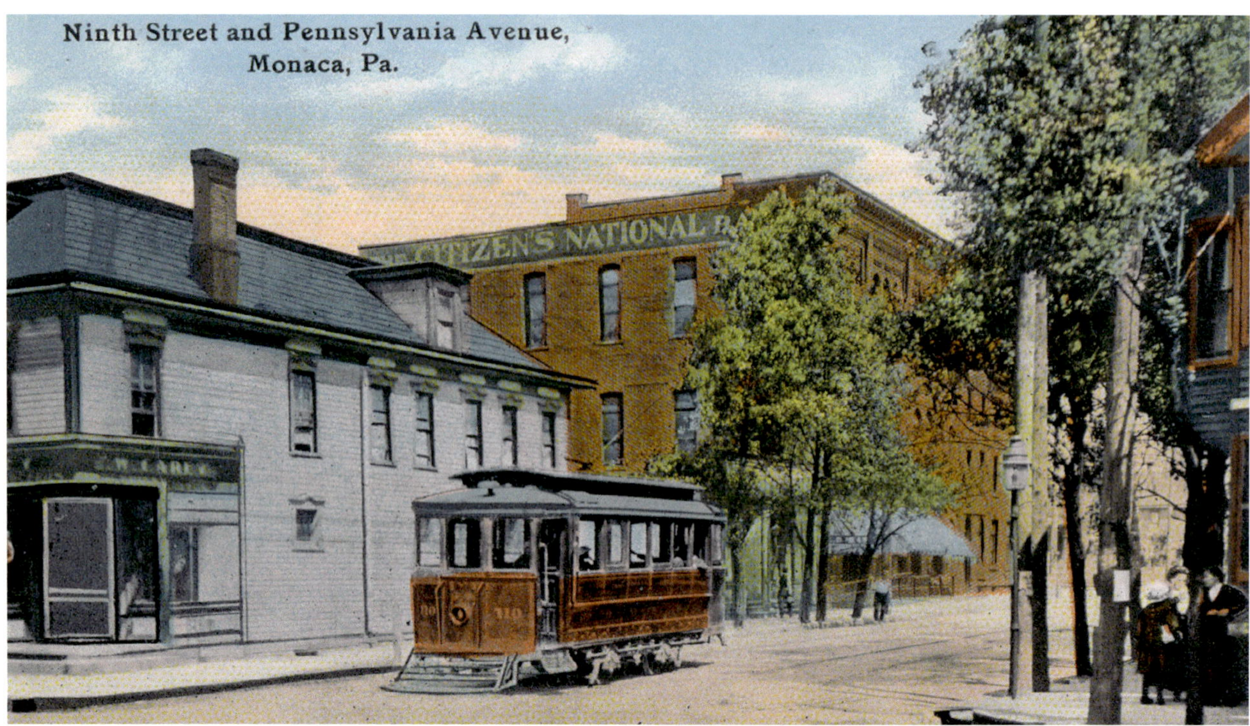

Ninth Street and Pennsylvania Avenue in Monaca is the location of a Beaver Valley Traction Company trolley car in this postcard postmarked July 25, 1919. On October 1, 1900 the Beaver Valley Traction Company was formed by a consolidation of the area's trolley car lines. According to the *McGraw Electric Railway List August 1918*, the Beaver Valley Traction Company had thirty-six miles of track and sixty-four cars.

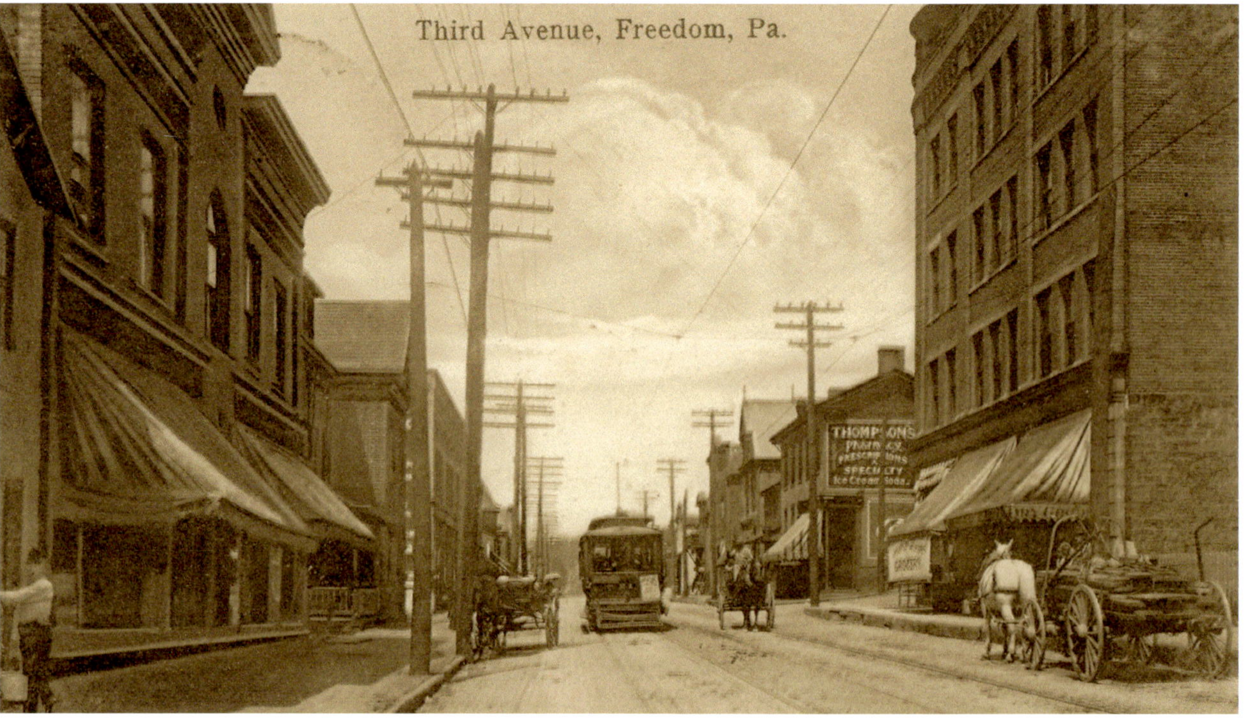

In this postcard postmarked September 9, 1910, a Beaver Valley Traction Company is on Third Avenue in Freedom. There was service every thirty minutes from Vanport to Beaver Falls, service every twenty minutes from Beaver to Leetsdale, service every ten minutes from Rochester to Monaca, service every twenty minutes from Beaver Falls to New Brighton, and service every twenty minutes from Rochester to Morado. There was good ridership in the Ohio River valley industrial area served by the trolley car system until the Great Depression when many of the industrial facilities closed. The system was converted to bus operation on August 10, 1937.

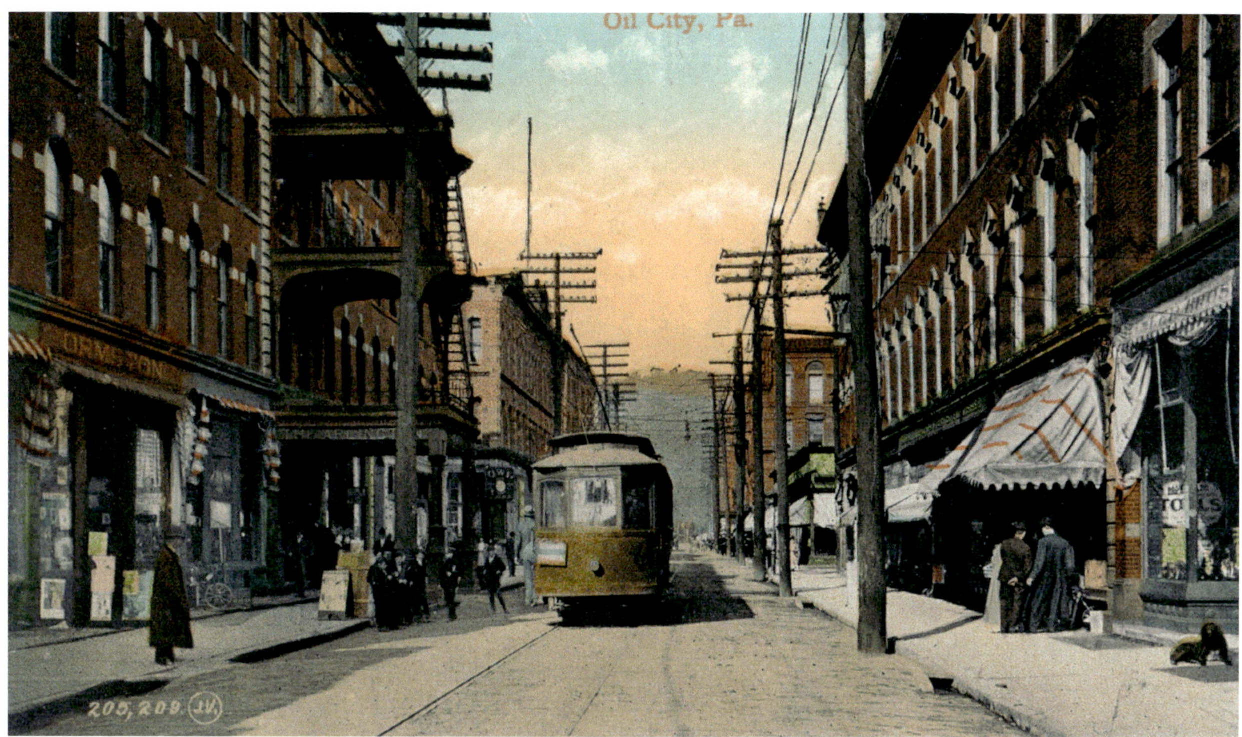

Seneca Street in Oil City is the location of a Citizens Traction Company trolley car heading for Rouseville in this postcard postmarked October 9, 1908. The Oil City Street Railway, founded by John B. Smithman, began electric trolley car operation on November 30, 1893. On January 14, 1901, Smithman sold his company to the Citizens Traction Company. According to the *McGraw Electric Railway Directory 1924*, the company operated 34.7 miles of track.

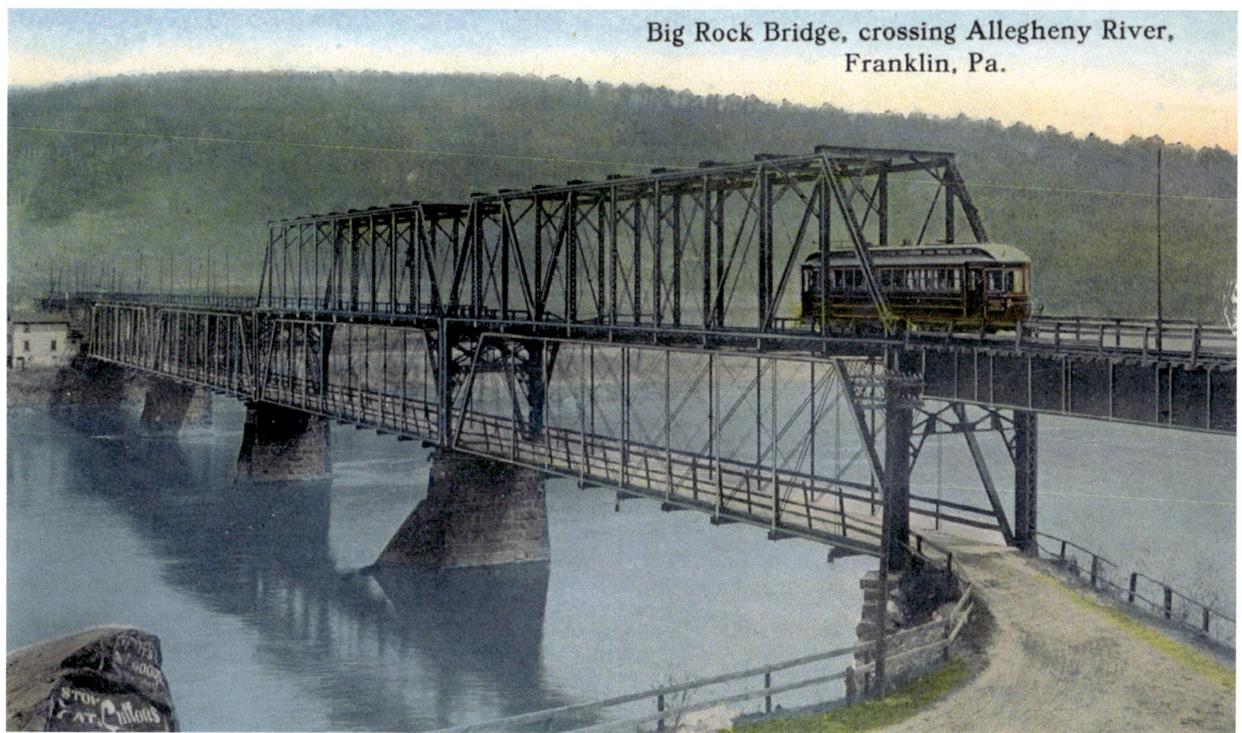

In this postcard, postmarked July 23, 1915, a Citizens Traction Company trolley car is on the Big Rock Bridge crossing the Allegheny River in Franklin. On February 9, 1895 the Franklin & Oil City Electric Street Railway was merged into the Franklin Electric Street Railway, which in May 1902 became part of Citizens Traction Company. The company operated two trolley routes connecting Oil City with Franklin. The southern route was south of the Allegheny River and served Monarch Park. The northern route crossed over to the north side of the Allegheny River to serve Reno. Trolley service ended on June 16, 1928.

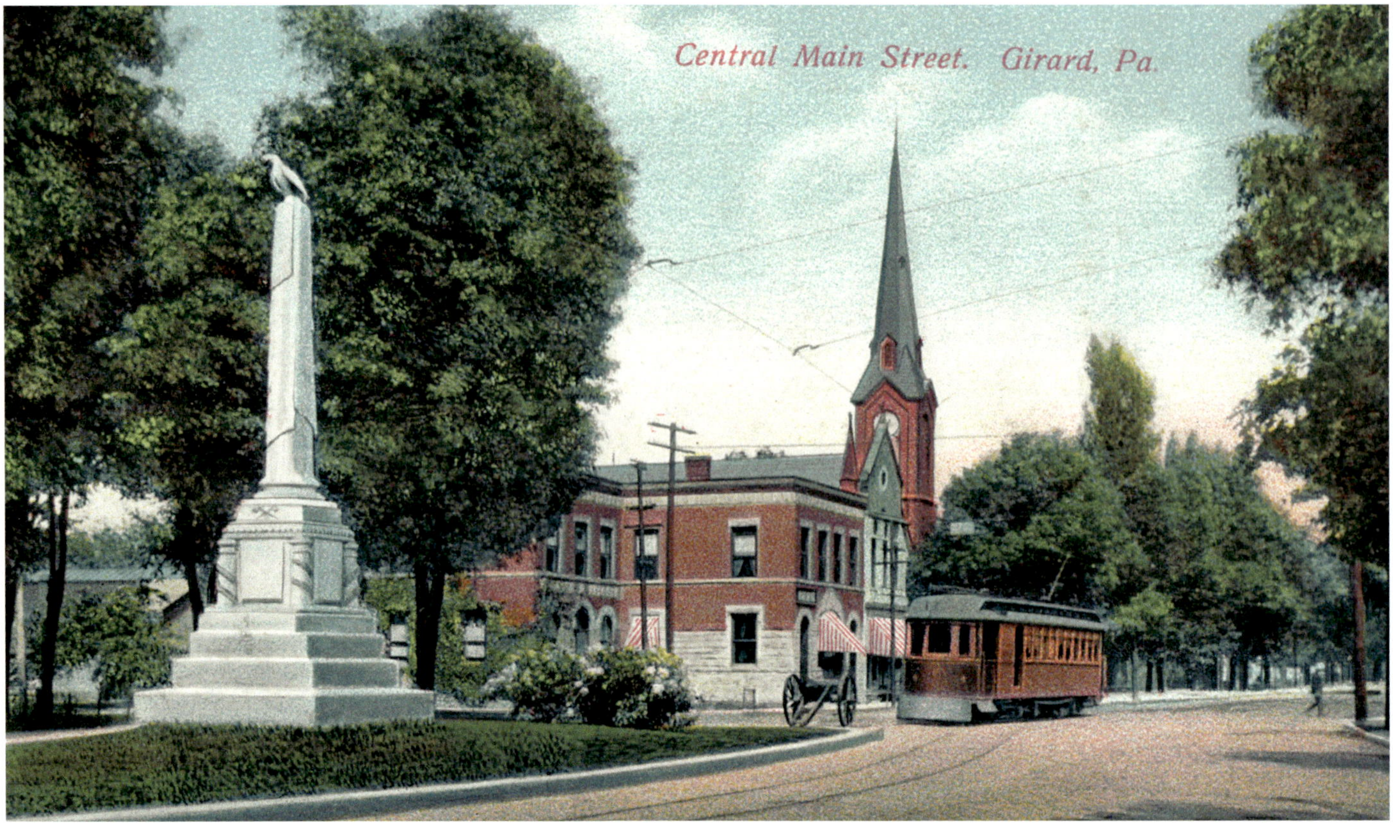

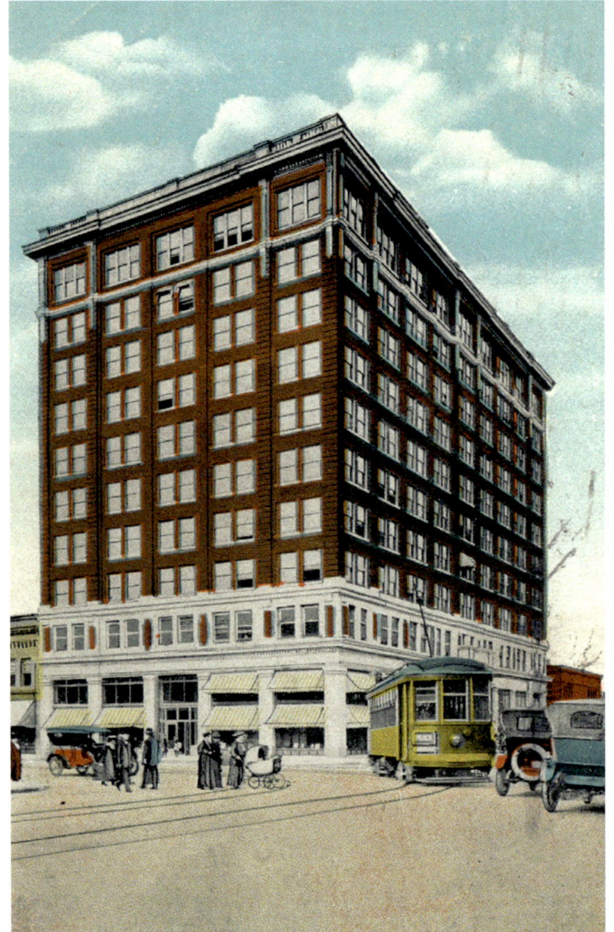

Above: A Conneaut & Erie Traction Company (CETC) trolley car is on Main Street passing the Dan Rice Monument in Girard in this postcard view around 1910. The CETC began through service from Erie, Pennsylvania, to Conneaut, Ohio, on November 8, 1903. Low ridership caused financial difficulties. The company was sold and became the Cleveland & Erie Railway Company on May 12, 1909. Unable to make payments for the use of Erie Railways trackage in Erie, the company went into receivership in 1920. Trolley car service ended on September 16, 1922.

Left: In this postcard postmarked June 8, 1923, an Erie Railways Company trolley car is turning from 12th Street onto State Street and will pass the Commerce Building in Erie. The Erie Electric Motor Company began electric trolley car service on June 25, 1889 and was merged into the Buffalo & Lake Erie Traction Company (BLETC) on December 24, 1906. Under an October 1, 1924 reorganization, the BLETC became the Buffalo & Erie Railway Company and the Erie Railways Company took over operation of the Erie, Pennsylvania, trolley car lines. Trolley cars made their last run in Erie on May 12, 1935.